THE
TRUTH
AGENDA

Making Sense of Unexplained Mysteries, Global Cover-Ups and 2012 Prophecies

D0551730

ANDY THOMAS

Dedicated to all those working for liberty and truth

First published in 2009 by Vital Signs Publishing
3 Old House Courtyard, Southover High Street,
Lewes, East Sussex, BN7 1HT, UK
Website: *www.vitalsignspublishing.co.uk*
E-mail: *info@vitalsignspublishing.co.uk*

Front cover design by Andy Thomas & Jason Porthouse

ISBN: 978-0-9550608-1-6

Other books by Andy Thomas:

Fields of Mystery
Quest for Contact (with Paul Bura)
Vital Signs
Swirled Harvest
A Oneness of Mind
An Introduction to Crop Circles

The Lewes 'Quadrilogy':
Streets of Fire / The Lewes Flood / Lewes - A Souvenir Guide / Lewes on the Fifth

As editor:
Joeb: Servant of Gaia (by Paul Bura)
Stepping to the Drummer (by Paul Bura)
Beyond 2012 (by Geoff Stray)

Printed by InPrint AS (Dardedze Holography), Latvia - *www.dardedze.lv*

CONTENTS

Introduction   *9*

PART ONE: MYSTERIES, MIRACLES AND GLOBAL DECEPTION

I   Making Sense of Our World   *17*
Western Discontent;   Understanding Conspiracy Theory;   New Times, Old
Suspicions; Applying the Truth Agenda

II   Mysteries Ancient and Modern   *27*
The Giza Challenge; The Crop Circle Controversy; Other Mysteries

III   UFOs   *37*
The Roswell Incident; Area 51; UFO Evidence; Contactee Experiences; Why
Would ETs Be Here?; Visions of the Future

IV   Miracles and Prophecies   *49*
Seers and Prophets; Religious Prophecies; The Apparition Phenomenon; The
Three Secrets of Fatima; The Miracle of the Sun; Fatima Under Analysis; Divine
Inspiration in the White House?; The Politics of Armageddon

V   Grand Conspiracies   *65*
Conspiracy - An Overall Picture; Weakening the Masses?; Reducing the Global
Population; The Georgia Guidestones; Paranoia as Legitimate Mistrust?; The
Aims of Global Conspiracy; Financial Manipulation?; The MPs' Expenses Scandal;
The European Stepping-Stone; Many Threads; A Society of Control; A Micro-
Chipped Population; The Fall and Rise of David Icke; The Extra-Terrestrial
Bloodline; The Genesis Gene; The Atlantis Connection; Secret Societies; The
Bohemian Grove Rituals; Breaking the Illusion

PART TWO: DECONSTRUCTING CONSENSUS REALITY

VI   One Giant Leap..?   *99*
Growing Doubts Over the Moon Landings; The Key Evidence; The Astronauts'
Testimony;   The Moon Rock Conundrum;   Anomalies in the Photographic

Record; The Classic Aldrin Photo; Camera Issues; Anomalies of the Lunar Lander; Video Issues; A Studio Hoax?; Choosing the Truth; The Radiation Problem; The Heat Problem; Could a NASA Hoax be Kept Secret?; 'Space Race' Secrets; Why a Lunar Deception?

VII Weapons of Mass Deception *131*

Peeling the Layers of Trust; The Afghanistan Campaign; Iraq and the Weapons of Mass Destruction; The David Kelly Affair; The Aftermath of the Gulf War; Why the WMD lie?; Faith and Mistrust

VIII 9/11 *141*

The Official Story; The Central Allegations; The Key Evidence; i) The Pentagon; ii) The Twin Towers; iii) WTC 7; Other Areas of Concern; Official Debunking; A Growing Movement

PART THREE: TOOLS OF CONTROL

IX The War on Liberty *181*

The Project for the New American Century; 'False-Flag' Terror; The War on Terror; The Patriot Act; The Death of Habeas Corpus; ID Cards Revisited; The Surveillance Society; Policing Cyberspace; Dealing With Real Threats; 7/7 Anomalies; A Difficult Choice

X Caging the Human Spirit *205*

The Bonds of Health and Safety; The Battle for Natural Health; Immunisation Choices; Policing Personal Beliefs; Political Correctness; The Fracturing of Community and Families; Media Influence and Propaganda; 'Dumbing Down'; Physical Barriers; The Caged Society - Evolution or Contrivance?

XI The Green Dilemma *223*

Policing Each Other Through Green Concerns; The Guilt of Climate Change; The Global Warming Conundrum; An Inconvenient Ruling; The Confusing Data of Climate Change; The Energy Crisis; The Common Sense of Preservation; The Control Agenda Unfolds

XII 2012 *239*

Millennial Transference; 2012 - The Key Elements; The Maya Countdown; The Maya Prophecies; Other Historical 2012 Predictions; Modern 2012 Insights;

Cosmic Waves; Solar Activity; Fluctuations in the Heliosphere; Geomagnetic Reversal; Galactic Alignment and Ascension; 2012 - the Year of... Nothing?; Tying the Threads Together; Readiness for Civil Unrest?; The Astrology of 2012; The Control Agenda Explained?; 2012 Squared

PART FOUR: SOLUTIONS AND INSPIRATIONS

XIII   Who Are We Dealing With? *267*
Lifting the Blindfold; The Elite and its Motivations; Openness as Mitigation?; Factions Within Factions; Consent by Apathy; Maintaining the Flame of Optimism

XIV   The Power of Collective Thought *281*
What Are We Fighting For?; The Evolution of Consciousness; The Power of the Mind; The Global Consciousness Project; Taking Back Collective Power; The Importance of Intention; The Proactive Use of the Collective; Taking Responsibility; Echoes From the Future; Stepping Up to the Task

XV   The Power of Positive Action *299*
Personal Responsibility; Facing the Fear of Ridicule; Personal Integrity; Guarding Against Mob Rule; The British Factor; The Waiting Game; Making a Stand; The Positive Lessons of Recent History; An Interlude; Prometheus Unbound; Confidence and High Spirits

APPENDIX 1: Notes *319*

APPENDIX 2: Further Resources *353*

PICTURE CREDITS *365*

INDEX *371*

THE AUTHOR *380*

ACKNOWLEDGEMENTS

Huge thanks to the following for helping *The Truth Agenda* come into being:

Helen Sewell for dedicated love and support for almost seven years, and for proofing and inspiration; *Piers Adams* for more diligent proofing, fact-checking and inspired suggestions (investigate *www.redpriest.com* for some truly extraordinary baroque pyrotechnics); *Sue Adams* for enthusiastic indexing skills; *Marcus Allen* for valuable help with the lunar content and his kind words; *Ian R Crane* for final checking and his own kind words; *Geoff Stray* for scrutiny of the 2012 content; *Terry Boardman* for the Steiner material; *Jason Porthouse* for his work on the front cover montage and other vital aid over the years; all the photographers [*Picture Credits*, page 365], especially *Andreas Müller*, *Tony and Ann Woodall* and *Heather and Ron Thomas*; *Ian Henshall* and the several other members of the 9/11 truth community who helped with image sourcing. Apologies to anyone inadvertantly missed out.

Thanks also to *Martin Noakes* for tech advice and all his crucial truth networking, *Lindsay Woods* of SB Publications for help with overseas transactions, and *Julia Bishop*, *Di Brown*, *Debbie Marriage* and *Sheila Martin* for support and kindness.

And, of course, great acknowledgement to the many, many people out there challenging convention and risking reputations, livelihoods and sometimes actual lives to create a better world, whose work has been wittingly (see Appendices) or unwittingly drawn on in this book.

'The truth is, there is something terribly wrong with this country, isn't there? Cruelty and injustice, intolerance and oppression. And where once you had the freedom to object, to think and speak as you saw fit, you now have censors and systems of surveillance coercing your conformity and soliciting your submission. How did this happen? Who's to blame? Well certainly there are those more responsible than others, and they will be held accountable, but again, truth be told, if you're looking for the guilty, you need only look into a mirror. I know why you did it. I know you were afraid. Who wouldn't be? War, terror, disease. There were a myriad of problems, which conspired to corrupt your reason and rob you of your common sense. Fear got the best of you, and in your panic you turned to the now high chancellor... ...He promised you order, he promised you peace, and all he demanded in return was your silent, obedient consent. Last night I sought to end that silence...'

'V' broadcasts to the British nation in the film *V For Vendetta* (2005, scripted by Laurence and Andrew Wachowski - see page 355)

'A long habit of not thinking a thing wrong
gives it a superficial appearance of being right'

Thomas Paine 1737-1809

INTRODUCTION

In the spring of 2008, I was asked to make an appearance on BBC 1's *The One Show*, alongside *Nexus Magazine*'s Marcus Allen and UFO investigator John Wickham. The British High Court had just rejected Mohammed Al Fayed's assertions that the tragic demise of Princess Diana and his son Dodi in a Paris underpass had been a co-ordinated assassination. Despite the straightforward verdict that 'gross negligence' from the driver and the paparazzi were all that were responsible, the polls were showing that much of the population still doubted this, and the BBC wanted to examine why a fascination with conspiracy theories persisted.

As ambassadors from the world of mysteries research, the three of us were thus looked after and interviewed at length in a nice London hotel by presenter (and ex-*Sun* editor) Kelvin MacKenzie. The discussion took in everything from the paranormal to persisting accusations that the whole truth about 9/11 had not been told. The conversation was affable, comprehensive and balanced.

A day later, finger poised on the video record button, I watched our interview air on prime-time evening television, knowing that millions would be watching. Well aware from past experience that no more than a few minutes, at best, would remain from the discussion, I braced myself to see what remained from our two hours of recording. 'Minutes' turned out to be very hopeful - instead, barely *half* a minute remained. I got to mention Guy Fawkes, Marcus asked whether we were alone in the universe, and John said nothing at all. And that was it - all the valuable discussion we had recorded about the more important themes had vanished into the ether. Then it was back to the studio presenters for condescending dismissal.

This sobering experience is a good example of how the so-called fringes of debate are always treated by the mainstream. It is far easier to sweep important issues under the carpet with jocularity and heavy editing than actually confront the reality of why so many people question what they are told to believe by a world that refuses to face uncomfortable questions. Yet a sizeable proportion of its inhabitants have at one time or another witnessed things they cannot understand or make sense of in everyday terms - or have met obstruction while trying to do so. We have it drummed into us time and again that nothing out of the ordinary can really happen, in the face of substantial evidence to the contrary. Those who insist on plying their convictions usually become freak show entertainments for a time, before fading back into obscurity or becoming minor stars in a paranormal research ghetto. Others, whose investigations lead them into mysteries of a more political kind, can find themselves attacked as delusional troublemakers by bitterly defensive press columnists, or even victimised by the state.

Why are things this way? Why are some topics considered 'respectable', while others are shunned as 'fringe' nonsense unworthy of investigation? Is this because they truly are nonsensical - or is it because a nameless stratum of authority would rather certain areas were left alone? The evidence, under analysis, suggests the latter as a very real possibility. *The Truth Agenda*, then, is a book concerned with mysteries and cover-ups of many kinds. Some of them reside within the realms of the parasciences, and others very much in the 'real world' - yet both genres appear to be distinctly connected when examined closely. Indeed, the higher echelons and power structures of our entire society seem obsessed with occult knowledge and a belief in the mystical realms - yet those lower down the ladder are ridiculed for making a show of investigating them, and often find themselves branded with a sneer as 'conspiracy theorists', a term increasingly employed in an abusive sense. Someone on high seems to feel threatened by these people. The application of a 'Truth Agenda' to these forbidden areas, by the simple method proposed in Chapter I, soon reveals hidden layers more than worthy of investigation.

What this book is *not* is an empty compendium of wacky beliefs listed in order and then unceremoniously debunked, like so many tomes of stocking-filler disinformation clogging up the shelves today. Instead, it tries to build, bit by bit, a coherent picture of the areas that have led people from many walks of life to consider that the times we are moving into now are important and that we are not being told the truth about them by hidden levels of authority. Part One lays the groundwork concerning mysteries and conspiracy theories, before Part Two selects three key events in (relatively) recent history to look at how the official evidence for their provenance stands up. Part Three examines the serious social consequences of the mandates engineered by some of the questionable areas exposed, and Part Four provides encouraging evidence that we can collectively turn all of this around to a more positive outlook - if we so choose.

For all the global sweep of the issues revealed by the Truth Agenda, two countries inevitably feature prominently in this

Filming for BBC 1's The One Show *[page 9]. A two-hour discussion on conspiracy theories resulted in less than half a minute's final broadcast.*

book - the UK and USA. It cannot be escaped that history and genes inseparably link the two, but beyond this the US, for all its current problems, obviously remains the dominant superpower in the world, hence its recurring profile in the analysis. What happens to America affects everybody, as the global recession so clearly illustrates. As a citizen of Albion I can, of course, do nothing but write from the British perspective. Yet the UK has long provided a cultural bridge between the United States and Europe, and there is a strong sense that what manifests here still makes a huge difference to the world (as explored in the concluding chapter), long-gone though Britain's questionable empire may be.

When people think of 'conspiracy theories', however, it is to the US that minds tend to leap. To some observers, the election of Barack Obama saw the old world inhabited by the former Bush administration, with all its uncomfortable roots in 9/11, dubious Middle Eastern wars and 'necessary' restrictions on freedom, conveniently recede into history, all conspiracy theories quietly forgotten

Barack Obama takes his inaugural presidential oath - subject of much controversy in itself [page 21]. Hopes are high for a new world under Obama, but just minutes after this moment, many of the old agendas were restated, leaving some of the Bush-era conspiracy theories intact.

in a new world of liberty and joy. The more realistic point out, however, that just three paragraphs into Obama's inaugural address - one which bore uncomfortable similarities to his predecessor's first speech - the new president was describing America as a nation 'at war, against a far-reaching network of violence and hatred'. This neatly announced a determination to continue the liberty-crushing 'War on Terror' that some had hoped might indeed recede into history, being a campaign that even the more conservative pundits acknowledge has made the world a far *more* terror-filled place to live in, not less. It is also a conflict that had its official beginnings in the baptismal fires of 11th September 2001 - a day of events which are mired, like so many other nexus points in history, in doubt, obfuscation and blatant lies, as we shall explore. Thus, the 'new' period of history we find ourselves in, for all the apparent (and hopefully genuine) good intentions of the Obama administration, far from being a break with the past appears at the moment to be simply a continuation of previous mandates in some areas, albeit with cosmetic changes. Therefore the need for the last decade's deep enquiries mounted by 'truthseekers', or conspiracy theorists (a term I doggedly adopt here, rather as Quakers successfully absorbed a name originally intended as an insult) remains entirely valid.

What, though, are these enquiries? This book exists to help untangle some of the matted threads of mysteries research, which can appear impenetrable to those on the outside, and attempts to, as the subtitle suggests, make sense of it all in as straightforward a way as is possible. In so doing, it presents a hypothesis, based on years of interaction and correspondence with those in this world of 'fringe' enquiry, that summarises and encapsulates its general belief system without gross over-simplification, but also without being the density of a telephone directory, as standard conspiracy texts tend to be. Along the way, some of my own personal fascinations are inevitably woven into the mix, but for the most part *The Truth Agenda* stands as an overview of what a minority - though a sizeable one - believe about their civilisation and planetary prospects here in the opening period of the 21st century. Coming to an absolute judgement on these beliefs is not the purpose of these pages, yet it was striking in their compilation how credible some of them can be made to seem without much effort, even in a hypothetical context.

The core of the conspiracy view is that knowledge of unexplained phenomena and occult beliefs underpin the central philosophy of a secret ruling class that has dominated for millennia, one which may be quietly expecting a potentially disruptive cosmological event to occur to the planet sometime soon, an expectation based on prophecies and visions. With that in mind, this elite cabal is installing a regime of control, using any means necessary, to ensure that it retains its power during or after such an upheaval. The odd thing is that, unhinged as some of this may first appear, in summarising the overall picture the hypothesis takes on a strangely convincing symmetry - even if some of it does eventually turn out to be myth born of collective paranoia. Yet from the darkest of those fears, a number of clear truths do seem to emerge, with the reality of control agendas, vast political lies and the power of hidden ideologies revealing themselves pretty plainly, even if the conclusions drawn by the truthseekers sometimes go too far.

The happy news about all of this is that even if the blackest visions *were* to be confirmed, there is enough human goodness and wisdom available to deal with them - given dedication and positive intent. If all that is achieved by fevered speculation on a hidden world of mysteries and cover-ups is an enhanced appreciation of the freedom and beauty in the lives that people do have - or must create - then none of it is in vain. The empowerment that comes with legitimate questioning, taking nothing at face value about our world or those we allow to govern it, is reason enough to take the journey.

The danger of all such projects is that the very engagement with some of the darker subjects can in itself generate gloom and exacerbate the problem. If all the tracts on positive thinking are correct, campaigning for peace, for instance, is inherently more likely to achieve its aim, on an energetic level, than protesting against war. Yet this cannot be used as an excuse for failing to call to account that which is wrong. Raising full awareness of dysfunctional fixtures, which we can too easily accept due to their sheer familiarity, as the opening Thomas Paine quote suggests, is a vital task if light is to dispel shadows. Hence it is unavoidable that many of these pages are devoted to lifting the layers on subjects which some may find uncomfortable, distasteful or even frightening to question, as we challenge some of history's sacred

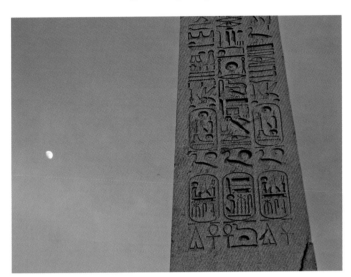

cows along the way. But challenge we must if we are to break out of the prison of illusion which has been built all around us, whether intentionally or by accident. Only through awareness can we avoid potential disaster - heading for a wall while blindfold provides merely temporary and delusional security. Opening our eyes to the hard reality of the danger zones is the

Egyptian needle and the Moon at the Place de la Concorde, Paris. Many believe that ancient mysteries and occult beliefs still underpin the philosophy of the power structures that run the world today, and that big secrets are kept from us.

only way we can avoid their worst excesses. Yet at the end of the journey we take through these pages, something wonderful lies - the realisation that collectively we are far more powerful than those so many credit with having caused the problems.

While readers new to questioning consensus reality may feel unsettled, the areas covered here will be less startling to seasoned truthseekers with fixed creeds, but alternative analysis needs to reach beyond the front stalls to make a difference, and the broad overview offered here is necessarily simplified. Sources for more detailed general information are listed in the Appendices. The book is also of its time and events will doubtless overtake some of the covered areas soon enough, especially in a now rapidly changing world, but the broad picture is likely to remain relevant for a while yet.

Much of the problem the fringe has in persuading the outside world of the validity of its convictions is that too often those teetering on the edge of interest can be discouraged by what can sometimes come across as partisan overload. With this in mind I have concentrated on more accessible areas of investigation, whilst omitting others that I feel lack definitive evidence or mask unpleasant racial scapegoating. I have also avoided dissecting the origins of the world's religions and their various claimed misdemeanours. That is too big a task for *The Truth Agenda* and I am assuming that open-minded readers will recognise for themselves the inherent weakness of any mindset that requires blind faith in 'God-given' rights to justify itself. It seems so well established that religions have been misused for authoritarian purposes through the ages, whatever their genuine spiritual values, that the subject doesn't warrant close attention here. Harmful fundamentalism, however, on any side of the debate, religious, political or scientific, is firmly called into question throughout.

A degree of moderation, then, is necessary for the purposes of spreading awareness of what may turn out to be the key issues of our times. Its employment should also ensure that each of us remains open-minded, ready to review opinions if discerning evidence is presented, in whatever direction it takes us, towards or away from convention. I have found, from my own experience as a lecturer sharing the mystery realms with mainstream audiences, that people are more comfortable with new ideas when alternative truths are offered, but not sold as absolutes. In that spirit, then, *The Truth Agenda*'s key purpose is simply to reach out to those who don't feel quite right about the slightly warped society around them and want to look just a little further outside the usual confines of mainstream thinking to see if any answers lie there. Readers must choose their own reality.

At the very least, the journey should provoke thought and discussion. That, if nothing else, should make it worthwhile, even if the reader violently disagrees with the content. It is better to have some opinion than none, with blandness and apathy being particularly virulent weakeners of the human spirit. Strength and substance always comes with healthy debate.

Andy Thomas

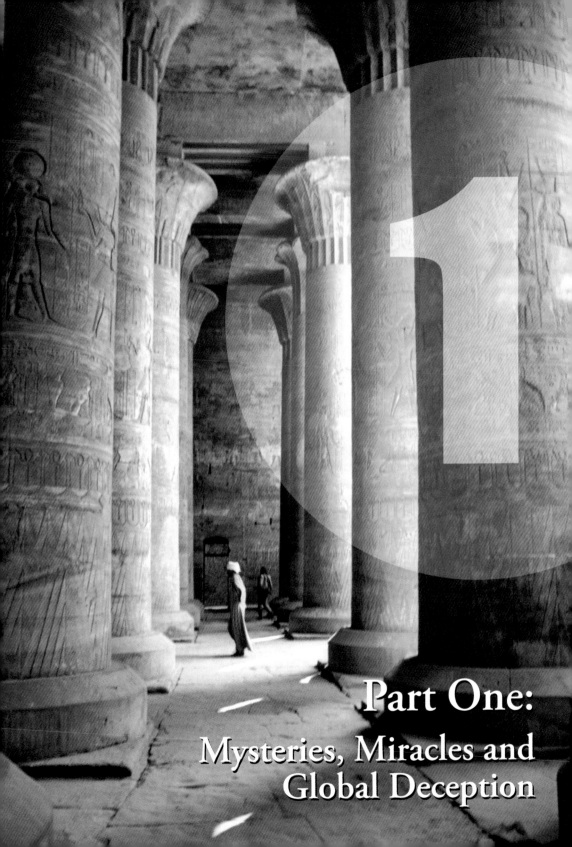

Part One:
Mysteries, Miracles and Global Deception

I   Making Sense of Our World

Is the somewhat fractured world we live in today a result of random developments - or a conspiracy? And is the picture we are presented with in the mainstream an accurate one? Given that so often it appears not to be, it is inevitable that many have begun to question the very foundations of the society in which they live.

Western Discontent

How many people are happy with the world we live in today? Ask any demographic the question, in Britain at least, and an overwhelming majority will answer in the negative. For all our scientific achievements, great discoveries and the many convenience comforts of the modern Western world, there is a pervading sense that civilisation has taken a wrong turn somewhere down the line. Secrets and lies seem rife within governments and institutions, countries go to war on very shaky grounds, and an agenda of control and suppression appears to be rapidly replacing the relative freedom the West once knew. Fear of climate change, fear of terrorism, fear of recession, fear of the outsider, fear of almost everything; all these threats seemingly dangled above our heads and actively inflated by media shock merchants mean we increasingly act from a place of threatened security rather than from expansion and joy. The prevailing impression is that we are poised on the brink of political, economic, spiritual and social breakdown as the family unit dissolves and the old foundations of respect and a sense of the sacred dwindle away into disorder, systemic corruption and crime. Meanwhile, heightened awareness of flu pandemics and the economic turmoil that is sweeping the world has focused many minds on the concept of loss (or in some cases just the fear of loss), rather than gain.

Positive thinking, then - a vital commodity in unstable times - is currently dwarfed by the seeming enormity of the problems that face us and the coverage given to them. Yet, despite the unquestionable reality of big issues to be dealt with, there is evidence that we are being disproportionately presented with a negative view of a world that may in truth be much brighter than we are being allowed to see. The version of society we perceive through our screens and papers almost unfailingly promotes fear and darkness, and tempts us to give our freedom away, almost as if encouraging hope and liberty would be an irresponsible thing to do. Almost as if there is an agenda.

The dark things are sometimes real enough - but so is hope and positivity. Yet the latter are without question downplayed as if, to those in control, a divided and unhappy society is far preferable. Either way, little in our world seems to make sense anymore - that is, if one assumes that the world is being run for the benefit of *us*. What if that is not the case?

Some say the current state of our civilisation is the result of a giant mistake, the product of error built upon error and rebounds from endless corrective manoeuvres born of desperation, as humankind evolves with depressing slowness. However, an increasing number of people believe that life has become the way it is because a hidden strata of our society *wants it to be that way*. After all, are we really so incompetent as a species? Have we learnt nothing? Many individuals and groups seem enlightened and intelligent, living positive lives and trying constantly to create positive change; yet society as a whole stubbornly refuses to move on from its litany of mistakes, continually repeating the faults of the past.

Understanding Conspiracy Theory

This is where we enter the world of 'conspiracy theory'. It has become an abusive expression in recent times, applied by the establishment to marginalise anyone who questions the status quo. An encouraged contempt for conspiracy theorists has allowed these questioners to be pushed neatly to the fringes as sad characters to be shunned, ridiculed or even feared. Books by mainstream journalists (like David Aaronovitch's recent *Voodoo Histories*)[1], which exist to knock down alternative views on recent history and falsely present all conspiracy theorists as far-right or even anti-Semitic extremists, are given massive media coverage, while the actual evidence presented by those being marginalised is given little or no airing and kept out of polite society. At the same time, fragile 'strawman' theories are forever pushed into the public eye via the tabloids and built up hugely, only to be quickly despatched. Mohammed Al Fayed's clearly doomed attempt - whatever the ultimate truth - to prove in the British High Court in 2008 that Princess Diana was murdered on the orders of Prince

The 'flame of Liberty' above the Pont de l'Alma underpass in Paris, where Princess Diana met her fate. Media hype over the 2008 inquest falsely inflated conspiracy speculation, only for it to be predictably knocked down by the final verdict - cleverly bringing all conspiracy theories into disrepute by association.

Philip provides a good example [pages 91 & 328]. With such an extreme accusation, and with important evidence oddly unpresented or deliberately withheld, it was clear from early on that a verdict to support the conspiracy view would be unlikely; yet certain tabloid newspapers screamed each new clue as sensational fact, before the predictable climbdown - or subsequent silence. By loudly fanfaring weaker cases before the inevitable public demolition, all conspiracy theories are brought into disrepute by simple association. Yet the theories for which there is substantial evidence, such as the anomalies surrounding 9/11 [Chapter VIII], are largely ignored or singled out for ignorant dismissal by sneering columnists - usually by failing to address the evidence itself and personally attacking or stereotyping the researchers instead.

Why is there such a stigma against those who question the establishment view? Is it because they are, in fact, asking pertinent questions no-one else dares to about the mysteries and cover-ups that seem to surround us? Even a superficial glance at both history and the patterns of today confirms that such things have long been indelible components of our

Bonfire Night in the UK. The annual parading of Guy Fawkes commemorates one of the most famous conspiracies of all time - yet we collectively struggle to accept that conspiracies still occur today.

world, yet we live in a culture of denial. Indeed, a wide belief in the unexplained, supernatural forces and conspiracy theory may be underpinning the society we live in to a much greater degree than anyone suspects.

For all the scorn regularly poured upon it, conspiracy theory seems to become perfectly mainstream when it suits a purpose; when English gardens see effigies of Guy Fawkes burnt or exploded each November the Fifth, for instance, we commemorate 'The Gunpowder Plot', one of the best-known historical conspiracies. At the other end of the spectrum, the widely accepted - and promoted - belief that bin Laden and Al Qaeda perpetrated the 9/11 attacks is a modern conspiracy theory writ large (yet is never presented as such). And how many today really believe that John F Kennedy was killed on the whim of a single fanatic with a personal agenda? Conspiracy theory only becomes a pariah when it's turned around and focused on the very people who want us to believe it of someone else.

The *Collins English Dictionary* defines 'conspiracy theory' as:

'The belief that the government or a covert organisation is responsible for an event that is unusual or unexplained, especially when any such involvement is denied'.

Given this definition and the lessons that history, both ancient and modern, has to tell us about global deception, who can seriously deny that conspiracies are rife and very real? Theorising about conspiracies is therefore a perfectly legitimate line of enquiry, and the term 'conspiracy theorist' is interchanged throughout this text with (the sometimes preferred) 'truthseeker' in a firmly non-abusive sense.

However, it is usually the conspiracy theorists that are held up to be the warped components of society, as far as the intellectuals we mysteriously appoint as our moral guardians in the media are concerned. Time and again we read cod-psychological treatise on the inherent dysfunctionality of conspiracy believers, often characterised as 'anoraks' with few social skills and troubled backgrounds - unlike journalists, of course, who must all, by implication, be impeccable bastions of wisdom. Typical of such scathing negation is this recent entry from UK columnist Polly Toynbee, who writes:

'Conspiracy theory journalism... abounds, assuming anything gleaned through a keyhole or leaked document reveals more truth than the big picture staring you in the face. Healthy scepticism easily tips into the conspiracy mindset, where dark motives lie behind everything... ...If no fact, history or official record can be trusted, then anything might be true and the world ceases to make sense or to be governable by common consent. It is a growing state of mind that, once it takes hold, spreads easily from small things to big beliefs. It needs a firm rebuttal, even when it invades relatively unimportant-seeming things - such as was Shakespeare really Shakespeare?' [2]

... The subtext of which would appear to be 'don't dare ask questions about anything that isn't obvious'. We clearly shouldn't trouble our undeveloped minds about such things. But why not? Why shouldn't we be curious as to whether Shakespeare really was Shakespeare? Why wouldn't we want to know why something as huge as the Moon landings appears to have such shaky evidence to support it? Why can't we ask why overt occult symbolism appears in so much architecture and iconography? Why shouldn't it be questioned as to how nearly 3000 people died so easily on 9/11 when normal procedures should have prevented it? Is asking these questions proof of a personality defect? If so, why is it that the people who are now calling society to account come from such a wide cross-section of class and education? Anoraks we will always have with us, and they can be loud and undiscerning sometimes, but in recent years the ranks of the challengers have been swelled by a quiet and largely sensible majority.

Toynbee does make an important point to express that if 'anything might be true' then 'the world ceases to make sense or to be governable by common consent'. Many people believe precisely that, but are not allowed to express it. Suppressing debate isn't healthy and can lead to extremism - something the world has too much of. Toynbee's typical journalistic contempt implies that nothing requires evidence to support it in the conspiracy world and that all who question official dogmas are agitating fantasists. But most self-respecting truthseekers accept the need for clear presentation of reasoned evidence, and it is this approach that we will take here. Much of that evidence is persuasive enough that it deserves a fuller examination. [Interestingly, when this author attended a lecture by Polly Toynbee - renowned for her acerbic pen - and held up 9/11 as an area worthy of more serious study, in the flesh she proved far less willing to defend her views on conspiracy theorists and made vaguely conciliatory noises to avoid a conflict.]

From people tired of such lazy media dismissal, a world of 'truth movements' and campaigns is proliferating in these obvious days of global deception and political obfuscation - a sure sign that we have collectively lost faith in those making the big decisions on our behalf.

New Times, Old Suspicions

Much of this book is necessarily focused on things past, concentrating on events which have shaped the world we live in now. But the temptation to think that a new era leaves behind the suspicions of old should be avoided. When Barack Obama had to re-swear his oath of allegiance as the 44th President of the United States of America the day after fluffing a line during his first attempt in front of millions of viewers on 20th January 2009 [photo, page 11], this was done 'out of an abundance of caution' and to avoid 'conspiracy theories'. This extraordinary action was a tacit acknowledgement of how widespread and influential conspiracy theorising has become in recent years.

Within hours of Obama's inauguration, in amongst the joyous celebrations from those hailing his historical accession, the Internet was also awash with speculation from those less sure: as Obama hadn't spoken the correct oath (the word 'faithfully' got transposed to a less solid place in a sentence), was he, in fact, president?[3] Was this a deliberate ploy so that he could not be held technically responsible for his actions if things went awry? With malicious rumours circulating that Obama's birth certificate might have been faked to enable him to take office (if born outside the USA, he would not be eligible as president - some claim his real place of birth was Kenya), unpleasant echoes of the events which marred George W Bush's 2001 presidential election 'victory', with its allegations of voting fraud, threatened to undermine the support of a minority, but clearly an influential one. The decision to re-take the oath illustrates that *every* action, no matter how small, is now under scrutiny from those who no longer trust authority - and those in power know it. Not that doing this in any way assuaged the doubts. If anything it raised further questions: Why was the second oath not filmed? Why did Obama not swear on a bible this time? Were any of the first orders signed by Obama in the hours before the second oath legally binding? And so on.[4]

Such is the climate of doubt we live in today. Let down so many times by a system that, well-meaning or not, appears so often to be corrupt, coldly authoritarian and

The White House, Washington DC. How much difference does a change of occupant really make to the way decisions are made? Is it always the same old hidden agendas at work, or does the election of Barack Obama really mean we can now hope for something new?

not running to programmes that seem to benefit the common person, people have lost faith in their leaders and confidence is at an all-time low. The current global financial disaster brought about by supposedly reckless bankers and negligent governments (but see page 71), together with the the 2009 British MPs' expenses scandal, have rudely awakened a new and more eclectic portion of the population to considering alternative views on the way the world is run. Those they thought they could trust have proved themselves unworthy of it, and the consequences of the betrayal have trickled into everyday lives in a very tangible way, as jobs, savings and pensions tumble. The election of President Obama, whose supporting masses, full of enthusiasm and bursting with genuine hope for something better this time, bucked the doubting trend for a short while, but the faith was wobbling in some just weeks after his inauguration. Who could, after all, live up to such high expectations, especially in a climate where only hard decisions, not crowd-pleasers, could be made?

Yet many outside of the polite mainstream, which had bordered on drooling hagiography during the presidential electioneering, were already pointing out that those who helped Obama to power behind the scenes appeared to be precisely the same characters who had helped create previous messes (such as political 'hawk' Zbigniew Brzezinski, credited by some with actually creating Al Qaeda by masterminding the training of Afghan 'freedom fighters' following the 1979 Soviet invasion), and those Obama appointed to office were the same breed of powermonger as before. Even George W Bush's Defence Secretary Robert M Gates, a member of the opposition Republican party, was retained from the previous administration.[5] These observations raised legitimate fears: was this just the same old agenda as before? Were the strings still being pulled from mysterious levels above? Those without faith in a system that appears always to be the same behind the scenes, no matter who is in charge, remain unconvinced that a political saviour has arrived. Indeed, some see Obama as quite the opposite.[6]

So the new times we find ourselves in seem no less prone to suspicion and conspiratorial musings than before. Indeed, if the global recession worsens and draconian measures to combat any subsequent unrest are stepped up (as vigilantes target bankers' properties, and street protests erupt, such as those seen - however contrived - at the London G20 summit in April 2009), the atmosphere of doubt may well deepen and evolve into something more proactive. We need to be careful how we respond, however, lest authorities are given the very mandates of control they may be looking for [more on this in Chapter XV].

Applying the Truth Agenda

If one turns around the naive assumption that the world is run for our collective benefit, and starts to consider just for a moment that it might, in fact, be run instead for the needs of an elite few, with their own murky plans, the uncomfortable effect is that everything begins to make a horrible kind of sense and some of the unexplained mysteries and many dark cover-ups begin to form a pattern. Some things are mysteries through the simple absence of an answer. But certain areas may remain obscure because somebody prefers it that way. The purpose of this book is to explore the possible patterns that might be falling into place before our very eyes in these times of growing doubt and subterfuge. Many believe we stand at a pivotal moment in human history. Understanding those patterns could hold the key to unlocking the cell of ignorance which has perhaps held us all prisoner for far too long.

If there is, then, an underlying global agenda that does not have our best interests at heart, how do we identify and expose it so that mass-awareness and subsequent action might dispel its worst effects? Perhaps, in response, we need to apply our own agenda - a 'truth agenda' - a process which simply looks again at the world as presented to us and asks whether the surface glamour and veneer of philanthropic intent holds up to logical scrutiny.

The Truth Agenda, then, is a straightforward method of selecting significant events that have shaped our modern world, and starkly and methodically peering just under the veneer to see what lies beneath. In so doing, different underlying motivations to surface appearances often present themselves, and underexposed details are revealed, as this book explores. Such analysis is not original - many other concerned individuals share the task today, and others will doubtless join in. But we appear to live in times where getting to the heart of what is really going on seems to matter more than ever, especially with such sweeping global means of communication, blatant economic manipulation and technological influence now available to those who may have ambitious plans for centralisation and concentration of power. The more who can raise awareness of what might be occurring to our collective detriment, the

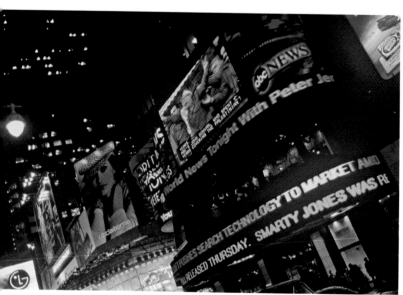

New York's Times Square announces the death of then Palestinian leader Yasser Arafat amongst the glitz of Broadway in 2004 - geopolitics and commercialism side by side in our new world of instant global communication. Yet such easy transmission of information also provides a perfect tool of universal propaganda for global elitists.

more chance there is of creating a positive collective solution. This book is but one more small contribution to the process, but the hope here is to encapsulate in an accessible and coherent way many of the key issues, as identified by the world of truthseeking, that can seem confusing and overwhelming to the uninitiated.

Over the years, investigation by many intrepid researchers (including this author) into unexplained phenomena have revealed how a systemic underlying belief in the supernatural, esoterica, and participation in - yes - conspiracies, has shaped our civilisation. This is denied, of course, and paradoxically a veneer of logical scientism is generally presented to us as the foundation of modern society - but the reality is that deeper scrutiny reveals something else altogether. By applying the Truth Agenda to a series of what may at first appear to be unrelated elements, it becomes apparent that there is a linking thread connecting many of the power and belief structures that shape the civilisation we live in today. These, in turn, almost certainly play a part in fuelling the control issues that increasingly bind us, as the unfolding of the subsequent chapters will hopefully demonstrate.

THE TRUTH AGENDA: *Doubts about the way the world is being run today are leading an increasing number of people to reconsider 'conspiracy theories' in a new light. If the world is not being run for our benefit, then whose? The recent change of administration in the White House has raised hopes of a new era, but continuing policies of old mean that many probing enquiries from the truthseekers remain legitimate. Applying a simple process of analysis to the key events of recent history may reveal important hidden layers, offering clues to the real agendas motivating our society.*

The monuments of Giza, Egypt. For all their reknown and the many archaeological guesses, no-one really knows how or why the pyramids were made - yet another mystery we take for granted.

II   MYSTERIES ANCIENT AND MODERN

There are many mysteries around us, which suggest that the world may not be quite as it seems - but as a culture we often like to pretend otherwise. It is always implied that everything is neatly explained and pigeonholed, and we are easily distracted from further investigation by intellectual snobbery or active debunking. Yet becoming more aware of unresolved enigmas can awaken people in unexpected ways. Two mysteries in particular provide good inspiration, one ancient, one modern; the pyramids and the crop circles.

The Giza Challenge

Mystery is in the fabric of everything around us, although we soon learn to co-exist with it and, eventually, forget it is there at all. The famous Egyptian pyramids on the Giza plateau stand as a perfect example of a mystery we all live with comfortably. Gigantic, awe-inspiring, they continue to fascinate each generation. Their images adorn calendars, book covers, posters and all manner of merchandise. With blocks so perfectly cut and placed that not even paper can go between them, the pyramids remain the finest example of human architectural genius. Although their original perfection has been marred (their gleamingly smooth outer walls having been largely removed), what we see today would still be a challenge for modern construction techniques. Indeed, the truth is that no-one knows for sure how they were made.

Yet despite this vacuum of knowledge, we continually see television reconstructions of how the pyramids *must* have been made - teams of sweating manual labour hauling massive slabs with ropes and rollers up gargantuan masonry ramps, almost as big as the pyramids themselves. We are more often than not told that ramps are the obvious solution. Indeed, a British television attempt to build a - very small - modern pyramid a few years ago could find no other way of lifting the blocks to the top. And yet there is no archaeological evidence whatsoever that ramps were ever built. Their scale and robustness would have been such that some trace of their structure would be left today in the sands beneath Giza - but excavations and numerous searches have revealed nothing. One recent suggestion is that *internal* ramps may have been used, but it all still remains highly speculative.[1]

When adventurous souls suggest the possibility that levitation techniques - perhaps using high-frequency sound - might have been used to construct the Egyptian monuments, the intellectuals and archaeological establishment laugh them down, despite some historical suggestions that such an art once existed (even Ian Lawton and Ian Ogilvie-Herald's otherwise sceptical 2001 book *Giza: The Truth* accepts the possibility of levitation, but the very act of considering this still pushes them into the realm of the 'alternative'). And so ramps and slaves parade across our screens again, and anyone who challenges is described as a 'pyramidiot'. Intellectualism and the darker side of 'peer review', as always, ensures nothing upsets the long-established hypotheses of the academic world - even when they are essentially assumptions and not necessarily supported by the facts.

In truth, we do not even know for certain when the pyramids were built, let alone how or why. Traditional Egyptology puts their construction between around 2589 and 2504 BCE during the Fourth Dynasty of the 'Old Kingdom', but others have claimed a date of much greater antiquity. The sphinx, certainly, displays stone weathering suggestive of a much older, wetter age, though all of this remains in heavy contention - or not. Standard archaeology simply dismisses each of the alternative theories on an equal basis. The dates have been set, the books have been written, and those who question the presumptions of the elder scholars are sidelined and ridiculed.

As to their purpose, the long-held view that the pyramids are simple, if elaborate, tombs continues to pervade the official doctrine, but many have challenged this simplistic take on these huge structures, which fails to take into account many unexplained aspects of their construction and placement. These include possible astronomical features, with many believing that the three main pyramids of Giza represent a huge ground plan of the belt of Orion and that thin shafts in the Great Pyramid were once aligned to specific stars.[2] Others vigorously disagree, of course, and there are far too many other 'alternative' theories to explore here, ranging from claims that the structures are 'power-plants', to the concept that they represent geometrical scale models of the planet and stand as a commemoration of a global axis tilt that took place around 10,500 BC. But the many astonishing mathematical correlations and coincidences in the angles and constructions at Giza do seem to demand attention,

The pyramids still stand as the most astounding structures ever built. While academic speculation gives the impression that their construction and purpose is explainable, the fact is that our understanding of them remains very limited - just one more global mystery we live with amongst many others.

not least the remarkable fact that the plateau (taking the latitude of 29.5 degrees and longitude of 31 degrees as the 'two lines that cover the most combined land area in the world') stands at the precise centre point of all the land masses of the Earth.[3]

While some proposals almost certainly strain credulity, the fact is that a large number of researchers believe there is a hidden purpose to the pyramids. Some of these ideas, at least, surely deserve a greater level of scrutiny - yet anything that falls even slightly outside the narrow parameters set by the establishment is not acceptable for investigation by the intellectual elite. (To answer the inevitable question here, these qualms do *not* equate to a promotion of the idea of extra-terrestrial influence in ancient Egyptian monument building, although some may be interested in the biblical references to the mysterious 'sons of God' and the Nephilim in Chapter V).

The Giza plateau stands at the exact centre of all the land masses on Earth - surely not a coincidence, but a fascinating observation that remains undiscussed by standard Egyptology.

The ultimate truth of all the pyramidal arguments is not the point here. The Giza challenge is merely illustrative of how the world tends to treat enduring mystery: it simply pretends there isn't any. When the Truth Agenda is applied to the pyramids, definitive answers are not forthcoming - yet the impression is given that all is understood and neatly wrapped-up. When events accumulate too far beyond the mundane and authorities can't pretend anymore, that's when the cover-ups begin (as with UFOs, as we shall see). Some, of course, believe the ancient wisdom (if not the technical wizardry), occult knowledge and system of authority displayed by the civilisation which worked so hard at Giza *is* preserved and coveted by secret societies and elite bodies who use it to further their own ends in today's world [Chapter V]. Whilst academic protectionism may explain some of the closed-mindedness, other hardcore doubters have alleged the operation of deliberate archaeological cover-ups to conceal humankind's true, and possibly much older, origins.[4]

The Crop Circle Controversy

Another mystery which the mainstream has managed to turn its back on in the hope that it will go away is the ever-enduring phenomenon of crop circles. For years now (indeed, centuries, according to records), increasingly elaborate shapes have been appearing swirled into crop fields around the globe, with the activity's epicentre being in the English heartlands of Wiltshire. Despite everything regularly heard about the circles - usually that all of them are made by clever artists, students or Young Farmers - the absolute truth is that the origins of a large number of them are completely unknown. For all the confirmed or suspected man-made designs, however many, there is a significant proportion of formations that seems impossible to explain so simply.

Yet, once again, any sense of mystery is brushed aside by self-appointed intellectuals at one end of the spectrum, and ill-informed journalists and television producers at the other. Seeing nothing more in the research community than speculative talk (largely in favour of a non-human origin) about forces of consciousness, extra-terrestrials or hitherto unknown natural processes, it

This staggering crop formation arrived at Milk Hill, Wiltshire on 12th August 2001. At 800 feet in diameter, it comprises 409 circles and is still considered one of the finest works of the phenomenon. The media assure us that all such designs are made by men with planks, but the evidence doesn't support this view.

is assumed by establishment pundits that the only real explanation can be the one demonstrated so often in front of cameras - man-made japery with planks, ropes and rollers. But in settling for this weak assumption, the sceptics ignore the large amounts of evidence comprising eye-witness sightings of formations appearing within seconds, biological changes occurring within the flattened plants, the many reports of bizarre aerial phenomena, the astonishingly complex geometry of many of the designs, and all manner of remarkable visual and physiological experiences recounted by many different people. How are these to be accounted for by the planker hypothesis, which would have it that all formations are of human origin? Numerous manual attempts to recreate many of the less explicable qualities of crop circles have failed or taken unrealistic time and effort, with limited results. Modest man-made formations can take several hours to construct, yet many exquisitely complex designs have been proven to have appeared within prohibitively short periods of time. Nonetheless, heroes are made of hoaxers and the important contrary evidence is simply brushed aside in the mainstream, restoring the cosy order of a 'normal' world with reassuring propaganda that tells us there is nothing in the fields to be interested in (or afraid of).

It is not for now to explore the ins and outs of the crop circle enigma, and this author has written extensively about it elsewhere (see *Appendix 2*). Readers must discover and assess the evidence for themselves. However, it is another example of a mystery we live with that is pushed to the fringes, ignored and very probably covered up. Without wanting to slip into paranoia, there is good reason to believe that some of the voracious debunking which has fallen on the circles has been deliberately organised by hands unknown, anxious that we should not be drawn to a phenomenon that might actually inspire people to *think* - which it does.

The 1991 claims of the two aging pranksters Doug and Dave that they had invented the entire circle mystery as a retirement activity succeeded in persuading much of the public that nothing of interest was going on - yet no evidence was ever presented to show that the duo had made more than a few very unimpressive formations. The non-existence of the press agency which put out the Doug and Dave story (the mysterious 'MBF Services' turned out not to be contactable, as a press agency at least, leading some to suspect MI5 involvement), together with other strange discrepancies and a general lack of conviction, led many to the view that the whole exercise was a distractive cover-up.[5] If so, it worked well, with a large fall of interest in the crop circles following publication.   However, the continuation and grand evolution of the phenomenon long after the comedy pensioners had retired from the scene reawakened a general interest which has endured, if reduced in scale from its previous heights. Some formations are clearly man-made, but

This formation appeared at Boxley, Kent, on 7th August 2006. Although Wiltshire is the epicentre of the crop circle mystery, other counties also receive patterns, as do many other countries outside the UK.

a significant proportion defy explanation in such terms. Perhaps that is why further debunking exercises and deceptions still occur from time to time, new claimants having replaced Doug and Dave.

With rumours of government 'D-notices' (official orders to the media to withhold information) being placed on circle experiments and everything from the Vatican to the military or CSICOP (the Committee for the Scientific Investigation of Claims of the Paranormal - today known as the Committee for Skeptical Inquiry - a self-appointed Inquisition-like group of savagely fundamentalist academics) being implicated as the source of the sceptic stories that do the rounds of the media, a lot of energy certainly seems to have been put into attacking something apparently harmless. All of which leads people to wonder why. Does someone on high know something we don't? A study of crop circles by the Ministry of Defence in the 1980s reportedly concluded that a phenomenon without mundane origins *was* occurring, and tests carried out by ADAS (Agricultural Development and Advisory Service, a division of the Ministry of Agriculture) in 1995 revealed unexplained anomalies in nitrogen and nitrate ratios in the soil beneath crop formations.[6] The military have also shown a notable interest over the years. It may well be authorities know full well that something of significance is happening in the fields, but they would rather the general populace didn't share their interest.

The fact is that the apparently engineered stigma of ridicule that has grown up around the circle phenomenon has allowed many to be turned away from the potential learning that could be gained from it. Any debunking policies have certainly been successful. Indeed, it is a given that the very act of including crop circles in this book of otherwise 'harder' subjects will be used by many to discredit all the other information within it. Perhaps that is why I purposefully include it - because applying the Truth Agenda

750 feet crop formation surrounded by round barrows (burial mounds) near Stonehenge, Wiltshire, 4th July 2002. Ancient sites and underground water seem to attract - or help generate - crop circles, perhaps through natural 'earth energies', leading some to speculate that a combination of forces are at work.

means being able to look anything in the eye with a fresh perspective. Certainly, it is a fact that some of the truthseekers now dealing with very real-world issues would not be there today without the original stimuli of thought provided by these exquisite glyphs, whatever their origins.

Like the pyramids, the awesome presence of the crop glyphs and the subsequent questioning they stimulate, even through simply contemplating the notions of higher intervention versus human art, have inspired many to more advanced levels of thinking - and changed the world as a result. Aside from the evolution of consciousness, which seems to arise from the inner debate each must have when faced with both beauty and enigma, there is also a direct influence, however. Some of the symbolism in the fields clearly echoes ancient wisdoms or archetypal psychological forms, and many aficionados speak of having been 'woken up' inside on a very deep, inexplicable level. The astronomical data contained within other designs have specifically indicated future dates and times which, when they have arrived, have coincided with unusual - and unpredictable - celestial events, sometimes referencing the cycles of the Sun [Chapter XII], factors which may play a key role in our near future.[7] Meanwhile, the recurring symbolic references to the year 2012 - subject of much prophecy

Many crop circles display complex detail even at close quarters, such as this tight swirl seen inside part of another formation at Milk Hill, Wiltshire, on 8th August 1997.

and speculation, as we shall see - have led many to accept the crop circles as just one more herald of some imminent and significant event for our planet. Indeed, the hopes and fears surrounding insights into our own future bind together many of the mysteries and cover-ups that may well be a major influence in the hidden agendas governing us today.

Other Mysteries

The pyramids and crop circles are just two examples of mysteries that are lightly dismissed, yet remain entirely unresolved. There are many others which could be listed here, outside of the usual novelties so often inappropriately lumped in with them by a lazy media; Bigfoot, the Loch Ness Monster, big cats, etc., all of which may or may not exist, but hardly carry the same weight of evidence or influence lives on any profound level.

The more relevant examples include religious apparitions [Chapter IV], ghosts (witnessed by so many reliable people, but scoffed at by the 'rationalists') and out-of-body experiences (verified as more than simple hallucination by much evidence, but similarly sidelined). The latter two phenomena seem strongly to suggest that consciousness can exist outside of the flesh under specific circumstances.

Many patients in hospitals have reported finding themselves floating above their own bodies while under general anaesthetic, and have been able to move their disembodied minds around, later describing seeing objects (verfied by staff) in high places that couldn't possibly have been seen from ground level. Some researchers have turned this ability into the directed art of 'remote viewing', in which minds are seemingly able to travel to far away or hidden places, often accurately describing layouts or objects, which are later confirmed. That extensive military experiments with remote viewing and other psychic techniques are known to have been conducted suggests that this is something taken seriously by higher authorities.

Crystal skull at the British Museum, one of several found across the globe. Although mercilessly debunked and now generally claimed to have been manufactured in 19th century Europe (as opposed to being from Aztec and Maya times, as many believed), the technique behind their perfect carving and finish has never been fully explained and many believe they remain a mystery worth further investigation.

A more physical manifestation of mystery is the disturbing animal mutilation enigma, in which cattle and other livestock are found with specific organs seamlessly and bloodlessly removed, often after sightings of strange aerial phenomena [page 45]. It says something that thousands of cases have been reported over the years, yet most everyday folk have never heard of the phenomenon.

Others are excited by speculation over the origins of the much-debunked but still enigmatic crystal skulls found around the world, or are fired by the joys of psychic questing and mediumistic channelling [page 50]. Some explore the possibilities offered by earth mysteries (the ethereal 'energies' around ancient stones and landmarks) and the curious geometrical connections of complexes like Avebury in Wiltshire (site of so many crop circles) with alleged remains of civilisations on Mars (the 'face' and pyramids on the Martian plains of Cydonia). There are many unexplained mysteries to investigate, but we do not need to sift the entire pantheon here. The point is that the world, which so often presents itself as neatly ordered and understood, may not be quite the tidy package of reason and honesty we are told it is. As such, we need to focus on specific areas that have something important to say about these times of unparalleled philosophical, social and political change.

Applying the Truth Agenda reveals holes in the official explanations for many of the mysteries that have been so lightly touched on by the mainstream, and there is good evidence to suggest full knowledge of them has been continually discouraged by intellectual elitism, distraction or active debunking, as with the crop circles. However, one area in particular shows very good evidence that full-blown cover-ups *are* instigated, and for this we must enter the twilight realm of ufology.

THE TRUTH AGENDA: *Academic elitism and a wide encouragement of scepticism too often prevents warranted enquiry into mysteries and phenomena that could provide valuable information or generate higher aspirations. A closed establishment prevents full investigation of archaeological monuments such as the pyramids, while fervent debunking seems designed to deflect interest away from 'paranormal' enigmas like crop circles, suggesting that important seams of knowledge are being kept from the general populace.*

The legendary military base Area 51, Nevada, USA. This official aerial shot was taken in 1968 and more runways have been constructed since. Many believe military technology is being reverse-engineered from recovered extra-terrestrial craft secretly stored here.

III   UFOS

Something strange is flying in our skies. Are UFOs extra-terrestrial or military? Either way, there is clear evidence that full knowledge of them is kept from us. The mystery surrounding this one phenomenon is confirmation that we are clearly NOT told the truth about everything. Yet many people claim to have had encounters with non-human creatures that have left them with a profound sense of expectation about the future.

The Roswell Incident

On 7th July 1947, the New Mexico-based newspaper, *The Roswell Daily Record*, sported an extraordinary headline - *RAAF Captures Flying Saucer on Ranch in Roswell Region*. In that decade this wasn't treated as a joke. Ever-increasing sightings of strange flying objects were being made then and, in a climate of post-war paranoia, any unusual craft or aerial light had the potential to be an unknown enemy threat. During World War II, bomber pilots even had a nick-name for the peculiar lights that would sometimes accompany their flight-paths - 'foo fighters'. These lights were never adequately explained.

Therefore, when a newspaper reported that a flying saucer had crashed in the desert near the town of Roswell, many in 1947 were happy to accept that this was exactly what had happened. Over time, other claimed details began to creep out - bodies of thin, grey alien creatures were reported to have been retrieved from the craft and the area of debris around it, and secretly carried to the local hospital. Military personnel had moved in and cordoned off the area and were planning to retrieve the crashed 'flying disk' for examination. Ever since that fateful headline, the Roswell incident has entered modern mythology; the subject of intense speculation, investigation - and denial. And deny it the authorities did. Aghast to see news of a direct alien intervention being splashed over the front pages, the Roswell Army Air Field (RAAF) public relations team sprang into action and the next day declared that the crash had involved nothing more than a 'weather balloon'. Soon, the attention around Roswell died down, leaving a vacuum of information which would be gradually filled by the curious, accurately or not, over the next few decades.

One of the RAAF officers who nervously displayed bits of wood and foil from the supposed weather balloon for the press cameras the day after the Roswell incident was Major Jesse Marcel. Marcel had been directly involved with cataloguing debris from the crash site and had seen for himself what had been retrieved. Interviewed in1978 by ufologist Stanton T Friedman, Marcel claimed that the weather balloon story was a decoy and that he had been ordered to front a debunking story. He maintained that he had indeed witnessed for himself unexplained artefacts at Roswell, which appeared to have non-terrestrial origins, and he described strange materials with unusual properties and objects with unrecognisable 'hieroglyphs' on them. In his opinion, an alien craft *was* recovered from the site, and he adhered to this claim until his death. Marcel's children, who were shown some of the debris by their father at the time, continue to support his story today.

As the Marcel testimony became public, so other witnesses from the Roswell event came forward to fill in more details. Although Marcel never saw the full crashed disk for himself, others said they did. Some military personnel and hospital staff claimed to remember five 'alien bodies' being brought in for autopsy, with more than one assertion that one of the creatures was still alive. Several staff reported being intimidated and threatened by sinister officials, who told them to keep quiet about what they had seen.

These are the claims, at least. As the decades have gone by, it has become more difficult to know what really happened at Roswell. Sceptics claim the various testimonies are misremembered minor incidents or full-blown fantasies, while others maintain that a massive cover-up took place. What is certain is that *something* came down near Roswell in 1947, exotic or mundane. It is also interesting to note that the official cover story has altered over the years. By 1995, the innocent weather balloon account had morphed into the object being a secret government device from Project Mogul, a programme to detect sound waves from Soviet atomic tests. Just two years after that it was being suggested that the retrieved 'bodies' might in fact have existed, but were nothing more than crash test dummies being used in an experiment. But why take a crash test dummy to an actual hospital? And what would that have to do with Project Mogul?

The Little A'le'inn *in Nevada, USA, the tourist-face of a subject some believe is a serious business. Just a little way from here is Area 51, a top secret base where many believe the craft retrieved from Roswell - amongst other artefacts - is stored.*

For all the clear mythologising and layers of misinformation regarding the Roswell incident, from both official and ufological sources, the fact is that stories of the event have been instrumental in stirring up interest in the many, many other reports of possible extra-terrestrial intrusions into our world. And what did happen to the supposed disk that was recovered? Some believe they know where it was taken.

Area 51

UFO folklore has it that the crashed Roswell craft is stored at the fabled US military base, code-named 'Area 51'. Situated in southern Nevada, and also sometimes known as 'Dreamland', Area 51 does exist, but such secrecy has surrounded its real purpose that it has become the subject of huge conspiracy speculation and has sparked several science fiction bonanzas (of which the alien-invasion blockbuster *Independence Day* is but one cheesy example).

Only acknowledged peripherally by the US military, Area 51 is ostensibly a test area for secret weapons and experimental aircraft. Nothing more is known. What is for sure is that a large no-fly area surrounds it and no-one gets in or out without major security clearance. That security has

Groom Lake Road, Nevada, USA. This dusty track leads to the mysterious Area 51, and is about as much as anyone can now see from the ground, its barbed perimeter fences having been greatly extended in recent years.

tightened in recent years. In previous decades it was possible to get close enough to Area 51 for several surreptitious camera crews and UFO investigators to have filmed clearly anomalous flying objects performing highly unusual manoeuvres over the base. Perhaps realising that it had become an attractive circus for truthseekers, the authorities eventually extended the perimeters beyond visual range. Anyone trying to get closer will soon find themselves under arrest.

A number of rumours and claims from supposed ex-insiders have surfaced over the years as to the purpose of Area 51 and its nearby bases. The recurring theme of the testimonies is that beneath the grim-looking runways and barracks is an extensive network of hangars holding within them retrieved craft from the likes of Roswell - and more besides, including organic specimens. The supposed intention behind all of this is to examine the extra-terrestrial technology and reverse-engineer it into new devices for military means. Some believe secrets from other-worldly technology have already been applied in useable vehicles, such as 'stealth' aircraft, which, oddly enough, bear a slight resemblance to some of the mysterious 'black triangles' that many have sighted in the skies over the years. Others think it has already gone a stage further, believing that most of the UFOs seen today are military experiments.

It is also speculated that less dangerous alien secrets may have already leaked into mainstream science - some believe the development of microchip and nano-technology could have been stimulated in the same way. If the US military has been using information from recovered UFOs to gain a military and economical advantage, there is, of course, no reason why other countries might not be doing the same - saucer crashes have been rumoured around the world. The whole recent history of technological progress may, in this view, have been influenced, albeit indirectly, by extra-terrestrial intervention, if the claims are to be believed. Some even hold that governments - the US, in particular - are actually working in cahoots with beings from other worlds, for reasons good or evil. (Television series *The X-Files* based much of its central concept around this idea, ending with the idea that a full alien invasion was being arranged for the year 2012.)

The sign that greets any would-be visitors to Area 51. What does go on inside has never been officially revealed, but the 'deadly force authorized' warnings make it clear that we are not supposed to try to find out.

The more incredulous, naturally, dismiss all talk of ETs, and hold that the entire UFO mystery is a product of purely human secret technology - or consider aerial sightings as nothing more than atmospheric phenomena and misreported mundanities. Others, such as Ian R Crane, without dismissing the possibility of real alien presences, have proposed that a deliberately stimulated cultural awareness of ETs is the first stage of a planned *faked* alien invasion [see also page 304] designed to further the ultimate aims of the global control agenda discussed in this book.

The important point here is that with Area 51 and the obvious withholding of information on UFOs in general (see below), we have clear evidence of a cover-up, whatever the truth. Although there are plenty of other secret research facilities hidden away in all major countries, there is usually some kind of official explanation to account for their existence. Even if it's just military technology that's being hidden, the fact that so little information about what goes on at Area 51 has ever been made available, and that all attempts at prising details from authorities are resisted, means that someone doesn't want anyone on the outside to know what's going on. By definition, this is a cover-up. It is clear evidence of one layer of our society - amongst many others - that is being kept from us, beyond the usual bureaucratic closets, knowledge of which is denied even to the taxpayers that support its existence. All of this secrecy is for our safety and 'national security', we are told.

UFO Evidence

What direct evidence is there that knowledge of UFOs is withheld from us? Whichever way it is looked at, something strange appears to be flying in our skies, despite the denials of the sceptics. This author, for example, has been approached at lectures more than once by commercial pilots who have witnessed craft and other aerial phenomena that seem to defy normal explanation, reports of which are without question kept quiet about in the aviation industry. Numerous people have recounted extraordinary sightings, and many thousands of seemingly rational people around the globe have witnessed flying disks, the aforementioned black triangles, clusters of lights and other objects that all seem to suggest something out of the ordinary is occurring, human or alien. Even when one takes the fantasists, frauds and the merely mistaken out of the equation (which admittedly makes up for a large percentage of reports), there is still a formidable body of sightings that cannot be ignored.

UFO 'flaps' (large numbers of reports in one area) have been going on around the world for many years. England had its own in the Warminster area in the 1970s, for instance, and the much-disputed incident at Rendlesham Forest, Suffolk, in 1980, where RAF personnel allegedly witnessed a conical craft hovering in the woods (which supposedly deactivated the nuclear missiles secretly stored there, a recurring and striking feature of military UFO reports), has become the UK's very own Roswell, equally prone to both denial and mythologising.[1] In the 1990s, Nick Pope, an ex-Ministry of Defence employee, insisted that one of his duties during his employment had been researching UFOs and that the MOD had been actively suppressing information. Although some have accused him of exaggeration (and even of spreading deliberate misinformation), it seems clear that those in power know far more about UFO-related events than anyone is prepared to let on.

It is interesting to note that one of the most pressured extradition cases in recent history, in which the US has been trying to bring UK resident Gary McKinnon to trial in the States, concerns McKinnon's (admitted) 'hacking' of US military databases, ostensibly to try to find information on UFOs and secret anti-gravity technology. He claims to have found proof for both by his actions. The disproportionate vigour with which the American legal teams have been trying to extradite McKinnon (despite his having been diagnosed as suffering from Asperger's Syndrome, a form of autism) suggests they are particularly keen to make an example of him, one which might dissuade others from pursuing the truth on UFOs, despite their claim that concerns merely revolve around 'national security'. More serious espionage has not received such attention, and any prosecutions have previously been allowed to take place in the native countries of the defendants. McKinnon faces a potential 70-year sentence if tried and found guilty in the US. The case is still hanging on appeals at the time of writing, with McKinnon's legal team having gone through both the British High Court and the European Court of Human Rights.[2]

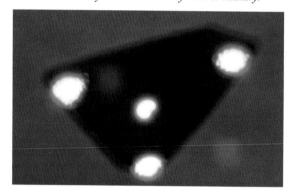

Alleged shot of the classic 'black triangle' variety of UFO, filmed at Wallonia, Belgium, 15th June 1990. Although saucer or cigar-shapes are the most commonly reported objects, the triangles have been seen many times - but are they alien or military?

As far as global UFO sightings go, in recent years Mexico City seems to have been the centre of a quite astonishing series of events. Whole fleets of shining spherical objects and other variations have been seen - and videoed - by many different people across the city at the same time. Aztec and Maya prophecies of imminent 'end times' due in 2012 [Chapter XII], and mystical intrigues surrounding the nearby volcanic mountain Popocatépetl, have all added to the portentous sense of mystery which has built up around the flap. Indeed, the Mexican Air Force (Fuerza Aérea Mexicana) is the only authoritative body in the world to have officially acknowledged the existence of the UFO phenomenon as something it is concerned by and interested in, although it remains open as to what the objects are.

Previously, the only authorised study of UFOs admitted to by a government was Project Blue Book, carried out by the United States Air Force (USAF), which documented and investigated over 12,000 sightings between 1952 and 1969 (and almost certainly beyond, but officially their interest stopped there). Perhaps predictably, the final report in 1970 dourly concluded that UFOs did not constitute 'a threat to national security' and that the vast majority of sightings were 'misidentifications of natural phenomena or conventional aircraft'. It completely brushed over the not insignificant 22% of cases that 'remained unsolved'. The British government has also from time to time (most recently in 2008) declassified reports of UFOs, but with equal lack of commitment or clarity.

However, we do have such a thing as the 'Freedom of Information Act', both in the USA and the UK. What happens when this is applied and hard-to-get official documents are sought so that the public can make up their own minds on the evidence? Are such documents ever released? Surprisingly, they are, if authorities are compelled enough by dedicated campaigners prepared to go through the layers of red tape. Unfortunately, in most cases where there is even a small suggestion of anything out of the ordinary, what enquirers get presented with are pages with vast swathes of text obscured by black blocks to prevent the crucial details from being read - in the name of protecting the 'national security' that Project Blue Book said UFOs weren't a threat to. So the documents get released, but the secrets stay put.

Sturdy campaigners like Dr Steven Greer have soldiered on with impressive efforts such as the Disclosure Project to stimulate governments into releasing the truth by helping 'military, intelligence, government, corporate and scientific' whistleblowers to testify publicly with their UFO and ET technology experiences.[3] However, debunkers do their worst and authorities simply ignore, so it's an uphill, if noble, struggle that's likely to continue for a while yet before any real recognition is gained, short of an extraordinary event occurring.

With the UFO mystery, then, there is clear evidence of an ongoing cover-up, plain and simple. If the governments of the world aren't going to speak up, however, then we have to turn to those who have claimed personal experiences with UFOs and their occupants to see what they have to say. And what some of them report has repercussions that lead us onto one of the most important underlying beliefs that might be shaping our world today - the expectation of imminent catastrophic change.

Contactee Experiences

One of the most controversial of all the UFO-related areas is that of 'contactees'; people who claim to have had direct encounters with extra-terrestrial beings. Some describe been physically abducted onto hovering craft, while others recount being taken from their beds at night by teleportation techniques or through some form of astral projection. Tales of strange physical examinations and even surgical operations being carried out on the abductees by alien creatures are widespread, particularly in the USA, where thousands of claimed abductions have been recorded. The beings described are typically (as at Roswell) the small, slender grey humanoid figures with dark almond-shaped eyes that have become the archetypal extra-terrestrial in the public mind. Other races have also been reported, such as the 'Nordics' (tall, handsome blonde figures), reptilian beings [page ??] and preying mantis-like presences - but the 'greys' remain the most prevalent visitors.

The first contactee story to reach wide attention concerned Betty and Barney Hill's claimed experience on 19th September 1961. While driving along a quiet road late at night in New Hampshire, USA, they observed a bright disc-shaped object approach their car. Frightened and curious, Barney stepped out into the road to observe it. Seeing 'humanoid figures' inside the craft, and feeling threatened by them, the couple decided to drive away, only to enter a strange state of altered consciousness instead. There is uncertainty about what happened next. From information based on disturbing dreams received by Betty after the experience, and hypnosis sessions held later to decipher what had happened during their altered state, they pieced together a scenario familiar from many other contactee accounts since; the medical procedures (which often centre around the reproductive organs), fragmented conversations with the beings, and even a moment where Betty was shown an astronomical map outlining the star system from where the visitors had originated.

So many people around the world have had similar experiences - often reported by children, unaware of others having had the same encounters - that it's hard to believe all of it could be lies or imagination. Yet on what level of 'reality' these abductions take place is debatable. Do they occur in physicality, or in the realm of the mind? Are they extra-terrestrial encounters or inner psychotic episodes triggered by psychic or electromagnetic stimuli (which has been shown to give rise to hallucinogenic visions - page 256)?

Extensive investigations by non-ufological enquirers have turned up interesting results. Before his tragic and untimely death in 2004 (run over by a drunken driver, raising inevitable conspiracy speculation), John E. Mack, a Harvard professor of psychiatry, endured peer ridicule and academic censure before succeeding in his quest to get the psychological community to acknowledge the scientific validity of the contactee/adbuctee phenomemon. During his studies, he interviewed sixty people and subjected them to rigorous interview and hypnotic regression. Mack found himself convinced that, whatever the exact nature of the contactees' experiences, *they* believed them to be real. With just a few exceptions, he concluded that most of those investigated were well-balanced and reliable witnesses doing their best to describe extraordinary events, which had occurred on at least some level of authenticity. Other studies, including the work of David M Jacobs, have supported these conclusions.

Something, therefore, appears to be happening on a very wide scale, which demands greater attention and not the mainstream dismissal that it usually receives. The similarity to traditional folk tales of people being abducted into the fairy realms, with attendant sexual and psychological overtones, has also not gone unnoticed. Either ETs have been among us for much longer than anyone suspects (and this may be the case - see Chapter V), or there is a mysterious esoteric stimulant at work that produces archetypal experiences for those affected, which are interpreted by individual minds into whatever frame of reference 'works' for them - fairies and demons in old times, aliens today.

Why Would ETs Be Here?

This treatise cannot determine definitively the true nature of the claimed experiences with apparently other-worldly beings. Instead, it is the beliefs and convictions that have resulted from some of these encounters that take us into the next important part of our general hypothesis. Yet there are many who do take the potential presence of ETs seriously, and it is worth a brief summing-up of some of the ideas around this.

If the ETs are real, one must speculate about why they are here. Some believe they are beings that have lost the ability to reproduce and are trying to extract genetic material from humans in an attempt to save themselves (perhaps explaining the fixation on the reproductive organs in many abduction accounts). The breeding of ET-human hybrids is often spoken about by contactees, and has interesting resonance with the ancient myths of the Nephilim [page 85]. The entirely strange and rather disturbing connection of UFO sightings with the many reports of mutilated cattle and other farm animals, in which organs (again, often reproductive) have been carefully removed with almost laser-precision and very little tissue damage, may also play into such an agenda, although secret military experiments cannot be discounted as another possible explanation.[4] Others think the visitors are trying to assess our species to see if we are ready to fit into an intergalactic community - or are weak enough to be invaded. Could there be a number of different ET species vying for control, some benevolent and others less so, with secret deals being made with some of our governments? Another view holds that the grey beings are not extra-

Traditional flying saucer allegedly photographed at Passoria, New Jersey in 1952. It is easy to be cynical about many of the UFO photographs offered as proof, but the level of eye-witness testimony is substantial, and tales of ET encounters are many.

terrestrial at all, but progressed versions of ourselves from the far future, coming back to regain something vital, which evolution or self-inflicted catastrophe has somehow eradicated.

However, what of the theory that the growing cultural awareness of supposed visits from ETs (nicely debunked for double-bluff purposes) may be part of an ongoing long-term plan to implement a faked alien invasion, as an incentive to create an enforced centralisation of power for our protection? This may sound an outlandish concept but, in the light of other controversial evidence we shall explore, the idea of such a massive deception being perpetrated on humanity may not be as entirely unlikely as it sounds. How we would know the difference between a real or hoaxed invasion is an argument for another time, though.

What matters here is not so much the reality or otherwise of the claimed ET contact experiences, but rather the consequences of how these people are affected by them - and the similarity of their visions to beliefs held in many different quarters.

Visions of the Future

As far as the ET contactee accounts go, what takes us towards the unpeeling of the next layer are the oft-repeated claims that their celestial captors have shown them visions of the future, either in words, projected images or psychic impressions. In many cases, the visions have either been apocalyptic or at least epic, depicting transformative global events that would come to pass and take humanity onto a new level of evolution - around *now*.

There are several noted examples of supposed extra-terrestrial prophecy. Claimed (if predictably disputed) contactees such as Billy Meier and Whitley Streiber have described being given information on approaching developments of huge significance including, in Meier's case, an apparent forewarning (in 1987) of 9/11 and the subsequent 'War on Terror', which would come to pass fourteen years later.[5] Ufologist Jon King, meanwhile, claims to have had an entire 'schedule' of how important evolutionary events would unfold (culminating in 'Earthshift' in 2013), telepathically transmitted to him during a series of encounters in the early 1980s.[6] At least some of the events made known to King (including an apparent prediction of complex crop formations, or 'energy codings' in Wiltshire) have come to pass, and the general schedule regarding global consciousness appears to tie in with many of the other prophecies made for the year 2012 - a phenomenon we shall explore more fully later. For quick reference, the predictions revolve around a 5125-year cycle of time recorded by independent cultures around the world, through folklore, prophecies and calendrical systems, all of which seem to indicate that each time the period comes around for renewal, a huge shift for the planet arrives with it. The turning of the next cycle, according to the most reliable calculators of the ancient calendars, occurs on 21st December 2012, and speculation is now rife as to what might transpire [Chapter XII].

Many other supposed ET-related encounters have had similar connotations of impending change for the world, and 'channelled' messages from all manner of proclaimed other-worldly intelligences [page 50] have spoken again and again of these times - late 20th, early 21st century - as being a crucial nexus point in history. Wherever these visions and messages come from, and whatever the real nature of the abduction experiences, they seem to fit a wider pattern of an upwelling awareness deep within the collective psyche of something big about to happen to our world, or at least to our civilisation.

This, then, is where we need to investigate other cross-referencing sources to see if there is a wider context into which these insights and prophecies fit.

THE TRUTH AGENDA: *Secret bases and whistleblowers' talk of recovered extra-terrestrial craft and non-human bodies have created a culture of myth-making and confusion. But it seems clear that there have been direct cover-ups concerning the existence of UFOs, and authorities clearly know far more than they are admitting, whatever the purpose of these mysterious visitations. There are simply too many reports for all of them to be dismissed, and individuals' encounters with apparently other-worldly beings seem to inspire a greater awareness of the importance of these times, or grant them direct visions of momentous near-future events.*

Statue of Our Lady of the Rosary at Fatima, Portugal, commemorating the remarkable apparitions of 1917. The final 'miracle' of Fatima is still one of the best-documented of its kind. But what was the exact nature of what occurred, and how much are the prophecies made here still influencing powerful people in the world today?

IV   MIRACLES AND PROPHECIES

Predictions of future times run through history, and are especially strong within Christianity. Belief in these prophecies, together with information gleaned from clairvoyant sources or direct messages from seemingly religious apparitions witnessed by thousands, may play a quiet but important role in influencing political decisions that affect us all.

Seers and Prophets

A recurring figure in historical and religious sagas is the prophet or soothsayer, one with the supernatural ability to foresee events that will shape the lives of monarchs and nations. The visions are often grand and apocalyptic - and specifically symbolic to the individual or party being addressed. But many also take the prophecies literally and apply their meaning directly to global events; hence the fundamentalist Christians currently promoting St John's book of Revelation as an actual prediction of things to come - events that believers claim are about to play out within our lifetime [page 51].

What kind of legacy have the prophets of old left for us, and how seriously should we take the overall picture of the future they have painted? The writings of the French 14th century mystic Nostradamus, for instance, are often held up as examples of successful prophecy, but in truth Nostradamus wrote his quatrains in such cryptic and esoterically multi-layered language that any attempt at interpretation in modern times is entirely subjective. When his words are applied to almost anything, some sort of meaning can be squeezed out, but with no absolute method of verification, their usefulness is questionable. As a result, the works of Nostradamus have been much abused - he may have accurately foreseen particular events, but no-one can really be sure. Similar grey areas hover over the writings of the likes of Mother Shipton, the well-known prophetess from the same historical period.[1] However, what does emerge from their writings is a sense that *these* times - again, the end of the 20th and the beginning of the 21st centuries - would be pivotal times of shift for humanity, and they are not alone amongst seers in suggesting this. Was it merely millennial superstition at work or was something else being picked up on?

In more recent times, there has been an upsurge of prediction and prophecy, which backs up the view that something of great importance is about to change the lives of the people of this time. The popular cultural emergence of clairvoyance and psychic studies from the late Victorian days onwards has led to a string of foretellings or channelled messages from the spiritual realms, all with a similar theme.

In the early 20th century, the American medium Edgar Cayce became the

Nostradamus of his day, anticipating much of the general shape the century would take on as it passed. Supporters claim he accurately predicted the Second World War, the 1929 stock market crash, the subsequent Great Depression and the creation of the State of Israel, amongst other important events.[2] Most significantly, Cayce spoke of a period of devastating 'Earth changes', both climatic and geophysical, which would sweep the world in the last decades of the century. Although events have clearly played out more slowly than Cayce foresaw, many feel his overall vision is beginning to unfold now. Was he right about everything? Clearly not, and sceptics, naturally, find ways to ignore it all. Yet, some areas are worth further thought. Although, for instance, Atlantis failed to dramatically rise again towards the century's end (at least in any overt fashion - some recently discovered underwater ruins have been claimed as remnants of Atlantis), perhaps Cayce's prediction that it would was fulfilled in a different way - through the growing awareness that ancient wisdom from a once higher civilisation (by whatever name) may have been quietly kept alive by secret societies and mystic traditions [Chapter V]. In any case, beyond the more grey areas, numerous soothsayers have agreed with Cayce's overall views on Earth changes.

Edgar Cayce, the famous psychic and visionary, as photographed in 1910. Cayce accurately predicted several of the important events of the 20th century, and his prophecies of significant 'Earth changes' tie in with information received through many other psychic channels.

Many times in more recent decades, channelled messages have been received from all kinds of spiritual realms or apparently extra-terrestrial sources speaking through human contacts - the Pleiadians, the Arcturans, the Council of Nine, the Ashtar Command [page 307], Ascended Masters, *et al* - all giving information and advice on our imminent future. Others have received insights through out-of-body experiences or drug-induced hallucinogenic trips. What trickles through all of these conduits is the assertion that the Earth is about to undergo some kind of shift, either physically, spiritually, or both, and that a period of tribulation and upheaval (as long-standing issues rise to the surface and polarise) will give way to a new 'Golden Age'. Those who practice serious astrology, meanwhile - another phenomenon too lightly dismissed by modern academics - believe that as the zodiacal wheel takes us into the Age of Aquarius, and other important planetary transits come into play [page 260], dramatic changes will, after a period of upheaval, give rise to a better realm of equality and wisdom, taking us away from the religious strife and shadowy politics that have punctuated the Age of Pisces for the last two thousand years.

How seriously should we take these messages and insinuations? With no way of verifying the claimed sources, should their channellers be trusted? Are all mediums frauds, or self-deluded egotists projecting their own psychological insecurities into fantasies of global change? Or is something genuine rising up into the collective, by whatever means necessary, to alert us to impending transformation? Throw into the mix the visions given to UFO contactees, inspirations gained by contemplation of crop circles, and all the multiple layers of the 2012 speculation, there seems to be a clear repeated theme to the insights gained from many contemporary mystical experiences.

Bearing in mind the implications of the ongoing Global Consciousness Project [Chapter XIV], in which science appears finally to be acknowledging the existence of a collective energy field, one that knows no boundaries of time, perhaps we would be wise to take heed of what *could* be a telepathic echo from our own future rippling back towards us from a huge event just around the corner. According to religious sources, especially, those ripples may have been reaching us for a long time.

Religious Prophecies

The most famous examples of future predictions can be found in Judaism and Christianity. Both Old and New Testaments are crammed full of prophets, seers and visionaries crying woe for kings and pharaohs, and hailing messianic figures to come. But the New Testament takes on a more specific theme - 'the Day of Judgement', in which the Earthly realm will be cleansed in a series of apocalyptic events, culminating in Christ's return.

Evangelical Christians are pinning a lot of hopes on St John's book of Revelation, in which vivid but rather obscure visions (which some consider might well have come to the author while imbibing hallucinogenic substances) are recorded in very mystical symbolism, believed by many scholars to be encoded as specific messages of encouragement to groups of persecuted early Christians. With their context massively expanded, modern believers are applying the visions as strict predictions of events occurring today - stepping stones to the eventual arrival of the 'New Jerusalem', which will vindicate their faith and leave behind non-believers.

And what of 'The Rapture', in which the devout believe they will be physically floated upwards into the heavens as the apocalyptic events of Judgement unfold? Anticipation for The Rapture, particularly in the USA, is now widespread and has added to the urgency and fanaticism felt by some awaiting the fulfilment of biblical prophecy, even though - perhaps surprisingly - the concept isn't based on any clear reference in the Bible. The Rapture is, in fact, a relatively modern construct, derived from a few disconnected poetic phrases scattered throughout the Old Testament. The origins of the concept's rise into mainstream fundamentalist doctrine is uncertain, though it first found its popularity in the 1800s. Many believers seem convinced it's all in the book of Revelation - but it isn't. Yet strong emotional attachment to Rapture prophecy continues to influence disturbingly influential people, as we shall see.

Current global events do, however, seem to have a little resonance with what *is* in Revelation, excitedly pointed out by religious eschatologists. Its vision of the 'mark of the beast' - 666 - branded onto people by a dark regime and without which no-one could buy or sell, is one example. The long-term plan to implant microchips into the population (which will eventually replace plastic cards with flesh swipes), could be seen as a fulfilment of this prophecy of restricted movement [pages 79 and 191]. Together with the universal use of commercial bar codes, stock-monitoring RFID (Radio-Frequency Identification) chips could also be seen in this light, although the oft-quoted conspiracy claim that bar codes

One of Matthias Gerung's (1500–1570) numerous interpretations of the biblical book of Revelation. The lurid and fantastical visions of St John the Divine continue to influence modern Christian thinking today and are seen by many as direct prophecies of our times.

incorporate the numbers 666 in the three longer strips that appear in every code is untrue.[3] On the environmental front, other believers point to pollution-stimulated algae growths - turning some lakes and rivers around the world a garish red - as a fulfilment of the vision in which 'a third of the sea turned into blood' (Revelation 8:8).

On the other hand, just as with Nostradamus, many of the key phrases in Revelation can be applied to many things and some apparent relevance will emerge if seen through the filters of faith. There may also be deliberate attempts to *fulfil* biblical prophecies, of course, so that believers are seen to be vindicated and ensuring that 'God's will' is implemented, a worrying notion we shall explore further.

Growing interest in the 'Bible Code' has seen another potential layer of religious prediction come to light. First popularised in Michael Drosnin's 1997 book *The Bible Code*, the titular cipher is allegedly to be found by isolating patterns of text characters in original Hebrew versions of the Bible. Doing this apparently reveals secret prophecies, which speak of current events or ones due in our near-future. Some anticipated occurrences are claimed to have already come to pass (the code is said to have foretold the assassination of Israeli Prime Minister Yitzhak Rabin in 1995, for instance), but all of the prophecies are prone to very subjective interpretation and some consider the whole thing a hoax. However, once again the Bible code ultimately threatens big transformative disasters to come.[4]

Radical interpretations and 'decodings' of religious texts is a deep and murky area. The key point is that whatever the truth of all this religious revelation, certain people in high positions appear to believe in it - which means that it must be having a profound effect on the world we live in, whether we personally subscribe to the views or not.

As for conventional biblical prophecy, it is clear from scholarly analysis that the writers and (importantly) the many editors of the Gospels and apostolic writings believed that the Second Coming was something imminent, possibly even expected within their lifetimes. Certainly, it is unlikely they thought they would have to wait another two thousand years for it. Yet, for some hitherto indefinable reason, believers in Christian prophecy seem to be expecting a fulfilment of the prophecies any day now. As a civilisation oddly fascinated by numerology and anniversaries of messianic births, the excited build-up to the Millennium [page 239] inevitably played a big role in cementing themes of religious expectation. There had been a similar hysteria as the year 1000 approached, of course. Back then, it could perhaps have been attributed to the more simplistic mindset of a medieval population, but a thousand years later little had moved on in this regard. Since nothing of great importance did occur in 2000, much of the focus moved instead to speculation over 2012, for which there is at least a serious body of cross-referencing prophecies and calendrical coincidences that invites some proper consideration [Chapter XII]. Perhaps, all along, the millennial speculations were in truth about 2012, but transposed a little earlier to a neater date.

However, Christian expectation of imminent change is not based solely on the word of ancient writings. There are examples of relatively recent prophecies, accompanied by dramatic miraculous phenomena, which have strong implications for a religious power structure that dominates much of the world today.

The Apparition Phenomenon

In October 1917, near the small town of Fatima in Portugal, a remarkable event occurred, which would have lasting repercussions for the Roman Catholic Church. For on that day, something that appeared to be the Sun 'danced' in the sky in front of thousands of spectators - as arranged by the biblical Virgin Mary herself, or at least a being that claimed to be her.

The Fatima events, described below, are generally regarded as the most substantial of all the many 'apparitions' of Mary, or 'Our Lady', which have been reported in relatively modern times, with other significant events taking place around the world, especially in Ireland and, in recent decades, Medjugorje in what is now Bosnia-Herzegovina. Some appearances are to individuals, while others, as at Medjugorje and Fatima, occur before thousands. There is a recurring theme to these experiences; while some see only inexplicable light phenomena, others experience heavenly figures and receive messages and visions concerning the importance of faith and the dangers of losing it in a world about to turn upside down.

What the true nature of these apparitions is has been the subject of much speculation. Many of the Christian faithful accept them at face value as direct visits from divine beings, but others have suspected them of being everything from projections of inner consciousness reacting to natural electromagnetic fields (dowsable 'Earth energy' is often very strong at apparition sites), to extra-terrestrials masquerading as religious figures.[5] It may be that some unknown force is attempting to get its central message across in whatever frame of reference may be necessary to gain attention. Certainly, the communications received resonate strongly with the similar themes transmitted to psychics and ET contactees, albeit with an overtly religious flavour. The message is nearly always one of needing to be prepared, spiritually and practically, for something big. The Fatima prophecies are particularly strong in this regard.

The Three Secrets of Fatima

Although accounts vary, essentially the dramatic events at Fatima began in 1915 when three local shepherd children, Lucia dos Santos, age nine, and her two younger cousins, Francisco and Jacinta Marto, witnessed a strange transparent cloud 'in the shape of a man' hovering above nearby pine trees. A year later, the cloud was seen again, this time forming fully into what seemed to the children to be an angel. Appearing three times to them and leading the children in devotional prayer, the angel was merely a herald for the strange woman dressed in 'brilliant white' who then appeared before them another year after that, on 17 May 1917. Claiming to be 'from heaven', the as-yet unnamed lady (only in her final apparition did she reveal herself as 'Our Lady of the Rosary') spoke softly and strangely during several meetings with the children, again leading them in prayer, but also divulging three 'secrets' that they must deliver to the Holy Father (the then Pope Benedict XV). Curiously enough, in May 1917, Pope Benedict had made a direct and very public appeal to Mary to intercede to stop the world war, which was currently tearing Europe apart. Was this his reply?

The first secret was a frightening vision of hell, a warning of what would come to those without faith; the second was an apparent prediction of another world war and a caution about the evils of rising communism. As for the third secret, Lucia was told that it could not be revealed to the Church until after 1960. Lucia became a nun and outlived her cousins, who both died in their youth. She continued to have visions, and decades later dutifully revealed the third secret in a written document. The popes who read it thereafter reportedly appeared deeply shocked. Yet this last secret remained officially hidden until 2000, when the Vatican announced that it was a simple prophecy of the assassination attempt on Pope John Paul II, which occurred in 1981. Many doubt that this is the full story of the third secret - after all, why wait so long to reveal something so straightforward and already years past? The nature of the third vision, as publicised, was rather vague and esoteric, and open to interpretations other

The three children who experienced visions of 'Our Lady of the Rosary' at Fatima, Portugal in 1917. The information shared with them is clearly taken very seriously by the Vatican. Only Lucia dos Santos (left) survived into old age - her cousins Francisco and Jacinta Marto both died in childhood.

than the one John Paul elected to believe about himself. In addition, there seemed to be an odd level of official Vatican obfuscation about the issue.

So was the third secret rather more than we were told? The evidence suggests so, for before John Paul's announcement the clear hints that had been dropped by high-level Vatican sources on several occasions about the other aspects of the third secret (see below) appeared to speak of a worldwide crisis of Christian faith, and of globally unsettling events due to happen... about now.

The Miracle of the Sun

When the children recounted their ongoing experiences at the time, some family members and local villagers were understandably hesitant in accepting the story. With Portugal then under the grip of a fervently secular regime, there was even local political resistance due to the overtly anti-communist flavour to some of the messages. As crowds increasingly gathered to witness the now monthly appearances of the mysterious woman to the children (although it is unclear what the people themselves saw at this point), the authorities grew ever-more uncomfortable; at one point the children were locked up by the local mayor and threatened with execution. Seemingly understanding of their need for proof, the woman promised the children that if they gathered as many people as they could at a certain time around the Fatima pasture-land known as the Cova da Iria (where the apparitions had been taking place), she would perform a miracle that would leave no-one in any doubt as to the provenance of her words. Few could have anticipated the extraordinary events that followed.

Photographs purporting to be of the events at Fatima on 13th October 1917. Above, the gathering crowds wait, as directed by the apparently divine messages passed through the children. Below, an actual shot of the phenomenon seen by the people on the day, photographed from several miles away. Presumed at the time to be the Sun, the object darkened and performed an extraordinary series of acrobatics across the sky. Was this a religious experience, or, as some suspect, a classic UFO performance?

On 13th October 1917, with only the word of three children to go on, but in hope for a sign that might liberate them from their agnostic masters, an incredible 70,000 or so believers from the village and its outlying regions gathered in heavy rain to wait for the promised miracle. Sure enough, soon after midday, it came. What appeared to the crowd to be the Sun behind a thin veil of cloud began to perform a series of outlandish and terrifying manoeuvres across the sky, at first revolving rapidly in a Catherine wheel-like manner, throwing out whirls of glowing colours.

The Lisbon-based (and usually anti-clerical) newspaper *O Dia* reported the events, which were witnessed by the faithful and the doubting alike:

Despite the evidence that the governments behind governments always ensure the 'right' candidate comes to power, George W Bush's particularly strong Christian convictions and underlying religious fervour (presumably held back by aides keen to play this down) do appear to set him apart from some of his peers. But if God wasn't personally whispering into Bush's ear in the night, instructing him in global policy, where did his claimed divine guidance come from? Is it more likely, in fact, that God was speaking to him through the advices of... one Pastor Ted Haggard?

The Politics of Armageddon

Evangelist Ted Haggard, known as 'Pastor Ted' to his followers, was the founder of the New Life Church In Colorado, as well as being a founder of the Association of Life-Giving Churches and the leader of the National Association of Evangelicals between 2003 and November 2006. His influence in the spiritual life of Christian fundamentalist America was profound - as was his influence in US politics. For it is on record that Haggard was a key advisor to George W Bush.[9] Not only did he rally massive support among evangelicals for both of Bush's 'successful' election campaigns, but Haggard also held weekly telephone conferences each Monday with Bush and his aides, advising them of the religious direction their global policies should be taking. In 2005, author Jeff Sharlet wrote of Haggard that 'no pastor in America holds more sway over the political direction of evangelicalism'.[10] So perhaps this is how God spoke to George W Bush.

The White House was predictably quiet when Haggard resigned from his church in 2006 after admitting involvement in a drugs and gay sex scandal, but that's not so important here. What is of concern is that for several years Ted Haggard - a man with a strong religious conviction that End Times and The Rapture are imminent - must have had an important hand in directing the course of world politics.

The evangelical 'End Timers' movement in the US, especially, is now so strong that a significant proportion of North America's population is expecting the Second Coming any minute now - which means that, overtly or candidly, they must be helping to encourage policies and ways of life that not only prepare them for it (in their eyes), but that actively *help bring the prophecies of apocalypse about*. Many end-timers see global chaos as a good thing - a fulfilment of the predicted 'tribulation' that will eventually pave the way for the New Jerusalem. If the Day of Judgement brings with it the glorious Rapture, every day closer to world peace and stability is a step *away* from what Christian fundamentalists actually want - which is a bit of a problem to those who don't subscribe to such beliefs, and would actually like a path to peace without prophecy-riddled struggle and strife.

The fact is, however, that for eight years we had a born-again Christian president -

a man in one of the highest positions on Earth, with a finger on the very button of the machinery of war - being regularly advised by an evangelical preacher not only expecting the end of the world, but who, by definition, must have seen it as his duty to actually help bring about the final battle of Armageddon, leading 'good' against 'evil'. Seen in this context, maybe some of the policies and mandates that seem to have caused such chaos in the Middle East in recent years begin to make a little more sense. Given Barack Obama's strong charismatic Christian leanings

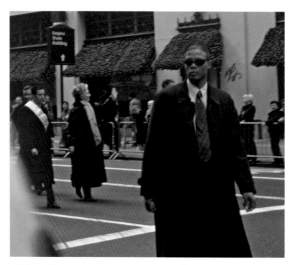

(despite having a Muslim father), and claims that Hillary Clinton is a member of the evangelical 'dominionist' group 'The Family', there seems little reason to presume the religious agenda will be subsiding in US politics any time soon.[11]

There is, incidentally, one more influential leader who was also advised on occasion by Pastor Ted Haggard - Tony Blair. His 2007 conversion to Roman Catholicism and his overtly public protestations of faith since leaving public office as Prime Minister of Britain leave little doubt that his own political direction must also

Hillary Clinton waves to supporters at the Veteran's Day parade, New York, 2004, while cautious minders prowl. Clinton is rumoured to be part of a strongly evangelical movement known as 'The Family'. Politics and religions seem as inseparable in the US as in the Islamic countries the US often criticises.

have been heavily, if quietly, influenced by his private religious convictions. It certainly explains much about his awkward and slyly deflective response to television interviewer Jeremy Paxman's probing question in a 2003 interview about whether he and George W Bush ever prayed together.[12] Blair's much-publicised closed meetings with Pope Benedict XVI, a key holder of prophetic religious secrets, also make the mind boggle at the nature of the conversations that might have taken place between them.

What is clear from recent events - and the whole of history - is that religion and state in the West have always gone together and still go together, with many people suspecting that fundamentalist agendas underlie many of the decisions which are made, through whatever denomination (note the significant number of strict Christians who have been in both Tony Blair's and, subsequently, Gordon Brown's cabinets, including Ruth Kelly - a member of the Catholic extremist group Opus Dei). This is not, of course, to say that Christianity, in its moderate form, is in any way wrong or that governments have no right to religious beliefs. In the Islamic countries, the religious fervour within the politics is at least honest and upfront, however misused and dangerous it may sometimes be. In the West the fervour seems equally keen, but is hidden. Many of the fingers that accusingly point to the perils of Islamic fundamentalism appear to be equally fundamentalist in a different direction.

Some conspiracy theorists reject the notion of religious influence in Western politics, claiming it is a cover for overtly power-and-money-based scheming, but the evidence would suggest the ultimate motivation is probably a mixture of both, perhaps in preparation for expected big changes and the coming fulfilment of ancient - and modern - prophecies.

THE TRUTH AGENDA: *Prophecies of disruptive but transformative events that will befall our planet seem endemic within ancient religious and mystical texts - but they are also welling up through modern clairvoyance and multiple-witness apparitions. People in high places, claiming divine inspiration or authority, appear to be the guardians of secrets that must surely influence the direction of the world we live in today, and undeclared religious agendas underpin Western politics far more than is admitted.*

Genuine Egyptian needle at the Place de la Concorde, Paris, topped with a golden pyramid [page 91]. The ubiquity of such powerful ancient symbolism is seen by some to be a statement of domination from a hidden ruling elite.

V   GRAND CONSPIRACIES

Is the method by which our civilisation is run the result of a massive manipulation from elite groups and secret societies with shadowy agendas? With so many people now doubting the true foundation of the West's supposedly democratic principles, what is the exact nature of those doubts and should we pay any heed to them? The speculation of the conspiracy theorists, whatever the final answers, raises important questions about both the world today and the potentially ancient origins of the power structure that may really govern us.

Conspiracy - An Overall Picture

The preceding chapters give a brief overview of just some areas where many people do not trust the motivations, or the words, of those who supposedly lead us. There so often seems to be disturbing evidence of wider agendas, whether religious, power-seeking or esoteric, running secretly beneath the veneer of normality that is presented to us. The media, in particular, is complicit in supporting this veneer by always refusing to rock the boat beyond certain limits; the scandals journalists reveal rarely touch the true levels of intrigue and deception that run far deeper. We are continually kept distracted and dumb by mind-numbing fascination with trivia and materialism so that most of us never have the time or the need to lift the corner of the carpet to see what has been swept underneath. When we do begin to look, our need for cosiness often snaps us back into place and our blinkers go on. That, or fear - of exclusion from society, of terrorism, of war, of climate change, of financial loss, of outsiders - holds us back from challenging our claimed protectors too much. But there is a sense that this is beginning to shift. A minority, yet a significant one, is now challenging many things that have been hitherto taken for granted, and that minority is implementing the Truth Agenda. The corner of the carpet is being lifted at last and many do not like what they see.

This is where we truly immerse ourselves in the realm of conspiracy theory, a place where polarities and extremism can run riot. Yet it is also a place where the right questions, at least, do get asked. Certain devotees of truthseeking see *everything* as a conspiracy, viewing the world as a tangled web of deceit, corruption, manipulation and elitism, convinced that someone out there is deliberately trying to make our lives miserable and mundane so that we never rise above the morass to become the powerful beings that we really are. Although for some this may be what is known as psychological projection (inner personal fears not being dealt with or 'owned', but conveniently disassociated from and projected onto people and events 'out there'), there is, unsettlingly, actual evidence to support the reality of a number of these concerns.

With the many prophecies of imminent change clearly believed in some very high places, it may be that someone wants to ensure they maintain the upper hand should anything come to pass that overturns the traditional order of things [Chapter XII]. If we are being treated as sheep, it may be important to our masters that we are kept in our pens while an anticipated storm passes through; or put in the slaughterhouse, according to the grimmest views.

In the conspiracy view, all political decisions, every election, every war, every economic crisis, every fuel shortage, every famine and food crisis, every terrorist group, every disaster, is manipulated and/or co-ordinated by a relatively small elite group of influential businessmen, industrialists, politicians, monarchs and intellectuals, to forward a secret agenda with occultist leanings that has *their* best interests at heart and not ours. Although the original secret society that adopted the name was a specific Bavarian group, the network of manipulators is now often generically referred to as 'The Illuminati' (Latin for 'enlightened'). Its influence is believed to be maintained through political and business-orientated power structures, international banking, global trading alliances and (especially, to the minds of many) the secret societies, which ensure that dynasties, bloodlines and ancient mystical beliefs endure, with knowledge passed on only to the chosen. In this way, the elite's power is never challenged and its grip on the world never weakens. Subscribers to this view maintain that no politician gets anywhere near a position of influence without the say-so of the Illuminati, and believe that elections are determined either with strategic manipulation of funding for campaigns, clever propaganda or, when forced, actual vote-rigging.

As evidence that many big decisions are made outside of parliaments, truthseekers point to the existence of unelected but powerful bodies such as The Bilderberg Group, The Council on Foreign Relations, The Club of Rome, The Trilateral Commission, the World Economic Forum, the Tavistock Institute and all the many other mysterious high-level clubs and quangos, often run by well-known political or business figures. Working with rich and influential families like the Rockefellers and the Rothschilds, these bodies launch significant global policies, which affect our lives yet by-pass the usual structures of democracy. It's certainly no secret that strange little boards and committees, accountable to no-one, have long pulled strings that jerk the actions of those supposedly making free decisions on our behalf, and the recent banking crisis has revealed where many of the really important decisions are made. Other influences, such as interactions at the bizarre annual Bohemian Grove gathering [page 92], may also play an important role.

Weakening the Masses?

At the more extreme end of conspiracy theory, some are concerned that active steps are being taken to ensure we are enslaved to the elite by plans to neuter not only our personal power but also our health, to weaken us all so that we become more controllable, more malleable to the desires of the few. Draconian controls such as the EU-proposed restrictions on alternative medicines, vitamins and minerals (courtesy of the 'Codex Alimentarius' food safety body - page 209) *do* seem to be taking away healthcare decisions from us, making us ever-more reliant on powerful pharmaceutical industries, which tend to treat symptoms but not the causes of conditions. Meanwhile, poor nutrition and the increased presence of junk food as a staple diet, particularly amongst the young (with sales of fast food rocketing in the economic recession), has become endemic, for all the lip-service paid towards healthier living, and we are targeted by an endless list of dubious additives in edible products and debatable chemicals in our water, such as fluoride.

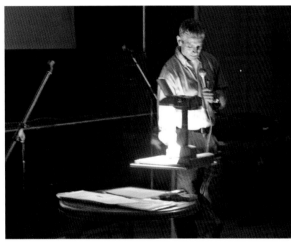

Many truthseekers believe the science of vaccination has at best been massively misunderstood and at worst is a deliberate attempt to weaken the immune system of the human race. Here, campaigner Trevor Gunn, author of the greatly influential Mass Immunisation - A Point in Question *[page 324] gives a presentation to raise awareness of the issues.*

Some believe the vaccination programme, MMR (Measles, Mumps and Rubella) and beyond, has also had dramatic negative effects on our immune systems. With both the safety and effectiveness of the procedure having been challenged by more educated health professionals than is reported, hardcore theorists believe this is a deliberate attempt to damage our natural resistance. We are told that immunisation has wiped out disease, but there are many who hold firmly that statistics don't support this and that the figures have been misrepresented to support the continuation of the programme. It is certainly a verifiable fact that most traditional childhood diseases were already in steep decline before vaccines for them were introduced.[1] The ever-growing cocktail of highly questionable substances (including mercury) that make up vaccines are considered by some to have contributed to behavioural and health problems in young people. Those who raise this, however, are quickly vilified in the media and attacked by mainstream professionals - or even accused of fostering a form of child abuse. Certainly, the claims of the questioners need vigorous scrutiny, but the fact is that doubts remain over the accepted science, and these concerns have not been definitively addressed. (See Chapter X for more on immunisation, Codex Alimentarius, and fluoridation.)

Others go even further and believe that mobile phones and many of the new microwave communication transmitters that have gone up around the world may help us talk to each other, but also act as neural suppressers. Then there are 'chemtrails', increased occurrences of unusual high-altitude vapour trails, which are believed by some to be evidence that governments are secretly seeding the atmosphere with dubious chemicals for reasons of their own (perhaps to do with climate control, or as further poisonous suppressants). There is also the HAARP project (High Frequency Active Auroral Research Program), by which US scientists have learnt to manipulate the ionosphere, supposedly for military communications. Doubters, however, see it as a potential mind-control weapon, along with all manner of secret Tesla technology and hidden devices that are supposedly being used against us.

All of this is speculation, of course, and readers must investigate the evidence for themselves, but the growing numbers prepared to believe such things is illustrative of the deepening erosion of trust in authority. For others, even the fear that someone out there wants to weaken humanity's health and well-being is not enough, believing instead that the ultimate aim is in fact to wipe most of us out. We will deal with this sticky area first before moving on to look at other areas of the conspiratorial view.

Reducing the Global Population

Many gloomier theorists are convinced there are plans afoot for a massive reduction of the world population, to be achieved through epidemics and viruses, deliberately spread. Some say that AIDS was but one lab-engineered attempt to get the ball rolling (although others have claimed it to be an entire fraud, a misunderstanding of a collection of immune diseases used to create more fear).[2] At the very least, a resurgence of eugenics programmes and enforced selective breeding might lie just beneath the surface of some curious policies floating around at the moment.

Wild paranoia? Over-population is claimed to be a serious issue for the governments of the world, with some models predicting a major food, water and energy disaster by 2030 - although there are also claims that these fears are a deliberately-spread myth, designed, like other fear stories [Part Three], to be used as a tool of control, and to justify elitist ambitions for a more 'selective' global population.[3] Much was made in the conspiracy world of a lecture given in 2006 at St Edwards University in Austin, Texas, when Dr Eric Pianka of the

Texas Academy of Sciences appeared to advocate the merits of thinning out the masses by the release of a genetically-enhanced strain of the Ebola virus. This story was screamed across the forums as evidence that we were indeed all seen as nothing more than 'useless eaters' by the intellectual elite. Pianka later denied this interpretation of his speech, saying that his comments had been taken out of context and that he was simply projecting the possibility that such a virus *could* take hold, not that it should.[4] The fact, however, that so many took his comments as they did was a telling sign of the serious misgivings some people harbour in these uncertain times.

The concerns - much spread in the media - over avian (bird) flu in the last few years have recently been supplanted by the swine flu pandemic, but both have been used to create great fear, which has seen people across the world rushing to have flu jabs and stock up on the oral anti-viral tablet Tamiflu (oseltamivir), even though neither specifically work on either of the two strains. Some consider swine flu to be one of the new engineered viruses that will aid the program of depopulation, although the global death toll has in truth been low at the time of writing. However, the pandemic was 'expected' to re-emerge in a stronger form from the end of 2009 onwards. Rather than the flu itself, many other truthseekers are more suspicious of the cocktail of drugs being fed to people panicked into demanding them. Dr Leonard Horowitz, author of *Emerging Viruses*, for instance, believes that the anti-virals and vaccines are deliberately designed to weaken our immune systems, not strengthen them, making us more vulnerable to - or actually activating - later, stronger strains of global pandemics, be they swine flu, avian flu or something new, tying in with views held by those who doubt the claimed good intentions of the vaccination program.[5] If nothing else, the known side effects of Tamiflu (accepted even by *Wikipedia*), which can include behavioural problems and hallucinations, should be cause for great apprehension, considering how much of the world population is now taking it.[6]

At the other end of the spectrum there are claims that swine flu in particular is another exaggerated threat to boost the grip - and profits - of the pharmaceutical industries [page 211]. In the (at least at that point) entirely disproportionate wave of fear that accompanied the first indications of a pandemic, the UK government alone spent £100 million to stockpile enough Tamiflu to be administered to 80% of the population. Assertions that Tamiflu's three-year lifespan meant that, by happy 'coincidence', masses of global stocks had to be used up or destroyed just as the new pandemic was being announced were denied when the sell-by dates were suddenly extended by two years, but many remain doubtful.[7] It is also a fact that Donald Rumsfeld, ex-US Secretary for Defense, considered by many to be a key architect of the darker global agenda, was once chairman of Gilead Sciences Inc., which owns the patent on Tamiflu, and he retains major stocks in the company today.[8] Rumsfeld was also connected with the production and US government approval of the controversial sweetener aspartame, which has crept into much food and drink today yet is considered by many to be very harmful [page 340].

It seems rather extreme to consider that there might really be those out there who would want to wipe many of us from the Earth, and perhaps some of these fears do reside in the realms of paranoia - yet little clues here and there do seem to suggest such an intention may not be beyond the realms of possibility. The global warming scare may also play into such an agenda [Chapter XI].

The Georgia Guidestones

In 1979, plans for a mysterious monument at Elbert County, Georgia (USA), known as The Georgia Guidestones, were submitted by an unknown designer (under the pseudonym 'R C Christian'). The resulting artwork was erected in 1980. Resembling a Stonehenge-like collection of vertical slabs, carved inscriptions on the stones (in a number of different languages) record a decree of the artist's aspirations for the world, but are seen by many as euphemisms to represent the ultimate intentions of the Illuminati. These include references to the formation of a 'world court' and utilise phrases implying the necessity for eugenics ('guide reproduction wisely - improving fitness and diversity'). Most unsettlingly, the stones proclaim that humanity should keep its numbers 'under 500,000,000'. If this recommendation was adhered to, it would mean reducing the current population of the world by nine-tenths. Who would have the right to decide who lives and who dies? Consequently, the Georgia Guidestones are seen by some as a celebration of something evil - which may explain why, in 2008, they were vandalised with (somewhat base) anti-Illuminati aerosol slogans. Certainly, many are incensed that such a public avocation of mass extermination is allowed to stand unchallenged.[9]

Paranoia as Legitimate Mistrust?

Some of the beliefs discussed above may have a basis in truth, some of them may not. Perhaps none of them do. However, the fact that so many are willing to consider such extreme scenarios does say much about how little we trust those in authority today. But have those authorities earned our trust?

By at least considering the reasoning behind all these conspiratorial assertions, even if we dispense with many of them, it is interesting to note how many valid areas for legitimate investigation remain.

The Aims of Global Conspiracy

What, then, if taken as a given, would be the ultimate aim of all this underhand manipulation? According to most conspiracy theorists, the most cherished long-term desire of the Illuminati is to impose upon the globe a 'one world government' - a body to supersede all individual sovereignty and administrations, controlled by one central source working to a universal agenda. The political euphemism for this is the 'New World Order' (NWO), an aspiration increasingly voiced in speeches by prime ministers (especially Gordon Brown) and presidents as the answer to all our troubles.

George Orwell (real name Eric Blair), one of the key writers of the 20th century. Orwell's nightmare vision of global superstates and a society governed by draconian control and surveillance is considered by some to be a frighteningly prescient anticipation of our world's current trajectory.

In truth, the long-term logical outcome of such a New World Order would seem to be one that will ultimately bring one currency, one authority and one mindset to be adhered to by all humankind - perhaps, if the worst fears are realised, with populations reduced in number and rendered harmless by societal controls, all maintained by a small overseeing body, pontificating from on high. Such a system would render us more controllable, and ensure that a tiny elite would retain its supremacy, untroubled by real democracy - just as George Orwell warned. Thus, the relentless gathering of European countries into one federal superstate, with the euro as just the beginning [page 75], and (admittedly denied) mutterings of plans to submit the USA, Mexico and Canada to a similar unified currency (sometimes referred to as 'The Amero') as part of a 'North American Union' are seen by many as slow but dogged steps towards One World Government - or at the very least a system of much greater regional centralisation.[10] Were the three global superstates of Oceania, Eurasia and Eastasia, as visualised in Orwell's *Nineteen Eighty-Four*, fictional after all?

Financial Manipulation?

The 'credit crisis' of 2008, which plunged countries across the world into recession and millions into misery and unemployment, may have been ostensibly due to a banking system out of control, but the fact that this obvious and inevitable situation was allowed to develop at all has led some to believe it was a contrived plot to benefit the New World Order agenda. For years, many observers of the Western financial system gave loud warnings that the increasingly reckless investments and wild speculating of arrogant bankers, falsely bloating the economy, were guaranteed to hit a brick wall. All were ignored. At the time of writing, for instance, it is becoming clear from emerging whistleblowers that several staff, approved personally by Gordon Brown (while Chancellor of the Exchequer) to regulate the UK banking system, knew of the impending financial disaster and where the mismanagement was taking place. However, either they failed to act and/or pass on the information - or they were themselves ignored, taking direct responsibility for the recession one step closer to the highest of offices. All the while government coffers were being filled, our supposed guardians were inevitably happy to turn a blind eye to malpractice - yet at the same time, if they truly believed in *sustainable* growth, why did they not intervene at a sensible juncture to ensure a more measured policy to safeguard the future, instead of allowing such a devastating and entirely predictable crash? Hence, when the Truth Agenda is applied to the bigger picture, it is perhaps not too big a leap to imagine that the current global financial crisis might actually be desirable to those with a hidden purpose to their actions.

Many point to international banking as being one of the key tools of the Illuminati, and many even challenge the very legal legitimacy of entirely unaccountable financial cornerstones such as the US Federal Reserve (the central US banking system) and other banks around the globe, pointing out that what are in truth privately-owned companies should never have been given such massive influence. In June 2009, Barack Obama gave even *more* control to the Federal Reserve.[11]   Globalisation, questionable trade agreements and the arms trade, meanwhile, increase the West's control of the 'developing world' at the expense of the people living there, and the bankers are never far away from the machinations. The recent documentary *The Money Masters: How International Bankers Gained Control of America*, includes two revealing quotes:

'*The powers of financial capitalism had a far-reaching plan, nothing less than to create a world system of financial control in private hands able to dominate the political system of each country and the economy of the world as a whole... Their secret is that they have annexed from governments, monarchies, and republics the power to create the world's money...*' - Prof. Carroll Quigley, author of *Tragedy & Hope: A History of the World in Our Time*

'*Banking was conceived in iniquity and was born in sin. The bankers own the Earth. Take it away from them, but leave them the power to create money, and with the flick of the pen they will create enough deposits to buy it back again. However, take it away from them, and all the great fortunes like mine will disappear and they ought to disappear, for this would be a happier and better world to live in. But, if you wish to remain the slaves of bankers and pay the cost of your own slavery, let them continue to create money'* - Sir Josiah Stamp, Director of the Bank of England in the 1920s [12]

If anyone doubted that money is indeed created 'with the flick of the pen', the recent UK tactic of deploying 'quantitative easing' as a risky way of kick-starting the economy should have dissolved any illusions. The fact is that we *have* given our power away to the banks, and without any doubt whatsoever this has allowed them to be run and/or manipulated by elite groups with something other than the public's well-being in mind. Money has indeed long been used as a method of social enslavement - today we have it through 'acceptable' but crushing debts such as student loans and mortgages, which hamper our freedom from the earliest stages of life. Now the question of who really owns that money - and thus who owns *us* - is coming to the fore for uncomfortable reappraisal. Banks may appear at the

Canary Wharf, London, the financial centre of Britain (complete with glass pyramid - see page 92), towering over its surroundings in more ways than one. International banking is widely considered to be behind many global manipulations, according to conspiracy theorists. If nothing else, it is clear that this is where real power resides.

moment to be taking the public rap for having allowed the recent crash to occur (with supposedly humbled board members appearing before Parliamentary select committees to shed porcelain tears), but this may be a distractive ruse to conceal what is effectively not only their continuing, but increasing power.

Under the pressures of the current economic crisis, several major governments have now effectively used taxpayers money to prop up the banking system in an undeclared form of nationalisation, creating a further blurring between the jurisdictions of banks and authorities (which some believe is a planned calculated risk on the part of the elite puppeteers). As such, banks have demonstrated the inherent entanglement they have with - and stranglehold they have on - governments. Unwise gambles with this money could see some countries risking total bankruptcy - making them more vulnerable to 'persuasion' on certain issues, such as entering unified currencies. Already, the UK, currently looking very weak

74

in its deepening recession, is finding it harder to resist the carrot being offered by those who believe we would be 'stronger' under the euro. Thus centralisation of the kind claimed to benefit the NWO is seen to become more attractive.

There is also a pervading suspicion amongst the cynical that the current 'bubble', which is giving the appearance that the global recession may be about to end (based on the injection of taxpayers' money and vast amounts hastily-borrowed from various global funds, which will put Britain in particular into crippling debt for decades to come), is in itself an attempt to create a false sense of security that will in fact result in a final and devastating crash. Into the wake of this, say some, will step the NWO, creating a financial system from scratch that will rescue the world - and more closely serve their purposes.

The MPs' Expenses Scandal

In the early summer of 2009, the *Daily Telegraph* broke a story that had a devastating effect on public confidence in British MPs - and perhaps a wider consequence. Outrages involving Lords admitting that they would accept bribes to influence legislation for lobbyists the year before had already hinted at unsavoury cracks in Westminster's facade of virtue.[13] However, when a whistleblower leaked details of individual MPs' erratic expenses claims it revealed systemic seams of financial corruption ranging from untenable claims for garden manure and pornographic videos to less forgiveable abuses such as mortages being claimed for when they had already been paid off. The huge and largely justified wave of public anger saw MPs resigning (including, astonishingly, the Speaker of the House), paying back what was effectively stolen public money, and making embarrassing apologies. More gravely, it left the British Parliamentary system looking weak and incapable of ruling itself.

Yet another protest passes by the UK Parliament buildings - but in 2009 the protests got personal when it was revealed that MPs were routinely abusing the expenses system. Although this was a necessary reality-check, was the ongoing scandal used to weaken the authority of British self-rule?

Perhaps it was just coincidence that this occurred in the run-up to the 2009 Euro-MP elections, taking any discussion of real and serious issues about Europe's creeping influence away from the front pages for several weeks, but some suspect it was a coordinated distraction. Labour's results in the final vote were predictably dire, but parties supporting independence from Europe didn't get the coverage they might have without the expenses furore consuming the media. It is also interesting to note that more than once, in all the broadcast public debates, the suggestion was mooted that perhaps it was time the UK allowed itself to be more closely regulated by Europe... Which may all along have been part of the strategy of so widely exposing the corruption. The irony here is that the European Parliament itself has never managed to balance its books or been properly audited since its inception, and accusations of expenses fraud there are just as rife - but not given so much coverage.

To some, the denigration of the UK Parliament is another attempt to demolish true British democracy, an institution that, although clearly far from perfect, has spent centuries of strife being built up and has inspired most other democracies around the world. Although it has probably always been vulnerable to manipulation from the puppet masters, and the current expenses situation obviously needs to be sorted out, we should perhaps think twice before allowing its reputation to be further besmirched. Otherwise, we risk losing even the last vestiges of independence and will become fully prey to the machinations of a New World Order keen to see the UK sidelined and absorbed.

Already the very low voter turnouts in British elections give the impression to the higher powers that no-one really cares how they are governed or who does the governing. Granted that it is hard for some to see what real difference votes make in a manipulated democracy, nonetheless it is the *only* system we currently have. The events currently creating a dangerous apathy leave the path more open to a complete replacement of that system with something even less democratic, and we should perhaps be on our guard for further potentially engineered scandals. When we stop caring, we avert our eyes and fall into distraction - and that is when illusionists tend to work their tricks.

The European Stepping-Stone

The EU agenda is further aided and abetted in the UK and other countries by those working for initiatives such as 'Common Purpose', which promotes federal European aims through insidious (and suspiciously shadowy) infiltration of local government and public services via 'educational' staff courses and financial backhanders.[14] The recent elevation of the unelected and often reviled Europhile Lord Peter Mandelson into a high position of influence in Gordon Brown's government is seen by many as another strategy to ensure Britain is gently but firmly guided into the arms of Europe. The increasingly federal-looking EU is seen by many as a key step to a global state, in which the idea of a small country retaining its own currency (and thus true control over its own policies) will become impossible to sustain. The denials of federalism often heard emanating from the Brussels and Strasbourg Parliaments were rendered hollow when an Irish referendum rejected the overtly federalist 'Treaty of Lisbon' in 2008 (with referenda in France and The Netherlands already having turned down a reworking of the EU constitution in 2005). Constitutionally, Ireland's rejection should have seen the treaty's implementation being halted; instead the 'no' vote was simply ignored. Its creeping influence has therefore continued, with the emerald isle having been bullied to imminently vote again (in the hope of a 'yes' vote this time, now that Ireland's economy is looking very fragile and a few little 'sweeteners' have been added into the mix). If other possible single

The Strasbourg Parliament, France, one of the two European Parliaments (the other is in Brussels) that have growing influence in an increasingly federal-looking EU superstate. Is this where the real seat of British power will soon lie, as a step towards one world government? Many fear so.

currencies such as the (thus far denied) Amero do threaten to well up, new areas of the world will presumably be able to look forward to their own 'unifying' projects.

Many of the suggested solutions to the global financial crisis could lead eventually to the development of a true world bank. How long, then, will it be before a one world government is suggested to go with it? With the consequences of the crash still unfolding, it is interesting to see how often the idea of increased centralisation of power is being publicly mooted as the answer to all our problems.

Some, of course, welcome the idea of globalised central administration. Surely this would end all wars, and create a new era of peace and harmony, such as that envisaged by Utopian writers for centuries (H G Wells and Bertrand Russell amongst them - pages 268-270)? On paper, perhaps it would. Perhaps there are even good intentions of a kind behind all this centralisation [Chapter XIII]. The problem comes with observing those who currently appear to be attempting to implement this system. Can we trust them? Unfortunately their actions so far, together with the lessons of history, suggest that we cannot. There does not yet appear to be anyone enlightened enough to be entrusted with such vast power, but that isn't stopping certain people trying to attain it.

Many Threads

How, some ask, could all this elite control operate without it being obvious? Answer: very subtly. Uniformed Illuminati officers would not openly stroll the corridors of power; they wouldn't need to. Merely pulling a few strings from above and having a few contacts in key places would be quite enough to foster their agendas to begin with - and they would be playing a long game, begun decades, perhaps centuries, ago. In any case, truthseekers claim it *is* all obvious - so obvious that the world doesn't take any notice. A simple glance at those openly attending meetings of democracy-averse groups such as the Bilderbergs - often mainstream politicians, and even royalty - soon makes it clear who the agents of global elitism might be.

It is traditional with this kind of subject matter to list here an unending series of potential conspiracies and manipulations that may be shaping our world, naming names, identifying backgrounds and getting into complex details about plots and schemes. But that would add hundreds of pages. Although specific examples will follow in this book, readers are advised to research the wider picture elsewhere and speculate as they will. There are numerous tomes and websites out there packed with information on just about any thread one wishes to follow, and readers are encouraged to do so (see the Appendix for some pointers) - while they still can. With the freedom of the Internet now under serious threat [Chapter IX], we may have only a short window left in which this information can be shared openly. Ignore the fear of cliché and read *Nineteen Eighty-Four* to understand the unfortunate blueprint that many of our governments seem to be working to, Illuminati or no Illuminati. What is important here is to apply the Truth Agenda to some of the bigger mysteries and cover-ups that most people can immediately relate to and that *do* appear to have some serious supporting evidence which demands investigation.

Above all, what the conspiracy speculation does incontrovertibly reveal is that a system of overbearing control is currently being foisted upon us. This, at the very least, appears to be undeniable whichever way it is looked at.

A Society of Control

Since 9/11, under the aegis of the 'War on Terror', and for reasons explored later, the Western nations have implemented a series of policies that have progressively whittled away the liberties that formerly held up our society - all in the name of our protection. This is particularly true in the USA and the UK. Our former freedom - of speech, movement and action - is rapidly being replaced with fear-based restrictions and a culture where people no longer feel able to speak out loud about their concerns. We are continually monitored by cameras and now governed by laws that give the state the right to pry into any area of our lives, no matter how private. This is analysed more fully in Chapter IX.

Defenders of the restrictions contend that someone with nothing to hide has no reason to fear them, and they welcome new measures such as the ID card scheme now being gradually introduced into the UK and expected to be in full swing by, curiously, 2012, unless a Tory government reverses it.[15] Initially voluntary (but effectively not - page 191), the scheme will link to a controversial National Identity Register (NIR). Surely, say the defenders, if we know who everyone is, all checked and approved, then we will be safer from terrorists, criminals and electoral fraud? On the surface, some justification for the scheme can be found. The problem, once again, comes with the observation that those implementing the new restrictions have not proved themselves reliable or trustworthy in the past, in addition to the fact that the proposed system seems perilously rigid and much open to abuse. All studies show it will not be immune to fraud, nor prevent terrorism or crime - but it will give authorities a crowbar of control and surveillance the likes of which no country has ever seen.

The ID cards now being pushed into British society (despite very mixed and cautious opinion polls) are 'bio-metric'. This means that they are not simply glorified passports or consumer loyalty cards, which is the usual defence. Instead, via the National Identity Register, they will help exchange DNA information, fingerprints, digitised facial and iris scans and other very personal information that in the wrong hands could be widely misused. Under the new scheme, fifty categories of personal information can be held on each citizen. When an ID-swipe becomes required, as it eventually will, for every public transport journey, every shopping and bank account transaction and every entry into a public place, then at that point all significant movements, purchases and decisions we ever make will be recorded via the ID system and the NIR. Although the official line is that the information will not be stored on a *centralised* database, the reality is that the NIR amounts to exactly that.

Once information goes onto a digital database of any kind, there is no way of indefinitely protecting it. Sooner or later it will become available to any authority, and probably any commercial enterprise that needs that information (such as life insurers keen to root out genetic disorders). The database will, at some point, have to become electronically tied in with others - otherwise, what is the point of the scheme and how will the system work? No satisfactory answers to these concerns have been forthcoming from ministers and bodies that have previously shown themselves incapable of protecting private information for long.

The 'accidental' loss of the two tax CDs in 2007 (and other official files since), containing detailed information on families across Britain, caused public scandal and illustrated how easily private data can be mishandled. However, this 'loss' was a double-edged sword. Decried by some as evidence of why the ID system could never work, the reality is that the public outcry over the CDs has actually allowed government departments to justify setting up *more secure and controlled* databases for the future - and enabled them to talk up ID cards as a solution to the problem. Which may have been the idea all along.

More serious is what will happen in an ID culture, where most day-to-day actions will be disallowed without a card or code. When someone in authority, however unfairly, decides that a member of the public has become a 'subversive' or undesirable element, it will become very easy to remove them from mainstream society simply by deactivating their entry in the database. This would restrict movement and essentially reduce the digitally dispossessed to the state of a social leper.[16] In the forthcoming cashless society, even going shopping won't be an option. You may not consider yourself a subversive, but if someone decides otherwise on your behalf, there will be little to be done about it. Given the increasingly fascistic and controlling tendencies of some Western governments since 9/11, how much of a stretch of the imagination is it to foresee a problematic regime coming to power that might be quite capable of making such decisions when faced with political critics? Already we hear tales of peace protestors, political truth campaigners and otherwise lawful members of society being intimidated by authorities and brutally removed from public meetings [page 192]. In an ID society, the threatened withdrawal of personal identity may become yet another useful persuader.

Beyond the more conspiratorial side of the issue, what would transpire if one were simply deleted from the ID system by accident? The proposed legislation would place the onus firmly on individuals to prove who they are and fight for reinstatement to the system, invoking the possibility of Kafka-esque nightmares in dealing with a faceless bureaucracy just to regain one's freedom of movement.

A Micro-Chipped Population

ID *cards*, of course, would soon be replaced by the second generation of ID technology - microchip implants. Already, electronic chip schemes are being pioneered both in the UK and the USA, with the likes of the police, universities and office workers being used as guinea pigs. Why have all the bother and inconvenience of a card when you can have a little chip inserted into your flesh, which can be 'swiped', like superstore barcodes? Fear of terrorism and crime is already being used to encourage support for the entire population to be chipped - no more unidentified bombers or shoplifters; no more straying Alzheimer's victims; no more missing children. The hysterically intense and slightly unsavoury media fascination with the apparent kidnapping in 2007 of the little girl Madeleine McCann in Portugal (still unsolved at the time of writing) provided just one of many justifications to the nervous as to why we would all be better off chipped. Fear, as ever, makes us consider the darkest of things through coloured filters - and it seems that everything possible is being done to keep us in the fear zone [Chapters IX & X].

The thought of a generation united by the presence of their very own microchip makes some people feel safe - but many others sense something inherently

Radiograph of a cat, showing its embedded ID microchip. ID chips for pets are now commonplace, and get us used to the idea of the benefits they can supposedly bring - people will certainly be next, however, and there are grave areas of concern over the potential misuse of such implants.

wrong with such a system. With little faith in those implementing it, who knows what the chips might really be used for and what they might be capable of? Just the thought that even an innocent moment on your own would not be possible without authorities knowing where you were and what you were doing, brings to mind poor Winston Smith cowering in the corner just out of view of the telescreen in Orwell's all-too-prescient parable. Already we have clusters of cameras on every street, more in the UK than any other country in the world - but the chips mean there will soon be no escape, not even in little corners of former privacy.

It sounds like sci-fi, but it isn't. Some clothing and other goods are already impregnated with RFID chips (Radio-Frequency Identification) for commercial tracking purposes, with the eventual intention that shops will be able to trace their goods from manufacture to sale to final ownership. Even before ID cards and people-chipping, soon every retailer will know what you bought and where you went with it, allowing them to bombard you with unwanted but specifically targeted advertising and promotional offers (as already happens with some web retail sites). Cars and lorries use RFID for toll gates in some countries and a system is being set up that will track all of our journeys (monitoring speed and driving quality) on government databases. Before long our bodies will be tagged in the same way, the minutiae of our lives available to any authority that wants it. The ID system, first card, then chip, will before very long be ruling British lives - and eventually those of all nations - unless a significant number of people stand up and hold out against it. This may well happen. But there is only a limited window of time in which the stand can be taken.

Who, then, are the people who will help make that stand? Who will lead the protests? Hasn't anyone been warning us about the dangers to liberty that suddenly seem to be upon us? Couldn't somebody have *done* something? These cries will become louder and more ubiquitous as ID schemes and other surveillance measures currently being developed really begin to take hold.

In truth, there have been several mainstream attempts to alert people to the type of society we are heading into. However, when their brave ambassadors arrive on our living room screens or printed pages, all too often people laugh at them - and we are encouraged to do so. What kind of people are these sacrificial jesters that we might have dismissed rather too easily? Here is one prominent example.

The Fall and Rise of David Icke

When former goalkeeper, TV sports presenter and Green Party spokesman David Icke suddenly announced a spiritual conversion in the early 1990s, it was perfect tabloid fodder. When a former statesman like Tony Blair becomes a Catholic, eyebrows may be raised, but no-one sniggers at the beliefs. But Icke had found a different kind of spirituality, of the New Age persuasion, which, inexplicably, is always seen as fair game for media hounds. Old religions, despite all their foibles, misdemeanours and strange mysticism, command respect, but new belief systems are never afforded the same treatment [page 212]. So when a favourite BBC sports personality started to talk about psychic channelling, higher guidance and our collective connection to a universal consciousness, out came the knives of ridicule.

David Icke's initial penchant for wearing turquoise shell-suits, together with his famous appearance on Terry Wogan's peak-time television show to tell viewers that he was the 'Son of God' has somehow lodged in the collective British memory. What few remember is that he did later qualify the latter statement by saying that we are all 'sons of God' - something agreed on by many world religions. But Icke-as-new-Messiah suited the media sensationalists and he was written off as a laughing stock who had just destroyed a promising career. Or had he?

With the turquoise gone, and a little less of the New Age rhetoric, David Icke turned his new-found spiritual insights into something directly practical. His media status, however much it was being used for chuckles, gave Icke an unusually high-profile conduit into the mainstream and he began to find his unconventional views and pronouncements about world events making their way onto the great British breakfast table at a level few others could achieve. As his interest in what could make the world a better place turned to deep explorations into what had made it so dark in the first place, he found himself becoming labelled a 'conspiracy theorist' and a fighter for liberty and freedom. This enabled the usual journalistic sidelining reserved for such areas, but it also won Icke new attention and support from many despondent truthseekers around the world, happy to have found someone who could represent them at last.

With those on high perhaps realising that things were going too far, there were attempts to neuter Icke in the mid-1990s. His risky strategy of quoting the *Protocols of the Elders of Zion* - an apparently forged document of supposedly Jewish plans for world domination created to stir up hatred towards Judaism in 1903 - saw Icke receiving very public accusations of anti-Semitism, despite his protestations that he did NOT believe Jews to be behind the protocols. Instead, he openly stated that the sentiments of the document, even if a hoax, were being used as a blueprint for global domination by other groups. His books made this more than clear, but the Nazi accusations stuck for some time before Icke was able to shake them off.

David Icke, conspiracy messiah to some, laughing stock to others. But many of Icke's extrapolated predictions have been proven right and his books have a wide global readership.

The belief of some that fundamentalist Zionism - as opposed to genuine Judaism - might be a component of New World Order machinations is often used by the mainstream as a stick with which to beat conspiracy theorists. The curious phenomenon by which rearranging the digits in the somewhat bizarre London 2012 Olympic logo creates the word 'Zion', for instance, has raised many eyebrows amongst truthseekers - but this hardly makes them anti-Semitic. The truth is that fundamentalism within nearly all of the Abrahamic religions is almost certainly involved with the global agenda somewhere down the line, as we have already seen, and allegations of anti-Semitism are too often abused to close down lines of perfectly legitimate enquiry, especially when it comes to scrutiny of American-Israeli political decisions, CIA-Mossad operations, or indeed elements of extremist Zionism.

Although misguided protestors stuck in a false past still occasionally turn up at David Icke lectures, eventually most of the negative citations faded and a new respect for Icke's uncannily accurate predictions (see below) won him a wide and dedicated following. Indeed, his PROBLEM-REACTION-SOLUTION equation has become a standard expression in the conspiracy world.

PROBLEM-REACTION-SOLUTION defines the manipulation pattern of the New World Order: 1) Create a problem (for example, encourage, allow or actively promote terrorist attacks - or engineer an economic crisis); 2) This generates a large reaction (the population, through fear or outrage, begs for action); 3) The authorities then happily provide the solution (usually more controls and restrictions, with wider powers granted to them, which is what they wanted all along). PROBLEM-REACTION-SOLUTION is a neat and frighteningly sense-making strategy for the power-hungry, which, once recognised, can be seen in action all around us if one cares to look for it.

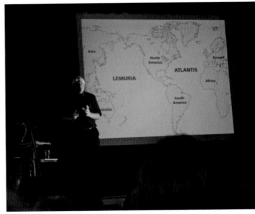

David Icke in action, speaking at the Alternative View conference, 2008. Icke's own all-day seminars can last several hours without a break, but his oratory skills command big audiences.

Over the years, David Icke's prolific books, passionate speeches and website commentary have become a powerful influence in the pantheon of truth movements and liberty campaigning. He sells out lecture halls throughout the world and finds his views repeated and pondered on by many other truthseekers. Yet many of those same supporters will not admit openly to having any interest in the man, let alone having had contact with him.

Here's why.

The Extra-Terrestrial Bloodline

The main contention with the views of David Icke, even amongst some otherwise loyal supporters, has been his belief that... the world is run by an elite group of extra-terrestrial reptilian beings. Icke - and other researchers, it must be said - gradually developed the view, based on (controversial) alleged eye-witness testimony, ancient records and clairvoyant sources.

Essentially, the reptile-theory runs that an extra-terrestrial gene was seeded amongst a ruling class in humankind aeons ago and that this same class, with the British monarchy as its central hub, runs the world today, helping to perpetuate all of the conspiratorial horrors outlined at the beginning of this chapter. According to this view, the reptilian bloodline is diligently maintained, and shape-shifting abilities mask the true nature of its carriers.

If the idea of the Queen being an alien lizard wasn't enough for some, the notion that she and her brethren (including all US presidents) carry out blood sacrifices and ritual child abuse in an extensive occult network was the final straw. This saw many part company with Icke's views, to the point of total denial that they had even looked at one of his books, when, in fact, their shelves were stacked with them.

Why, then, does anyone give David Icke the time of day at all? Is all the reptile stuff not evidence enough that he is the madman many proclaim? The reason for Icke's continuing mitigation amongst the loyal - however uncomfortable it may be - is that he has been proven to be right on many things he predicted years ago.

The surveillance state, ID cards, human micro-chipping, a war on terrorism sparked by a massively-orchestrated attack, the rise of a federal Europe, all manner of global political shifts that have come to pass or are in the planning now - all of these and much more were anticipated by David Icke over a decade before they began in earnest. Perhaps anyone with foresight could have extrapolated the logical conclusion of some of the policies and social trends quietly being implemented in the early 1990s, and Icke has certainly not been alone, nor was he the first, in sounding warnings (see also William Cooper, Alex Jones, Jeff Rense, Jim Marrs, *et al*). Yet Icke's take on it all has turned out to be the most fully-formed and shrewd. Hence, for all the concern over his more extreme beliefs, many concerned followers of truth and liberty movements have never quite been able to resist tuning into the latest opinions of this sometimes bullish, yet somehow surprisingly grounded modern prophet with formidable skills of oration.

And what of those extreme beliefs? Is the notion that an elite bloodline has been passed down through the ages by a ruling class with occult tendencies truly such a hard thing to accept? Royal families and dynasties amongst the wealthy have always guarded bloodlines and performed rituals of a mystical nature. The higher secret societies, which clearly have significant social influence, vet members closely (admitting them with the bizarrest of ceremonies) and jealously protect their own power and welfare. And it does appear to be true, as any researcher can determine, that many US presidents (and past prospective presidential candidates, such as John Kerry) have had direct genealogical links to the British monarchy, including, of course, the Bush family. With a recent mainstream research project stating that just 6000 powerful people effectively run the world, even if the extra-terrestrial gene is taken simply as a metaphor, the scenario of the global situation and who might be running it today can be seen as much the same thing.[17]

But, for all the controversy, there are those who refuse to fully relinquish the notion that some members of the human race may carry an extra-terrestrial gene. Why? Perhaps because it's explicitly implied in The Bible.

The Genesis Gene

Genesis, Chapter 6, verses 1-4, very clearly implies that humankind once interbred with a race not of our world - the 'sons of God' - and suggests that the influence of that new gene pool continued on through the ages. With a mysterious spin-off hybrid race, the 'Nephilim', also mentioned, the references to possible extra-terrestrial intervention are too compelling to be ignored. The *New American Standard Bible* translates it thus:

'Now it came about, when men began to multiply on the face of the land, and daughters were born to them, that the sons of God saw that the daughters of men were beautiful; and they took wives for themselves, whomever they chose. Then the Lord said, "My Spirit shall not strive with man forever, because he also is flesh; nevertheless his days shall be one hundred and twenty years." The Nephilim were on the Earth in those days, and also afterward, when the sons of God came in to the daughters of men, and they bore children to them. Those were the mighty men who were of old, men of renown.'

The 'sons of God' clearly implies angelic beings - for which many read extra-terrestrials - interbreeding with humans. They are referred to as 'giants' in some texts. However, some Abrahamic folklore (especially the Ethiopian *Book of Enoch*) has it that the latterly-mentioned Nephilim were the offspring of fallen angels who broke the rules and lusted for human females. Various other biblically-related ancient texts refer to similar stories. Some see the Nephilim as a malign race that God attempted to wipe out with the flood escaped by Noah (the story of which follows on directly from the above bible passage), although the phrase 'the Nephilim were on the Earth in those days, and also afterward' suggests their bloodline may have survived. Could this be the seed of the so-called reptilian agenda of today? We may never know exactly what this brief passage in the Bible refers to. Perhaps there is an entirely mundane origin (some hold that the Nephilim were simply a race of tall tribal warriors), but it has inevitably led to much speculation amongst those who believe we are still under the influence of the Genesis gene, not least because so many other ancient cultures have similar references to past interference from outside of our Earthly realm.

A number of old civilisations held that their gods originated from the stars, especially the Egyptians and the Sumerians, whose records have been best preserved. (Tribal traditions also tap the same seam - elders of the African Dogon tribe believe that they are directly descended from beings of the star system Sirius, and have long known uncannily accurate information about that region of space, which modern science is only now discovering.) The Sumerian legend of the 'Annunaki' - their gods - has many parallels with the story of the biblical Nephilim. Ancient mysteries speculator Zecharia Sitchin interprets Sumerian records to read that the Annunaki were, in fact, extra-terrestrial beings from the legendary planet Nibiru, who genetically engineered humankind as a slave race for manual labour. Though some scholars have criticised his translations, this interpretation of Sumerian

myth, put together with the biblical references, is compelling in its general scope. Sitchin and his adherents believe Nibiru is on a long elliptical orbit in our solar system, which will bring it back into close contact with Earth any day now (tying in to some people's interpretations of the 2012 prophecies - see Chapter XII). They assert that a pure bloodline left by the Annunaki amongst a dominating class long ago has been waiting in the wings to preserve control for the return of their masters. (Others

Sumerian carvings showing the arrival of the Annunaki in spaceship-like vessels. Many ancient myths and legends, including The Bible, record god-like beings arriving on Earth and interbreeding with humankind.

believe that some of the *same* beings, hidden by their shape-shifting abilities, remain with us today in places of power.) As ever, the truth is less important than belief in the myth; what matters is that certain people in positions of power may hold these stories to be real, and thus act on them with potentially unfortunate consequences. The veracity of Nibiru aside, the Sumerian texts speak of a scenario that could easily be applied to David Icke's reptilian agenda.

Interestingly, the heart of the Sumerian empire, one of the first great advanced cultures, lay in the area once known as Mesopotamia, sometimes referred to as 'the cradle of civilisation'. Is it coincidence that this is where modern Iraq is today - the focus of so much world attention and struggle for control? During the 2003 invasion, the US military even placed their most major base (Camp Alpha, south of Baghdad) on the precise location of ancient Babylon, destroying important archaeological evidence in the process and causing outrage amongst historians.[18] Perhaps there is more mystical significance to gaining dominance over this area then may at first meet the eye, especially if someone on high is expecting the imminent return of their gods - or the fallen angels - to ancient seats of power.

In this context, the detail of information from apparently extra-terrestrial sources, and consequent cover-ups surrounding awareness of UFOs, begins to take on a more important resonance. If our former masters are returning, is there a secret plan from those in the know to welcome and re-install them - or to fight them in a slave's revolt?

Aside from all the talk of extra-terrestrial genes, there is certainly evidence that mystical wisdom has been preserved by ongoing channels of information and passed down by elite encoding throughout the ages. Even without proof of bloodlines, it is clear that esoteric knowledge from antiquity continues to shape our world today.

The Atlantis Connection

Another Genesis reference may have relevance to the continuation of ancient agendas, albeit more obliquely. Genesis 11, verses 1-9, recounts the story of the Tower of Babel, impressing on the reader how powerful humankind was becoming, post-flood. With 'one language' uniting the peoples of the Earth, plans to build a 'tower with its top in the heavens' attracts the jealousy of 'the Lord', who makes clear his disapproval:

'Behold, they are one people, and they have all one language; and this is only the beginning of what they will do; and nothing that they propose to do will now be impossible for them. Come, let us go down, and there confuse their language, that they may not understand one another's speech.' [19]

Pieter Bruegel's 1563 painting of the Tower of Babel. The story of the tower, halted when God struck down humanity so that men were no longer able to communicate with each other in one tongue, has resonance with the story of Atlantis. Most cultures have myths of a once enlightened but lost civilisation.

Struck down with the sudden inability to communicate properly with each other, humans were scattered across 'the face of all the Earth' and the building of the tower was abandoned. (Interestingly, the Lord's thoughts here could sum up the attitude of the alleged Illuminati - a self-aware and united population is inherently powerful and ambitious, so must be kept divided, uncommunicative and distracted - divide and rule.) Noting the reference 'let us go down', which again implies beings coming from somewhere above, the tale of the Tower of Babel could be taken as a reference to the Atlantis myth. Again and again, ancient legends (and indeed modern clairvoyance and channellings) speak of today's global culture having originally derived from one centralised advanced civilisation, be it Atlantis, Lemuria or Mu. Many of these stories speak of a fall from enlightenment and a forced scattering of inhabitants, fleeing from a disaster or banishment of some kind.

Original Egyptian needle in situ. Needles and pyramids are still used today to denote power over society.

There are many today who believe that the curious similarities of legends, religious beliefs and construction techniques (pyramids in Egypt, China and South America, for instance), which link otherwise disconnected cultures around the world, speak of refugees or settlers from one previously united civilisation setting up anew. Some genetic commonalities also support the idea - plus the similarities of ancient symbolism and belief systems that appear to have seeped down even into modern culture.

Secret Societies

The arcane knowledge, symbols and myths of otherwise lost times are thought by some to be encoded in the writings and teachings of mystic traditions and secret societies, especially amongst the higher echelons of Freemasonry, and

The Washington Monument, Washington DC. Constructed to emulate classic Egyptian architecture, it is the largest obelisk of its kind in the world at (a numerologically curious) 555 feet and five inches tall - and is considered by many to be a straight statement of Masonic domination.

ruling-class 'orders' like 'Skull and Bones', which began at Yale University in Connecticut and has included such alumnae as George W Bush (and indeed his one-time electoral rival John Kerry). This jealously guarded information may be a fragment of a bygone age preserved for the elite few, believing themselves to be distant descendants of the survivors who were perhaps chosen as guardians of that knowledge for its eventual application in times of upheaval. This is why some conspiracy theorists point to the likes of Freemasonry as being the core of the dark elite, although it's pretty clear lower degrees (happy with a bit of ritual, local influence and some nice dinners) wouldn't know much about it, nor would they consider themselves a negative influence in society. Some would also argue that Freemasonry's roots cannot be traced back much beyond a few centuries, and assert that it simply adopted the esoterica of ancient cultures as an affectation to add gravitas.

The 'all seeing eye' on a standard dollar bill, with obvious ancient and secret society connotations. The multi-layered meanings of this banknote alone could take a whole chapter to discuss.

Other critics of the secret society-connection have claimed that the likes of Freemasonry's principles would be at odds with those of a born-again Christian such as George W Bush (various religious bodies have attacked Freemasonry as being incompatible with mainstream faiths); however, prominently religious people are known to be members of various 'lodges' and Freemasonry does not discourage belief in God. Indeed, as *Wikipedia* has it:

'Candidates for regular Freemasonry are required to declare a belief in a Supreme Being. However, the candidate is not asked to expand on, or explain, his interpretation of Supreme Being. The discussion of politics and religion is forbidden within a Masonic Lodge, in part so a Mason will not be placed in the situation of having to justify his personal interpretation. Thus, reference to the Supreme Being will mean the Christian Trinity to a Christian Mason, Allah to a Muslim Mason, Para Brahman to a Hindu Mason, etc. And while most Freemasons would take the view that the term Supreme Being equates to God, others may hold a more complex or philosophical interpretation of the term.' [20]

The fact is that membership of secret societies does seem to be a linking thread amongst many influential people on the world stage, and anything hidden is bound to generate fear of cronyism and underhand dealings. Some of Freemasonry's strange and guarded traditions are guaranteed to raise questions from the outside, and the symbols of ancient power that it may share with whatever other questionable forces might be operating do seem to be everywhere.

It doesn't take much searching to find Masonic and other secret society symbolism in some pretty obvious settings: the profusion of stone 'needles' (often genuine Egyptian imports) and other curious monuments placed at key locations across the world; corporate and political logos with overt mystical references; and, most famously, the 'all-seeing-eye' over the pyramid on the dollar bill (amongst other heavy hints on banknotes of many countries). Some believe that the modern layouts of entire cities also incorporate occult significance, with Paris (France) and

Glass pyramid at the Louvre, Paris, a modern addition to the many mystical and occult symbols across the city. Most of the great cities of the world appear to embody specific layouts and architecture as signs of power.

Washington DC providing particularly good fuel for conspiracy theorists and numerologists alike. With both those cities having had strong Masonic links during the French Revolutionary years of the late 1700s, the secret society emblems in each do seem to be especially overt, with the requisite needles, pyramids, claimed mystical alignments of road layouts and cryptically significant architectural proportions provoking huge, if not always accurate, speculation.[21] Pyramids in particular have long been associated with strange properties and used as symbols of dominance (representing the levels of true power, with the ignorant masses at the lowest level). The erection, therefore, of a huge glass pyramid at the Louvre (completed in 1989, the bicentenary of the Revolution), with smaller pyramidal satellites and an underground inverted version, was bound to cause the biggest stir of all and remains the subject of much dark muttering amongst anti-NWO factions.

The phenomenal success of Dan Brown's novel *The Da Vinci Code* in 2003 (in which the remains of Mary Magdalene are hinted to lie beneath the Louvre's inverted pyramid, a secret concealed by a series of cryptic clues and conspiracies) compounded

Tip of the inverted pyramid at the Louvre, scene of a fictional conspiracy in The Da Vinci Code, *but full of connotations in its own right.*

the tangled conjecture and gave weight to the urban myth that the main surface pyramid is comprised of 666 glass panes. Although it is a tantalising fact that the official Louvre brochure did indeed claim this biblically prophetic number during initial construction, a modern count shows that there are in truth at least 673 panes in the completed version. Nonetheless, put together with all the other claimed Parisian occult connections, the arrival of an actual pyramid in their midst was bound to raise eyebrows - eyebrows which arched even higher when the

Egyptian needle at the Place de la Concorde [page 64] was, with great ceremony, mysteriously crowned with a smaller golden pyramid in 1998.

Paris found itself under further conspiratorial scrutiny when Princess Diana died there in the infamous car crash of 31st August 1997. According to varying claims, the Pont de l'Alma underpass where the shocking incident took place is built either on the site of an ancient Roman temple dedicated, pointedly, to the goddess Diana (the Louvre statue of whom looks oddly

The underpass at the Pont de l'Alma, Paris, where Princess Diana's car crashed in uncertain circumstances that will be debated forever. With the Flame of Liberty monument standing above it, some believe her death was a ritual killing.

similar to the princess), and/or on top of an underground chamber of Merovingian kings (500-751 AD) where ritual sacrifices were once made. The presence above the underpass of the gold 'flame of liberty' monument (now generally presumed by tourists to commemorate Diana's death, but in fact erected in 1987 - page 18) gave rise to other fevered speculation from those who believe the princess's death was essentially an occult-layered assassination. Was a crash engineered at a meaningful sacrificial site to represent an icon of 'liberty' being extinguished? Or is this all fanciful fantasy born of strange coincidence?[22] Others believe Dealey Plaza in Dallas, where President Kennedy was shot in 1963, is similarly laden with occult symbolism.

Much of the ancient knowledge kept by today's secret societies and embodied in public architecture is generally believed to have been passed down to modernity by the likes of medieval religious orders such as the Knights Templars and the Rosicrucians (bearing secrets learnt during the crusades), with various bloodlines and dynasties sharing many connections. Paris and Washington DC are considered the most prominent examples of that arcane knowledge being given physical form, with all the energetic power such symbolism is believed to hold, but the layout of London is also suspected to have been built with a similar agenda. This is highlighted by the fact that Sir Christopher Wren - a prominent Freemason - had direct influence over the reconstruction of London after the Great Fire of 1666 (the numerology of which has inevitably been seen as more than coincidence by many).

One Canada Square, Canary Wharf, London, topped with a pyramid of its own and allegedly aligned with the longitude and latitude of several ancient sites in Egypt.

Present-day UK architecture seems equally prone to the inclusion of barely-hidden ancient symbolism: Canary Wharf Tower (officially One Canada Square, Britain's tallest building), the distinctive skyscraper at a key financial centre of London, is topped by a perfect glass pyramid of apparently the same geometrical proportions as the Great Pyramid of Giza [Chapter II].[23] Correlation has also been claimed between Canary Wharf and the longitude and latitude of various Egyptian monuments (indeed, an entire global web of Illuminati-inspired mystical alignments is presumed to exist by many), while accusations of occult influence in the local politics of the surrounding borough of Tower Hamlets even reached mainstream news in the 1990s.

This is but a tiny selection of the ancient esoteric knowledge believed by some to be making its presence felt in the modern world. If it is indeed a conspiracy in operation, those at work on its behalf don't seem to mind boasting about it through overt representation in architecture and public monuments, seemingly rife with multi-layered meaning. Some would say it's a straight thumbing of the nose to the dumb masses.

Others, of course, laugh at the suggestion that secret societies are the guardians of real power or any kind of ancient wisdom. Is there, after all, any proof whatsoever that they get up to anything remotely worrying or subversive? With this in mind, let's have a look at one such organisation in more detail.

The Bohemian Grove Rituals

In 1872, a group of Californian journalists, musicians and artists founded a secret society which they christened The Bohemian Club, reflecting its then avant-garde roots. As time went by, the club began to attract wealthy businessmen, media moguls and politicians, and this mix soon became its primary focus. Exclusively male, it was the classic fraternal society lampooned more than once by the likes of Laurel and Hardy and *The Flintstones*, with strict vows of secrecy and complex rituals, balanced by 'hi-jinx' and 'low-jinx' entertainments.

Each July, the Bohemian Club would hold an annual summer encampment in beautiful woods outside of Los Angeles purchased especially for its activities. This place became known as Bohemian Grove. At the camp, plays and musical performances would be staged at different arenas throughout the woods, and club members would drink, 'bond', discuss business deals and get up to who knows what else around campfires beneath the stars.

The centrepiece of the summer camp, held on the first Saturday of each three-week event, was a ritual known as 'The Cremation of Care', in which selected members would... *dress in robes and sacrifice the effigy of a child to a giant stone owl.* By so doing, attendees would dispense with the 'dull cares' of the world outside, leaving them free to frolic without conscience.

It might all sound like some eccentric piece of Victoriana, the kind of thing long ago left behind by reason and enlightenment - were it not for the fact that The Bohemian Club is still alive and well and that the Cremation of Care ceremony is to this day conducted each July to massive attendances. Amongst the crowd are always influential politicians, leading magnates, corporate executives and selected celebrities; the people who shape our society today. This, then, is what some of our world leaders do on their holidays - watch effigies of children being sacrificed to large stone owls. Readers may be tempted at this point to dismiss this as mad fantasy. Remarkably, it isn't.

Although it is rarely spoken about in public, it is well-known - and acknowledged - that many key political figures of each generation have made appearances at Bohemian Grove, often upcoming presidents, prime ministers or congressmen; Richard Nixon, Ronald Reagan, Henry Kissinger and Dick Cheney are just a handful of 'names' known to have attended or regularly attended. George W Bush and Tony Blair are also rumoured (and generally assumed) to have passed through the Grove. With camp attendance figures approaching 3000 in some years, it's a fair bet that many of the aforementioned 6000-people-who-run-the-world will have attended Bohemian Grove at some time or another. Interestingly, Bill Clinton claimed *not* to have ever been there, and famously appeared to mock the Bohemian Club, but if this wasn't a diversionary tactic it might explain why his tenancy in the White House was allowed to be the one of the most publicly vilified in history (despite positive opinion polls), complete with exposed sex scandals and impeachment attempts.[24] Perhaps one is either 'in' or 'out'. [Not that the Clintons should in any way be excused from their own inevitable part in any underlying agendas, especially given that Hillary Clinton is now US Secretary of State, one of the highest places of office in the world. The ominous string of untimely deaths (around 50, through mysterious suicides, accidents and murders) amongst those with close knowledge of the Clintons' business and political dealings suggests - at the very least - a jinx that makes them worth avoiding.][24]

How do we know about the Cremation of Care ceremony if it's all so secret? Tellingly, one of the key exposures on the Bohemian Grove activities was made not by a conspiracy theorist, but by UK television and press journalist Jon Ronson. In 2000, whilst researching a book and television series (Channel Four's *The Secret Rulers of the World*), Ronson joined fervent US truthseeker Alex Jones in breaking into the woods, and successfully filmed parts of the Cremation of Care ritual before having to make a hasty exit as suspicions were aroused. Doubtful at first, but convinced by the evidence of his own eyes, Ronson conceded that the presence of prominent leaders at the Bohemian Grove rituals was at the very least rather odd, and devoted a chapter of his bestselling book *Them* to the subject.[25] Was this really what our supposed role models should be doing? His was not the first attempted exposé, nor the last, but certainly the most prominent.

So is the Bohemian ceremony just a harmless pageant, or something darker? In the ritual, a small boat ferries the effigy across a lake, where it is received by hooded figures and consumed in fire on an altar beneath the imposing statue of the giant owl, which supposedly signifies 'knowledge'. There has been much speculation about the meaning of the owl, with Alex Jones claiming it is a representation of the ancient Hebrew god 'Moloch' (although Moloch is traditionally a bull-headed creature) and that it has Satanic overtones. In truth, the ritual seems deliberately over-blown and melodramatic, with music and a voice-over (presumably pre-recorded) from former US television anchorman Walter Cronkite. It's almost laughable. Almost.

If the Bohemian Club rituals were openly spoken of and happily explained away as a harmless pageant, a bit of fun for our leaders on vacation, one might be able to accept this as a just another part of the ceremonial fabric of our society. And indeed, when pressed, the little that has been said by club members attempts to convey exactly this. But the lack of openness can only create more sinister speculation. The fact that another statue in the grove shows the club's chosen patron saint, St John of Nepomuk, with a finger held to his lips in a 'keep-quiet' pose, doesn't exactly speak of inclusiveness to the rest of the population.

Claims that it is all a bit of fun, with no meaningful discussion of the outside world around the campfires, is plainly nonsensical, especially given that it is acknowledged that a key preparative meeting for the Manhattan Project, which developed the first atomic bomb, was held during the Grove camp of 1942. It is almost certain that amongst all the admittedly juvenile humour and male-bonding that must go on ('there's no end to the pee-pee and penis jokes, suggesting that these men, advanced in so many other ways, were emotionally arrested sometime during adolescence', wrote Philip Weiss of *Spy Magazine*, who also broke into the Grove in 1989), some pretty serious discussions about global events and underlying agendas must also take place.

All this, put together with the presumably less ritualistic closed meetings at the likes of the Bilderberg Group, The Council for Foreign Relations, The Trilateral Commission and the many other mysterious high-level 'think-tanks' that influence global politics, makes it increasingly likely that parliaments and congresses are merely shop-windows for decisions essentially made elsewhere, far out of the gaze of any who may naively hope that democracy is still a going concern.

Next time you hear of some new grand global policy being announced, consider, then, that it may well have been devised by the type of people who sit around campfires in the shadow of a large stone owl. For this is the reality - not a fiction - that we are dealing with. What the motives and intentions of these people are is far from clear, but perhaps it becomes

The Bohemian Grove rituals could be passed off as a harmless pageant, yet it is known that high-level meetings also take place there, away from the prying eyes of democracy and the public. A key early meeting to develop the first atomic bomb is known to have taken place during the Bohemian Grove camp of 1942.

more obvious as to why so many people do now subscribe to many of the conspiracy 'theories' stirred by an application of the Truth Agenda. With so much that is so very plainly lied about or at least heavily played down, it really does appear that there are crucial things going on that are hidden from us, and not just in the realms of the paranormal.

Breaking the Illusion

What, then, can we trust? If the illusion we have been fed for so long about the nature of our civilisation and those who run it is so very skewed from the reality, is any of our official history reliable or true? Why should we believe *anything* we are told by people who seem to place their interests far above ours? What do we find when we apply the Truth Agenda to the 'authorised' view of even the most major events and achievements?

Here is a test. Stick a pin, while blindfolded, on a chart showing a list of recent historical moments or important global events. Take that randomly chosen selection and then scrutinise it in every detail, spending time looking at the official record versus the reality of what actually happened. Look at the evidence presented to justify the official record and put it through a vigorous analysis of logic, questioning its reliability. Then consider why we are being asked to believe that official record and question who or what benefits most from that belief. This is the Truth Agenda in action.

It is surprising to find from this process that very few things are what they first appear to be. At the very least, the evidence proffered in the mainstream to support an official view is often shockingly fragile - and sometimes plainly deceptive.

As a demonstration, we will look in the next part at three major examples of events celebrated by 'consensus reality', but which, under scrutiny, become disturbingly tenuous in terms of the evidence that supposedly supports them. If just one thing we took for granted as a reality can be shown to be even slightly unreliable, then the hypothesis presented in this book moves one step closer to deserving at least some consideration.

THE TRUTH AGENDA: *Mistrust in our leaders and the systems they manage has led many to suspect the very worst of both, to the point where some believe a regime of financial and political manipulation is creating a centralised global state designed to maintain power for a small but influential elite. The overt occult symbolism and bizarre rituals employed by those appearing to implement this suggest a firm belief in ancient lore and a total conviction of their right to rule, while the common people are seen as disposable pawns. Those who attempt to expose this scheme are vilified and ridiculed, and may sometimes go too far in their speculation - yet it is hard to dismiss the clear observation that important truths about the way the world is governed are being kept from us. If the fundamental basis of our society is so rooted in deception, why should we trust any story fed to us by officialdom?*

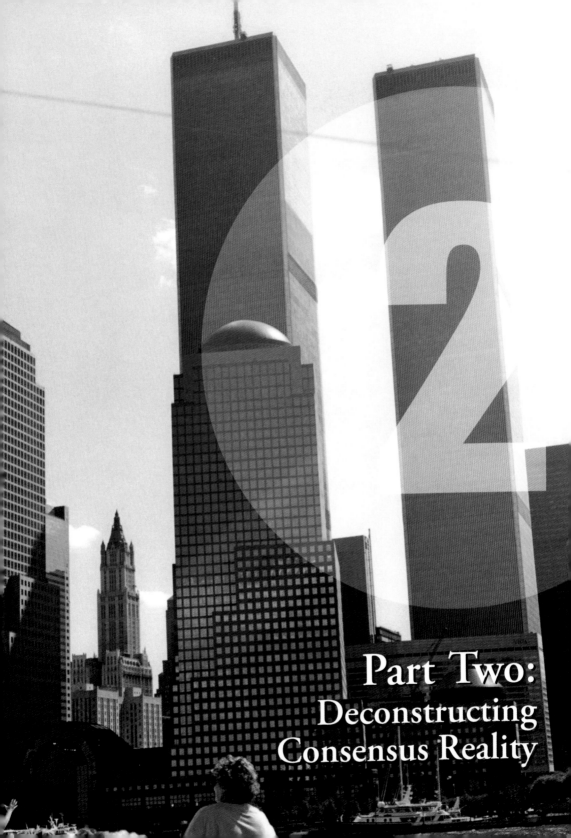

Part Two:
Deconstructing
Consensus Reality

The colossal Saturn V rocket at the Kennedy Space Centre, Florida. Rockets such as this were unquestionably seen to take off - but did their payloads really make it to the Moon? If they did, have we been shown the real evidence?

VI   ONE GIANT LEAP..?

The first pin we will stick into the board of famous historical events, for the application of the Truth Agenda, concerns what is often spoken of as humankind's greatest achievement. The Moon landings are frequently held up as an example of the spirit of adventure, ingenuity and determination that gives our sometimes flawed species validation. Yet a surprisingly large number of people doubt the evidence for the lunar expeditions. Has the truth of the Apollo missions really been told, and if not what are the implications for our view of consensus reality?

Growing Doubts Over the Moon Landings

On 20th July 1969, possibly the most famous celebratory moment in modern history occurred when Neil Armstrong, NASA astronaut, landed on Earth's natural satellite and became the first human being ever to stand on another world. Five further missions, with different crews, would follow. In an age of angst, civil unrest and atrocities in Vietnam it was the perfect distraction for a jaded US society, and encouraged all of us to believe there was a better side to the human race that could put triumph above tragedy.

Why, then, have so many people expressed such doubt in the authenticity of the Moon landings? It's one of the most famous conspiracy theories of all, often chuckled about in the mainstream, yet widely discussed. Even in 1969, polls showed a surprisingly large proportion of the global population had reservations about what had really happened, with some television viewers phoning in with bizarre claims of seeing Coke bottles on the Moon's surface or catching glimpses of wires and lighting rigs. It was dismissed then as psychological denial from simple folk who couldn't come to terms with the huge technical achievements of the modern world.

However, as the media loudly celebrates the fortieth anniversary year of the first landing, not only has the doubt not gone away, it has actually grown.

Although satellite technology is finally expected to photograph the Moon landing sites in detail to mark the grand anniversary, the fact is that until independent researchers physically stand on the lunar surface to examine the artefacts supposedly left by the astronauts (which, given the easy availability of advanced photo-editing software, will probably be the only thing to really settle the arguments), the doubts are going to remain. The absence of aerial pictures thus far has in itself been a huge puzzle, given the long presence of many sophisticated lunar orbiters. Doubters believe the time has been used to work on some very good fakes.

Although it seems upsetting to have to question a human achievement held closely to our hearts for so long, sadly we do seem to live in a world of habitual deception where nothing official can be completely relied on. As a consequence, many seemingly unquestionable things become open to re-evaluation.

Naturally, not only is the lunar hoax one of the best known conspiracy theories, it is also one of the most attacked. There are vast swathes of the Internet devoted to believers and non-believers battling it out to challenge each other's explanations for anomalies in the NASA record of evidence. Tellingly, though, all this debate has not settled the divisions.

Those unwilling to have their higher hopes for humankind dashed tend to get very emotive when the Moon landings are questioned, and bitter exchanges with the heretics are common. Defenders of official records on any subject tend to take on an unhelpful tone of haughtiness and do what is always done when under fire - pick on the weaker areas of the conspiracy theories (the 'straw man' arguments), which indeed *don't* stand up, and ignore the stronger areas, which can then be dismissed by simple association and quietly forgotten about. One example of this regarding the evidence for the Moon landings is the question of why stars can't be seen in the lunar surface photos, a point sometimes shouted by the less sharp of the doubters, and rightly pounced on by defenders. The - in this case quite correct - answer is that the comparatively faint stars wouldn't show up, because of the reduced exposure level necessary to capture the detail of the brighter surface. Such easy knock-downs are trumpeted as being typical of the holes in lunar conspiracy theories. However, the more serious points, such as why the astronauts seem to be standing in anomalous pools of light or have been photographed from impossible angles (as we shall see), are rather conveniently either never addressed, or waved away with explanations that may sound scientific to the lay person ('light scatters differently on the Moon'), but are actually suspect when analysed.

We will not thrash out every argument around the lunar hoax theory - the interested reader should explore the sources recommended in *Appendix 2* to discover all the many disputed areas - but it is worth looking at some of the major arguments that have simply not been settled or satisfactorily explained by defenders. It is a very complex business, and this chapter is a necessarily simplified look at the main issues to help reveal an important example of something sold as a given which, when put under scrutiny, begins to look a little shaky.

The Key Evidence

The NASA Moon landing claims - and they *are* claims - are particularly unusual in the field of human endeavour, because there is so little evidence available to prove what happened. With no accompanying journalists or independent observers, there is simply no outside corroboration of what happened on the Moon - we just have to take the word of a very few people that NASA went there.

What we know for sure is this: huge Saturn V rockets took off (witnessed by tens of thousands), and indeed an unused version of one impressively lies on display today at the Kennedy Space Centre in Florida [page 98], so there is no doubt of their existence, nor of a space programme in general. At the end of the missions, capsules then sailed down from the sky on parachutes into the Pacific Ocean. This much is certain. What is missing is clear evidence of what occurred in-between.

Approximately 400,000 people were involved in the space missions, most of them sincere, technically-adept personnel, all clearly believing in their work and its aims. The intention to go to the Moon, and the attempted development of the technology to allow it was plainly genuine. Indeed, national prestige was riding on it. In 1961, President John F Kennedy had famously stated his aim of 'achieving the goal, before this decade is out, of landing a man on the Moon and returning him safely to the Earth'.[1]

Exhibits and unused Apollo craft at the Kennedy Space Centre, Florida, commemorating the missions to the Moon. How could anyone think that such a huge venture could possibly have been faked? Yet an alarming number of people now question the evidence for the landings.

In the wake of JFK's untimely death in 1963, what respectable US citizen would not want to try to honour that goal?

But what if this lofty aspiration turned out to be unattainable within such a time frame? What if technical disasters and unanticipated problems proved insurmountable? With the Cold War at its height, and an unsavoury Asian war going badly, to fail would be a blow beyond measure to the US psyche. What could one do? The conspiracy theorists think they know the answer.

With such a large hole in the demonstrable public record of the Moon landings, outside of take-off and splash-down, we have to rely on three essential pieces of evidence to accept the official story that NASA went to the Moon. We have: 1) the testimony of the astronauts themselves; 2) Moon rocks; and 3) the photographs.

It might be imagined that these three key exhibits should stand up to some pretty serious analysis as criteria on which to base our belief in this grand achievement - yet the curious fact is that they don't.

The Astronauts' Testimony

The collected testimony of the astronauts is... interesting. Although some *have* spoken of the profound nature of their experience (more than one 'got' God and became highly religious afterwards), others sometimes sound oddly blasé and matter-of-fact about it; not what you might expect from people who had stood for the first time on another world, looking back up at a now distant Earth. Some, like Neil Armstrong, have been strangely quiet about it all, coming forward now and then to make script-prepared anniversary statements, but not with the joy and conviction that might be anticipated. Other testimony is plainly contradictory - some astronauts speak of how bright the stars looked from space (indeed, some of the navigation was achieved by the remarkably archaic method of using a sextant to read the position of stars), while others say they could barely see the stars at all.[2] There are many other inconsistencies and apparent errors in the verbal record, which don't appear to make sense if they had all shared a similar experience, albeit on different missions.

The uncomfortable truth is that people have been known to lie throughout history. Whether it be for patriotic reasons, through respect of oaths, or fear of threats to them and their families, there are many examples of people who have willingly or unwillingly fronted stories to save king and country (Major Jesse Marcel at Roswell being a minor example - page 37). With all NASA astronauts of the 1960s having come from good military stock, patriotic allegiance at the expense of the truth might come easily if they believed the safety and prestige of America was at stake. And if their own families' safety and reputation was also at stake, the compulsion to do their duty might be even stronger.

The crew of the ill-fated Apollo 1. L-R: Virgil Grissom, Edward White and Roger Chaffee. All died during a launch pad fire in 1967. Grissom was a very vocal critic of the Moon missions, loudly questioning their feasibility. Years later, his son Scott uncovered evidence to suggest the crew were murdered.

Surely, though, at least one of the astronauts might have been tempted to blow the whistle if a scam was in operation? Perhaps they tried to; there has been much speculation on more than one NASA figure.

Virgil 'Gus' Grissom, officially the third human to go into space (after Yuri Gagarin and Alan Shepard), in a Mercury capsule in 1961, was originally scheduled to be the first man on the Moon, not Armstrong. However, reports from colleagues and family show that Grissom - a qualified aircraft engineer - had become an increasingly vocal critic of not only the poor safety specifications of the proposed Moon missions, but even of its entire technical feasibility. With controversy surrounding his own Mercury flight, in which the safety hatch inexplicably blew out on splash-down, there is evidence that Grissom was increasingly seen as a liability. Grissom felt unfairly blamed for the hatch incident, but he pointed to poor technology as the culprit, beginning a running critique of the space programmes he himself was closely involved in. This extended even to hanging a lemon on an Apollo test module in front of press reporters as a sign of his contempt, rating the Moon mission's chances of success as 'pretty slim'. In fact, on the evidence of his first flight (especially when the sunken Mercury capsule, *Liberty Bell 7*, was finally recovered for examination in 1999 and showed no signs of its necessary heat-shield), some doubt that Grissom even made it into space proper, perhaps explaining further his resentment at having to front something he didn't believe could really work.

The remains of the Apollo 1 capsule after the fire. Scott Grissom later discovered an anomalous metal plate had been deliberately inserted into the wiring, almost certainly causing the fire.

On 27th January 1967, Grissom and his two colleagues Edward White and Roger Chaffee died in a terrible fire that raged through the cockpit of Apollo 1 during training. An inadvisably sealed atmosphere of almost pure oxygen had become ignited by, apparently, poor wiring. Years later, Grissom's son Scott, a qualified engineer, mounted his own investigation and managed to examine the remains of his father's death capsule - and the faulty switch responsible for the fire. He discovered a small and functionless metal plate with it that appeared to fit into the switch - the insertion of which would almost guarantee the production of a dangerous spark. In 1999, Scott went public with his belief that his father was murdered. According to Virgil's wife, Betty Grissom, her husband - who had received death threats he believed came from within NASA - once warned her that 'if there is ever a serious accident in the space program, it's likely to be me'.[3]

Another dubious end awaited one Thomas Ronald Baron, an inspector at Cape Kennedy (now Cape Canaveral) who had compiled a highly critical report on the poor safety record and inefficiency at North American Aviation (NAA - contracted by NASA to work on the Apollo programme), which led up to the Apollo 1 tragedy. Stating in front of a congressional subcommittee that one NAA employee 'knew exactly what caused the fire' (although the employee denied this), Baron never got a chance to say more because he and his family died when their car was struck by a train just a week later. Coincidence? The crash was ruled as 'suicide'. With only Baron's short - and highly damning - preliminary paper having been published, the full 500-page report he was compiling before his death never saw the light of day.[4]

Draw your own conclusions. Could it be that someone did indeed do away with a unsettlingly critical astronaut threatening to expose the unfeasibility of the Moon missions, and then tried to cover up an all-too revealing inquiry? If so, who would dare try to reveal further shortcomings after Grissom and his colleagues, followed by Baron and his family, met such hideous fates?

Rumours also persist that Apollo 15 veteran James Irwin was about to go public with information about a lunar cover-up, when he died suddenly of cardiac arrest in 1991. Although it is true that Irwin did already have a heart condition, it's interesting that he was the first of the Moon astronauts to pass away.[5] Irwin was also one of the several lunar pioneers who had become evangelical Christian preachers; a response to the wonder of space, or an attempt to find redemption?

The Grissom case illustrates at the very least that there *were* voices raised at the time trying to draw attention to the fact that the Moon mission was far more flawed and risky than the NASA publicity machine was letting on. Nearly all US space shots before the Apollo programme, merely low-orbital ones at that, had run into major technical difficulties and had succeeded - just - on a wing and a prayer. Even the formal Apollo training exercises rarely worked properly, with *not one* successful trial of a lunar lander test craft before the real thing set off (Armstrong was nearly killed when such a device span out of control in 1968; he managed to eject just seconds before disaster). Yet six Moon landing missions - with only the highly publicised Apollo 13 as the exception (see below) - seemed to run smoothly and without major error. Getting men in tin cans into low orbit

Neil Armstrong's Lunar Lander Training Vehicle spins to its doom in 1968. Armstrong ejected safely. Not a single LLTV test was ever successful - yet the landers all worked perfectly on the Moon.

stretched NASA's capabilities to breaking point, but a voyage to another world was suddenly a breeze.

The testimony of astronauts, therefore, has to be taken on the same level as the testimony of early mountaineers and explorers (some of whom did fake claims of their conquests) - we simply have to accept their word that they went to the Moon. And perhaps they did, but is the evidence presented for it reliable? This may be a separate issue, for there are plenty who believe the missions went ahead, but that the photographic record was faked, for reasons we will discuss later. However, concerns over human survivability in the harshness of space using primitive 1960s technology clouds this compromise theory for others.

At the time (especially before the exposure of Richard Nixon's misdemeanours in 1974, which was a major blow to American faith in the word of prominent figures), few thought to question the word of the astronautic heroes, but in these days of mass-media deceptions, routine political lies, dodgy dossiers that lead us into war [Chapter VII] and buildings that fall down for no convincing reason [Chapter VIII], it's now more understandable why people feel they need a little more substantial back-up for extraordinary claims. So the word of the astronauts, unfortunately, is no longer enough to sustain total belief.

We need to look, therefore, at the second piece of evidence regularly presented as proof for the Moon odyssey, to see how that stands up to the Truth Agenda.

The Moon Rock Conundrum

If words are not enough, should not a solid piece of geology show that we did actually go to the Moon? When doubts over photographs and testimonies are expressed, rocks retrieved from the lunar surface are usually proffered as the ultimate mitigation. But are they what scientists claim?

There are two major problems with the Moon rock issue. One concerns scientific presumption, and the other, methods of retrieval.

Very few people have ever examined Moon debris. The distribution of material collected by the lunar missions has been extremely limited, and when samples are occasionally released for analysis it is usually only to close associates of NASA or mainstream scientific bodies unlikely to challenge convention. Even then, samples are never allowed to be physically touched, but handled only under strict laboratory conditions. Those who *have* examined rocks or dust have often expressed how similar the samples are to terrestrial geology, with just a few supposed differences. Is this because, as scientists currently claim, Earth and Moon were once joined, split asunder by a massive collision when the solar system was young - or could it be because the samples actually come from Earth itself?

Scientific fraud has been known in many avenues of research. What proof have we that samples released by NASA come from the Moon? If a cover-up of the kind claimed by doubters is in operation, the rocks could come from anywhere. Who would know the difference?

Virtually no analysis of lunar materials has been genuinely scientific, *because the assumption is always made from the start that the sample comes from the Moon*. With that very strong impression in mind, it must be hard for even the best laboratory worker to approach their work with a clear perspective. Instead of testing blind samples to see what is there, comparing them to controls without bias (as science claims should always occur), analyses of lunar material always begin with a preconception (rather like the restrictive thinking inherent in mainstream Egyptology - Chapter II). In other words, there have been very few, if any, proper investigations to determine whether or not Moon rock is actually from the Moon.

Moon rocks, collected by the crew of Apollo 11 - or were they? Could lunar material have been collected by automated probes instead? Some doubt that the rocks even come from the Moon.

Even when official analysis is conducted within the usual parameters, anomalies still arise, ones that should raise more questions than are ever aired. When eminent UK astrobiologist Andrew Steele of the University of Portsmouth managed to scrutinise Moon material at close quarters, his examinations revealed several components of Earthly contamination; tiny particles of plastic, Teflon and micro-animal remains were clearly present in the samples he was sent.[6] Given the tight strictures over delivery and handling described above, how could such contamination occur? Or was the sample of dirt simply from more terrestrial climes in the first place? There are many unanswered questions about where these supposed Moon samples really come from.

But let's assume for a moment that the rock samples do come from the lunar surface - the presumption that they could only have been brought back by the astronauts is a narrow one. Unmanned probes have been a major - indeed, *the* major - part of space exploration since it began. There are far fewer problems accepting the reality of this, because making technology function in deep space is infinitely easier than preserving the fragile life systems of human beings - and there are no clear reasons why anyone would need to fake it.

Several unmanned probes were sent to the Moon before and after the Apollo missions, by both NASA and the Soviet space programme. Indeed, as early as 1970, the Soviets claimed to have retrieved small urns of Moon dust, sent back to Earth from an unmanned craft. It is not impossible that scoops of lunar material could have been retrieved by secret NASA probes in the same way. [Similarly, the laser-calibration 'mirrors' left on the Moon by three Apollo crews - another criteria often used as proof that man once stood there - could also have also been placed by unmanned craft (as the Soviets achieved with their own mirrors, twice), although when Gerhard Wisnewski attempted to find out *exactly* where on the lunar surface these mirrors were, no-one was able to tell him.][7] It is even possible that NASA could have bargained with the Soviets for access to lunar soil - not as unlikely as it may sound, despite all the Cold War race-into-space propaganda we were fed in the 1960s and 70s. There is evidence to show that there was quiet co-operation and collusion between the two sides in more than one area [page ??].

Another source of Moon material could be from meteorites. It is now well-known that we have had rocks raining down on us from the planets in our solar system for millions of years, with both Moon and Mars-originated meteorites (we are told) having been clearly identified. Antarctica, for instance, is littered with them. So, if automated probes or outright faking using earthly rocks aren't responsible, this is another way extra-terrestrial geology could be legitimately presented for analysis.

Consequently, lunar rock is not the panacea of authentication that defenders of the official NASA record would wish to us believe. Like the testimony of the astronauts, it cannot be accepted as definitive proof that we once stood on the Moon.

Two supposedly key pieces of evidence for the Moon landings are therefore more questionable than one might like to believe, with neither astronautic testimony nor geological samples being watertight criteria. All we are left to turn to for final reassurance is the one major area remaining - the photographs and films.

Anomalies in the Photographic Record

They are arguably the most famous photos in history; men standing on another world, crystal-clear images of humankind's gleaming technology set against the grey, barren wastelands of the Moon. They have inspired pride and the spirit of adventure in many over the last forty years - as they did in this author at the time. In my first decade of life while the Moon landings were seemingly taking place, I viewed the astronauts as heroes, and rockets and lunar landers were my transports of delight. This enthusiasm went as far as writing in for James Irwin's autograph when he was in London as an ITV commentator for one of the later missions, and I was duly rewarded. Whether he scribbled his own name (three times on one piece of paper, oddly), or whether someone in the television offices did it to keep a impressionable boy happy, I will never know, but it was a cherished keepsake for many years.

The point here is that it gives this author little pleasure to look now at those photos which so fired the imagination and see... flaws. Like many who first become aware of the potential NASA cover-up, there is shock and a grieving process one has to go through before being able to see the official record more objectively - but once the veil is lifted it is hard to see these iconic images in quite the same way again.

One of the doubters' central accusations against the Moon missions is that some or all of the photos were faked in a studio, or at the very least were taken during legitimate training exercises and presented, with a little doctoring, as the real thing. This idea is so prevalent in the public mind that it has been successfully used as a mainstream source of fiction (the movie *Capricorn One*, in which the Moon is substituted by Mars) as well as satirically lampooned (everything from the James Bond movie *Diamonds are Forever*, to *The Simpsons*), and everyone knows what they are getting at. In fact, the idea is so popularised that this is one of the very aspects used to knock the theory down; it becomes nothing more than a joke after a while. However, could one of the reasons for the high profile of the studio forgery theory be because there is actually a plausible case to be investigated?

It doesn't take too much knowledge of photography to find difficulties in accepting that all of the lunar surface photos were taken in natural light - the central claim of the official story. People with good photographic experience, such as Marcus Allen (who has become one of the key questioners of the NASA claims) - and this author (I have had books of photographs published) - point to very clear anomalies in the lunar photos, which challenge the notion that they were simple snapshots taken on a quick jaunt around the Moon.

So what are these anomalies? Ignoring some of the weaker critiques (debatable shadow angles, the visibility or non-visibility of stars, etc.), we shall explore the stronger evidence that something is not right in these pictures by looking at a few specific examples. Some of the arguments are necessarily of a technical nature, but the issues present themselves clearly enough.

The Classic Aldrin Photo

(See Fig. 1): One of the most famous images of all time, often used in NASA publicity and history books, is of Edwin 'Buzz' Aldrin, the second person ever to stand on the Moon, supposedly photographed by Neil Armstrong during the Apollo 11 mission [taken on a Hasselblad 500 EL camera, as all the Moon photos were, using Kodak Ektachrome transparency film, ISO 160 - more on the cameras on page 112]. It's a beautiful composition and an iconic image, with the foot of the lunar lander just visible to the right of the shot. However, there are four major problems with this picture.

Fig. 1: Apollo 11's 'Buzz' Aldrin standing on the Moon, one of the most iconic and most-reproduced NASA images of all time. But there are many lighting and angle anomalies [see text] that make many believe it was taken in a studio. The image has not been cropped - this is the exact original. Compare to the NASA Media Services version in Fig. 4 [page 111], where a large slab of black sky has been added in.

Anomaly Number One: The front of Aldrin's suit is lit up very clearly here, apparently by reflected light. According to NASA, the light is being bounced from the lunar surface. This might be believable were it not for some rudimentary rules concerning photography and light. The Sun is very clearly behind Aldrin, to the right of the picture. Given the exposure, which has left his foreground shadow very dark, either the astronaut should look much the same (a stark back-lit silhouette) or his ground shadow should also be lighter and exhibit detail in the dust; instead, we see the full features of his suit, glowing with secondary light, while his shadow is densely impenetrable. The only way to ensure such detail would be revealed on a back-lit standing object (i.e. Aldrin) *without* a great amount of reflected light would be to bring up the exposure of the shot - but this would also bring out detail on the area in his shadow and leave the lit parts of the lunar surface glowing bright. Instead, Aldrin's foreground shadow is completely black and the Moon's lit areas are fairly dull, apart from a peculiar brighter region to the right (see Anomaly Number Two).

With no atmosphere to help distribute light, it is difficult to explain the visible detail on Aldrin's suit. The lunar surface has the reflectivity of tarmac - the Moon may look bright in our skies, but at close quarters its albedo (degree of reflectivity) is very weak. Reflected light would be unable to account for Aldrin's body detail as we see it here. In other words, it is almost as if some kind of artificial light source has been used to specifically 'fill-in' the parts of the astronaut not in the glare of the bright Sun - but NASA says no extra lighting was used. Some say the fill comes from Earthlight, but (especially as Earth was directly overhead for Apollo 11 - the fill-in light clearly comes from the side, as it does in most of the lunar photos), any such light would be so feeble as to make no photographic difference (and again, even if it did, and even allowing that a space suit is more reflective than Moon dust, why would it not also show up some detail in Aldrin's ground shadow?).

Fig. 2: The same image as Fig. 1, but with the contrast increased (and no other editing). This reveals without any doubt that Aldrin is standing with a pool of light behind him to the right - an impossibility if this is natural sunlight.

Anomaly Number Two: Looking at the overall picture, made more obvious when the contrast is adjusted [Fig. 2], we see another clearly observed - and almost entirely inexplicable - phenomenon: Aldrin is in a clear pool of light, a bright spot focused on an area just behind him, to the right (his left). How can this be so, if the only light source is the Sun? The Sun does not produce pools of light in an open space, as can be demonstrated on any clear terrestrial day. Instead, it gives a uniform, evenly-spread light. This would be especially so in a cloudless vacuum. Yet this NASA photo shows a clear fall-off of luminosity toward both the foreground and the background. The horizon is almost in darkness in the increased contrast version, which shouldn't be the case in an even light. Photographing someone standing on a sandy beach or desert (the best equivalent of the Moon we can get down here) does not result in a bright spot in the middle and a darkening to the front and to the horizon.

This is just one of several NASA photos in which an entirely anomalous pool of light is clearly visible. There can really only be one explanation for this - Aldrin (and his counterparts in other pictures) must be lit by spotlights and reflective techniques. But no spotlights or any other lighting equipment were officially taken to the Moon. Interestingly, the photographic bright spots are one of the least-mentioned areas by the many defenders of the official record, yet they are among the most glaring - literally - of all the anomalies.

Fig. 3: Close-up of the reflection from Aldrin's visor, showing Neil Armstrong supposedly taking the picture - but he could not possibly have done so given the high angle of the shot.

Anomaly Number Three: A third major problem with this photo of Aldrin was first pointed out by Mary Bennett and David Percy, authors of the NASA-debunking book *Dark Moon*. The photograph has been taken from a surprisingly high-angle viewpoint (i.e. looking down), clearly revealed by the level of the background horizon and the visibility of the top of Aldrin's back-pack. This could not have been taken by an astronaut with a camera immovably strapped to his chest (the system used in most of the missions).

Given the apparently flat lunar surface at this location, whoever took this photo must have been poised with the lens at least at eye level - or higher - and was thus *not* the astronaut visible in Aldrin's visor reflection (supposedly Armstrong - Fig. 3). Experiments by Bennett and Percy reveal that the horizon line, if taken by a body-strapped camera, should come somewhere around Aldrin's chest, not at the artistically-pleasing level of his helmet, which makes for a perfect compositional continuation of the horizon line either side of him, a phenomenon seen in a number of NASA images [see also Fig. 5 & Fig. 6].[8]

Fig. 4: The NASA Media Services version of the same classic Aldrin photo, which crops the image and adds extra sky at the top.

Anomaly Number Four: In fact, aside from all the above issues, the Aldrin portrait is one of the photos that has very definitely been tampered with in PR versions of the same image issued by NASA Media Services [Fig. 4], which have a larger slab of additional black sky above Aldrin's head (making the middle cross-hair, or calibration 'reticle', included on all the lunar images, appear vertically off-centre). Comparing with Fig. 1, it can be seen that the original version of the picture shows very little sky above Aldrin (with the cross-hair directly central), and his helmet is uncomfortably close to the top of the frame, which is far less pleasing to the eye, but is as originally taken. If just one image can have been so obviously tampered with, why could it not have happened in more ambitious ways with many of the others? It is claimed, however, that no re-touching occurred.

This fourth anomaly is fairly explicable, and plainly down to NASA manipulating the image for aesthetic purposes. However, it is hard to find easy solutions for the other troubling difficulties - and this is just one photograph. Others raise similar questions. Whether the classic Aldrin photo was taken on the Moon or in a studio, it seems to have been realised after the fact that this was the best image to be used for PR, despite it being, annoyingly for NASA, one of the very few examples of bad composition - for it is in itself a mystery how the vast majority of pictures were so perfectly framed on a camera without a viewfinder.

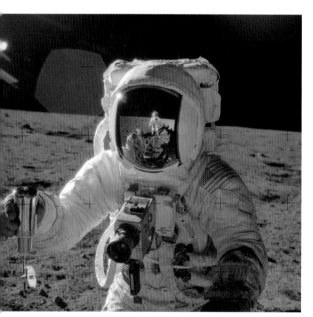

Fig. 5: Alan Bean, Apollo 12. Another photo taken from a higher angle than possible if the astronaut in the reflection was taking it. There are also more lighting anomalies. The standard chest-height Hasselblad camera can be clearly seen.

Camera Issues

(See Fig. 5): This photograph of Alan Bean from Apollo 12 shows another very clear example of sunshine seen to one side (left), while fill-in light has seemingly been used to illuminate areas that should be in black shadow (right). Again, the photo has been taken from a high angle to ensure the horizon line reflected in the visor pleasingly continues the one in the background - thus it could not have been taken by the astronaut seen in the reflection. If it was, the horizon behind Bean would run through his chest, so either the photo was taken by someone else from another, more elevated, angle or the visor image has simply been spliced into the picture (as the contrast differences would appear to suggest).

The angle and extra illumination, however, helpfully reveals for us the Hasselblad 500 EL camera used on all the Moon missions (see also Fig. 7). A normal if expensive camera, only slightly modified for use in the harsh lunar environment, it was attached firmly to the chest of the astronauts and had no useable viewfinder. With only basic aperture, focusing and exposure controls operated through thick pressurised gloves, and shots composed by guesswork and body movements alone, all the Moon photos were taken - once again, as with many NASA achievements

Fig. 6: Testing camera levels. Above - photo taken at chest height. Below - photo taken at eye level. Note the line of the background fence and compare to Figs. 1 & 5. Chest-level shots could not possibly result in the horizon lines seen in such lunar images. Yet we are told all the shots were taken at chest height.

- on a wing and a prayer. Yet so many of the lunar surface photographs are perfect - rather like studio portraits. This is especially remarkable given that no 'bracketing' of exposures took place (taking three or more shots of the same thing at different light levels to ensure at least one useable image, as practiced by most professional photographers). The unknown photographic conditions on the Moon would have been a particular trial for the Apollo 11 crew who were the first to set foot there.

If one were to spend a day patrolling a dusty wilderness with a camera held firmly at chest-height, photographing friends and their paraphernalia with only basic controls and no viewfinder - and had to achieve this wearing gardening gloves - it would soon become clear that gaining useable results would be something of a trial. Most likely, even using a wide angle lens, the odd head might be cut off, the tilt of many of the images might be skewed and the occasional exposure (manual only and unbracketed, remember) would surely be wrong. But on the Moon, none of this seemed to be a problem, beyond a bit of extra sky needing to be added here and there for compositional purposes.

Defenders of the official line state that a large number of lunar photos *didn't* come out well and were held back from publication, but this claim is not held up by the released contact sheets (which supposedly can't be edited) from the original rolls of film. These, despite a few apparent misfires here and there, demonstrate that the majority of shots achieve near-perfection of exposure, focus and composition, another mystery of this astonishing historical accomplishment.

Fig. 7: A Hasselblad 500 EL camera, as allegedly used on the Moon, strapped to the chest with no viewfinder and controls that had to be operated wearing pressurised gloves. The high quality of the lunar photos is truly remarkable.

The actual films inside the Hasselblad cameras were protected from the extremes of intense heat and intense cold only by a thin layer of 'reflective coating'. But given that lunar temperatures reach over 100°C in direct sunlight, and under -100°C in the shadows (a vacuum doesn't convect heat), and that the Moon is flooded by potentially film-fogging radiation that never gets to earthly environs (more on radiation soon), it is a wonder that any films - vulnerable 1960s stock, not today's more resilient grades - made it back intact at all. Experiments by doubters using ovens, freezers and irradiation suggest severe problems resulting from exposure to these extremes. Some say the films never were useable and that technicians were unable to fix it on each subsequent mission, which is perhaps why they might have had to re-stage the photos in a studio or doctor images from training exercises to justify the vast expense of the Moon programme; a programme that had cost lives as well as money, as with the unfortunates of the Apollo 1 affair and other training personnel. Others, of course, say there's more to it than that.

Fig. 8: Another clear lighting anomaly. The Sun is behind the LEM, yet all but the shadow is brightly lit.

Fig. 9: Aldrin descends Apollo 11 on the shadow *side - yet a specific light source creates highlights on his boot.*

Anomalies of the Lunar Lander

(See Fig. 8): In this photo, we see another clear example of fill-in light having been used, and all the same arguments apply as in the previous examples. The lander (or Lunar Excursion Module - LEM) has the Sun visibly behind it to the left, and casts a large jet black shadow towards the bottom right of the photo, in which no detail can be seen at all. Yet the craft itself is brightly lit from the right so that colourful detail can be seen and the United States logo shows up clearly (the latter observation being a notable feature of many of the photos). It is almost impossible to believe that this illumination can be from reflected light, especially given how large the dark area of ground shadow is. Similar issues arise with Fig. 9, in which Buzz Aldrin can be seen descending the ladder of Apollo 11. Given that we are seeing the shadow side of the LM (i.e. again with the Sun behind it), the levels of light are astonishing - and Aldrin's boot appears to be showing a clear reflection of a single bright light source; a spotlight or flash, perhaps?

Fig. 10: The lunar surface beneath Apollo 11 (with refuse sack). In none of the mission shots can disturbance of any kind be seen beneath the LEMs. We are told the thrusters were cut before they touched down, but pre-mission NASA visualisations showed something quite different was anticipated.

Fig. 11: Above - clean foot of Apollo 11. Below - dusty foot of the Phoenix Mars lander in 2008. Is the lack of any visible Moon dust reasonable?

Another curious observation made by many regarding images of the LEM is that there appears to be neither blown dust anywhere on the feet of the craft (Fig. 11 - compare this to the photo of the 2008 Phoenix probe on Mars, showing clear deposits of dust and soil), nor evidence of the slightest crater or scorch mark beneath the central engine [Fig. 10]. Official defenders state that most of the thrust to brake the descent of the lander was expended before it reached ground level, but it is interesting to note that from all the pre-mission artwork produced by NASA, the craft was *expected* to be descending on a huge jet of flame until the surface was reached [page 128]. Even if the defence is partly valid, it seems peculiar that no disturbance of any kind is visible in the Moon dust beneath the craft in any of the six mission photograph sets, and that no scattered dust seems to have been thrown up by what still must have been something of a jolt as it impacted.

There are other anomalies concerning the thrust required to pilot the LEM. Again, pre-mission conceptual artwork suggests that the lifting off of the top part of the craft on departure (leaving the landing gear on the Moon's surface) would produce a notably large and visible flame. Even allowing for the fact that thrusters do not burn in a vacuum as they do in an atmosphere, the famous automatic video images of an ascending capsule [Fig. 12] show no light, signs of heat or any visible exhaust at all from such a high temperature rocket - just ejected debris from the explosive bolts. Yet NASA footage of the same thrusters being tested on Earth shows an incredible force being expended; one

Deconstructing Consensus Reality

would expect something to be seen, especially as the fuel used for Apollo was the same as that still used for the space shuttle today - which produces visible effects in a vacuum, filmed on many missions [also Fig. 12].

One would also expect something to be *heard* from the engines; not in silent space, of course, but through the helmet-radios of the astronauts in the cabin of the lunar lander. Given that the astronauts were literally standing on top of an incredibly powerful propulsion engine, just feet away from them, it is

very strange that no released recordings of astronaut dialogue at the moments when the engines were firing exhibit any background sound at all - instead, all that can be heard are calm voices against silence, with no hint of what at the very least could be expected to be an audible rumble or vibration conducted through the spacesuits, even allowing for the fact that the cabin was reportedly depressurised at the time. [This point raises other questions - how were complex switches, dials and keyboards operated so easily while wearing stiff pressurised gauntlets, when the astronauts' lives depended on very fine accuracy of control?]

Everything from the questionable storage capacity of the LEM, heating/cooling problems [page 123] and its remarkably amateur and fragile-looking construction have been called into question by critics, and not without justification.

Fig. 12: Above - Apollo 11 lifting off from the lunar surface with no visible exhaust or flame of any kind. Below - the space shuttle firing its main thrusters, with clearly visible effects. Yet the same fuel is used in both. The LEM appears to lift upwards almost as if by crane.

Coming back to the photographs, it is alarming to note that many of the problems with the selections under discussion can be detected throughout the entire NASA image record of the Moon landings. There is one potential mitigation, though - what about the video footage? Surely that backs up the veracity of the still shots?

Video Issues

(See Fig. 13): In this image, we see astronaut John Young from Apollo 16 leaping up two feet or so off the ground, held in momentary suspension, supposedly using the low lunar gravity to salute the US flag before him in a rather novel way. Looking closely, we can see there is a loose flap on the top of his backpack, sticking up like a little triangle. There is clear space between him and the lunar surface. We can also note the angle of the flag. To the left is the LEM with the wheeled lunar 'rover' in front of it.

This is an interesting example, because the moment the photo was taken was simultaneously recorded on video - presumably from a camera on the rover, from the angles visible in the footage. But instead of being a secondary-source confirmation of the reliability of the pictures, we simply have more anomalies.

 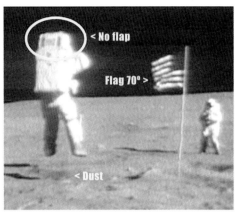

Fig. 13: Left - Still photograph of the Apollo 16 'jump salute', showing John Young leaping up whilst saluting the flag. Right - Video image of the same moment, filmed from a reverse angle. But is it the same moment? The highlighted top of the backpack shows a flap clearly sticking up in the still shot which is absent in the video, the flag is hanging at a different angle and the dust cloud seen in the moving image is not present in its counterpart.

In the video version of this moment, the triangular backpack flap, so clearly visible in the photo, is hardly sticking up at all, even allowing for the reverse angle. Also in the video, there is a clearly visible puff of dust thrown up at the moment the astronaut jumps - yet there is no dust at all in the photograph. The flag, meanwhile, is hanging at a notably more sloped angle than in the photo (there are various anomalies apertaining to flags throughout the whole image record, in fact - see *Dark Moon* for more). In other words, it seems that the video version of the jump salute was re-staged and not taken at the same time as the photo (or vice-versa). It is not impossible that this was the case, of course, but the point is that we are *told* it is the same moment, when apparently it isn't. Other still shots supposedly taken simultaneously with video footage can be shown to be inconsistent, suggesting that photographs and moving images must have been staged in separate sessions, no matter what is claimed and regardless of whether they were on the Moon or not.

The dust-beneath-the-feet in the jump salute raises another interesting issue. Considering what we are told about the very fine quality of lunar surface material, in such low gravity one would expect any disturbance of it to leave clouds of dust hanging for a little while before re-settling. Instead, in video footage of roving buggies and other astronaut activity (such as the salute) the dust is seen to fall quickly back to the ground. It has also been pointed out that in the absence of any moisture at all on the Moon, such clear footprints and tyre-tracks as visible in the photos and films would be unlikely to form in the way seen.

As for the general presence of 'low gravity', this is supposedly proven by the leaden nature of astronaut movement exhibited in the videos. However, some have suggested that all the apparent gravity effects could be accounted for by the simple act of slightly slowing down normal footage (a technique used in many science fiction entertainments). When tests have been run to speed up Moon videos just a little, it is curious to note that the movements and postures of astronauts and the objects they manhandle suddenly take on quite a mundane appearance - as it would look on Earth, in fact. There are also occasional bright flashes above the astronauts in some of the videos, which some have suggested may be wires catching the light. In one scene, an astronaut is clearly seen to stumble, yet is suspended for a brief moment at a miraculously peculiar angle before regaining balance, something unlikely to occur even in reduced gravity.

The videos of the Moon missions shown on our televisions at the time were low-grade versions broadcast by simply pointing a camera at a NASA monitor screen, hence some of the 'ghosting' and general poor image quality that prevented clear viewing of what was going on. Analysis of the original, much higher-resolution, videotapes would have been an obvious line of enquiry to settle some arguments. However, this was not possible for a while. In 2006, it was officially announced that - incredibly, for arguably the single greatest scientific achievement of the 20th century - the original videotapes for all of the Moon missions had been... lost. Lost? Well, possibly misfiled or administratively buried somewhere.[9] So all we had for a while were cruder copies. However, mysteriously enough, the videos were found again just in time for the fortieth anniversary celebrations, so that the legend of NASA's intrepid explorers could be reinforced again - perhaps after edits?

A Studio Hoax?

What is the evidence that a studio could have stood in for the lunar surface, with wires and changed camera speeds to evoke the feeling of a lower gravity environment? More than one might imagine, in fact. Astronaut training was openly held in quite elaborate mock-lunar landscapes, and huge and very convincing models of the Moon were made for various purposes. Some of the training photographs are uncannily like the claimed real ones, with just a little less detail.

In his 1968 film *2001: A Space Odyssey*, Stanley Kubrick had already demonstrated that special effects could convincingly stand in for real-life space activity. (Indeed, some have attempted to implicate Kubrick and/or his effects team as being part of the lunar deception - others have suggested that Walt Disney, who was a close friend of former Nazi scientist turned NASA rocket-genius Wernher Von Braun from the 1950s onwards, might also have been involved.) With enough time and money, therefore - and with much prestige at stake - it's not too difficult to imagine a studio hoax could be made believable. A convincing replica of a lunar

surface had already been built for Apollo 11 training at Flagstaff, Arizona, while a huge assembly of gantries, girders and cranes had been constructed at Langley, Virginia, to simulate low gravity for LEM tests. Both of these places could easily have been utilised for the purposes of a hoax. In any case, with remote bases like Area 51 available to the US authorities [Chapter III], there would be no shortage of large, secret spaces in which to mount such a venture - if they even needed to be large,

Fig. 14: Left - Michael Collins apparently spacewalking outside Gemini 10, as published in his book Carrying The Fire. *Right - Michael Collins inside a NASA training plane, simulating zero gravity. This is plainly the same photo, with the background replaced by blackness for the spacewalk version and then presented as something it isn't. Some NASA images are easily provable fakes.*

that is; the horizons in some of the Apollo photographs do seem rather near, even allowing for the smaller diameter of the Moon as compared with Earth, and hard lines sometimes mark the joining of the ground landscape to distant mountains, almost as if they could be scenery flats creating the illusion of vastness. In some images there is strong evidence of the *same* background scenery being used to represent supposedly different locations, or shifted to be visible in what should be mutually-exclusive compositional shots. Some vistas could also have been convincingly mounted using miniatures, as Kubrick's film makes plain, which might explain the perspective and scale paradoxes that present themselves when comparing some of the images.

It is a proven fact that at least some photographs purporting to show astronauts in space HAVE been fabricated. One famous shot showing Michael Collins apparently space-walking outside Gemini 10 can clearly be proven to be a cut-and-paste image from a terrestrial training mission, reversed and with its background replaced with space-like blackness [Fig. 14].[10]   Another publicised shot of golf being played on the Moon [Fig. 15] can be equally unmasked. As Mary Bennett and David Percy write at *www.aulis.com*:

'In the 1994 British hardback version of Moon Shot *by Al Shepard and Deke Slayton there is a large photograph of Al Shepard playing golf on the lunar surface. In this picture is his companion astronaut. A total impossibility if this was a photograph taken on the Moon during the mission* [as no-one else could have been taking the still picture - no automatic Hasselblads were used on the Moon]. *It was not taken at the time. It is a composite of several other NASA pictures. Yet, this fact was not signalled as such within the pages of this particular edition of* Moon Shot; *it was presented as a photograph of the actual event.'* [11]

Fig. 15: *Alan Shepard and Stuart Roosa playing golf during the Apollo 14 mission - except that the photo is a provable composite pasted together from several different images, as Mary Bennett and David Percy have shown.*

After this was pointed out, it is curious to note that the photo in question was omitted from the 1995 paperback version of the book.

If handy PR shots can be so easily generated and carelessly thrown into the public domain, why might it not be a regular NASA habit?

So is the questioning of humankind's greatest claimed conquest the madness it may seem? Or is it a valid concern in response to very obvious inconsistencies and glaring impossibilities, which have never been properly addressed by either NASA or its defenders, despite all their attempts to dismiss the critics?

Choosing the Truth

The depressing reality is that the three main areas of evidence that supposedly support the authenticity of the Moon missions can all be found to be unreliable when analysed closely. Neither testimony, geology or photography makes the solid case we are told exists. So it all comes down to what one chooses to believe.

What about Apollo 13, some say? That mission in 1970 was aborted after an in-flight explosion caused the crew to retreat to the inadequate lunar module to survive, and a landing wasn't made. Some point to this dramatic event as evidence that the Moon missions were indeed full of genuine peril and unplanned difficulties. Why would anyone hoax that? But even this case isn't clear-cut. With public Moon interest on the wane and budget cuts being threatened (see the conclusion to this chapter to see why that might be more important than at first meets the eye), the Apollo 13 crisis was certainly used as the perfect PR story to re-focus attention onto these gallant pioneers, to justify a few more missions. When Bennett and Percy investigated the planned location at which Apollo 13 *should* have touched down if it had been successful, they discovered that the area known as Fra Mauro would have been in total darkness at the time (hence, in part, their book title *Dark Moon*) - a completely untenable condition for any useful science trip.

If one dismisses all of the lunar conspiracy theories, one does so in the light of several unexplained and major anomalies. Maybe there really are unusual but mundane explanations for these problems, which haven't yet become clear, even to NASA staff. So defenders attack the doubters' easy targets, but ignore the tougher ones, perhaps because they don't know the answers themselves but assume that explanations will emerge. But what if sensible explanations don't emerge? Those emotionally attached to humankind's achievements in space may never be able to assess objectively the merits or otherwise of the NASA evidence. Thus they will always take part in circular arguments on the Internet and forever be in conflict with those they see as uneducated paranoid miscreants, even when their own arguments don't stand up to logical - or scientific - analysis.

The mid-way position taken by some is to believe that we did go to the Moon, but couldn't make the cameras work there. Perhaps some of the pictures are real, but many of the ones that survived weren't considered good enough to make the case to the world and therefore had to be re-staged? Or did the astronauts see something they couldn't share with us? There are plenty of UFO-related theories in this area.

In 2008, Ed Mitchell himself, lunar module pilot of Apollo 14 in 1971, went on record to say that NASA had covered up UFO reports made by the supposed lunar explorers and claimed that the US had withheld firm knowledge of extra-terrestrials for years.[12] While ufologists celebrated the announcement, the more cautious lunar doubters felt that this might be a deliberate distraction in itself. To infer that evidence of aliens was found on the Moon reinforces the view that astronauts *did* land there. This concerns some, for there are also those who feel that we never did go to the Moon, or at least not in the way we were shown.

The Radiation Problem

The notion that astronauts didn't visit the Moon at all seems too much for some, but there is interesting evidence to be considered here. Radiation, for instance, is a major hazard in space outside of the Earth's protective fields, and on the Moon

Deconstructing Consensus Reality

there is no atmospheric protection. Given that some of the missions took place during high solar activity, when radiation levels were extreme (as Bennett and Percy demonstrate)[13], how did the astronauts survive with just a few millimetres of aluminium between them and space while in the craft (raising also the question of how the capsule survived a cabin pressure of 700 lbs per square foot without exploding), and relatively thin and apparently not radiation-proof suits when outside?[14] Why expose the astronauts to such potentially lethal doses when far less dangerous flight windows could have been chosen? Did NASA really play such a risky game of Russian Roulette with the lives of their heroic front-men?

The construction of the lunar lander in particular seems strangely flimsy and ramshackle [Fig. 16], especially given the very substantial and deep walls of radiation protection being proposed for today's developing (and questionable, in the light of these issues) manned Mars missions. The LEM had a 'protective' aluminium skin just three sheets of foil thick. Even the supersonic airliner Concorde carried a radiation measuring device and there have been renewed media concerns of late that regular aeroplane crews at high altitudes may be exposed to too much radiation. Astronauts working on the International Space Station have also had to develop significant shielding, despite being in a relatively low orbit, safely beneath the Earth's natural protection.

Fig. 16: The Apollo 16 LEM approaches the command module after its trip to the lunar surface. Did men really survive the harsh radioactive environment of space in such flimsy (and in this case apparently beaten-up) tin boxes?

Even before they entered into deeper space, the astronauts would have had to pass through the highly radioactive 'Van Allen' belts that shield us from harmful Sun effects and cosmic rays. Although NASA states that the astronauts' passage through them (for a duration of at least an hour and a half) was too brief to be harmful, outside research - based on official figures of the radiation present there - strongly suggests that the dose received could not possibly leave those exposed to it unaffected. Yet there seems to be no statistical evidence to show that astronauts have been prone to increased cancer or other radiation-enhanced conditions in their later lives.

However, even if the astronauts avoided the radiation problems by some miracle, it is unlikely that the films in the cameras would have remained unaffected, given that they had no special protection. As we have already seen, in the 1960s photographic stock was especially sensitive to damage from radiation of any kind, which was why people would not put undeveloped films through old-style airport X-ray scanners, to avoid the high risk of fogging or the complete obliteration of images. It seems almost impossible that the lunar photos could have been safely returned without a single blemish from exposure to unfiltered solar radiation and cosmic rays. It is interesting to note that as recently as 2001 large-format IMAX film canisters taken into low-level orbit on the space shuttle had to be carefully stored between special protective water containers to prevent the effects of radiation - yet missions to the Moon and back, with zero protection, seemed to pose no problem.

The Heat Problem

Aside from radiation, how the astronauts were protected from the extreme heat of the Sun on the lunar surface has never been satisfactorily explained either. The spacesuits used a water cooling system to maintain a comfortable body temperature, yet the LEM itself employed a process that required the occasional expulsion of moisture into the surrounding vacuum. From this, a small cloud of gas or ice crystals could reasonably be expected to be seen venting outside the craft from time to time, but this doesn't seem to have been the case. Marcus Allen writes:

'How was the heat generated in the space craft removed if air conditioning cannot work in the vacuum of space? The lunar landers sat on the Moon's surface for up to 72 hours in direct sunlight, the temperature of which, on the Moon, is higher than the boiling point of water. How did the astronauts keep cool? We are told it was by the use of heat-sinks and the evaporation of water from porous plates, yet no photographic evidence of this occuring has ever been seen.' [15]

The issue of heat regulation, then, is another lunar mystery to add to the long list.

Could a NASA Hoax be Kept Secret?

We are used to believing what we are told to believe. Or at least we agree to believe until events like the Weapons of Mass Destruction debacle unfold [next chapter]. Even now, though, few like to lift the lid of the Pandora's Box of global deception, because it is too painful and unsettling to consider that those running our world may not be trustworthy. Especially in the slightly more innocent 1960s, and despite some minor doubts expressed at the time, few thought to really question something as huge as men landing on the Moon. After all, how could anyone fake something so big? Even now, in more cynical times, many believe it would be impossible to maintain a cover-up over something as significant as a mission to another world, and argue that there would surely have been whistleblowers. But some believe there were.

Bennett and Percy assert that some of the bizarre anomalies in the NASA record (and there are many, many more anomalies than we have covered here) were deliberately left there by otherwise silenced personnel, in the hope that someone might spot the errors and begin to question them somewhere down the line - as indeed they have. Jack White's detailed analysis of the Moon mission anomalies (including lunar rovers leaving no tyre tracks [Fig. 17], many shadow, lighting and angle problems, clearly manipulated images, inconsistencies with equipment and spacesuit details in photos supposedly taken on the same excursions and, bizarrely, printed photographs of previous missions seen lying on a foot of a LEM) can be studied on the *www.aulis.com* website.[16] Even if some of these observances are dismissed or put down to optical illusion, it is hard to feel entirely secure about the official record after perusing them all.

Fig. 17: The lunar rover of Apollo 17. The 'Moon buggy' appears to leave barely any tracks at all in some images, as if it has just been placed into position rather than being driven. Yet clear footprints and dust markings seem to result from all other compressions. The NASA record shows the Apollo 17 rover had already been used before this picture was taken, so it is not, as some have argued, that the lack of tracks is due to its only just having been assembled.

Despite the oft-heard scoffing from defenders of the official story, research suggests that it wouldn't actually require many people to operate a mass deception around the Moon landings. Mission Control almost certainly did believe it was communicating with people on the Moon (the signals from the astronauts were relayed in an unusual way, incidentally, which would have made it quite hard to define exactly where they might have been coming from). The many technicians and administrative staff almost certainly worked genuinely towards a goal; rockets took off and capsules splashed down. But if the conspiracy theorists are right, only a limited number of insiders would be needed to perpetrate a studio fake and keep it a secret, even from most of those working in the programme. As with the events of 9/11 [Chapter VIII], someone manipulated into perpetrating a tiny but important part of a confusion tactic may not have known themselves that they were doing so. Keeping people rigidly compartmentalised in work environments is a well-established way of maintaining order in the workplace and ensuring industrial secrets are held.

If the hoax hypothesis is true, there would have been good enough reason why those few people involved with the Moon missions who *did* know what was really going on would keep quiet, especially if patriotic fervour was strongly instilled, or the known consequence of any betrayal was heavy enough. Perhaps guilt did prey on the perpetrators, though; some of the conversations recorded from astronauts during their missions seem almost cynical in tone, with some of them remarking on more than one occasion that things in space don't look real. As Pete Conrad exclaims loudly during the Apollo 12 mission:

'That Sun's bright, it's like somebody is shining a spotlight on your hands! ... I tell you ... it really is. It's like somebody's got a super-bright spotlight!' [17]

Exuberance on a sunny lunar day, or subtle whistleblowing?

A more famous line may also indicate an interesting Freudian slip. Neil Armstrong, stepping onto the lunar surface for the very first time, notably managed to fumble one of the most iconic lines in history. 'That's one small step for Man; one giant leap for Mankind' *should* have been 'That's one small step for *a* man...' While popular culture has recorded it as a charming (and often unnoticed) blunder in the confusion of great responsibility, some think he was trying to indicate that it really was just a small step for Man.

'Space Race' Secrets

Yuri Gagarin, famously the first man into space. But have we been told the truth about his trip and the entire Soviet/US 'space race'?

But if whistleblowers are notably few and far between, why, then, would the likes of the Soviets, at least, not try to expose NASA if something obviously suspect was going on? Surely it would have been in their interests to have called into question the supposed conquests of their rivals, especially if they knew themselves what was feasible in space and what wasn't? Perhaps not. The acceptance of Yuri Gagarin's history-shattering first-man-in-space flight on 12th April 1961 might have been equally challenged by the US, given that NO evidence whatsoever was presented at the time to prove its reality (and very little has been offered since). Indeed, there is compelling evidence that the early Soviet space programme was itself prone to massive fraud and covered-up disasters, with much doubt as to whether it was really Gagarin who made that flight.[18] Yet the US stayed oddly quiet.

The answer to why the space scientists on both sides may have kept hush about each other's possible misdemeanours, despite all the 'space-race' front of the Cold War, can probably be derived from observing the kindred spirits of the ex-Nazi scientists who were divided up by the Americans and the Soviets to work on their respective space programmes at the end of World War II. (Space travel effectively began with German V2 missiles). With each bloc knowing that the conquest - and ultimately the militarisation - of space would be crucial to the future balance of power (with long-running programmes coming fully to fruition only today, the majority of space shuttle missions being quietly military in purpose and responsible for releasing many of the US spy satellites that float above us as we speak), they used the knowledge of those who had once been their enemies. But there seems no reason why the likes of Wernher von Braun and his colleagues, albeit now in different continents, wouldn't still be happy to covertly exchange technological knowledge with each other (as evidence suggests they did). Nor would there be any reason why they would try to expose each other. Old allegiances die hard. Shouting about the potential cover-ups of another might well draw attention to their own.

The country of origin was proudly displayed on the Saturn 5 rockets, but President Kennedy himself thought that cooperation with the Soviets was the way forward into space.

Shortly before his assassination, it is interesting to note that John F Kennedy, who had long supported the idea of joint space ventures, openly instructed NASA to participate with the USSR space programme. His Confidential National Security Action Memorandum (no. 271) of 12th November 1963, headed *Cooperation with the USSR on Outer Space Matters* clearly states:

'I would like you to assume personally the initiative and central responsibility within the government for the development of a program of substantive cooperation with the Soviet Union in the field of outer space, including the development of specific technical proposals.' [19]

Curiously - and true, though it may sound

like a conspiracist's fantasy - Kennedy also issued another memorandum the same day asking the CIA to release classified UFO documents to NASA to aid its new era of cooperation with the Soviets. When Kennedy was shot dead just two weeks later (which readers can add to their own list of suspicions if they wish), the idea of official cooperation seemed to die with him, and the 'Space Race' appeared, publicly at least, to resume - but who knows what lines of communication had already been set up?

Why a Lunar Deception?

There are many other concerns that have been raised over the Moon missions, from the ability of the Saturn V rockets to carry the payloads claimed, to the sheer wonder that any of the primitive technology, scorned by even the likes of Gus Grissom, worked at all. But the point has been made here - the solidity of something we all take for granted suddenly seems weak and uncertain when put under the microscope, whatever the ultimate truth.

The huge silo at Cape Canaveral today, where the space shuttles are refitted for launch. Yet for all the pretence of NASA being a civilian operation, a large proportion of NASA's work today, particularly with the shuttle, is military in purpose.

Why would NASA really mount such a huge undertaking, only to have to fake all or part of it? Was it just to look big on the world stage and distract from its darker activities? To honour a dead president's wishes? Or was it something more sinister? Gerhard Wisnewski's book *One Small Step* points out that the huge fiscal allowances approved and supported on the back of public enthusiasm for the Moon missions and subsequent manned orbital programmes have enabled massive amounts of cash to fall into military budgets (and almost certainly secret 'black-op' developments) that might otherwise never have been generated or sanctioned. A deception could not endure forever, but perhaps the financial ball was rolling enough by the time of the last mission in 1972 to let its initial spark go. After all, why didn't the Moon programme continue, with so many claimed advantages to having bases there? Perhaps because it was never truly viable in the first place? With talk of returning to the Moon growing again now (including proposed missions from several different countries, which could prove interesting), and indeed going on to Mars, perhaps the technology has caught up at last to make it a reality - or the coffers need refilling with public support. If so, much of the renewed initiative will now probably be military at heart, whatever impression the PR gives.

It is true that NASA today is essentially a military outfit, despite the cosmetic appearance of being a civilian operation. Black budgets, kicked off by all the gee-whizz aspirations for the 'final frontier' encouraged so massively in the 1960s, may have been used to develop secret weapons planned to give the US (and, presumably, the wider governments behind the governments) armed domination of our skies - and control over our lives. Already the ionosphere is clogged with non-commercial satellites, the purposes of which are entirely unknown to the general public, leading to much worried speculation from hardcore truthseekers.

Conceptual pre-mission artwork for the Apollo programme, ironically showing the huge and exciting plumes the landers were expected to produce, instead of nothing [Fig. 12, page 116]. Were the gung-ho dreams of the early space age genuine, only to be soured by technical disappointment and the need to cover up failure? Or was the long-term plan always to use public excitement for unlikely manned missions to generate huge black budgets to support dreams of military domination?

Once again, we're back at the idea of an unfolding agenda of control. Something as seemingly innocent as the idea of putting a man on the Moon - even if it *was* just an idea - may have been part of a wider remit, one that fits into all the theories of elite plans for intense centralisation and global domination.

The ability to dominate, whichever way it is looked at, has been given a massive step-up by one event in particular. That event took place on 11th September 2001. It has changed everybody's lives, and must be looked at squarely in the face, as we soon shall do. Distressingly, it is one more example - and a major one - where the official version falls apart when put under the most rudimentary analysis.

With belief in the Moon landings so integral to our faith in the recent historical record, and to our self-image as a civilisation, becoming aware of the evidential anomalies can make people deeply upset and shakes them to their core. It is a profound process that has woken many up to a new awareness that they might have been lied to in other areas too. Investigating 9/11 shakes people's faith in authority in a similar, if more sinister, way.

But should we really be so surprised at the concept of such massive deceptions?

As a prologue to looking at the events of 9/11, let us first remind ourselves of a very clear-cut instance in which very few are in doubt that the world was deceived - something that was originally fired by those events of September 2001.

THE TRUTH AGENDA: *Mankind's greatest achievement is supported by surprisingly flimsy evidence, and we have to take the word of plainly unreliable authorities that it occurred at all. Something of unquestionable veracity would effortlessly support itself with self-consistency - yet the anomalies in the record of the Moon landings are impossible to ignore. Better official explanations are deserved, but questioners are brushed aside as delusional fools. If we did go to the Moon, it seems that the whole story has not been told and that some parts of the evidential record, at least, have been tampered with or fabricated. If so, why? Was support for the manned Moon missions necessary to enable massive black budgets to be generated for secret projects, masking yet another tier of a growing control programme? Awaking to credible doubts over something as familiar as the Moon landings makes people more open to the possibility that they may have been lied to in other important areas.*

The annual Veteran's Day parade passes the Empire State Building in New York, as troops commemorate genuine bravery and service - but the event is also a statement of US military might, its impetus now reborn to fight a never-ending 'War on Terror'.

VII   WEAPONS OF MASS DECEPTION

As another example of a key global event that doesn't stand up to the Truth Agenda, we can look to a more contemporary public deception - one that actually is being widely exposed. The invasion of Iraq, courtesy of a US/British-led alliance in 2003, was based on a claim that turned out to be palpably false. Through fear of 'weapons of mass destruction', people were cowed into lowering their opposition to a disastrous war that has since opened many eyes, in a very real-world way, to an awareness of how popular opinion is manipulated.

Peeling the Layers of Trust

Just occasionally, an unmistakable mass-deception breaks out of the realm of conspiracy theory and enters the mainstream (whereby, of course, it is classified as something else). When this happens, it peels off a layer of public trust in our leaders that can take many years to grow back. Sometimes it never does.

The revelations concerning Richard Nixon's Watergate misdemeanours in the early 1970s, for example, notably reduced the average American's confidence in their leaders (with the result that every public scandal since has had the word 'gate' affixed to it). In the UK, the secret machinations that fired the Suez crisis in 1956 (in which the UK and France secretly persuaded Israel to attack Egypt as a ruse to justify annexing the Suez canal, which the Egyptians had just 'nationalised'), damaged British public confidence before that, and has been cited as a major step in the final fall of the colonial Empire.[1] There are other historical examples. More recently, however, and with consequences far more dire, the debacle regarding the Iraqi 'weapons of mass destruction' blasted a crucial chink in the facade of trustworthy government. Now everyone was granted an unholy glimpse into how public opinion is manipulated into supporting questionable global actions.

The Afghanistan Campaign

From the day that aeroplanes slammed into major US buildings on 11th September 2001 [next chapter], two countries, Afghanistan and Iraq, were specifically targeted for war by (mainly) the US and the UK under the blanket remit of the new 'War on Terror' - this, despite the fact that neither country could be shown to be directly responsible for the atrocities. This was especially true of Iraq, its alleged links with Jihadist group Al Qaeda being extremely tenuous to say the least. The public wave of grief and anger over 9/11 enabled obstacles to military action in both these nations to be removed with ease. In any case, both operations had long been in the planning, with an Afghan invasion actually poised to go even before the attacks. Fortuitous mistrust of Islamic nations was now cemented firmly in the public mind, enabling first Afghanistan, and then Iraq, to be effectively annexed, with a hanging threat over the other Muslim member states of the 'axis of evil'. It was surely no mistake that George W Bush, a fundamentalist Christian, described the War on Terror as a 'crusade'. We live with the messy and terrible results of that crusade today.

The operation in Afghanistan could, on one level, be sold as a positive and necessary action. Told that Osama bin Laden and his fundamentalist supporters were responsible for the horrors of 9/11 (despite the Bush and bin Laden families having many proven business connections), people were more easily persuaded into seeing a need for some kind of action in the country where the Al Qaeda chief was allegedly hiding. He was never found. To this day, in fact - incredible as it may seem - bin Laden still does not officially appear on the FBI's wanted list for 9/11 terror suspects. Tellingly, the official reason given for this is 'lack of evidence'. Many suspect the alleged '9/11 confession' video of bin Laden to be faked, and with good reason. The plumper, darker-skinned character in the fuzzy images bears little resemblance to the bin Laden seen in previous interviews - who had denied involvement in the attacks.[2] More recent confessions, from the likes of Khalid Sheik Mohammed and compatriots, extracted at the Guantanamo Bay detention centre using torture and who knows what other brainwashing techniques, are hardly to be relied on either. Given the unlikelihood of their release, there is also a high chance that these characters are playing the martyr card for maximum effect. Even if they were involved with 9/11, they are unlikely to have been the major players, as we shall see. Yet despite the absence of firm links to the US attacks, the Afghan campaign continues to this day at full velocity, with mounting casualties and horrific atrocities on both sides. Ironically, the world has become a far more dangerous place since the War on Terror began, with reprisals and extremism stirred to new heights [Chapter IX].

Western troops in Afghanistan. The 9/11 attacks were used as the reason to enter the country, ostensibly to find bin Laden, but an invasion had long been in the planning, and the motives for going in were far more complex.

With no sign of victory over the Taliban or Al

THE TRUTH AGENDA

Qaeda and little chance of it occurring, despite Barack Obama's recent commitment of another 30,000 troops, some are led to wonder what the real agenda behind the West's role in Afghanistan really is. Predictably, the need to create a new network of important oil pipelines is at least one of the likely reasons. The US has long made it clear that it would like to see a pipeline running from Turkmenistan, through Afghanistan and into the persecuted Baluchistan (or Balochistan) region of Pakistan (which may help explain the recent elevation of Pakistan into the big picture in the War on Terror - page 187), while helping to prevent one being run from Iran, through Baluchistan and into India. With China also pursuing interests in the region, the growth of a 'free Baluchistan' movement in the West to aid the protection of US influence seems likely in the next few years.[3] But before anything could happen a foothold was needed in Afghanistan, and the hunt for bin Laden happily provided this.

The more cynical theorists also see the ensured continuation of Afghanistan's biggest export - opium (a crucial ingredient of heroin) - as another. Many believe Western governments secretly create funds by working with drug cartels, and claim that they actually *protect* the global flow of illegal drugs, for all the public show of opposition. If this seems incredible, it should

America's most wanted... Osama bin Laden. Except that he isn't. The Al Qaeda leader has never been on the FBI's suspect list for the 9/11 attacks, due to 'lack of evidence'.

be remembered that it wasn't too far back in history when Britain went to war with China to openly maintain the opium trade, netting Hong Kong along the way. Others believe the ruling elite are happier for people to be distracted and marginalised by drugs, as another way of suppressing people's full potential. All this could be dismissed as conspiracy paranoia were it not for the provable fact that Afghan opium production has massively soared since the arrival of Western troops, leading to inevitable suspicions.[4]

Iraq and the Weapons of Mass Destruction

Action in Afghanistan at least had a grain of demonstrable justification, as far as the public was concerned. The operation in Iraq was a different matter. In the run-up to the events which would see its borders crossed by a shaky US-led alliance in 2003, the public were visibly unconvinced by the rather vague reasons being given for the necessity of war. The largest peace protests ever witnessed (the numbers played down by governments, naturally) filled the streets of several major cities around the world in February that year, with London alone seeing something approaching two million marchers. The world did not want another war. But it got another war,

Deconstructing Consensus Reality

because the ultimate decision makers, perhaps around the campfires of Bohemian Grove and at the tables of closed cabals, had decided to have one.

With the masses growing ever-more uncomfortable at the impending conflict in the Gulf, Tony Blair looking ever-more haggard and inwardly-torn by the day, and George W Bush and his neo-conservative sponsors becoming ever-more gung-ho, rather oddly the advertised motives for going to war with Iraq kept changing. When humanitarian platitudes and crocodile tears for the (without doubt) oppressed Iraqi population weren't quite enough to convince the masses (after all, why not deal with a few other cruel regimes around the world at the same time?), our secret and not-so-secret rulers reached for the usual solution - the instillation of fear.

When the overwhelming reason for needing to deal with Saddam Hussein suddenly became his apparent acquisition of 'weapons of mass destruction' (never fully defined), technology which could be called into action to strike Western targets within '45 minutes', some of the global opposition to the war subsided - not much, but it reduced just enough for people *not* to be able to stop all sides of their parliaments, most notably in the UK, voting to give support for what was effectively US action under a very thin smokescreen of an international alliance.

The evidence for these terrible weapons, as presented in the UK, was contained in a dossier, supposedly gathered from informed intelligence sources. The dossier was loudly proclaimed as the ultimate proof that war against Iraq was now entirely necessary. Yet even while this was occurring, there were clear indications that the weapons did not actually exist. In 2008, Pulitzer prize-winning political journalist Ron Suskind claimed that a key Iraqi intelligence official, Tahir Jalil Habbush al Takriti, had even communicated secretly with US and UK intelligence staff (including MI6 chief Richard Dearlove) on the eve of war and exchanged credible intelligence that there were no WMDs. Though Dearlove and the US have denied this, other supporting evidence, including damning Whitehall e-mails finally released in 2009, together with the refusal to release minutes of key cabinet meetings, strongly suggests that the US and the UK knew full well that their given reasons for invading Iraq were bogus.[5]

Nonetheless, what would become known as the 'dodgy dossier' was held up in both Parliament and Congress as all the evidence needed as to why Iraq must

America's next most wanted... Saddam Hussein, seen here in captivity before being executed. Clearly a tyrant few miss today, was his removal, however, really about weapons of mass destruction?

be dealt with (without any of the fine details being revealed, mind), and the machinery of war rumbled unstoppably into life. Blair lost his scruples and the neo-cons got their way. And so, in March 2003, war against Iraq began, and the rest is... the usual web of deceit and the rewriting of history.

The David Kelly Affair

Yet loud - and qualified - voices *were* raised against the reliability of the crucial dossier, even as the war was raging. When experienced UN weapons inspector Dr David Kelly secretly informed BBC radio journalist Andrew Gilligan that he believed the information in the dossier had been considerably exaggerated ('sexed up', as the suddenly concerned media put it) from its original source, three things occurred: first, someone in Downing Street surreptitiously released Kelly's name to the press, thus breaking his anonymity, and then Blair's cronies proceeded to besmirch Kelly's reputation, describing him as a 'Walter Mitty'-like fantasist. Following this, cabinet spin doctors, led by Alastair Campbell, lambasted the BBC as liars (fatally neutering their news output from thereon, the Beeb ever-fearful of losing the public licence fee) and hounded first Gilligan and, eventually, BBC Director-General Greg Dyke out of their jobs.

And on 18 July 2003, Dr David Kelly was found dead in woods near his Oxfordshire home.

With death apparently resulting from a combination of a drugs overdose and wounds to the wrists, it was widely reported that the one official who had dared to speak out against the reasons for conflict in Iraq had taken his own life. But had he? Kelly's death immediately aroused suspicion. Investigations by Liberal Democrat MP Norman Baker (who bravely voted against action in Iraq and whose 2007 book *The Strange Death of David Kelly* is essential reading) soon revealed serious anomalies in the suicide story.[6] Kelly's body, as officially found, had provably been moved from where it was originally reported to have been. Both the drug intake found in his blood and the wounds to his arteries were too minor for death to have resulted from them, and nothing in Kelly's behaviour that day or before had suggested suicidal thoughts. Other unexplained aspects, such as a strong police presence near his home *before* Kelly's disappearance was reported, and the

Norman Baker MP, whose tireless crusade to get to the bottom of the David Kelly affair made national headlines. Baker concluded that Kelly's death was almost certainly murder and not suicide.

erection of huge aerials in his garden after, add to the strangeness. Allegedly compelled to take his own life by depression over the criticism he had received on exposure as the BBC inside source, the reality was that Kelly had no reasons to kill himself, nor did he give any signs that he wanted to. He simply went for a walk in the woods one afternoon, and never returned.

It seems that Kelly himself, neither fool nor fantasist, already had a pretty clear intimation of what might happen to him. Baker writes:

'British diplomat David Broucher told the Hutton inquiry that, some months before Dr Kelly's death, he had asked him what would happen if Iraq were invaded. Rather chillingly, Dr Kelly replied that he "would probably be found dead in the woods".' [7]

Shoehorned by Blairites into supporting the case for proof of Kelly's suicidal intentions, this statement is more realistically seen by most who knew him as his guess at what might be done to shut him up (rather like the intimation Princess Diana had, expressed in a letter to her ex-butler Paul Burrell, that someone might try to assassinate her in a staged car crash). If so, it was an accurate prediction.

It seems clear from Norman Baker's thorough investigation that David Kelly was murdered. Baker puts it down to Iraqi dissidents, keen for an invasion to take place and not wanting anything to stop it, but others point the finger of blame much closer to home. Either way, the truth about Kelly was not told, and the supposed taking of his own life appears to have been falsified. The nauseous hand-wringing of regret from those apparently devastated by his 'suicide' - the same people who had revealed Kelly's name to the media - simply added one more indignity to the affair.

One thing was for sure; Kelly's grisly demise ensured no other informants would raise any serious voices against the weapons of mass destruction dossier.

The Aftermath of the Gulf War

Just a year later, however, the mandate for war in Iraq had fallen apart all by itself. No weapons of mass-destruction were found, despite the (claimed) extensive searching. The protestors had been right to question the motives for war, and T-shirts with the slogan 'Tony B-liar' became ubiquitous. It was to little joy that the unfortunate David Kelly was posthumously vindicated, and much of what was now known as the 'dodgy dossier' was found to have been based on an old student thesis downloaded from the Internet and embellished accordingly. The usual things occurred thereafter. A government-sponsored report into the Iraq action and the Kelly affair (the Hutton Inquiry, published in January 2004) was a predictable whitewash, with all guilty parties effectively acquitted, the

WMD promoters having been apparently misled by incompetence on the part of conveniently unnamed intelligence agents. The whole debacle was swept under the carpet - and both the UK and the US public re-voted back into power the very leaders who had taken them into the situation (*un*like the not entirely dissimilar Suez crisis of 1956, over which prime minister Anthony Eden at least had the decency to resign). [In June 2009 a new and full inquiry into the war was finally announced, but with arguments erupting almost immediately over whether to hold it publicly or 'behind closed doors', few had hope for any real result or accountablility.]

Meanwhile, Iraq was devastated and reduced to a weakened faction-torn wasteland, its people killed or injured in many thousands, while the US and its allies, hidden and overt, had greater access to another country's oil reserves. Tellingly this oil was now sold in dollars again, and not in euros - according to some, one of the main undeclared issues that led to the war (and one that may be firing up the growing desire for US action in Iran, which has also ceased to use the dollar as its sole trading currency).

The 2003 invasion of Iraq rages, An astonishing number of people died, were maimed or succumbed to disease because of this action. Yet almost everyone suspected at the time that the war was based on a false premise. Despite this, both Blair and Bush were re-elected to power in the aftermath.

The Western warmongers also gained a stronger political foothold in the Middle East, at the very heart of 'the cradle of civilisation', where some mystic traditions say the gods first arrived on Earth [page ??]. The siting of a US military camp directly on top of the historical remains of Babylon (where legend has it the Tower of Babel once stood) outraged archaeologists, but the gesture may have been highly symbolic.

The mainstream view holds that the invasion of Iraq, carried out without a clear plan for any power structure to replace the Hussein regime, was a massive debacle stemming from more 'incompetence'. Some, however, believe that not even the Bush administration could have been that short-sighted. Was the destabilisation of the region all part of a wider plan, a much-weakened oil-producing country enabling the dominoes of neighbouring Iran, and perhaps Syria, to be next to tumble? And with so many religious end-timers [Chapter IV] having powerful influence over US policies, was it yet another unfortunate blow to the prospect of a peaceful and thriving Middle East or actually a happy step closer to The Rapture?

Why the WMD Lie?

Why was the weapons of mass destruction issue focused on so intensely if those pushing for war knew it to be a bogus criterion? Why expose themselves so clearly as liars? Some have used this as evidence that it was a genuine mistake on the part of the warmongers, but there is another aspect to consider: bad intentions aren't forgiven very lightly, but human error can be overlooked.

Perhaps those behind the action gambled that the public would grant them absolution for their apparent sloppiness - the usual mitigation, as with the supposed intelligence 'errors' that allowed the 9/11 attacks to occur. If the West had gone into Iraq with all guns blazing for anything even slightly ideologically questionable, the necessary support might not have been there. Taking action to protect us all from potential harm, however, was something far harder for peaceniks to challenge. Some have wondered why a few weapons weren't surreptitiously planted in Iraq to justify the war, but that might have raised too many enquiries and exposed uncomfortable trails of responsibility. Far better to rely on the public granting forgiveness for mistakes, which, shockingly, it did - to a degree.

Faith and Mistrust

Despite voter forgiveness (or at least apathy), the weapons of mass-destruction disaster did seriously challenge the faith of many in the West that their leaders were reliable and trustworthy. That faith has not yet recovered, which may be why military action in Iran - clearly one of the next targets on the hit-list - has been slower than perhaps it might have been, although the wheels are firmly in motion and still gaining speed at the time of writing. Recent overtures of dialogue from a new US president with a Muslim father suggest more subtle ploys, and recent Iranian political instability might require different strategies, but the sights still seem trained on Tehran. However, far more support from a doubting public would be needed this time to grease the path of any military action, raising fears in some that further underhand measures might be employed to 'manufacture consent', as Noam Chomsky puts it.

Not everyone forgave Blair so easily. Here, childrens shoes are piled up at the Cenotaph at a protest march a few years later. The shoes and the mock coffin say it all.

The collective weakening of confidence resulting from the WMD scandal, however, doesn't seem to have prevented a kind of lazy pseudo-trust being reinvested in governments. People's memories are alarmingly short, something surely relied on by those in power; the blind optimism that our leaders might get it right next time always allows the same old faces to continue on. If not, how did Bush and Blair get a second chance in the polls, with so many thousands of men, women and children tragically and unnecessarily dead, injured or sick (particularly through the obscene and much covered-up use of depleted uranium) as a direct result of the policies they ushered through? The irony of Blair now being the West's Middle East 'peace envoy' (and perhaps soon to be rewarded with the presidency of the EU) seems lost on many, and his recent religious platitudes are hard to swallow without cynicism.

Nonetheless, for all the blind eyes being turned by voters the Iraq catastrophe *has* helped create a sizeable demographic that now questions the power structures that shape our world. Campaigners like Brian Haw, who has been camped outside the Houses of Parliament with his protest stalls now for an incredible eight years, help keep the flame of awareness and remembrance alive.[8] The WMD fairy-tale is a firm piece of evidence that we are indeed regularly deceived (even with the deceptions written off as ineptitude) - evidence that needs no analysis of photographs or esoteric investigation to comprehend. What more proof do we need that we are consistently misled into supporting situations that benefit the agendas of the few against the wishes of the many (unless one subscribes to the view that those few operate to genuinely protect the wider good, however questionable their techniques - Chapter XIII)? If analysis of more obscure and mystical realms doesn't shake some readers, the process that leads to a necessary deconstruction of 'consensus reality' may start instead with a memory of this spectacular diversion.

The invasion of Iraq was a direct offshoot of the War on Terror that began with the dramatic events of 9/11. But if no-one now trusts the reasons given for the war in Iraq, why should anyone trust those given for the War on Terror in the first place? Sure enough, by applying the Truth Agenda to the events that put the world on the road to today's control programmes, we soon find clear evidence to challenge the entire basis of our current culture of fear.

THE TRUTH AGENDA: *In a very tangible way, the weapons of mass destruction catastrophe illustrates how easily public opinion falls prey to deception. The wide feeling of doubt at the time, and the evidence revealed since, make it clear that Western governments knew very well that the reasons given for invading Iraq were false. Somebody was even prepared to kill to ensure that information was not exposed, as Dr David Kelly discovered. The campaigns in Iraq and Afghanistan are seen by many as necessary steps in the New World Order plans. With such a plainly underhand lie about WMDs being employed to win popular consent, can anyone seriously doubt that a manipulation of the masses is taking place?*

Deconstructing Consensus Reality

The World Trade
Center in its heyday.
How could such an
important complex
be attacked and
destroyed so easily?

VIII   9/11

The events of 11th September 2001 turned the world upside down and generated the 'War on Terror', which has encroached on our lives in ways that many still don't appreciate. Yet the official story of 9/11 is full of holes and anomalies, to a degree that makes it almost impossible to believe when scrutinised in detail. Shocking to behold, the lies and cover-ups surrounding this epochal moment in history reveal even more clearly than the WMD fraud that a significant deception must be taking place. With 9/11, however, authorities and the media are doing their utmost to keep a lid on a growing - and justified - public unease.

IMPORTANT NOTE: The following chapter takes a necessarily forensic look at the evidence surrounding the events of 9/11. It must be stressed here that at no point is it being overlooked that these events involved massive distress, tragedy and heartache to both the victims and their relatives (this is also true for the innocent victims of the WMD lies, of course). Indeed, it is because of these very factors that getting to the truth of the detail matters so much - so that such an appalling occurrence can never be allowed to happen again.

Besides my own observations, the sources drawn on here are the most reliable and thorough, with particular - though not sole - reference to the investigations of David Ray Griffin, who has been the most prolific and convincing of all the academics who have challenged the authorised account of 9/11 (see the Appendix notes for a fuller bibliography of these and other sources). This is not in any way to suggest that the researchers quoted would necessarily support the wider hypothesis of this book (although some do), and no such inference should be made here.

The Official Story

On the bright morning of 11th September 2001, four jet liners were hijacked in north-eastern US airspace. Now piloted by Middle-Eastern terrorists working for Osama bin Laden's Al Qaeda terrorist network, two of the planes were flown into the World Trade Centre in Manhattan, destroying its twin towers completely; another struck the Pentagon, damaging one side of it, and another crashed into woods in Pennsylvania, apparently after passengers attempted to wrestle control back from the hijackers. Around 3000 people died in the attacks.

That is the story that has been told to the world, the one which apparently unfolded before our very eyes on that awful day, and the one to which most people subscribed as the truth - at least to begin with.

As we have already seen, under the mandate of 9/11 the War on Terror was ushered in, ensuring an eternal conflict that would swell defence budgets and allow battles on foreign shores which might never otherwise have been acceptable to the electorate of America and Europe. Under that mandate, regardless of the recent election of Barack Obama, freedom of speech, belief and movement is still being crushed out of all recognition, with many seeing this as a stage towards the 'New World Order' of centralisation and domination.

But what if it could be shown that what we are told happened that day is unreliable? The ghastly conclusion reached by applying the Truth Agenda to this example of a high-profile, yet deeply questionable, occurrence is that the official story of 9/11 may be one of the most serious lies ever told in history. For, shockingly, the details of the 'orthodox' version of events, as set against what actually happened, simply don't stand up to scrutiny.

The Central Allegations

Are the main allegations of those who doubt what we have been told about 9/11 just paranoid sensationalism? The evidence says not, and the calibre of the doubters is formidable. Far beyond the predictable conspiracy community, an increasing number of well-educated scholars, scientists and academics (not to mention film directors, celebrities and artists), from an impressive range of respected professions, are raising very loud voices to call attention to glaring anomalies concerning 9/11. By doing so, they challenge not only obvious lies and suspicious discrepancies in the record, but also events that appear to subvert both the laws of physics and common sense. Not for nothing has the 9/11 truth movement become one of the fastest-growing clarions of political activism in modern times, with groups around the world campaigning for a truly independent inquiry to reveal what really happened. The official inquiry, effectively sponsored by the Bush administration, is hardly to be relied on, as we shall see. Only mainstream journalists seem gullible enough still to accept its demonstrably skewed findings in full today and the media's undying complicity has allowed the myth of the orthodox version to propagate.

The passing of the Bush era should not be seen as an excuse to lessen the intense analysis of 9/11. The Obama tenancy of the White House, for all

The World Trade Center in happier times. Little could anyone guess that not just one but both towers and the surrounding complex would eventually be entirely destroyed. 9/11 changed the world - but have we been told the true story?

the cosmetic changes, appears to be no less rooted in the global mandate begun on 9/11 than the previous administration, and thus attempts conveniently to consign the attacks to 'the history books' (a desire voiced by several pundits during the hand-over from Bush to Obama) should be firmly resisted. The devastating political and social reverberations from 9/11 are still far too strong to be moved on from lightly.

The central accusation of the doubters is that the evidence demonstrates that the 9/11 attacks could *only* have occurred with the aid of insiders holding advantageous roles within the Bush administration and/or the US military intelligence systems. The plotters either comprised a small rogue element acting in isolation or, worse, represented an institutional conspiracy conducted from the highest places. Many more fear the latter, but either way we have reasons to feel very uncomfortable, especially given that some of the names and faces from the Bush era still remain in places of influence today.

Some say bin Laden's agents were merely 'patsies', unsuspecting martyr-fanatics surreptitiously set up by the real plotters to indict the Muslim world, while others believe the entire scheme was conducted from within the US. It's a shocking charge for those new to the concept, and the knee-jerk reaction is to dismiss the notion that anyone could do such an appalling thing to 'their own people', as most journalists and mainstream pundits tend to do. Yet the unsettling truth is that history is littered with similar examples [Chapter IX]; extreme actions that sacrifice citizens in the name of a higher cause or hidden agenda.

It is worth remembering here that the 9/11 accusations may have a direct precedent. Emad Salem, an FBI agent who infiltrated the Arab terrorist group that detonated a truck bomb in the basement car park of the World Trade Centre on 26th February 1993, openly accused the FBI of giving genuine explosives to the group in place of the dummy ones that were supposed to help to frame them.[1] According to Salem, instead of preventing it, the attack (which has mostly been forgotten by the public in the shadow of the 2001 events) was inexplicably allowed to take place, killing six people and injuring over a thousand. Although the allegation was denied by US authorities, it is hard to dismiss the testimony in the light of the 9/11 qualms. Was this an earlier failed attempt covertly to engineer a situation that finally succeeded eight years later?

What, then, are the key reasons to question the official story of 9/11? Although the many areas of doubt are too deep and complex to cover here, and readers must follow-up other sources to get the full picture, we will concentrate (as with the Moon landings) on some of the more solid and seemingly inexplicable anomalies of the dark day that changed our world.

The Key Evidence

Given that one of the main criticisms of the NASA Moon landing evidence is that so few people were there to verify what really did or didn't happen (with only a few live blurry television images to go on until the questionable photos were later released), one might think, by contrast, that the nature of the 9/11 events would be beyond any doubt. So widely televised and repeated that the images are burned indelibly in our minds, the sheer availability of indisputably clear visual evidence of 9/11, which many people witnessed on their televisions and in the streets of New York and Washington DC all at the same time, has been the very thing that has enabled greater concerns over the truth to emerge. Like the NASA images, full independent analysis can be made by any informed observer using recordings of what can be seen happening, but what makes 9/11 different is that most people (a few 'hologram'/special-effects theorists aside), thanks to the multiple-witnesses, are happy to accept that the images themselves are not fake. Thus much of the central argument over the 9/11 story (with the exception of the mysterious Flight 93) becomes not one of pondering the entire authenticity of what we are seeing, but instead of questioning the exact nature of what we are *told* we are seeing.

We are told we see the twin towers pancaking down into dust because a combination of the aeroplane impacts and subsequent fires weakened the structures to collapse levels. We are told that the hole in the Pentagon is the result of a Boeing 757 having crashed into it. We are told that Building Seven of the World Trade Center fell down due to fire damage initiated by falling debris from its neighbours. (In fact, until recently, we were not told much at all about Building Seven, but we will come to this.)

There are many, many reasons, beyond the more iconic features, to doubt the official account of 9/11, some of which we will look at later, but these three very visible factors have been key to igniting the arguments. Superficially, what we are *told* to believe with regard to these most public aspects of the attacks at first appears to make sense - until one starts to look a little closer, and thinks with a little less of a tabloid mentality. Which is, of course, what few are ever encouraged to do. But when one breaks out of conditioned convention, that's when the veil lifts and the facade of artifice carefully built up in the mainstream begins to crumble under the Truth Agenda.

With this in mind, let's examine the major areas that first ignited the challenges to what people were being told they were seeing.

i) The Pentagon

THE HOLE: One of the first discrepancies to be noticed regarding the very visual evidence of the 9/11 attacks was the impact damage to the Pentagon. Supposedly the hole where Flight 77 (a hefty 228-passenger Boeing 757) entered the building, what we actually see in the early shots (Fig. 1 - before the upper wall collapsed in shortly after) is a horizontal scar, at ground floor level, with a central entry-point of little more than twenty feet across and perhaps twenty feet high. Either side of the hole, there is an extended area of lesser damage approaching a maximum of 120 feet. It didn't take too long for a number of websites, alternative radio stations and eventually the whole world of conspiracy theory and beyond, to wonder, quite justifiably, how a jet liner with a wingspan of nearly 125 feet and a vertical tail of 44 feet in height could have left such a relatively small area of impact.

Basic trigonometry alone suggests that the width of the entire area of damage should be at least 164 feet across, not 120 feet. The second floor of the Pentagon is hardly even damaged, with *unbroken* windows clearly visible in the immediate post-

Fig. 1: *The main area of impact at the Pentagon, shortly after the strike (before the roof fell in). The general area of main impact (centre) is remarkably small - and the circular objects in front of it are cable spools that were there before the crash. The spools are untouched and there is no visible debris on the lawn. Did a Boeing 757 really hit this building?*

impact photographs. Why didn't the tall vertical tail tear a scar into the second floor? And how could the bulk of such a large aircraft enter the building through such a tiny central area?

Government-sponsored studies provide computer reconstructions in which the wings of the aircraft are seen to simply melt away into the infrastructure of the Pentagon as the aircraft strikes, as if the vaporisation of aeroplanes were an everyday feature of air crashes. Other official explanations suggest the wings somehow folding back against the fuselage as the plane enters the building - yet the widely-publicised footage shows this very plainly didn't occur when the planes hit the World Trade Centre. In most well-publicised air disasters, wing-parts are usually very visible scattered in the debris field, but not at the Pentagon. It is hard to see how such little visible entry damage could have resulted when Flight 77 hit the building.

LACK OF DEBRIS AND FIRE DAMAGE: A central observation that has been made regarding the Pentagon crash concerns the remarkable lack of aeroplane remains. In most photographs of the impact zone, there is barely any wreckage visible near the walls or on the lawn. Indeed, large cable spools being used by workmen who were - curiously - restoring that very block of the Pentagon when the aircraft struck are very clearly visible in front of the entry point, undamaged and barely misplaced by what must have been a significant explosion. There is no evidence of a huge 757 tail lying anywhere, no engines or wing parts.

We are told that most of the debris distributed itself inside the building, and there are a few photographs showing some of this. But these images raise more questions than they answer: what purport to be components of the jet engines, for instance, are far too small to have come from a 757, as many informed aircraft enthusiasts have pointed out. Even credible eye-witnesses on the day have spoken of the remarkable lack of large debris even inside the Pentagon.[2] The very few shots that do exhibit small crumpled parts of the fuselage on the outer lawn make it look, as many have exclaimed, as if they have just been neatly placed there for show. Also, as we are told that most of the plane was absorbed into the building (including all of both wings), how did these bits suddenly find themselves far outside?

Photographs showing the entry point *after* the top walls have collapsed (tellingly, the ones most publicised, perhaps because the initial damage looks worse that way) also display another curiosity. Very clean severing of the infrastructure can be seen, with offices on one side of the collapse suddenly exposed to the elements. Yet there is almost no visible fire damage to these rooms. Famously, one of these offices clearly displays a stool with a book or papers still on it, not even displaced or singed [Fig. 2]. Given that a large jet liner, loaded with highly inflammable fuel, had just plunged into the building only feet away, this is rather extraordinary, especially when one considers how much the authorities have made of the extensive 'fireballs' and intense heat from

Fig. 2: Close-up of the Pentagon damage. Even allowing for the fact that the roof has collapsed in on top of the entry damage, tearing the walls open to expose offices to the elements (rather than it being a direct result of the explosion) it is still hard to see how a stool with papers on it (highlighted) survived a fireball just feet away as Flight 77 struck.

subsequent burning, which supposedly brought down the twin towers.

With these observations, and many more not covered here, many have found themselves speculating that what hit the Pentagon must have been something far smaller than a Boeing 757, with much less fuel onboard and, seemingly, a remarkable clean-strike capability.

HOW WAS THE PLANE MANOEUVRED?: Even if one considers the official view that what hit the Pentagon *was* a 757, this in itself raises many unexplained questions, particularly concerning how it was manoeuvred down to an incredibly low position at such a high velocity. We are told that the plane entered the building at a speed of around 500 mph, supposedly taking down street lamps on the nearby freeway as it came in (which some people, interestingly, described as looking as if they had been unscrewed from the ground). However, simulations of how this flight path could have been attained, when coming from the plane's original altitude, raise serious questions.

To get the 757 down to the virtually lawn-skimming height described, the plane would need to have executed what has been described as one of the most extraordinary acrobatics in aviation history, with an extremely tight turn in a very small area of airspace, simultaneously dropping 7000 feet within two minutes. Jet aircraft are built to achieve certain speeds only at very high altitudes where the air pressure is very different, and do not function in the same way at ground level. How, then, did the 757 continue to perform well enough to execute the manoeuvre and maintain the claimed speed of 500 mph, without stalling, as it came in? And how - and why - was it positioned so exactly as to hit precisely the block it did (a largely unstaffed one under restoration), when it would have been much easier to plough into the inner rings of the building from the top? Did someone only want limited damage and casualties here? 125 fatalities at the Pentagon was bad enough, but was it as bad as it should have been if Al Qaeda had really wanted to make their point?

At the helm of the 757, we are told, was Al Qaeda terrorist Hani Hanjour, a man so inept at flying even light aircraft that at the time he was having lessons more than one of the US flight instructors who unsuspectingly trained him expressed the view that he 'could not handle basic air manoeuvres'. Yet on 9/11, just months later, Hanjour somehow managed to improvise one of the most astonishing aerial feats ever performed.

WHAT DID REALLY HIT THE PENTAGON?: All this doubt leaves a big puzzle - if not a 757, what then did strike this most guarded of buildings, and how? The Pentagon is surrounded by a sophisticated missile defence system which, puzzlingly, was not employed that day, even though by the time it was struck the twin towers had already been hit and it was known that hijacked aircraft were in the skies. How could the US military have left themselves so unprotected as to allow a 757 to descend upon their headquarters? Or was it not such a large aircraft? Even in the small-plane scenario, however, it should have been successfully intercepted.

The eye-witness accounts are very contradictory. It seems that a large aeroplane did fly close to the Pentagon just before the much-witnessed explosion, perhaps giving rise to the assumption that it was this that hit the building. But plenty of other people have described a much smaller plane coming in - or perhaps even a missile. If whatever did hit the Pentagon was indeed flying at around 500 mph, at ground level no-one would be able to say for sure what they saw as it would simply be too fast for the brain to register. However, *told* that it was a 757, perhaps their minds filled in the rest.

Fig. 3: A frame from the CCTV video showing the moment of impact at the Pentagon. Officials claim the very few frames ever released from this tape show Flight 77 entering the building - but the vague object is impossible to identify. With the Pentagon surrounded by cameras, why has definitive footage of the crash never been released?

The many security cameras clustered around the Pentagon should surely have put the matter to rest? But even here there is confusion and obfuscation. The very few image frames ever released from these security videos show simply a flash of *something*, which might be an aeroplane coming in, followed by an explosion [Fig. 3]. Nowhere is there evidence that the craft was a 757. The very lack of publicised security images raises great suspicion. With so many cameras trained on the building, one would expect there would be irrefutable visual proof of what happened - but this has not been shared. The authorities seemed eager that the world should see images of exactly what happened at the World Trade Center, but not, strangely, at the Pentagon. Neither, by the way, is there any civilian proof of the Pentagon impact available, as on the day of the attack all local businesses in the vicinity had their security footage taken away by government agents, and none of it was ever returned. Now, so long after the event and with such sophisticated image-manipulation software available, any seemingly convincing images that do get released will understandably not be accepted by the doubters.

Official shots of the aftermath showing the damage further inside the Pentagon reveal something else of interest. From these images, it can be seen that the front of the impacting craft managed to make its way through three protective rings (blocks with large open courtyards between them) of the building, finally exiting in a neat hole around ten feet in diameter. This suggests something of great penetrative power having struck, rather than the relatively light construction of a 757 nose.

So was it a cruise missile or a smaller aircraft, perhaps of military specifications, that really took down the walls of the Pentagon? Most theorists are increasingly drawn towards the latter, but investigation continues, with the most recent speculation centring on the little-known A3 Sky Warrior fighter plane, parts of which seem to match some of the debris that *is* visible in the wreckage. For certain, there is not much evidence to show that Flight 77 was what hit the Pentagon on 9/11. It would seem there is a high chance it was substituted by a more suitable vehicle, perhaps something guaranteed to make

Fig. 4: The final exit hole inside the Pentagon. The object that managed to pierce several rings of the building would appear to be more the result of something sharply penetrative rather than the soft nose of a Boeing 757. And what did really happen to the wings on its way through?

a more 'surgical' strike - less devastating than what was needed at the twin towers, but enough to look impressive and make the point. (What then did happen to the hijacked Boeing? Some ideas are explored below.) With this act, the world was left in no doubt that, on the surface at least, Islamic fundamentalists could now threaten the very core of US stability and its military protectors.

ii) The Twin Towers

The overriding image of 9/11 that has been imprinted in most people's minds is of Flight 75 striking the south tower of the World Trade Center (WTC) at 9.03 am. With the north tower already having been hit by Flight 11 at 8.46 am, all cameras were trained on the WTC for this astonishing event, making it probably the most televised live disaster in history. Soon after, further devastating scenes scarred themselves into our collective consciousness as both towers collapsed from their tops downwards in horrific tumbles into their own footprints.

With these images now so familiar, and the message pounded into us (even before the dubious evidence was presented) that this was the work of Al Qaeda terrorists, one might consider what happened at the WTC to be beyond question. However, the more these images are viewed in a spirit of open-minded analysis, the less this scenario makes sense.

Before 9/11, no modern building had ever collapsed due to fire damage. Yet on this day, *three* huge structures came down in their entirety at the WTC complex, effectively due, we are told, to weakened infrastructures and fire. We will concentrate on the twin towers here and then look at the third tower in the section titled *WTC 7*.

DID FIRE MAKE THE TOWERS FALL?: The official explanation for the falling of each tower can be summed-up thus: the impact of the planes damaged core supports and removed fireproofing insulation, enabling the subsequent build up of heat from the resulting fires to weaken the steel infrastructure, resulting in the collapses we all know so well. Yet there are so many problems with this hypothesis - widely disseminated as a fact - that the rest of this book could be devoted to discussing it. But here are some of the key issues.

Whether fireproofing really was removed from the core supports by the initial impact of the aeroplanes, and if so how much, can never be known. The damage was never observed by survivors up close, let alone forensically examined, during or after the disaster, so most of the official theories are based on supposition and unsettlingly unscientific experiments by the likes of the National Institute of Standards and Technology (NIST), which simply 'came up with its estimates by firing shotgun rounds at steel plates in a plywood box'.[3] NIST and the US technology magazine *Popular Mechanics* have been the key defenders of the science of the official story (and were effectively mouthpieces for the Bush administration to many minds), but as truth-campaigning author David Ray Griffin devastatingly

The terrible sight of the World Trade Center burning, shortly before both towers fell to the ground. But why did they fall? The official explanations fail to make sense, and would appear to contravene too many laws of physics - and challenge basic common sense - according to many architects and engineers.

demonstrates in his indispensable books on 9/11, too often they play with figures and twist semantics to make the incredible sound credible.

Even assuming that fireproofing was removed, exposing steel to heat, it has become clear that the constant high temperatures required to weaken the steel supports could never have been reached by the types of fires we see burning in the available footage. Simplifying things, steel begins to seriously weaken at about 2732°F [1500°C], but despite deceptive insinuations from the likes of NIST, there is no evidence to show that the kerosene fires from the exploded jets could have burned for long enough to reach anywhere near that temperature. The fiercest kerosene blazes might just reach around 1832°F [1000°C] at the very most, even with added fuel from office furniture, carpets, etc.[4] Defenders of the official account use the notion of lashings of jet fuel running down the corridors and lift-shafts to justify all of the structure-weakening damage they say occurred, but this simply doesn't make sense under scrutiny. Even some official sources acknowledge that the very black smoke that pours from the towers is evidence that the fires there in fact burned at relatively low, oxygen-starved levels. Most of the kerosene fuel can be seen burning itself out almost immediately in the huge orange fireballs resulting from the initial aeroplane strikes, so the subsequent fires were probably composed of building material smouldering at much lower temperatures than a continuous kerosene fire.

Although it is clear that some of the tragic victims in the towers found the heat in their areas unbearable, and chose to leap to a quicker, if appalling, end, the visual evidence suggests far less of a 'raging inferno' (the standard employed terminology) than has been promoted. In one heart-rending news image, a woman can be seen standing at the very edge of an aeroplane-torn scar, forlornly looking outwards. Although she is at the centre of the initial destruction, the heat has clearly died down enough to allow her this reflective moment. This does not suggest the levels of temperature that would be weakening steel to the massive extent required.

HOW DID THE STEEL SUPPORTS FAIL?: To result in the type of collapse we see, floor coming down upon floor, each level's core support would have to fail at exactly the same time. Is this credible? Independent analysis from qualified physicists such as Dr Steven Jones and architects like Richard Gage suggests it isn't - without an artificially introduced force.[5] Even accepting the possibility of heat weakening the steel beyond durability in certain places, there is a problem. With clearly uneven and relatively sparse fires seen to be burning in the towers, what could generate this almost unheard-of simultaneous structural failure?

The weakness of the original 'pancaking' theory, which holds that the added weight of each floor coming down then brought down the next and so on, as the floors became disconnected from the support columns, has even been acknowledged by the likes of NIST, but its tinkering with alternative plays on the idea are barely more convincing (it now says that 'global collapse' occurred, precisely because the support columns did *not* become disconnected, thus progressively dragging each one inwards). Whichever way officials say the collapses occurred, we are still being asked to believe that buildings specifically designed to withstand the impact of more than one Boeing 707 (the largest plane at the time the WTC was constructed), were, in fact, little more than card houses with no serious inner support structure.

Wreckage at 'Ground Zero' - thousands of girders, smothered in toxic dust. But how did so many support columns and beams fail so utterly? Many believe that only strategically placed explosives could have resulted in such total devastation.

It is interesting to note that the initial authorised computer models of how the towers collapsed, widely disseminated to the media in the wake of 9/11, managed to omit the key central support columns completely, showing instead just an empty void in the middle of the tower, and floors mysteriously sliding down around them. This was clearly manipulative. In fact, as the eventual release of the WTC blueprints in March 2007 confirmed (suspiciously held back from public view from the attack date until then), each tower had 47 core columns and 240 perimeter (exterior) columns.[6] Even allowing that several of these columns may have been damaged by the initial impact, the fact is that the buildings were designed to withstand the severing of many of them and they should not have fallen in the way we see. MIT professor Thomas Eagar - generally a supporter of the official view - himself writes:

'The number of columns lost on the initial impact was not large and the loads were shifted to remaining columns...'[7]

It is clear, for instance, that Flight 75 actually impacted WTC 2, the second tower to be hit, near the corner of the building. This should have caused far less damage to the central supports than occurred at WTC 1, which was struck nearer the centre of its north face - yet WTC 2 collapsed *first*, after only 56 minutes (WTC 1 fell after 102 minutes). How did this occur?

In any case, why wasn't the progressive collapse of each tower eventually halted, or at least hindered and slowed, by the floors below, which had not been damaged by fire or impact? How could *every* previously undamaged support on *every* floor fail all at the same time as the one above came down, even given the combined weight tugging on the supports in the revised 'global collapse' theory?

Many independent physicists (i.e. not connected to the US authorities) who have analysed the falls of the towers have severely challenged the official explanation. Sooner or later the collapse should have halted itself by the simple laws of gravity, density and mass, as Richard Gage has demonstrated.[8] If nothing else, one might expect to see some kind of uneven descent at work, even if its progression was relatively swift. Instead, what actually occurs is a virtually 'free-fall' total failure of both towers (i.e. falling at the rate that something would drop, without atmospheric resistance, in normal gravity), each entire structure unstoppably coming down within ten seconds. This is something unheard of in architectural history - apart from in controlled demolitions.

WERE THE TOWERS BROUGHT DOWN BY CONTROLLED DEMOLITION?: Aside from all the many other areas of dispute, the most discussed aspect of the 9/11 anomalies are the claims that the bizarre collapse of the twin towers indicate the strong likelihood of controlled demolition techniques being employed that day. This is a serious contention, because it unequivocally implies that the towers must have been laced with explosives before the attacks - something which could not, presumably, have been achieved by the direct presence of Middle Eastern terrorists, and would also require time and qualified skills. Accepting this scenario demands that some kind of 'insider' assistance must have been involved to ensure the successful destruction of the WTC. What, then, is the evidence to support the demolition view?

The entire nature of the tower collapses is anomalous. For instance, as the South Tower falls, we clearly see the first thirty floors or so begin to topple over steeply towards the ground, only for the leaning block to unexpectedly *correct itself* (or at least just dissolve into dust) and fall instead into the 'footprint' of the rest of the building. We also see the tall crowning transmission antenna on the North Tower suddenly descend inwards into the centre of the falling roof at a rate slightly *faster* than the general collapse going on around it. Neither of these oddities, nor any of the other strange phenomena observed during the collapses (see below), are consistent with what would be expected from a natural fall, nor with any variation of either the pancaking or global collapse theory. Instead, they strongly suggest that forces within the building are being engineered to disintegrate the internal support columns, thus accounting for the angle correction and the unexpected acceleration of the transmission tower. Only explosives placed within the building could credibly account for this.

Critics of truthseekers ask how such explosives could have been placed without anyone noticing - but it could have been a long and slow process, masked by any kind of maintenance procedure. Indeed, Scott Forbes, an office worker at the WTC (attacked as a fantasist by official defenders), has claimed there was a thirty-hour 'power down' of the WTC on 8-9th September 2001 for a 'cabling upgrade', during which electricity was sporadically off and CCTV cameras did not function. There are also reports that the status of 'heightened security alert' was lifted just two days before that, with reports of sniffer dogs being abruptly removed from the premises. These claims remain unconfirmed, but even if this information is ignored Richard Gage has suggested that extensive lift-shaft maintenance work carried out in the months before 9/11 could have comfortably masked the planting of explosives, and believes that the shafts would have given good access to critical structural points. The truly cynical may also wish to note that Marvin Bush, one of George W Bush's brothers, was at one point a co-owner of Securicom, the company in charge of security at the WTC.

When all is said and done, however, any arguments over the 'how' must be looked at in the light of the available *direct* evidence that explosives might have been used to bring down the twin towers - and that evidence is persuasive.

EVIDENCE OF EXPLOSIVES: In truth, the word 'collapse' is not really accurate for the destruction of the twin towers. Even the most cursory observation of what happens when they fall reveals that they effectively *explode* from the aeroplane entry floor levels downwards, with substantial amounts of debris being cast far outside of the general collapse area with what must be incredible force, certainly beyond that expected from a simple gravitational fall. Large chunks of rubble and beams were found several blocks away in the aftermath, together with other wreckage, including fragments of human remains on tops of buildings so far away from the WTC site that they were only discovered years later.[9] Applying the laws of physics to the filmed ejections of material demonstrates that the angles and momentum of larger objects seen flying outwards could not occur without an additional force of propulsion - which explosives would provide.[10] Evidence that large amounts of heat and energy were expended during the destruction of the towers can be seen from the 'pyroclastic' nature of the clouds of white dust, which so dramatically pursued fleeing citizens through the streets in a far more expansive manner than one might expect from a straightforward fall. The clouds billow upwards and outwards, suggesting to some researchers the presence of a great motivating upsurge, probably from intense heat, just as in a volcanic eruption.

The state of the fallen buildings showed such an extreme level of destruction that the term 'pulverisation' was used by several 'Ground Zero' workers - the buildings had not merely collapsed, but had literally been reduced to dust. Barely anything survived the fall. Bobby Gray, a crane operator who was part of the clear-up team, exclaimed:

'I don't remember seeing carpeting or furniture. You'd think a metal file cabinet would make it, but I don't remember seeing any, or phones, computers, none of that stuff... ...Even in areas that never burned we didn't find anything. It was just so hard to comprehend that everything could have been pulverised to that extent. How do you pulverise carpet or filing cabinets?'[11]

All that remained of the towers were sections of the outer lattice at ground level. Clearance workers reported a remarkable dearth of actual objects, such as filing cabinets or telephones, almost as if everything had literally crumbled to dust - more evidence that high temperature explosives may well have been employed here.

All this can justifiably be considered as evidence that a very intense form of explosive was used to destroy the towers. Dr Steven Jones is one of several physicists who believe that some kind of inflammatory substance such as thermite, which enables materials to burn at far higher temperatures than normal, might have been used to weaken the structure first. This may explain how the steel core supports were able to snap so easily, once a final explosive impetus was applied. An example of evidence of thermite, or a similar substance, would be the presence of molten metal - and sure enough we see molten metal literally running down from the smoking towers in some footage, despite the relatively low temperature fires caused by the plane impacts, which couldn't possibly have altered the nature of steel in this way. Large amounts of molten metal (which official mouthpieces have tried to suggest is glass, but there is too much eye-witness evidence to the contrary from wreckage clearance crews) were found in the rubble even days after the collapses, and subsequent aerial thermal imaging revealed very high lingering temperatures at Ground Zero, far above that which could be explained by the remnants of jet-fuel fires. More evidence of thermite has recently come to light in an analysis of the dust from the destruction of the towers, carried out by seven scientists, including Jones, and published in April 2009 in the paper *Active Thermitic Material Discovered in Dust from the 9/11 World Trade Center Catastrophe*. Gregg Roberts of Architects and Engineers for 9/11 Truth reports:

'The team analyzed dust samples that were collected from four locations near Ground Zero. One sample was collected ten minutes after the North Tower exploded, so it could not have been contaminated with particles from the cleanup efforts. All four samples contained the same unusual, tiny red/gray chips, which turned out to consist not only of the ingredients of conventional thermite but also carbon, silicon, and other elements.'[12]

A fireman clears some of the very fine and highly poisonous dust at Ground Zero. The firemen were rightly hailed as heroes by authorities on 9/11, but those same authorities were quite happy to send their heroes and others back into the danger zone long before the toxicity had settled, causing severe health problems since.

[Even without the thermite, the issue of toxic dust (containing many other dangerous contaminates) is another outrage of 9/11. Firemen, rescue workers and New York civilians were inexplicably assured by authorities that it was safe to re-enter the area long before it was actually was, leading almost certainly to health issues and many subsequent deaths caused by respiratory and other problems.][13]

Another notable feature suggesting the use of explosives to bring down the towers, which can clearly be seen in photographs of the WTC rubble, is the remains of steel beams exhibiting ends that seem to have been sliced neatly across at 45° angles, almost as if they have been sawn. Official defenders claim this is simply where recovery crews cut the beams to clear wreckage, but comparing these to stock promotional photos of 'cutter charges' and their results, used in controlled demolitions to take out the infrastructures of buildings in neat portions, one can see that the observed angular slicings are virtually identical. It is certainly noteworthy that nearly all of the steel beams at Ground Zero seemed to fall as neatly severed, manageable and regimented-size pieces that were easy to pick up and take away afterwards. It is hard to imagine that a random structural failure would have produced this level of organisation.

DEMOLITION SQUIBS?: One of the most debated visual anomalies in the collapse footage concerns what some describe as 'squibs' - large puffs of smoke and ejected material, which can clearly be seen blossoming at different places along the entire height of both WTC towers as they fall, far below the level of the descending disintegration. No adequate explanation has yet been presented for what these are. Defenders have claimed they are the result of an air pressure-wave pushing through the building as the floors come down from above, blowing out glass windows. Others have suggested they are gas canisters or air ducts exploding, but these explanations are little more than empty guesses, especially given that air ducts don't generally explode under pressure, and no industrial gas canisters were present in either of the twin towers. The pressure-wave theory sounds more feasible, but doesn't really convince, for two main reasons: 1) the puffs are far bigger and more violent than such an innocuous word suggests, ejecting large amounts of rubble - more than would result from just air pushing out office materials, as the pressure-wave theory would suggest, and 2) some of the ejections are so far down from the collapsing floors that any pressure-effect could not yet have reached those levels (especially given that each tower is coming down at the maximum speed possible, known as 'free-fall').

It is hard to see how the official explanation can account for this phenomena. Yet comparison of these puffs with film of squibs resulting from explosive charges placed in buildings that *have* been brought down by controlled demolition reveals an uncanny likeness between the two, leading many to conclude that what we are seeing as the towers fall are strategically-placed explosives going off to weaken each floor, ensuring total collapse.

In addition to the squibs, there is also footage showing rapid flashes of light running in vertical strips along the corners of each tower, like firecrackers - or little explosive charges. All this could be dismissed as electric cables breaking, were it not for the fact that, again, they are actually sizeable discharges and occur at a notable distance below the collapsing floors.

Put together with the fact that many people described hearing and seeing explosions going off in the towers both during and *before* the collapse, there is a substantial case to be answered here.

TESTIMONY OF EXPLOSIONS: In the original news footage of 9/11, as broadcast on the day, it is notable how many firemen, rescue workers and civilians all reported witnessing what seemed like explosions *inside* the twin towers while they were still standing - and then as they came down. TV stations across America reported these in unambiguous terms at the time, with interviews and even live footage of clouds of smoke coming up from the *basement* of one of the towers (before it fell) after a particularly loud boom. Yet in the days after, references to any of this began to be dropped until at last it was as if these reports had never been. There seems to have been a concerted mass-edit ever since, with no mention of internal explosions whatsoever in any of today's available mainstream archive footage. Indeed, even the French Naudet brothers, who were famously filming New York firemen for a documentary on the day of the attacks (and took the only officially available footage of the first tower strike) have, in the most recent version of their tribute film *9/11*, deliberately removed a striking sequence where a group of returning firemen animatedly discuss how the collapsing towers were like explosions taking out the floors ('Boom, boom, boom'). This can only raise further suspicion that a rewriting of history is taking place.

Yet, on record, are astonishing testimonies such as this, from fire captain Karin Deshore, describing (allowing for excited grammar) the phenomena he witnessed at the moment one of the towers fell:

'Somewhere around the middle of the [North Tower of the] World Trade Center, there was this orange and red flash coming out. Then this flash just kept popping all the way around the building and that building had started to explode. The popping sound, and with each popping sound it was initially an orange and then a red flash came out of the building and then it would just go all around the building on both sides as far as I could see. These popping sounds and the explosions were getting bigger, going both up and down and then all around the building.'[14]

This is just one of many similar accounts. Firemen, in particular, being the closest witnesses, documented many such reports. Many confirm descriptions of explosions taking place far below the line of the plane impact damage before and during the falls. It is also clear from fire crew testimony (and the Naudet footage) that explosions *did* occur in the basement of the towers, causing visible damage in the lobby. This is often put down to burning jet fuel pouring down the lift shafts, but given the extreme length of the lift shafts it is hard to see how such extensive damage could occur at ground level.

The firemen's testimony in all this is crucial to getting to the truth of what happened at the WTC. Yet most firemen will no longer discuss their experiences openly. Why should this be? Perhaps because of the concerns expressed by auxiliary lieutenant fireman Paul Isaac:

'Many other firemen [besides me] know there were bombs in the buildings, but they're afraid for their jobs to admit it because the 'higher-ups' forbid discussion of this fact.'[15]

THE JANITOR'S TALE: In the light of reluctance amongst the rescue services to speak out, we therefore have to turn to civilian testimony for back-up evidence concerning explosives at the WTC, and here one man's story stands out. William Rodriguez was a janitor in the North Tower on the day of 9/11, and was decorated by George W Bush himself for his bravery in re-entering the tower with firemen after the plane strike and helping to release trapped workers by opening fire doors and acting as an informed guide. The testimony of Rodriguez is important, because he is one of those who witnessed a huge explosion in the basement of the North Tower just before the plane hit the building.

Rodriguez and his staff were in the first sub-level office at the time, when a large blast rocked the floor below them. A burned and bloodied staff member staggered in, shouting 'Explosion! Explosion! Explosion!' Other co-workers have confirmed the basement blast (describing extensive damage reminiscent of the 1993 truck bomb, which first attempted to bring down the towers).[16] The almost immediate plane strike afterwards, and the subsequent drama, distracted from this event at the time, but Rodriguez didn't forget.

Other basement explosions were described and felt by many witnesses, including the aforementioned live broadcast (since mysteriously removed from media circulation), showing large pre-collapse clouds of smoke coming up from the ground.

In Rick Seigel's interesting amateur footage of the burning towers, taken from one of the wharfs across the water at Hoboken, a mile or so away, the fall of each tower appears to be markedly preceded by a deep boom, which shakes the ground about ten seconds before.[17] Although this remains to be corroborated by other witnesses, in the video smoke can be seen to rise from the basements after each boom. Taking out the roots of a building's basement just before pulling down the infrastructure above it is a known controlled demolition procedure.

William Rodriguez and the firemen with him all heard explosions in the tower around them as they attempted to rescue office workers. They also became aware of strange movements of what sounded like heavy equipment on a service floor usually closed off to normal staff, noises that have never been explained. Managing to survive the final collapse of the tower by incredible chance (protecting himself by diving under a nearby fire truck), Rodriguez was sure that someone would want to document his important testimony when the officially-appointed 9/11 Commission was preparing its reports, but neither he nor his staff were ever called to give evidence:

'I contacted NIST... ...four times without a response. Finally (at a public hearing), I asked them before they came up with their conclusion... ...if they ever considered my statements or the statements of any of the other survivors who heard the explosions. They just stared at me with blank faces.'[18]

Incensed at the refusal of any authority to acknowledge his experiences, Rodriguez embarked on an ongoing global lecture tour in which he has since shared his full and heartfelt account with thousands, in an attempt to by-pass the clearly partisan establishment filters. As such, he has probably done more than many conspiracy theorists to spread awareness that someone may have placed explosives in the twin towers to help to bring them down.

However, given that no construction has ever fallen due to fire damage in the whole of modern architectural history (including hotels and tower blocks which have burned for up to 24 hours without collapsing, as in Madrid in 2005) it is a remarkable thing that not two, but three buildings apparently did so on 9/11. For most people forget, and have been encouraged to forget, the fall of WTC 7.

iii) WTC 7

At 5.20pm on 11th September 2001, after several harrowing hours since the morning attacks, the fall of one more, unoccupied, office block at Ground Zero was barely noticed. Building Seven - WTC 7 - was just more collateral in a long day of death and destruction.

Yet 9/11 truthseekers believe that the collapse of WTC 7 is one of the most anomalous aspects of all - because it was never hit by an aeroplane. Partially but not substantially damaged by falling debris from the twin towers, and exhibiting limited fires on one or two floors, its sudden and total collapse into its own footprint seems completely inexplicable.

Official defenders say that both the fires and debris damage were far more extensive than was apparent, but the reality is that in almost no available footage of WTC 7 can anything other than minor impairment and modest burning be observed

The Federal Emergency Management Agency's demonstration of the position of WTC 7 as the second of the twin towers collapses nearby. Some damage to Building 7 might be expected, but why did it later fall down like a pack of cards when it was never hit by an aeroplane and exhibited only limited fires?

WTC 7

(new testimony and film was suspiciously held back until broadcast by the BBC in 2008, but have to be taken on trust and still don't prove the case). If major buildings fall down with such little provocation, then every block in Manhattan should have been emptied of occupants then and there for safety reasons alone. But they weren't. Neither have any fears ever been expressed since that a building might collapse due to fire or exterior damage, even when a light aircraft accidentally struck a New York apartment block in October 2006, causing an extensive blaze on two floors.[19] Neighbourhoods were not evacuated.

HOW COULD WTC 7 FALL?: WTC 7 was built specifically to withstand every imaginable hazard, especially as, significantly, it housed a number of important occupants, including Mayor Rudi Giuliani's Emergency Command Center for the City of New York, offices for the US Department of Defense, the CIA and the US Secret Service. In addition, it also hosted the Inland Revenue Service (IRS) and the Security and Exchange Commission, which were both at that point investigating the unfolding Enron corruption scandal.

How then, was such a crucial building able to come down so easily, again at free-fall speed and with no unevenness of collapse? How could 24 core and 57 perimeter support columns simultaneously fail, level by level, without even aeroplane impact damage to explain such a failure, but with only minor structural compromise? Debris hitting the outside of the building could not possibly have removed fireproofing from the internal support columns - one of the central arguments claimed for the fall of the twin towers - so how could modest fires, with not even kerosene to fuel them, have weakened the floors in this way?

Unlike the twin towers, which seem to explode with great force from the top downwards, the fall of WTC 7 in available footage is far more sedate, and much more like a conventional implosion demolition, gracefully descending to the ground with a minimum of fuss. It seems that the twin towers were meant to go down in a dramatic spectacle never to be forgotten, whilst WTC 7 was removed as quietly and as simply as possible. Its disintegration received only limited television coverage, through all the media obsession with the bigger events of the day, and most people forgot that it even occurred. Incredibly, in the final 9/11 Commission report WTC 7's entirely puzzling demise doesn't even warrant a single mention.

A large number of physicists with no ties to US authorities have expressed the view that instant structural failure of a building in this way is simply not possible without an explosive impetus. Several demolition companies, shown the footage of WTC 7's fall by 9/11 researchers, who did not at first tell them the time, place or nature of what they were looking at, expressed the view that the images must be film of expert demolition at work. All were amazed when told the real location and circumstances, and all stated the impossibility of such a collapse resulting from fire or debris damage.[20] Even NIST hesitated in publishing a final report on WTC 7, perhaps because even they were struggling to come up with an official explanation that could make any sense.

In summer 2008, the BBC's *Conspiracy Files* programme (which had already launched what amounted to a manipulative debunk of 9/11 truth claims in a previous 2007 episode) broadcast new footage taken by firemen of the 'raging infernos' in WTC 7, together with alleged new testimony that the internal fires were far greater than anyone could see from the outside. The official NIST report finally followed shortly after in August 2008, saying much the same thing, and describing the building's fall (conveniently) as a 'new phenomenon', in which, floor by floor, the heat-weakened connections to the steel supports simultaneously snapped (rather than being pulled inwards, as in the 'global collapse' explanation for the twin towers). Given the seven years it had taken for this theory to emerge, with its very sparse supportive footage and suspiciously late testimony, many were dubious of the claims. In any case, even allowing for their possible veracity, and the 'more-fire-than-anyone-realises' emphasis on the reasons for the building's destruction, it remains that no modern structure should possibly have fallen in this way due to heat and flames alone.

WTC 7 exhibited some fire during the day - but not much. Why should it have so effortlessly fallen down just a few hours later? And why was such an important building, home to several high-profile occupants, including Mayor Giuliani's Office of Emergency Management, abandoned to its fate so early in the day?

Moreover, the evidence that controlled explosives were very probably employed is once again made clear by scrutiny of the footage. Very suspicious puffs can be seen emanating from the side of WTC 7, almost exactly at the moment it begins to fall, with no possibility of their being pressure-wave effects this time (because nothing is yet coming down). A ripple that passes across the main face of the building suggests a blast shockwave of some kind in progress, and witnesses reported seeing glass windows 'busting out' just before it began its straight descent into rubble.

OFFICIAL ACKNOWLEDGEMENT OF DEMOLITION?: There seems to be some confusion amongst even the authorities at the core of the 9/11 events as to what happened regarding WTC 7. Although the official line now says that fire and debris damage caused its collapse, it seems that the idea of admitting deliberate demolition with regard to this block *was* toyed with. Otherwise, how do we make sense of WTC owner Larry Silverstein's now notorious comments on Building Seven in the 2002 PBS television documentary *America Rebuilds*, in which he states the following?:

'I said, "We've had such terrible loss of life, maybe the smartest thing to do is pull it." And they made that decision to pull and we watched the building collapse.'

Given that 'pull it' is a traditional demolition term used to describe the moment that a building is pulled down, at first sight this would appear to be confirmation that WTC 7 was indeed demolished, ostensibly for safety reasons (rather than it just falling down), and Silverstein's comments were leapt on by truthseekers as such. But if WTC 7 could have been destroyed in this way, why not the twin towers also?

All this began to raise uncomfortable speculation. After all, lacing a building with explosives is something that couldn't possibly have been done in an afternoon, in all the chaos of a disaster zone. Controlled demolition can take weeks to plan. Were office workers always sitting just feet away from officially-sanctioned explosive charges, designed as part of the infrastructure just in case emergency demolition was ever needed (an argument which has also been made for the twin towers)? Such a contingency measure would be unheard of. If not, however, how could WTC 7 have possibly been brought down that day?

With conspiracy theorists now calling WTC 7 the 'smoking gun' of 9/11, and officials perhaps realising the revealing and potentially disastrous nature of the 'pull it' statement, attempts were made to rescind or at least re-clarify Silverstein's words, which were hastily explained as meaning that he was simply referring to the decision to 'pull' the firemen out of the dangerous building. But this raised more questions than it answered. With demolition experts confirming that the phrase 'pull it' was pretty unambiguous in its industry meaning, to use such a term to refer to removing rescue crews from a danger zone was highly unusual to say the least.

FOREKNOWLEDGE OF WTC 7'S COLLAPSE: Accepting for the sake of argument that Silverstein *was* only referring to the removal of the firemen from WTC 7, this still leaves a major anomaly, because it is very clear that officials knew well in advance that this building would collapse. But how did they know?

WTC 7 was set back some distance from the twin towers, with Buildings Five and

Six in-between. Even allowing for the fact that these nine-storey blocks were much lower than Seven's 47 storeys, why would anyone think that WTC 7 was about to come down when there seemed to be no great concern over the potential collapse of these other substantial surrounding blocks of the WTC, which were far more damaged by falling debris? Also, with no steel-frame construction ever having collapsed due to fires on a few floors in the whole history of modern architecture (and with no aeroplane impact), why did anyone think this would happen now?

Yet officials were plainly aware that WTC 7 would be coming down, up to seven hours in advance, according to the testimony of fire officers. Captain Michael Currid, president of the Uniformed Fire Officers Association, reported Mayor Giuliani's Office of Emergency Management as having warned that WTC 7 was 'basically a lost cause and we should not lose anyone trying to save it'.[21] Other officers received the same message and fire crews were removed from the building and a safety cordon set up several hours before it fell. But why should this be? With firemen having tackled far worse blazes in New York before then, why single out WTC 7 as a 'lost cause', especially for such a vital administrative building?

Given that the building was actually *home* to the command centre of the Office of Emergency Management, it seems to have been evacuated extremely early on - even before the towers next to it fell, according to City Housing Authority worker Barry Jennings, who claims that he and Michael Hess, New York's 'corporation counsel', entered the command centre shortly before 9.03am (after the North tower was struck, but before the South was hit) only to find it already deserted.

FEMA's annotated aerial shot showing the remains of the WTC complex. The twin tower areas are just below the bottom of the picture. It can be seen that parts of WTC 5 and WTC 6 survived, but WTC 7 - set back further - didn't.

Yet the official story says the evacuation did not occur until 9.30am. It should be noted here that Jennings and Hess also reported a large explosion taking place inside WTC 7 as they tried to leave the mysteriously empty building. The blast destroyed the stairs beneath them. Other sounds of explosions followed. If true, this suggests that a systematic weakening of the structure may have been taking place throughout the day before WTC 7's eventual collapse in the late afternoon.[22]

Interestingly, some communicative cross-wires seem to have occurred in the hour before WTC 7 did finally come down at 5.20pm, which again speak not only of foreknowledge of its destruction, but also a direct planning of it. In 2007, footage from BBC World News' live coverage of 9/11 re-emerged on the Internet, showing reporter Jane Standley describing the collapse of WTC 7 a full twenty-three minutes *before* it actually fell. Ironically, the still-intact block can be clearly seen in shot on the horizon behind her. All this speaks of a pre-prepared statement accidentally going out a little too soon. Just a mistake on the part of those who had been warned of the building's supposedly dangerous condition, or a demolition schedule going a little awry?

WHY DESTROY WTC 7?: Why bring WTC 7 down as well as the twin towers? Some 9/11 truthseekers hold that the events of the day may have been co-ordinated from WTC 7, with unknown occupants using it as a central hub to control the outcome of the attacks. This belief is held especially amongst those who suggest the planes were guided in by remote control, with command perhaps even taken out of the hands of the supposed hijackers - not as outlandish as it may sound when the evidence is examined.[23] Perhaps, with the job now done, having allowed time to remove all useful items, it was safer

The smoke plume from the fall of WTC 7, exhibiting the 'pyroclastic' flows seen on 9/11. These suggest extensive heat in the dust clouds not typical of natural collapses.

and more convenient to destroy all remaining evidence than risk rescue crews and investigators finding incriminating clues in the aftermath.

If nothing else - although this still suggests pre-planning, and therefore foreknowledge of the day's attacks - the rather serendipitous loss of crucial Enron investigation documents (and who knows what else) may have been a good enough reason for someone to bring down the building, in the hope that its destruction might not be noticed in amongst all the tumult. And mostly it wasn't, despite WTC 7 being one of the most mysterious and suspicious elements of 9/11.

Other Areas of Concern

All of the above points, in themselves, stand as good enough justification for a new and totally independent public investigation into 9/11, which is the central aim of most of the truth campaigners. With the official 9/11 Commission having been effectively staffed by close associates of the Bush administration, such an independent inquiry has not yet occurred. These included, as Executive Director of the Commission, Philip Zelikow, a long-time friend and colleague of Condoleezza Rice.[24] Anyone in doubt over the obvious partiality of the supposed inquiry should invest in a copy of David Ray Griffin's 2004 book *The 9/11 Commission Report: Omissions and Distortions*, which outlines, point by point, every failure of the Commission to address the truth of what really occurred on 9/11. The title of Griffin's book tells you all you need to know here about the official report's reliability.

Those who attack 9/11 truthers often accuse them of putting unnatural focus on contentious minutiae taken out of context. However, when challenging the truth of something, one should always look for 'clusters' of anomalies and inconsistencies - and there is more than enough evidence of such clusters with regard to 9/11. Applying the Truth Agenda to this subject reveals some of the largest evidential holes to be found in any historical event. Before we move on to exploring the bigger picture of where all the mysteries and cover-ups discussed in this book are taking us, it would be remiss, therefore, not to touch at least briefly on some other areas of concern over 9/11.

Hijacker Mohammed Atta, supposedly a devout Muslim fanatic, was seen cavorting in lap dancing clubs just days before 9/11. Was he really a religious martyr?

DO WE REALLY KNOW WHO THE HIJACKERS WERE?: If members of Al Qaeda were involved at all with the attacks, even merely as patsies, were the hijackers the ones we were told about in the news? Mohammed Atta, for example (held to be the ringleader on the day), far from being a devout Muslim as claimed, appears to have enjoyed himself at lap-dancing clubs and casinos in the preceding week - behaviour hardly befitting a religious martyr. Also, given that Hani Hanjour could barely handle a light aircraft, let alone a jet airliner, how was he able to execute the extraordinary manoeuvre into the Pentagon (see above) - unless someone else was piloting the plane or remote control had been imposed on Flight 77?

The appearance of the supposed hijackers passing through airport gates in security video footage is inconsistent with descriptions given by the ground staff at the time, and security 'time-coding' on the tapes appears to have been tampered with. Although there has been some mysterious and not entirely convincing backtracking on the story since, it's interesting to note that, in the weeks after 9/11, BBC News reported that seven of the alleged hijackers were claiming to be both innocent and alive and well in their native countries.

The identification of the hijackers - as claimed by the US authorities - always seemed fortuitously easy; as well as suspiciously over-incriminating evidence apparently having been left in their parked cars, we are also asked to believe that some of the hijackers' passports were picked up from pavements below the WTC, having survived the huge fireballs of the aeroplane impacts. Little else escaped intact in the otherwise pulverised remains.

As already mentioned, the 'confessions' of those currently incarcerated by US authorities and accused of plotting of 9/11 cannot be relied upon either, with accusations of both plea-bargaining and brainwashing being rife.

HOW WERE THE HIJACKS SO SUCCESSFUL?: With only small boxcutters (Stanley Knife-like blades) as their weapons, and very restricted access to the cockpits, is it reasonable to believe that four aeroplanes were successfully hijacked in the way claimed, and so quickly? Why, for instance, did not one of the pilots have the time or the initiative to press the emergency mayday button fitted into every plane, just a finger-click away?

In addition, for every plane, the transponders (automatic beacons) were switched off - almost unheard of in any previous hijacking case. Although NORAD (North American Aerospace Defense Command) and the FAA (Federal Aviation Administration) claim this is why they were unable to trace the flight paths of the aeroplanes, this simply cannot be true, as the craft would have shown up clearly as radar blips at least - otherwise, as David Ray Griffin has pointed out, how has the US ever protected its airspace? Russian bombers, for instance, would hardly have been likely to have been broadcasting convenient transponder signals.

On 9/11, the suspicious NORAD exercise 'Operation Vigilant Guardian', which concerned hypothetical aeroplanes hitting well-known US buildings (including the WTC), was being conducted *that very day* - amongst several other oddly-timed national drills. This enabled genuine confusion to reign amongst air traffic controllers ('is this real-world or exercise?', says one, when being told of the hijackings), and created a good cover for officialdom to explain why proper intercepts were not made. NORAD's own tapes of air traffic control conversations are controversial in themselves, with inconsistencies and evidence of selective editing having occurred (with changes made to the record in recent years), perhaps to obfuscate the facts about who knew what - and when - about the hijacked planes, raising serious doubts about the official claim that they didn't have enough time to stop the attacks.[25]

Even allowing for genuine disorganisation, it is an incredible anomaly that fighter planes - until 9/11, always scrambled within minutes of even a suspected hijack - were not sent up until far too late. No action was taken even after the first WTC tower had been hit and other planes were known to have been hijacked. When fighters were finally launched (and official times are inconsistent as to when this happened, but it was at least thirty minutes after the first tower strike), they flew too slowly, and from a *more distant* base than was available, consequently achieving nothing.

Evidence that the hijacked planes may indeed have been deliberately permitted to continue to their targets came from an unexpected source during the 9/11 Commission interviews. Norman Mineta, United States Secretary of Transportation at the time, made the following fascinating statement in his testimony regarding what he experienced in the Presidential Emergency Operating Center as Flight 77 approached the Pentagon:

'There was a young man who had come in and said to the vice president [Dick Cheney], 'The plane is 50 miles out. The plane is 30 miles out.' And when it got down to, 'The plane is 10 miles out,' the young man also said to the vice president, 'Do the orders still stand?' And the vice president turned and whipped his neck around and said, 'Of course the orders still stand. Have you heard anything to the contrary?' Well, at the time I didn't know what all that meant. [26]

Many consider that they *do* know what it meant, believing that Flight 77, or whatever replaced it, was being allowed to do its worst. Other interpretations could be placed on this strange anecdote, but given that no 'orders' at all seem to have been acted on in the authorised version of events (with no interception nor activation of the Pentagon's defences), Mineta's testimony seems to confirm that officials knew full-well that a plane was on its way to the Pentagon and chose not to intercept it; indeed, it is hard to see what else this exchange could have meant. The fact that the 9/11 Commission failed to document this surely important information in its final report also suggests they saw it in the same light.

HOW DO WE KNOW WHAT HAPPENED ON THE PLANES?: Although tales of what supposedly occurred on the hijacked aeroplanes have now passed into popular folklore, the reality is that there is very little available evidence to support them. This is especially the case given that the Flight Data Recorders ('black boxes') from Flights 11, 175 & 93 were, officially, 'never found', presumed destroyed, so telemetry about the way the planes were handled is unavailable. (Some workers at Ground Zero have claimed the boxes there were indeed recovered, but there has been no official recognition of this.) The Cockpit Voice Recorders for Flights 11 & 175 were also 'never found' but, interestingly, given how much contention there is over what hit it, both recorders for Flight 77 *were* found at the Pentagon, as if to confirm the presence of a Boeing 757. Only the voice recorder was found for Flight 93, which crashed in woods in Pennsylvania - and from this, and a few phone calls supposedly made by the passengers and cabin crew, has been constructed the heroic story of passengers storming the cockpit

The remains of Flight 175 on the roof of WTC 5. Despite hijackers' passports having survived the impact fireballs, the Flight Data Recorders and Cockpit Voice Recorders from the WTC crashes have never officially been recovered...

('let's roll'), which inspired so much patriotic fervour in the media.

HOW WERE THE CELL PHONE CALLS MADE?: Almost all we have to prove the presence of Al Qaeda terrorists on the hijacked craft comes from details given in the now fabled cell phone (mobile) calls from frightened passengers and crew. Although in-flight back-of-the-seat calls may have been possible from some of the planes (though there is confusion about this), many have raised questions about how mobile calls - officially the main source of the conversations - could possibly have been made in 2001, when no mechanism then existed to enable them to be used at the altitudes claimed for the hijacked planes. Only now are commercial systems being introduced to allow this. The biggest doubts have been cast over the Flight 93 conversations, in which nine mobile calls were allegedly made.

Puzzled at these claims, Canadian science writer A K Dewdney decided to put this to the test with a number of experiments and concluded that the possibility of *any* cell phone calls being successful above a height of 8000 feet was highly unlikely.[27] Given that the officially-acknowledged altitude of Flight 93 was between 34,000 feet and 40,000 feet, calls from this plane should have been impossible. Perhaps realising the proven unfeasibility of the cell phone claims, more recently the FBI has mysteriously changed its data to state that in fact all but two of Flight 93's calls were in fact made from seat phones, going against all their previous statements - but even the two remaining cell calls are very unlikely to have taken place.

The odd nature of some of the alleged communications (only one of which has ever been publicly broadcast) also raises doubts, as with the transcript of the now

Deconstructing Consensus Reality

infamous call from Flight 93 passenger Mark Bingham to his mother, in which he opens a weirdly stilted conversation with the words 'Mom, this is Mark Bingham'. Would anyone really feel the need to give their surname to their own mother, even under stress? Given that voice-synthesiser technology, which can reproduce basic sentences in an authentic copy of someone's individual tones, certainly does exist, is it too extreme to consider that these calls could have been faked? Many researchers, even cautious ones, believe they may well have been.

Most famously, CNN television pundit Barbara Olson reputedly made two calls to her husband Ted (United States Solicitor General at the time of 9/11 and a close Bush supporter), on which much has been based. David Ray Griffin writes of this claim:

'According to this story, Olson reported that his wife had "called him twice on a cell phone from American Airlines Flight 77," saying that "all passengers and flight personnel, including the pilots, were herded to the back of the plane by armed hijackers. The only weapons she mentioned were knives and cardboard cutters... ...Ted Olson's report was very important. It provided the only evidence that American 77, which was said to have struck the Pentagon, had still been aloft after it had disappeared from FAA radar around 9:00 AM... ...Also, Barbara Olson had been a very well-known commentator on CNN. The report that she died in a plane that had been hijacked by Arab Muslims was an important factor in getting the nation's support for the Bush administration's "war on terror." Ted Olson's report was important in still another way, being the sole source of the widely accepted idea that the hijackers had box cutters.' [28]

However, Ted Olson's account has been undermined by the FBI's data, which records that Barbara Olson attempted one mobile call that didn't connect. Ted Olson later changed his story to say that the call must have been from a seat-back phone - but American Airlines has confirmed that Flight 77 did not have such facilities. Neither does the Pentagon agree with Barbara Olson's supposed version of what happened on the plane, prompting Griffin to add:

'This rejection of Ted Olson's story by American Airlines, the Pentagon, and especially the FBI is a development of utmost importance. Without the alleged calls from Barbara Olson, there is no evidence that Flight 77 returned to Washington. Also, if Ted Olson's claim was false, then there are only two possibilities: Either he lied or he was duped by someone using voice-morphing technology to pretend to be his wife. In either case, the official story about the calls from Barbara Olson was based on deception. And if that part of the official account of 9/11 was based on deception, should we not suspect that other parts were as well?'

WHAT REALLY HAPPENED TO THE AEROPLANES?: There are even doubts amongst the more ardent questioners as to which planes really hit the twin towers. These issues are far more contentious, but are included here for the sake of completeness. Several witnesses remarked on the day that the planes at the WTC did not resemble commercial aircraft, and video analysis doesn't rule out the possibility that the hijacked planes may have been switched at some point to similar but augmented military-type versions better suited to the task. (There are many arguments about anomalous undercarriage 'pods' visible in some shots of the supposed Flight 175 hitting WTC 2, and curious flashes are visible just before impact both there and in the Naudet footage of WTC 1 being struck, suggesting to some that something is being fired from the planes to ensure maximum penetration). The switched-plane theory is unproven, but, if true, raises the question as to what happened to the real planes and passengers if they were not the ones involved in the strikes? This is a pertinent question, if only for Flight 77, which, in the light of the evidence, is hard to accept as being the object that struck the Pentagon.

There have been claims that the actual craft we were told were used in the attacks were, having been switched, just quietly re-fitted, re-registered and sent back into service. One school of thought holds that the planes, having been hijacked, landed safely in secret, perhaps at military bases. (On the day of 9/11, US television station WCPO-TV did also report that Flight 93 had landed safely at Cleveland Hopkins Airport, Ohio, although this has since been vigorously debunked as a reporting error.) In this hypothesis, the passengers from all the planes were packed into Flight 93, which was then flown off and dispatched by a missile or fighter over Pennsylvania. An extreme belief, perhaps, but given the many other difficulties with the official story, such potential atrocities cannot be entirely ruled out.

It is certainly curious that every flight involved in the hijackings was unusually very low in passenger numbers that day, with Flight 93 in particular operating at only 19% capacity - just 45 people onboard a plane that seated 239. Was this a deliberate ploy to guarantee that all the hijacked passengers would eventually fit onto one plane? It is also interesting to note that apart from the dubious and inconsistent airport security images of the supposed hijackers, no images have ever been released showing any of the other passengers boarding. In addition, it is said that not one relative of any of the claimed nine local inhabitants due to arrive from Flight 93 was waiting at San Francisco when airport staff tried to inform people of what had happened - almost as if their arrival wasn't expected. This raises curious questions, and to this day no definitive passenger list for any of the hijacked flights has ever been agreed, nor have the names that were allegedly the hijackers' 'false IDs' been revealed.

WHAT DID HAPPEN TO FLIGHT 93?: Even dispensing with the more controversial theories, there is huge confusion over the ultimate fate of Flight 93. The government deny shooting it down, even for reasons of protecting the public, and support instead the heroic tale of passengers forcing the plane into the woods while trying to stop the hijackers - yet eye-witness evidence suggests otherwise, with clear reports of pursuing planes and an aerial explosion. The debris field from Flight 93's destruction was spread over several miles and there

was almost no visible wreckage or human remains left at all at the plane's supposed final resting place; just an anomalous hole in the ground. The apparently vaporising force of such destruction seems far beyond that which one would expect from a plane coming down by itself, especially when compared to footage of other air crash sites in recent decades, which usually displays visible aeroplane parts and artefacts strewn around. At least two Hollywood takes on the Flight 93 story have now firmly cemented the official version in the public mind, but the evidence speaks of something less noble occurring.

The bizarre impact crater caused by Flight 93 in Pennsylvania. The astonishing lack of debris or aeroplane parts at the site is highly anomalous, suggesting the bulk of the plane was destroyed before it hit the ground. The authorities deny shooting it down, but the physical evidence and eye-witness testimony speaks differently.

WAS THERE FOREKNOWLEDGE OF THE ATTACKS?: On a general level, the Bush administration's weak claims that no-one could have foreseen that planes could ever be used as missiles in such a way were provably false, as intelligence reports had warned more than once that such a ploy might one day be used. Condoleezza Rice, however, claimed that such reports were 'never briefed to us' - leaving responsibility for failure once again with unnamed intelligence staff.[29] The fact that one Samuel Byck had attempted to hijack a plane to fly into the White House as early as 1974 (dramatised in the movie *The Assassination of Richard Nixon* in 2004) also seemed to escape attention.

It has been publicly admitted that intelligence warnings of specific and imminent aeroplane attacks *were* received by US authorities in the run-up to 9/11, but their failure to act on them has been sidelined under the same blanket of 'incompetence' and bad communications, which somehow always sees politicians being reluctantly forgiven by voters. Some within the US, however, clearly did take serious notice of whatever was bubbling up from 'deep throat' sources - or acted in the absolute confidence of their own plans - as unusual stock market 'insider trading' in the days before the attacks demonstrates beyond doubt. Beginning a week before, and peaking on 6th September, there was an unprecedented 1200% increase in trading activities on the two airlines involved in the attacks, as a large amount of 'put options' (basically, financial 'bets' that the stock of a particular company will go down) were placed on them. Sure enough, in the immediate wake of 9/11, $2.5 million profits were made as the stock fell by 43% on American Airlines and by 39% on United Airlines. Strange trading in connection with other companies that would suffer due to the attacks also occurred. The official investigation into these serendipitous transactions mysteriously absolved the traders in question with the somewhat circular reasoning that they had 'no possible ties to Al Qaeda' - rather missing the point that Al Qaeda may not have been the main players.

Meanwhile, some have pointed out the further serendipity of owner Larry Silverstein taking out insurance against terrorist destruction of the WTC complex just six weeks before 9/11. This was indeed lucky, as even after the previous basement bombing of the North Tower in 1993 no-one had thought to do this. The insurers consequently paid out millions of dollars to Silverstein. The latter example could, of course, be chance, but there is enough general evidence to confirm that there *was* solid information floating around that something big was about to happen. San Francisco mayor Willie Brown, for instance, was reportedly warned to be 'cautious' about flying on September 11th.

Despite all this evidence of foreknowledge in many areas, the media has often preferred to concentrate on the unproven, but much-whispered (especially in the Islamic world, predictably enough) claim that a large Jewish contingent of WTC-based staff didn't turn up for work on 9/11 - thus neatly implying that questioning 9/11 is essentially an anti-Semitic exercise, when it most certainly isn't. It has been asserted that a strangely large number of WTC workers were absent that day, suggesting that some at least had been party to a sixth sense - or a tip-off - but Jewishness probably wasn't a connecting factor. Meanwhile, those who do believe Zionist elements of Mossad may have been involved with whatever unknown criminal cartel was at work on 9/11 can hardly be labelled anti-Semitic for speculating on the possible participation of one of the world's most powerful and shadowy intelligence organisations, which has close links with the not-exactly-spotless CIA.

WHAT DID THE PRESIDENT KNOW?: The much-lampooned and oft-criticised response of George W Bush to the news that America was 'under attack', whispered into his ear by presidential aide Andrew Card, has now entered cultural infamy (much of it courtesy of Michael Moore's film *Fahrenheit 9/11*). Sat on a chair telling stories to children in a classroom of the Emma E Booker Elementary School in Florida, Bush looks confused and unable to respond appropriately. Instead of excusing himself, politely breaking off to address the nation, he continues to read for several more minutes. What did he really know at this point?

Despite accusations from some, there are those who suspect that Bush may have been initially ignorant about the larger agenda unfolding that day, hence his confusion. If there was knowledge of, or involvement in, the attacks at a government level (many accuse Dick Cheney of being a key architect), was Bush informed a little later in the day, once in the 'safety' of the presidential plane Air Force One? If so, did he go along with the revealed plans willingly, or was there an implicit threat to his safety if he didn't? (It was publicly stated on the day that there was a coded terrorist threat to shoot down Air Force One, but did the threat in fact come from closer to home, as a blackmail strategy? This element of 9/11 has since been played down to the point of denial.)[30]

Further confusion has been added by later comments from Bush, in which he states that he already knew of the first WTC strike before he entered the classroom - he had seen the footage and thought 'that's one terrible pilot'. But how could Bush or anyone have seen this footage? The only officially acknowledged video of the first impact was taken by the French Naudet brothers - and *wasn't televised on the day of 9/11*, only being released later. The tape stayed trapped within its camera with the film crew as the traumatic day progressed. So how could Bush have seen it that morning? Is he lying about this for some complicated reason, or was there a secret camera bizarrely trained on the WTC to capture the moment for inside conspirators? If the latter, this would implicate Bush's involvement from the start, but many feel his reaction in the schoolroom suggests a man who doesn't really know what's going on. Either way, Bush should have then responded to the crash in front of journalists before he entered the class, if only to voice supportive sympathy to the families of the victims.

When the second impact at the WTC occurred, another important thing failed to happen. Given the absolute certainty that America was now indeed under attack, and with Bush surely a prime target and his presence at the school widely revealed by news coverage, why was he not immediately whisked away for his own safety - and to protect the schoolchildren from potential attack? Yet the story of the pet goat continued. Was this inaction because those in command of the situation (officially or unofficially) knew full well that no aeroplane would be heading in that particular direction that morning? Questions within questions reveal no clear answers to any of this, but it is very clear that something is not right.

WHY WAS WTC WRECKAGE ILLEGALLY REMOVED?: Given that on 9/11 the WTC became the USA's biggest-ever crime scene, why was no proper forensic examination of the wreckage ever carried out? Instead, it was cleared with almost disrespectful haste, and the remains (including the vital steel supports, which could once and for all have settled the matter of what made them snap) were - quite illegally - removed and hurriedly shipped out to the far east for recycling, after only the most perfunctory survey by a chosen few. The much circulated assumption seems to have been that as it was a 'fact' that bin Laden and his associates were responsible for the attacks, then why waste valuable time proving what was already known? As a result, the evidence was destroyed and inconvenient questions will now never be answered, at least not through forensic analysis.

The removal of wreckage at the WTC occurred with indecent haste and no proper forensic examination - unheard of in any previous criminal investigation. Most of the metal was shipped out to the Far East for recycling before anyone could examine it.

Official Debunking

We could go on, and other sources [see *Appendix 2*] provide much more. But enough has been stated here to make clear that at the very least there are many, many unanswered questions about 9/11 that should seriously concern us. On the events of this day are based the entire rationale of the war against liberty that we have seen ever since. Yet there is overwhelming evidence of falsity, subversion and distraction from official channels in almost every area concerning this vital keystone of history. Who exactly *was* behind the co-ordination of the attacks is unknown at this stage (although some fairly obvious prime suspects amongst the neo-cons have been directly cited by researchers like Webster Tarpley), but it is clear there is a substantial case to be re-investigated.

The usual defence - that such a huge fraud couldn't possibly be perpetrated without the knowledge of thousands at a highly involved level - doesn't stand up under analysis (as with the NASA arguments). The suspiciously 'coincidental' NORAD exercises occurring on 9/11 probably helped cover a multitude of sins on the day, with any intentionally dubious decisions neatly lost in the confusion. Only a very few people in the chain of command would have to be involved to ensure that the attacks would be successful - and spectacular enough to rest in the consciousness

Deconstructing Consensus Reality

of civilisation forever. Perhaps that's why both towers (WTC 7 aside) had to come down completely - blackened holes in the sides of buildings that could be repaired might not be enough to make the point. The total destruction of one of the most famous landmarks in the world, together with a shocking loss of life, would be.

The aforementioned defence often offered up against the 'inside help' theory - how could anyone do such a thing to their own people? - is also flawed when held up against the depressing legacy of history. There have been many well-documented cases of the power-hungry making what they see as 'necessary sacrifices' for the foment of some wider agenda, as we shall explore in the next chapter. Why should 9/11 have been any different? A halfway-house theory put forward by some, that the authorities merely stood back and let the attacks of 9/11 occur for political gain but didn't actively plan it, is also unsatisfactory. There is too much evidence to show proactive manipulation on the part of some hidden cabal with access to high places of authority. But even if the halfway idea is considered, is letting something happen on purpose any less lamentable than directly aiding and abetting it?

9/11 campaigner and author David Ray Griffin, seen here relaxing after a lecture, is a prominent and highly credible challenger of the official story. His several books on the subject [see Appendix 2] make an unarguable case that we have not been told the truth about the attacks.

Official - and highly flawed - attempts at debunking what George W Bush laughably described as 'outrageous conspiracy theories' (not realising that the official bin Laden story, even if taken as true, is in itself a conspiracy theory) have become louder and more desperate as the public clamour to get to the reality of 9/11 mounts. But the arguments put forward to combat the outrageous - or, more accurately, outraged - theorists are all too often weak and evasive, with the defenders simply ignoring anything embarrassingly stark that can't be answered by the authorised account (read David Ray Griffin's *Debunking 9/11 Debunking* for a convincing point-for-point rebuttal of virtually all of the attempted official defences).

A Growing Movement

It may still be considered fringe today, and the passing of the Bush era threatens to weaken the momentum, but the still-growing ranks of the now global 9/11 truth movement, and the ever-ascending Internet hits on documentaries questioning the official line (with statistics provably cranked down from time to time by seemingly concerned hosts) are testament to the obvious fragility of the story we have been fed. Polls, meanwhile, suggest that the majority of the US population itself now doubts the official story, or at least believes that authorities allowed the attacks to occur.[31] There is a not-insignificant network of web-surfing, DVD-swapping and pamphleteering that is beginning to tip the balance of popular thinking and will only spread further if convincing answers to the (literally) burning questions are not eventually forthcoming.

Soon, the word 'fringe' will no longer serve to describe an upsurge of people who feel they have had their intelligence insulted for too long by arrogant and evasive authorities, in themselves supported by a complicit (and intimidated?) media, which does everything it can to belittle 9/11 truthseekers. Believing in '9/11 conspiracy' is regularly held up to be proof of eccentricity or delusion. Why should this be the case, though, with so many convincing arguments

A member of the London 9/11 Truth Campaign shows the determined dedication that many campaigners have to uncover the real details of the events, spending time distributing leaflets and raising awareness. Why? Because the control agendas affecting our lives today are inextricably bound up in the legacy of 9/11. If it can be incontrovertibly demonstrated that we have been lied to, a major keystone of the 'war on liberty' will be shaken loose. [See Appendix 2 for many 9/11 resources.]

and perfectly legitimate lines of enquiry to support the doubts? Mainstream pundits have failed the public regarding open-minded analysis of 9/11, with some pompously dismissive columnists (including, in the UK, David Aaronovitch, Polly Toynbee and environmentalist George Monbiot, who described 9/11 questioners as 'morons' prey to an 'epidemic of gibberish') demonstrating a state of utter denial that merely illustrates the hollowness of popular journalism's supposedly investigative ideals.[32] Television, meanwhile, also produces ignorant dismissals of impressive evidence and omits all of the important details, as ever. The atrocious entries in the BBC *Conspiracy Files* series in particular provides final evidence that, since the David Kelly affair [Chapter VII], this once-great broadcasting institution has been well and truly neutered when it comes to incisive investigation of sensitive areas, specialising instead in debunking documentaries.

But then 9/11 has had a number of far-reaching consequences, some depressingly mundane and some distressingly massive, which we shall now explore in Part Three before coming to the good news of how easily all this deception and doubt might be turned around at last.

THE TRUTH AGENDA: *The event that created the mandate for the 'War on Terror', a campaign that has crushed liberties and created havoc around the world, demonstrates serious anomalies when the details are examined. Important questions about the logic, timing and physics of most of the occurrences on 9/11 have been too lightly dismissed, with plain evidence of obfuscation from both authorities and the media. The official 9/11 Commission Report omits crucial evidence that paints quite a different picture to the official view and implies layers of complicity and deception. This troubling and unavoidable conclusion strongly suggests that the attacks were engineered either partially or wholly by a criminal cabal with influence in the US political or intelligence infrastructure. 9/11 presents one of the most powerful cases that the view of the world we are presented with by the mainstream is a manipulated construct, masking deeper machinations that are secretly shaping our lives.*

Part Three:
Tools of Control

The Liberty Bell hangs in Philadelphia, Pennsylvania, and was made to represent the freedom of the USA and its people. Yet, in the wake of 9/11, the Patriot Act and other supposed anti-terror legislation wiped away almost overnight many of the old protections of the Constitution. Perhaps the famous crack, which dogged the bell from its first use, was a symbolic omen.

IX   THE WAR ON LIBERTY

The 'War on Terror', might be better described as the 'War on Liberty', given the mandate of control it has created for Western governments, with everyday freedoms previously taken for granted having been greatly eroded away in less than a decade - through the instillation of fear. No conspiracy thinking is necessary to see the reality of this happening all around us. Are the tools of control that have been created by this process being put into place as a key element in the ruling elite's long-term plans?

The Project for the New American Century

If 9/11 was co-ordinated partially or fully by internal US influences or indeed agents of any secret agenda, what might the aim have been? It is compulsory at this point for all truthseekers to cite the Project for the New American Century (PNAC), a think-tank of fervent US neo-conservatives, which produced a document in the late 1990s entitled *Rebuilding America's Defenses: Strategy, Forces and Resources for a New Century*. In it, the future of American power is discussed with disturbingly frank self-awareness. Amongst its expressions of concern that the US would lose influence without a refreshed conquering spirit and an appropriate mandate for expansion, the following line proved serendipitously prophetic in the wake of the 9/11 attacks:

'The process of transformation, even if it brings revolutionary change, is likely to be a long one, absent some catastrophic and catalysing event - like a new Pearl Harbor.'

It is notable that within hours of 9/11, George W Bush himself was likening the attacks to the events at Pearl Harbor during World War II, drawing a renewed attention to the original PNAC document from those who knew its contents. Suddenly the desired 'process of transformation' had indeed been boosted by the very kind of catalysing event it had visualised, and the public references made to 'the new Pearl Harbor' in the rush of patriotic speeches were none-too-subtle for those on the alert. In the wake of the developments which have ensued since, to some the PNAC musings look ever-more like a blueprint for the new wave of American Imperialism we have experienced since 9/11, and another step in the unfolding journey towards the New World Order.

The Pearl Harbor comparison is eerily resonant in more than one respect; despite cries of outrage from patriots, revisionist investigators are revealing details that make it increasingly likely that covert decisions within the US were involved in 'allowing' the Japanese attack to occur in 1941.[1] The curious and unusual absence of the best Naval vessels from the docks that day seems to add credence to this, in a situation perhaps analogous with the 2001 strike on the Pentagon seemingly being targeted only at its most expendable block [page 147]. If nothing else, as with 9/11, it seems clear that intelligence warnings of the Japanese attack were received, but no action was taken. The spectacular tragedy which unfolded did the trick in raising the necessary impetus for the US to join the global conflict and dissolved the previous public resistance.

Pearl Harbor, 1941. Many now believe the infamous Japanese attack on the US base was deliberately allowed to occur, as important intelligence warnings were given in advance, but nothing was done to stop it. The evidence shows that this kind of approach to global politics for the foment of wider plans may be disturbingly common.

'False-Flag' Terror

For critics of 9/11 conspiracy theories, the major sticking point is this: how could even the most power-hungry manipulators in such a nationalistic country be persuaded to sacrifice around 3000 of their own people to make a point? Yet the awful truth is that throughout history this kind of technique has been used time and again to create military and political advantage. The enduring name for such actions - 'false-flag' attacks - stems from the ancient practice of ships attacking their own allies under the flags and colours of their collective enemies, stirring hatred against the foe and giving rise to the required public backing for what might otherwise be unpopular wars and 'necessary' withdrawals of freedom. There have been many historical variations of mandates being engineered for otherwise unjustifiable actions, and we don't even need to look back to ancient times to find examples.

We have already seen [Chapter I] how it is increasingly believed that the English Gunpowder Plot of 1605 may have been deliberately co-ordinated by Protestant officials to stir up ill-feeling towards Catholics and thus initiate a new reign of persecution. But even in more recent times there is suspicious evidence of this type of policy being pursued. It is likely, for instance, that the sinking of the luxury liner *Lusitania* in 1915, an event which was instrumental in encouraging public support for the Americans joining World War I, was manipulated in a not entirely dissimilar manner to the Pearl Harbor incident twenty-five years later.

The *Lusitania* seems to have been deliberately sent into waters that were known to be patrolled by German U-boats, leading to its predictable destruction and the loss of over 1200 civilian lives. The truly cynical have suggested it may even have been torpedoed by our own vessels.

During the Arab-Israeli 'Six-Day War' of 1967, the supposedly accidental air and sea attack by Israel on the American ship *USS Liberty* off the Sinai Peninsular coast is seen by many as a botched attempt to implicate Egypt in its destruction, to encourage a US attack on that country. When the *Liberty* failed to sink, and too many survivors could testify as to who was responsible, an apology from Israel helped cover-up any darker revelations - but many remain dubious.

The 9/11 resonance most regularly invoked, however, is the burning of the Reichstag parliament building in Berlin in 1933. Blamed on communist forces, apparently led by Dutch insurrectionist Marinus van der Lubbe, the huge fire precipitated an almost overnight suspension of civil liberties that wouldn't be fully restored until after World War II. Yet there is much evidence to suggest that the Nazis themselves started the fire, or were at least instrumental in manipulating the communists into action. Whichever, it was a crucial event in the rise to power of Adolf Hitler and was used massively to promote his violent campaign against all opposition. Indeed, the style of rule adopted by Nazi Germany in the years after the fire, with its dissolution of common freedoms and increased militarism, has alarming parallels with what has occurred in the West since 9/11.

Those who react in horror to the notion that the Land of the Free would ever resort to the depths of such false-flag tactics would do well to examine the now freely-available US documents concerning Operation Northwoods in 1962, another 'smoking gun' oft-cited by truthseekers. At the height of North America's long-running stand-off with Fidel Castro's communist Cuba, a plan was put forward to justify a full-scale assault against the country, which involved the staged shooting-down of a dummy US airliner. Although the scheme did not involve the actual killing of US citizens, and was never implemented, the seed of an idea which might have eventually blossomed into the 9/11 attacks can be clearly discerned. Above all, the Operation Northwoods papers categorically demonstrate that our governing administrations (and/or whichever higher powers might be pulling the strings) *will* consider any tactic, however low, if it results in military and political advantage.

Given this, those who suspect inside involvement in 9/11 tend also to doubt that Timothy McVeigh and two other conspirators acted alone in bombing the Alfred P Murrah Federal Building in Oklahoma City on 19th April 1995. This atrocity saw an entire office complex destroyed in a powerful blast that claimed 168 lives - until 9/11, the worst act of terrorism in the US. Supposedly an attack to avenge the victims of the 1993 Waco siege (in which religious guru

David Koresh and seventy-six others were shot or burned to death by FBI teams, apparently deliberately),[2] many consider the Oklahoma incident as being an early step towards creating a mandate for liberty infringements through legislations that would be stepped up massively in the wake of 9/11. As with the WTC complex, the extensive damage to the Oklahoma offices suggests to many doubters that a single truck bomb could not have caused so much devastation. Open

The devastation caused at the Alfred P Murrah building, Oklahoma, in 1995. Yet, as with 9/11, there is evidence that pre-placed explosives were also used in addition to the truck bomb blamed for the blast, with more than one detonation recorded on the day. If so, who could have placed them?

reports of secondary explosions on the day (initially broadcast across the media, and then omitted in later edits), together with audio tapes from office dictation machines, which recorded more than one blast, have also been cited as important evidence of underhand action.[3] The strong conviction of many that pre-placed explosive charges must also have been deployed at the Alfred P Murrah building has obvious echoes with the concerns over 9/11, and some point the finger of blame once again at inside forces somewhere within the infrastructure of US authority.

Allegations of false-flag actions are not restricted to the West; there are plenty (including *Observer* journalist John Sweeney) who also believe that the 1999 apartment block bombings in Moscow, for example, supposedly perpetrated by Chechen terrorists, were in fact partially or wholly co-ordinated by Russian intelligence forces to create the necessary mandate for the military incursions into Chechnya which followed.[4]

Going to the trouble of staging a false-flag event may not even be necessary when straight disinformation can sometimes perform the same trick. The Gulf of Tonkin incident on 4th August 1964, a supposed major attack by South Vietnamese forces on US destroyers, was long held up as a key trigger in the horrific war that troubled the world for the next decade. In 2005, the US National Security Agency (NSA) quietly released documents that finally confirmed long-held suspicions that, beyond one minor skirmish two days before the alleged incident, the attacks *never actually occurred*. Once again, the confusion was put down to 'intelligence errors' and sonar irregularities on the night in question. Many people suffered and died for those errors. Sooner or later some kind of trigger for war would doubtless have been found, but error or deliberate ploy, the fact is that maintaining the myth that an attack had indeed occurred was a beneficial justification to keep in the public eye.[5]

Creating the conditions and necessary support for wars and restrictions on liberty - always to 'protect' the population from the enemy - by means of staged, openly provoked or merely claimed atrocities has a long history. There seems no reason to believe the 21st century is immune to the same games, difficult though it is to accept that anyone could still inflict such engineered horrors. Yet that seems to be the cold reality we must face when the Truth Agenda is applied and the shortcomings of so many official accounts and claimed motivations are exposed.

Even if our elected leaders are not directly creating the harm, those manipulating them from somewhere in the background, be they the Illuminati, elite dynasties, scheming bankers or merely the rich and influential, would appear to think that carnage and chaos is fully justified in the name of some loftier cause. The nuances of what that cause might be are explored in Chapter XII.

What seems beyond dispute, whatever its impetus, is that the War on Terror also inflicted on us a War on Liberty that is taking away, day by day, openly or by stealth, many of the joys of being a free human being that we have previously taken for granted in the West.

The War on Terror

In many ways the War on Terror, launched by the US in the wake of the 9/11 attacks and supported by most Western countries, was a stroke of genius on the part of those behind it. With the Soviet Union rather inconveniently dissolved after 1991, leaving no common foe to unite against, the elevation of Osama bin Laden to the role of Public Enemy Number One and the promotion of the lurking threat of Al Qaeda in every country was the perfect replacement. Now, once again, a control agenda and the global economy, so reliant on the unholy manufacture and export of armaments, could be kept bubbling along forever under the umbrella of a war that *could never end*. Who seriously believed, when the War on Terror was launched, that its aims could ever be reached, with Middle Eastern terrorism such a nebulous and apparently insidious fixture? On the basis of attempting to 'fix' this problem, first Afghanistan, then Iraq, fell to Western corrective procedures, neatly giving our leaders a niche of influence in some useful geographical and energy-rich places along the way. Iran appears to be next on the wish-list, although the Indian Mumbai hotel attacks in 2008, seemingly carried out by Pakistani extremists, and the ongoing import of Taliban insurgents across the Afghan border into near all-out war situations with Pakistani troops, have also placed India's unstable neighbour into the potential running order.

Whether Al Qaeda before 9/11 was merely a phantom menace or a genuine threat will probably now never be resolved. Many suspect the Al Qaeda we were all told to fear in the wake of the attacks was initially a created myth, a convenient catch-all facade thrown up by US intelligence services over an essentially ragged and divided series of tin-pot militias, then of little threat to the West. Even the otherwise toothless post-David Kelly BBC dared to air a series in 2004, *The Power of Nightmares*, very convincingly exposing this frank reality about Al Qaeda, before the channel pretended it had never broadcast it and returned to airing the usual War on Terror propaganda.[6] With the Western governments drumming bin Laden's culpability for 9/11 into everyone's heads (despite his own denials - as we have seen, only later very doubtful 'recordings' of someone purporting to be 'bin Laden' make his supposed claim on 9/11 explicit), the irony is that the motley Jihadist groups all now branded cells of 'Al Qaeda' actually *became* more powerful and began to play up to the myth being created for them. Even mainstream pundits accept that the world is now a less stable place since the War on Terror began, not a safer one, which would appear to be a self-defeating policy - unless this was the idea all along.

Doubting the origins of Al Qaeda is not to say that Islamic fundamentalism, which seeks to impose its repressive values on everything else through violent means, is not a problem in itself, but its prominence on the world stage has almost certainly been elevated to unimagined heights by the very powers that claim to oppose it. And so the West, for a while, had a perfect replacement for the vanished Soviet threat.

This said, more recent years have seen a renewed demonisation of Russia, especially since the Ossetia crisis with Georgia and Russia in 2008 - blamed by some on US interference - which delivered the traditional sabre-rattling from both East and West. The need to rebrand an old enemy may in itself have been an acknowledgement that the Al Qaeda 'threat' was outliving its usefulness a little too soon. With bin Laden never found and essentially inactive (indeed, reported dead by many sources, despite the occasional and very doubtful tapes purporting to be from him), a replacement collective foe was required and Vladimir Putin's (in whatever position of power) re-energised Russia seemed to fit the bill once more. Barack Obama's administration has been employing a softer rhetoric towards Russia of late, and how it will deal with the Eastern bloc remains to be seen at the time of writing, but powerful societies always need enemies, as George Orwell knew when he imagined the overarching and engineered threat of the subversive Albert Goldstein and his followers in his all-too prescient novel *Nineteen Eighty-Four*.

The depressing rise of what seemed to be a new Cold War appeared to be entirely desirable to the West during the latter George W Bush years. With US missiles planned for placement into Poland (under the guise of defending US allies from the likes of Iran) - a provocative act of a kind that would never be accepted if Russia was stationing missiles less than 100 miles from the US - and other previously Soviet states making new pacts with NATO rather than their old masters, it was inevitable that Russia would feel encircled and humiliated, rise to the bait and start to fight back. The irony of the US condemning Russia for invading a sovereign state during the Ossetia skirmish seemed lost on Bush and his cohorts. David Icke has long written of an Illuminati-engineered conflict with China that would help bring about the much planned for one-world government, but the last few years have seen Russia brought central stage instead to fulfil the role of Big Enemy. Wittingly or unwittingly, it began to play that role again perfectly, and began to freeze-out the West in return. However, the global financial crisis, and a new thawing from the Obama administration appears to have levelled or altered some of the Bush agendas, with Al Qaeda and the Taliban back on the main menu again through a renewed effort in Afghanistan, and a newly-beligerent North Korea offering itself once more in a convenient role as a clearly-identifiable enemy. But whatever occurs will be considered by many to be part of the ongoing NWO plan. None of this is to say that no action at all should be taken in the likes of Afghanistan if evidence suggested the need, but that evidence has been lacking so far and the motives remain shadowy or questionable at the very least [Chapter VII]. Meanwhile, Afghans and British troops are dying. The failure of the substantial military Afghan campaign so far, resulting instead in an actual *spread* of the conflict into Pakistan, suggests we are not being told the whole story.

The political fallout from the War on Terror and the subsequent muscle-flexing of the US and its allies, in Europe and the Middle East, has been pretty clear for all to see, then. But what of the effect on our everyday lives?

The other major casualty of this war has been the liberty of the individual, that rather annoying little feature, which is supposedly such a keystone of Western democracy. After 9/11, with dangerous terrorists now potentially on every corner, even in mainland America, that liberty could be neatly curtailed in the name of our protection - and it duly was.

The Patriot Act

The introduction of the entirely mis-named US 'Patriot Act' in the fear-stricken climate of post-9/11 America saw the abrupt removal of rights and freedoms that had been written into US law since 1776. The Bill of Rights, which underpinned the ground-breaking Declaration of Independence, is in many ways a perfect blueprint of how the balance between government and its citizens should be - at least, if it were lived to the letter. Americans have rightfully boasted of the bill's importance over the centuries, in its protection of the individual and the enshrining of basic civil liberties against governmental interference. We'll put aside here the belief of some conspiracy theorists that America was itself founded by the Illuminati as a step towards the New World Order. Either way, it's clear there were some genuinely positive aims in the original Bill of Rights, however warped things might have become. Yet in less than five years after 9/11, incredibly, that crucial bill saw many of its central pillars dissolved or sidelined in the name of protecting US citizens from terrorism. As John Whitehead of the Rutherford Institute writes:

'The Patriot Act violates at least six of the ten original amendments known as the Bill of Rights - the First, Fourth, Fifth, Sixth, Seventh and Eighth Amendments - and possibly the Thirteenth and Fourteenth as well.' [7]

Rushed through as an emergency measure within weeks of 9/11, and finally written into law in 2006, the Patriot Act was a convoluted acronym for 'Uniting and Strengthening America by Providing Appropriate Tools Required to Intercept and Obstruct Terrorism Act of 2001'. This, and the many further legislations that followed it, basically gave US authorities carte blanche to pry into all private communications without court orders, increase blanket surveillance of its citizens, restrict freedom of movement, limit the rights of protest and grant indefinite detention on any immigrant deemed a potential threat. In essence, it enabled the authorities to do whatever they wanted, anywhere, anytime, and allowed them to target anyone they suddenly considered dangerous or undesirable.

Guantanamo Bay in its 'heyday', with inmates bound in restrictive suits to prevent freedom of movement. The physical psychological pressures put on supposed terror suspects, together with dubious interrogation practices like 'waterboarding' (simulated drowning), were torture by any other name and a blot on a supposedly civilised society. The base is now closing, but to be replaced by what?

The outrages and injustices of Guantanamo Bay and the obscenity of 'Extraordinary Rendition', in which terror suspects are secretly flown to scruple-free countries to evade international laws on torture, are just two of the depressing abuses of these powers we have seen since the new Act was introduced.

So far it is prisoners of war and foreign - usually Islamic - suspects who have been the prime targets, but already the net is widening. Despite Barack Obama's move to close Guantanamo, it is doubtful that the powers behind the throne will allow much real change. Whatever the cosmetic adjustments, all the signs are that the (supposed) anti-terror strategies begun by the preceding administration remain firmly in place, as Obama's inaugural address (see *Introduction*) made clear.

As a result of the Patriot Act and its subsequent additions and amendments, many law-abiding US peace protesters and truth campaigners have unexpectedly found themselves at the wrong end of this all-too-flexible law, victimised and intimidated by an administration that, through fear of terrorism instilled in the masses, has been given the foundation of every tool of control it could possibly want. Most senators and congressmen never even read the Patriot Act bill before passing it. Who was likely to, presented with 342 pages full of dense legalese in small print? Fear, and/or the appeal of increased control, seemed to be the primary motivator in pushing the act through, not sensible consideration of its wider implications; something those behind it were presumably banking on.

The Death of Habeas Corpus

New and draconian restrictions on previously acceptable social activities and freedoms were not the sole domain of the US. In particular, the UK saw similar post-9/11 withdrawals of liberty, albeit implemented in a more surreptitious way. Perhaps realising that its population wouldn't sit still for such an overt measure as a British Patriot Act, in which people would realise too soon what was being taken away from them, the government introduced the same restrictions through a series of little legislations, altered small print and shifted goalposts. In this way, in the last few years the everyday liberties we once took for granted have been almost eradicated without too many noticing - yet.

When basic legalities that have protected human rights since the Dark Ages are suddenly taken away or twisted beyond all recognition, it is time to start worrying. The official acceptance of *habeas corpus* [literally, Latin for 'you must have the body'] has long protected citizens of civilised countries from tyranny and unlawful imprisonment by preventing authorities from detaining anyone without charge. It was being practiced in England from as early as the 12th century and was definitively enshrined in British law with the Habeas Corpus Act of 1679. Only in extreme times of national emergency or war has it been suspended. By calling the nebulous and seemingly unendable fight against terrorism a 'War', both the US and UK authorities have cleverly been able to continue to stretch and abuse habeas corpus beyond recognition when it suits them, effectively dispensing with it in any meaningful sense.

The attempted erosion of this crucial protection reached its culmination in the British House of Commons where (after much dubious tearoom lobbying and deal-making), as part of the 2008 Counter-Terrorism Bill, Parliament voted to extend to forty-two days the period in which terror suspects could be held without charge - an enormous increase on any previous benchmark. All of the many public protests and concerns over the potential abuses of this measure were ignored, and enough of the population, especially after the London bombings of 7th July 2005 (see below), were fearful enough not to resist the result too much. Only the House of Lords stepped in to prevent this part of the Bill becoming law, refreshingly defeating it by a huge 309 votes to 118.[8] Even a former head of MI5 (of all people), a former Lord Chief Justice and a former Metropolitan Police Commissioner felt it went too far - but the very intention to introduce such a law makes clear the direction in which the UK is heading. Climbing down, Home Secretary Jacqui Smith subsequently announced that the forty-two day proposal 'would be published in a separate draft Bill that could be voted on in the event of a national emergency'.

Before the Lords acted, reaction to the crow-barring in of the forty-two day rule was enough to trigger a by-election in the Yorkshire constituency of Haltemprice and Howden, when Conservative MP David Davis resigned in protest, supposedly in an effort to draw attention to this further assault on civil liberties. Any real issues were neatly sidelined in the media, however, when the main parties declined to put up any candidates, ensuring Davis' return to office but also taking any

David Icke prepares a presentation during the weeks of his standing in the Haltemprice and Howden by-election, supposedly called by David Davis MP to raise awareness of liberty issues. Only Icke's policies really tackled the issues, but the media ignored them.

serious focus away from the campaign. News reports concentrated less on the issues and more on the high financial cost of what they saw as a questionable election, focusing on its wackier and/ or celebrity candidates (including Miss Great Britain). Strangely, there was very little coverage of one of the few candidates who did put himself up for election on the issues, and not for the fun of the circus - one David Icke. Turning down the chance to have a chuckle about alien lizards and conspiracies, the media chose instead to largely ignore him - perhaps because what he said about the liberty issues during his (knowingly) doomed campaign made so much sense.

ID Cards Revisited

The most major and visible UK measure to be inspired by the War on Terror has been the launching of the biometric ID card scheme, due to be fully implemented in stages from 2010 onwards, together with the creation of the interactive National Identity Register (NIR), a central database that will include all personal details of each individual, including their DNA profile. Despite the tactical announcement in June 2009 (with Labour sagging badly in the polls) that it might not be made compulsory after all, the foment of extreme social disadvantages to *not* having an ID will doubtless achieve the same end. Liberty campaigners will be keenly watching the Conservative party's promise to withdraw the scheme in the (likely) event of their coming to power at the next general election, but the record of such policies being reversed in times past is not promising.

If a biometric ID scheme of any kind does arrive, however, it will have a huge potential for both direct misuse and simple misadventure by bureaucratic error. We have already explored in Chapter V the dark possibilities of the ID card scheme as it is currently being planned, together with its intended successor, the imbedded micro-chip. Suffice it to restate here that a system that has the potential to enable any authority anywhere to know of every movement, every transaction, every genetic detail and personal history of every individual alive is one that can only be operated by wise, well-intentioned and reliable bastions of total integrity. With corruption and intrigue endemic from the lowest ranks of local government to the higher echelons of Parliament (as regularly revealed by the likes of the otherwise conspiracy-denying *Private Eye* magazine)[9], it is clear from the most cursory application of the Truth Agenda that nowhere in the world do we have anything even approaching the kind of enlightened management necessary to manage a system of this kind. Placing such power into the hands of authorities that are showing disturbing tendencies towards fascistic control cannot be the sensible thing to do.

The ID scheme and NIR as they currently stand run the high risk of creating a system which, once it controls entrance to every workplace, shop, station or public building, and is necessary for every monetary transaction, will allow the elimination of any 'undesirables' from mainstream existence simply by selective electronic blocking or deletion. Life could be made terribly hard for any political or social heretics, who could soon find themselves living as down and outs if pushed to the fringes of society by the restriction of ID access.

If the reader is at this point feeling a little put out at the thought that anyone might ever come to think of them as an 'undesirable', it is worth considering that if the current trajectory is not checked, a time may come when the very act of reading a book like this could be considered a subversive act. We now live in a society where the likes of Walter Wolfgang, a loyal 82-year old Labour Party activist, found himself forcibly ejected by security heavies from the 2005 Labour conference for merely calling out the word 'nonsense' when confronted by then foreign secretary Jack Straw's weak justifications for the Iraq war. He was prevented from re-entering the hall under Terrorism Act powers, just one more misuse amongst many of these supposedly emergency legislations. It was recently revealed that of 1,271 arrests made under the same Act between 2007-2008, only 73 were actually for suspected terror offences.[10]

Other abuses of terror laws include new rules under Section 76 of the 2009 Counter Terrorism Act that, if implemented to their fullest, could effectively outlaw public photography of police activities (neatly making any visual evidence of police corruption or violence inadmissible in court) and indeed restrict the use of cameras in many places.[11] Train and plane-spotters have already found themselves targeted as possible criminals under existing anti-terrorism laws, and even innocent sight-seers in London have found themselves being taken in for questioning. The irony is that while the civilian use of cameras becomes more restricted, the presence of those installed by authorities grows.

The signs are, especially in the UK, that *all* of us are already held to be potential undesirables, as the myriad of cameras and other surveillance devices that have infested our streets in the last decade testify. With new measures which effectively sanction the automatic and sustained monitoring (without the need to apply for warrants) of all our e-mail activity, web surfing and telephone calls coming into being in both the US and UK as this book is being written, even the sanctity of our homes, personal interests and communications is no longer respected. Every one of us is now routinely treated as a potential criminal - and privacy has become a thing of the past.

The Surveillance Society

It is a fact that mainland Britain now has more security cameras than any other country in the world (although the US is fast catching up), with an estimated four and a half million CCTV cameras in operation - one for every fourteen people. With these intrusive eyes perched over nearly every high street, every major road and every shopping centre, as well as numerous private premises, it is estimated that an average trip outside our houses sees us being captured on camera around 300 times. But why?

We are told, continually, that these cameras are there for our protection - largely from crime and terrorism. Yet all studies thus far have shown that whilst these images may help identify some faces after an event, there is no evidence at all that CCTV prevents crime or increases our safety. ABC News journalist Marcus Baram writes:

'According to a British Home Office review of dozens of studies analysing the cameras' value at reducing crime, half showed a negative or negligible effect and the other half showed a negligible decrease of 4 percent at most. Researchers found that crime in Glasgow, Scotland, actually increased by 9 percent after cameras were installed there.' [12]

So the central, oft-repeated claim that our day to day privacy is only being violated for our own good is not supported by the evidence gathered by the very authorities who are creating this surveillance state.

So we must look for other explanations to make sense of why our rulers feel they need to keep such close tabs on their own citizens. George Orwell reached his own fairly clear conclusions as to why this might happen way back in 1948, and now that this nightmare vision has become reality (including the cameras that can shout instructions from faceless security teams, which are currently being installed in some public places) we must ask ourselves some very stiff questions about the motives of those in charge.

Surveillance cameras are now a common sight across the world, but Britain has more of them than any other country - and this despite statistical evidence that they do not prevent crime. So what are they really for?

The UK has always had an element of the 'nanny state' in its make-up, its ruling class feeling that it knows better than its apparently plebeian citizens what is best for them, but with the War on Terror propelling it, and entirely disproportionate fear of terrorism and crime being pushed on us almost daily through media manipulation and government policies, the control agenda is now seriously... out of control.

Outcries over plans to set up a British centralised database to keep records of all e-mails, Internet visits and phone calls did at least result in another government climbdown in 2009, but then-Home Secretary Jacqui Smith's subsequent 'request' to all communications firms to keep records of all such contacts, to be made available to authorities, established the same concept by stealth.[13] Targeting suspected criminals or terrorists by obtaining court orders to allow surveillance of individuals is one thing - blanket monitoring of all citizens is quite another. Now anyone even slightly suspected of being a 'danger' to society may unwittingly find themselves under the microscope. But who gets to decide who and what is dangerous? We may believe ourselves to be law-abiding and undeserving of state suspicion, but what if the state thinks otherwise? Those authorities calling the shots at the moment have hardly proved themselves fair or trustworthy thus far.

Policing Cyberspace

The world of electronic communications has been a gift to those who wish to keep an eye on who we all are. To reiterate, in addition to knowing who we are in contact with and when, the new surveillance regime means that every website we look at, and the subject of every Google search we make, will now be available to government databases, with profiles of each individual gradually being drawn up and documented. Reading books instead will not be a solution; all library records must now also be routinely shared with authorities, while titles ordered from Internet retailers or bought on credit or debit cards will be known from the electronic records. Many people may not realise that our shopping habits are already closely monitored, through records of credit card transactions or use of loyalty cards, which is how personalised special offers can be so specifically targeted (by Internet retailers in particular). Now our everyday habits, interests and beliefs are being equally profiled. Soon it will become impossible to live one's truth without its nature being known by a very real Big Brother.

The freedom of speech engendered by the unexpected advent of the Internet in the late 1980s is seen by some as a lifeline against any totalitarian force that would prevent us speaking our minds; indeed 'cyberspace' has been a phenomenal opportunity for the airing of truth and liberty issues. But it may prove to be a very short-lived shaft of light if current legislation and reforms of the Net being proposed go ahead. Aware that some kind of genie of liberation was released from the bottle by the availability of unfettered communication, there is every indication that the powers that be are trying to push it back in again.

Current plans will eventually bring the Internet under new regulations, which could see websites treated the same way as television stations. If this were to go ahead, a paid licence would be needed to operate a website, which would have to follow strict guidelines about content and form.[14] This could put non-profit-making hobbyist or campaigning web platforms out of the reach of the average person. Wading through layers of bureaucracy and paying fees just to put up a new piece about flower-arranging or collectable kettles could make running a site unviable for many, leaving only major commercial web pages up and running. In a country where the right to mount even street protests is becoming harder by the day, having to pass every new entry for a truth website or simple blog through the regulatory channels to see what is permissible would pretty much see the end of the Net as a campaigning tool. In an increasingly repressive system, the expression of views seen as merely fringe annoyances today could become major heresy tomorrow. More than one US neo-conservative has expounded the - inexplicable and entirely untrue - view that Internet truth forums that promote revisionist views and 'outrageous conspiracy theories' foster and encourage 'terrorism', and these warped characters have done little to conceal their aims to shut down the Net as we know it today.

The cleverness of the repressive Net regulations being proposed would be that there wouldn't be one key moment where any particular views would be banned or restricted - causing instant adverse reaction. Instead, the same effect would be quietly achieved with the gradual introduction of apparently beneficial 'improvements', the pill sugared by promises of a faster and easier-to-use system, dubbed 'Internet 2' by some. There would reside all the new licensed and regulated sites - by default, largely commercial ones - with slick, flashy and fully interactive facilities, leaving the old Internet looking slow, complex and old-fashioned by comparison and deemed to be full of the old dross, criminal porn and extremist elements that people would be encouraged to think was all that was there, eventually seeing its end.

It is not just at the webmaster end that the way we use the Internet could change. Another proposal already being pioneered by servers in Canada is that website accessibility could be regulated like satellite TV channels are today. Instead of free access to any website anywhere, surfers would be encouraged to sign up for 'packages' of the sites they already liked to use. Benefits and good hosting deals would be offered to make it worthwhile. Viewing any sites outside of those signed-up for would see extra charges of a much higher tariff, or they would simply not be accessible, depending on which package the viewer chooses. In this way, again rather cleverly, the freedom to seek out or accidentally discover little sites with unexpectedly astonishing or hard-to-get information would be greatly curtailed. In the last few years, we have already seen Google agree to block certain human rights websites so as to be able to operate in China (with similar deals struck in other restrictive countries). Now the same philosophy of selective omission is starting to be applied in the West, but using carrots, not sticks.

The constant media harassment of the Internet, so often characterised entirely disproportionately as nothing more than a playground for paedophiles and Jihadist groups, is helping to create the climate of fear that will strangle the freedom of the Internet. Any form of communication is open to abuse from a minority, and there is no question that there have been some abuses - but in the eyes of many the entirely beneficial and liberating effect of people being able to express their honest opinions about global events and voice concerns about those running our lives has made living with the relatively few violations of good sense and humanity a necessary price.

Caution is advised against the mob-mentality so often stimulated in the tabloid press against the Internet.   Given the media's often partisan and complicit role in peddling myths and half-truths (especially in regard to 9/11 and other questionable authorised versions of big events), only the Net has allowed a public voice to question the propaganda, and it has been a crucial tool of liberation in times of growing oppression. That window of free speech is in danger of closing all-too-soon and it should be used to its fullest while it still can be, to fight for its continued existence as a platform for all, not just the sanitised few.

But, some may say here, what about the real threat from terrorism and crime? Surely it cannot all be false-flag action and obfuscation? Do we not need at least some of these privacy intrusions and information filters to protect us all?

Dealing With Real Threats

A trap fallen into by some conspiracy theorists is to assume that *every* terrorist act or political shenanigan must be a fabricated step towards an evil New World Order. But this perhaps assumes too much power on the part of those who might be behind such plans, as we shall explore more in the last chapters. There is evidence that there are squabbling factions even amongst those who might be pulling the global strings - and therefore unpredictable elements at large in the world. There is also basic human nature to contend with, and terrorism is something that is going to arise in particular circumstances at certain times without the impetus of any background manipulation. So how do we deal with genuine threats without shutting down basic human liberties?

Especially in the UK, the War on Terror has revealed a fundamental philosophical shift in how authority deals with those who might harm or disrupt us (indicating that there may well be a wider plan at work). Those who lived through the 1970s and 1980s will remember the appalling campaign of terror operated by the IRA and opposing outfits from Northern Ireland. It is interesting to note that whilst there were some

The scar caused by the bomb planted by the IRA at the Grand Hotel, Brighton, on 12th October 1984. The attempt to wipe out Margaret Thatcher and her cabinet failed - but came very close. Despite this and other audacious attacks during the IRA campaign, the country did not close itself down into the fear-bound siege mentality that has been fostered under the War on Terror.

restrictions of movement in mainland Britain during those times, and checking of bags in city department stores and public places (especially after the Harrods bomb of 1983), there was *not* that sense of all-pervading fear that has been placed on us since 9/11 and, specifically in the UK, '7/7'. An air of sensible caution has been replaced by something grimmer and more socially debilitating this time around, as we appear to be encouraged to allow fear to rule our lives. During the IRA campaign, there was outrage at the killings and injuries that took place, but also a sense of common resistance, of refusing to give in to the coercive tactics of an extremist minority. Even when the British government was targeted with the Brighton bomb of 1984, which nearly assassinated Margaret Thatcher in her conference hotel, British society did not lock itself into a fearful siege mentality, where everyday freedoms were dispensed with to deal with the evil of the few. In the 'blitz-spirit', necessary care and security was taken, but life and the spirit of liberty went on. Why should that not be the case now?

Even if we dispense with the inside-job suspicions for a moment and take 9/11 at face value, what we have done by allowing the War on Terror to dominate Western life since is to capitulate to the intentions of the minority threats that genuinely do exist. By indulging in the very climate of terror they require, we hand our power over. There is a balance to be struck between common-sense measures and fear-based restriction, but we are not achieving the right balance at the moment, either because society is going through a dark night of the soul, or because it doesn't suit some murkier purpose.

There will always be people who will want to hurt or kill for some fanatical cause. But how common these fanatics are is questionable. Since the IRA ended its attacks, the 7/7 bombings have been the only major mainland incident in Britain. Since 9/11, thus far, the US has remained free from such assaults. Despite the occasional atrocity around the world, we seem to be much safer than we are told. Yet we are continually given the impression that killer terrorists are on every corner, and that only secret intelligence squads and complex police operations, with all their new surveillance powers, keep us protected. The evidence for this is very often unclear, however, and explanations oddly elusive. Public 'Terror Alert' scales go up and down in an abstract dance of mysterious figures, tanks suddenly appear outside airports and then vanish again for no apparent reason, and politicians talk of raised threats and then never mention them again.[15] Bomb plots and discoveries of new 'terrorist cells' make headlines for a few days, and then melt away with no explanation and few apologies for the consternation caused. A report in May 2009 concluded that just one in eight terror arrests ever results in a conviction.[16] If it is true that we are kept cushioned from the real threats of terrorism by undercover intelligence, the low conviction rate is a major anomaly, unless people are being quietly executed outside of the law. But then why shout things to the media about new 'plots' so loudly before being sure - and when that intelligence so often appears to be wrong? It is almost as if someone does want us to be kept in a state of fear.

When it looks like we might be relaxing again about security and control, something always seems to be activated or re-inflated to crank up the alarm again. Hence widely publicised plots involving aeroplanes being blown out of the sky using water or baby-milk containers as bomb-making equipment mean we now queue even longer at airports and put up with cold intimidation that would never otherwise be accepted. As well as having obviously harmless containers taken away from us to join the vats of assault-potential household objects, mothers are asked to take sips of their own bottled breast milk to prove its harmlessness or children are forced to take off their shoes. Precautions of some kind are necessary - without question - but a sensible balance has to be struck and the petrified society that has now been created is no longer operating from a centred place of wisdom.

7/7 Anomalies

When real terror attacks do occur, of course, such as the bombings on 7th July 2005, which exploded three underground trains and a bus in London, killing 52 people and injuring hundreds, we naturally fear for the safety of ourselves and our loved ones.

However, hard though it is to voice in the UK, it's worth mentioning that even here there are a number of strange anomalies, which have called the origins of this event into question from various truthseekers (crudely 'debunked' as ever by the always-reliable BBC *Conspiracy Files* series in 2009), who have once again accused secret forces of background involvement. It seems likely from investigations that Islamic fundamentalists were involved in the attacks, but doubters base their allegations on a series of errors and contradictions in the official story surrounding the commuter trains that were supposedly caught by the bombers on their way to London, suspicious changes made several times to the official narrative, lack of clear CCTV evidence - and the nature of the explosions themselves.[17] Some witnesses reported blasts seemingly coming up from *beneath* the trains, rather than from the claimed rucksacks, and photographic evidence of the aftermath seems to support this. Strangest of all is the fact that Peter Power, a supposedly independent 'crisis management specialist' and security expert, claimed that his firm, Visor Consultants, was operating a terror alert rehearsal at the *very times and very places where the real attacks occurred*. Broadcast on BBC Radio 5 Live's *Drivetime* programme on the day of the events, the following comments from Power are worth relating:

POWER: ...at half-past nine this morning we were actually running an exercise for, er, over, a company of over a thousand people in London based on simultaneous bombs going off precisely at the railway stations where it happened this morning, so I still have the hairs on the back of my neck standing upright!

PETER ALLEN (DJ): To get this quite straight, you were running an exercise to see how you would cope with this and it happened while you were running the exercise?

POWER: Precisely, and it was, er, about half-past nine this morning, we planned this for a company and for obvious reasons I don't want to reveal their name but they're listening and they'll know it. And we had a room full of crisis managers for the first time they'd met and so within five minutes we made a pretty rapid decision, 'this is the real one' and so we went through the correct drills of activating crisis management procedures to jump from 'slow time' to 'quick time' thinking and so on.[18]

Terrified passengers escape from a smoke-filled London tube train on the day of the 7/7 bombings. But with even these events, strange anomalies and unlikely 'coincidences' have presented themselves.

So, just as with 9/11, we are asked to accept that the events of 7/7, by complete coincidence, unfolded simultaneously with a drill that posited almost exactly the same scenario, at the same places. Did the bombers somehow know about the 'exercise' taking place that day, and choose to align their attack with it as some kind of cover? If so, how did they know of the terror rehearsal without inside information or help? Did the individuals involved simply believe they were taking part in an exercise, only to discover too late that their rucksack bombs were real? (This would have resonance with Emad Salem being given real explosives instead of dummies in the alleged FBI set-up of the 1993 World Trade Center truck bomb - page 143) The videos we have been shown of some of the alleged 7/7 bombers speaking to camera suggest real martyrdom intentions, but there could be more to the story. Or was the whole thing instigated by black op intelligences, using patsies and terror drills to create maximum confusion (as on 9/11, it would seem), which would make later attempts at getting to the truth almost impossible?

Only the bus in Tavistock Square doesn't seem to fit with the exercise locations - allegedly the terrorist there had intended to target the nearest underground station, but changed his plan, detonating the bomb nearly an hour after the other explosions. One claimed, if controversial, eye-witness account of what happened on the bus is very at odds with the official version, with talk of it being deliberately 'diverted' into the Square by two unmarked cars, as if it were being set up in some way.[19]

Were the circumstances surrounding 7/7 and the exercises truly just a bizarre coincidence? The Truth Agenda requires a clustering of anomalies to reveal deeper layers of deception beneath, and 7/7 is certainly far less of a clear-cut case than 9/11, with most of its events having happened deep underground and off-camera. But the odds against coincidence in the terror drill scenario alone suggest something is not quite right. As with Building Seven on 9/11, the official response to this aspect of the events has been to completely ignore it, as if Peter Power never made his very clear statements. Power himself later played down his own comments, making the exercises sound much vaguer, despite researchers having since verified that they certainly *were* taking place that day.

Needless to say, the anomalies (and there are many more - see *Appendix 2*) and the continued refusal of the government to launch a full independent public enquiry has left some truthseekers very doubtful about the events of 7/7.

Regardless of the reality, 7/7 was undoubtedly used to bring home to the British public that without the War on Terror and its necessary homeland security restrictions on life and liberty, more of this kind of thing might occur. Spain had already received its own reminder when commuter trains in Madrid were hideously exploded in March 2004. Blamed loosely on Al Qaeda, those attacks seemed intended (though unsuccessfully) to restore a wavering Spanish public to supporting their government's involvement in the Afghanistan and Iraq campaigns. Likewise, events in New York seemed far away to some in the UK, but bombs in London helped bring them 'on message' and encouraged yet more suspicion of the Muslim world, creating further division and social unrest. Not for nothing, perhaps, was 7/7 described several times in the media as 'the British 9/11'.

The 7/7 bombings and the police shooting of an innocent man in the terror hysteria that followed created an intense climate of fear for commuters and visitors to London - yet life went on. How much are we prepared to sacrifice for a safety we can never in any case guarantee?

The police's killing of Jean Charles de Menezes, mistaken for a potential suicide bomber on the London Underground and shot in the head at point-blank range less than two weeks after 7/7, despite being entirely innocent, sent out a further message. The police marksmen claimed that they shouted a warning to de Menezes, and that he advanced 'aggressively' towards them before they opened fire. Despite the fact that not one witness who appeared at the subsequent inquest verified this claim (all denied that de Menezes was given a warning or that he approached the police first) - which was also rejected by the jury - the Crown Prosecution Service, in a mockery of justice, refused to allow a verdict of unlawful killing, forcing the return of an 'open' verdict instead. Outraged protests from the jury and de Menezes' family failed to make a difference.[20]

With this edict, it was made quite clear to the population that anything which occurred in the name of anti-terrorism was above the law and not to be questioned, even if unfortunate civilians had their brains blown out in the process. Anyone concluding from any this that we were now definitively living in a 'police state' was, of course, merely misguided. Similarly, the global over-use of the control regime's dangerous new toy, the Taser stun gun, has resulted in the unnecessary 'accidental' deaths of an increasing number of unarmed civilians with apparently weak constitutions - but these regrettable incidents also reinforce a warning; mess with the authorities and this could be you.[21]

The control state's new weapon of choice, the Taser gun (seen here brandished by a US soldier). Supposedly a 'safe' stun-gun, the high charge electrical shocks administered by Tasers have now killed many people around the world. Their supposedly 'safe' status has encouraged a wide over-use of the gun, often in totally inappropriate situations, against unarmed civilians or non-threatening protestors.

A Difficult Choice

We have to make a choice. Terrorism, false-flag or genuine, is something we have to deal with. Some might argue that it makes no difference - it's real, wherever it comes from, and we have to protect ourselves. But what we give away to ensure that protection has to be thought about very carefully. If this is truly a war on terror, then that war has also to be fought philosophically and in a spirit of defiance. Fundamentalism that kills, be it Muslim, Hindu, Christian, Zionist, or whatever creed of justification, must be challenged and discouraged. But the terrorists win when we change our whole style of life to accommodate them. How far do we want to go down that path? At what point do we decide we must take a risk to preserve our freedom?

We can openly walk down our streets and into shops and offices and say we will take a calculated risk while doing so, for the sake of living the liberty of which the West so often boasts - or we can choose ID cards, embedded microchips, more security guards and metal-detectors, more cameras and surveillance of our private lives, to save us from religious fanatics. (On one level, of course, we have already seen in Chapter IV that some Western countries are effectively being run by religious fundamentalists.) We can choose to show contempt for the minority of criminals that demonstrate no respect for life and property, and hold our heads up high and live positive lives in the hope that positive thought proliferates (and it does - see Chapter XIV) - or we can cave into the fear continually drummed into us by tabloids and television that knife crime and muggings are growing by the day (statistically ambiguous, despite event clusters in certain areas and much increased news *coverage*).[22] Then we demand detection equipment at the doorways of shops and schools and stations, and build our whole lives around trepidation and negativity. Already, some live cowering behind their front doors, scared to emerge. We can take wise precautions to protect our children and loved ones, but allow them to live freely and openly and

Watching us watching them. Police filming the crowds at Brighton's annual Gay Pride parade - though from the surveillance and strong security presence one might think it was a protest march rather than a celebration. The more we collectively fear, the more we will be controlled - and allow ourselves to be controlled.

try to build a world where dire concerns are not so necessary - or we can buy into the terror-fuelled myth spread by endless headlines on the likes of poor Madeline McCann, one little girl sadly lost, that all our children are in danger and that paedophiles and killers lurk in every park and Internet chatroom. By doing this we inadvertently embrace the 'safety' that will come with the microchipping schemes already being pioneered, and keep our children behind closed doors; never again will people be lost, but never again will they be truly free either.

It's all a question of where we choose to draw the line. It is a collective decision that has more power than perhaps we know, as we shall see. What price our safety and security? If we decide to live in darkness and alarm, at the expense of all else, protected but effectively imprisoned in a police state, darkness and alarm is what we shall have. But is that really all we want?

Fear must not be given into, or it takes over. Positive thinking is a tangible and forceful power as we shall see, not just a New Age concept. Yet fear seems to be the thing most widely encouraged in our current society, and not solely residing within the realms of crime and terror.

THE TRUTH AGENDA: *The War on Terror has been one of the greatest coups on human liberty ever staged. In the name of our protection, fundamental freedoms have been eroded or taken away, leaving us prone to unhealthy state intervention or surveillance. False-flag terrorism to create states of fear is something with a long history and still seems to be occurring now. But whether the terror and crime we have to deal with is real or false, it is clear that fear of it is being used to control us. Striking the right balance between sensible precautions and a self-defeating climate of alarm is the only way to break free of this trap - which means we must not fall prey to the manipulative fear currently being foisted on us.*

Modern technology has given us many wonderful things... but are we being made too reliant on pharmaceuticals and additives, while natural alternatives are being taken away from us..?

X   CAGING THE HUMAN SPIRIT

With growing fear engendered by terrorism and crime, other factors in our society also seem geared to control and suppress the human spirit through disproportionate health and safety regulations, the abuse of political correctness and burgeoning restrictions on personal health choices, which enslave us to pharmaceutical solutions and weaken our immunity. Is this a further policy being operated to prevent us from stepping into our true power as human beings?

The Bonds of Health and Safety

The current erosion of liberties in our day to day lives seems to be accompanied by another dimension to the control agenda; a crushing of the human spirit, a dampening of our essentially adventurous natures. Under a system that seems to prefer us nicely contained, harmlessly shored up behind our front doors, hypnotised each night by soaps, game shows and electronic recreation, or depressed into inaction by an endless parade of negative news, the person who stands up and shines, takes a risk or merely ventures out in some proactive way, seems frowned upon. No great laws are required to generate this climate; a simple reliance on concerned jobsworths excited by the minutiae of small print can achieve the same thing.

Yet again for our protection, we are told, the ever-growing catalogue of health and safety rules, for example, increasingly suppress the harmless everyday activities we once took for granted, watering some of them down to near-pointlessness. Life itself is a risk, and sometimes unfortunate accidents will occur, but taking a risk of any kind is a diminishing option in a system that seems unable to bear anyone taking responsibility for themselves; witness the ever-shrinking equipment at children's playgrounds, all thrills removed, all adventure neutered. No-one would want to see a child harmed, but in an ever-more litigious world the disproportionate reduction would seem to have more to do with council fears of legal action than genuine concern for health, as most 'risk assessment' decisions do. Several studies have shown that a surfeit of risk-reduction actually damages child development.[1]

Woods and parks that might once have been packed with adventuring kids on sunny days are already now often deserted, with children absorbed in electronic worlds instead, or grounded by parental fear sparked by tabloid paedophile hysteria. Now fear of litigation has added to the disconnection with the outside world, with skateboard parks and adventure playgrounds suddenly removed in the middle of the night in some towns, beyond the vision of those who might protest. Carried out without discussion or local consultation, these decisions are made by the same authorities who then spend thousands trying to control hooligans at a loose end. But 'Health and Safety' must prevail, and the human spirit must acquiesce.

Thus, beyond the obvious common sense codes of practice offered to the public, come edicts of the absurd that encroach by the day on normal folk. As a prolific lecturer, this author can testify to the growing number of halls and venues where organisers are no longer permitted to boil kettles without official caterers being present, or handbags cannot be kept under seats. Nearly every week the news is full of examples of Health and Safety banning the likes of pencil cases from schools (because they might contain sharp objects) or the removal of goalposts from village greens (because people might run into them and hurt themselves). Invent a bizarre example and it will probably be a reality somewhere. These are the small-minded restrictions that people begin to rebel against, because it credits them with no intelligence and takes away all self-responsibility. If society is increasingly acting in a childish way, perhaps we shouldn't be surprised when even senior citizens are treated like irresponsible children. But is this crushing of the spirit accident - or design? Some truthseekers believe the latter.

Some of the supposed health and safety rules are nothing more than misinterpretations by petty-minded small-time authorities (often the risk-assessors rather than the H&S officers), intent on controlling others, as they themselves are unwittingly being controlled. But there are plenty of demonstrably insane rules officially being imposed on things that previously ran without fuss, which appear to make no sense beyond being there to outrage the soul and dull the independent spirit. It can carry a high financial burden for self-employed traders, for instance - who may have traded happily and successfully for years - to get newly required Health and Safety certificates in the UK. Thus many independent electricians and plumbers are going into bankruptcy (especially in the current economic downturn) because the several-thousand pound licences or certificates of the obvious they now need to trade are beyond their means. To get the 'cowboys', the law is wiping out the indians at the same time. It is almost as if being self-employed - and therefore less dependent on more easily-regulated bigger companies - is being discouraged in today's society, which prefers a safer hive mentality, not independence.

All this has been exacerbated - created? - by the tendency to treat people as statistics, not individual souls with feelings. The misplaced obsession with targets, ratings and administration (especially in the UK) has resulted in a culture where standards are too often twisted or 'dumbed down' to get students through exams, viewers to tune in, staff into the right category or patients through the hospital system (leaving too many reports each year of people suffering in their own filth while nurses prioritise the tasks that meet targets - instead of meeting human needs).

This reductionist approach to life can only generate distancing and dysfunction in society, which some believe is a key part of the elite plan. If the quality of education, social sophistication and human care had provably risen with all the mountains of form-filling, these fears could perhaps be lightly dismissed, but the opposite appears to be true.

Some readers may suspect too much paranoia here, especially those who struggle with the notion that our authorities may not have our best interests at heart. Almost certainly, some repressive regulations are simply good intentions gone too far. However, a look at the wider picture does begin to raise questions as to whether our health and safety really is the primary concern of a system that reduces us to numbers, or whether it actually suits those who may have fascistic plans for the world for people to be enslaved by red tape and restrictions in every stratum of life. For if our good health is genuinely the main focus of the rules and regulations that bind us, some very strange decisions are being made that seem to promote the opposite outcome.

The Battle for Natural Health

In recent decades, one of the largest growth areas in health-care has been the awareness that natural supplements and 'complementary' medicine can have a highly positive influence on our well-being and resistance to disease. Millions testify as to their effectiveness, and have been liberated from reliance on sometimes harmful pharmaceutical solutions. Often the successful results speak for themselves.

One might imagine governments concerned for our health and safety would welcome this development, with its plainly beneficial effects. Instead, there has been a sustained attack on the natural health industry courtesy of a self-elected mainstream body of intellectuals who have declared it quackery unworthy of scientific respect. Each month, the media loudly trumpets another supposedly scientific study that discounts any meaningful results from a predictable range of targets, usually high-dose vitamins, health supplements, homeopathy, or all manner of alternative therapies, sneered at in superior tones. Yet the non-effectiveness of many conventional medicines (astonishingly, only a minority of pharmaceutical products can be scientifically proven to be effective) and their many unfortunate 'side' effects seem not to fill pages of newspapers and minutes of air-time to the same degree. Few doubt the important and efficacious role mainstream medicine plays in our civilisation, but too many of its supporters seem blind to its faults, and are over-fervent in their censorship of alternative methods.

Scientific verification of areas that seem to fall outside of straightforward cause and effect is inevitably going to be controversial, and there is no reason why science shouldn't mount investigations into natural health claims. But the strong impression given with such studies is that a negative outcome is anticipated from the outset - which, by definition, is an unscientific approach. This is similar to the analyses of Moon rock being flawed by the pre-experiment assumption that it *is* Moon rock in the first place [Chapter VI]. If science doesn't find anything within the usually very narrow parameters it has set for itself, the phenomenon under investigation is declared as non-existent - or fraudulent. Sometimes, as with crop circles (or psi investigation - Chapter XIV), when peer-review science does begin to support the veracity of an unusual area it can suddenly find itself dismissed as 'fringe', and qualified academics are unexpectedly marginalised by the wider scientific community. Given the noted observation in quantum physics that the experimenter is somehow inextricably entangled with the outcome of the experiment itself, perhaps unsurprisingly no supportive results on natural health are ever produced by scientists of a sceptical mindset - and most mainstream tests are inevitably carried out by such people. The fact remains, however, that many seem to benefit from natural health practices, and double-blind tests carried out by more open-minded investigators (admittedly fewer, largely because they don't receive the same kind of commercial funding as the doubters) *do* show supportive results.[2]

Robert Verkerk of the Alliance for Natural Health, just one of several campaigners who has been fighting new EU legislation, which threatens to hugely reduce the number of high-dose vitamins and natural supplements available to the public, courtesy of the Codex Alimentarius food safety body.

Sceptics assert that any positive effects of non-conventional practices are merely the placebo effect in action (omitting to address the interesting successes reported on animals - and babies - which presumably fall outside this explanation). This ignores the fact that official medicine itself often operates on the placebo principle, as many doctors will confirm. And even *if* the placebo effect is all that is going on with complementary health, it is still *an* effect with a positive outcome. Yet every effort is seemingly being made to stamp out alternative medicine and naturally advantageous products.

There has been a massive rise in obesity and heart disease in our increasingly sedentary Western culture. With so many addicted to junk food and force-fed deadly additives such as the sweetener aspartame, which laces many popular drinks and foodstuffs,[3] the encouragement of healthy diets and good eating from the likes of TV chef Jamie Oliver receives much publicity and gets lip-service support from the UK government. Yet, paradoxically, those who believe, based on experience and evidence, that certain high-dose vitamins or natural supplements can also make a huge difference to health and well-being, are about to be penalised by new European directives, courtesy of the Codex Alimentarius, a long-established food safety think-tank founded in 1963 as part of the Food and Agriculture Organisation of the UN, and connected to the World Health Organisation. These rules will effectively remove the right to choose this path of dietary care, and they will also find their way into US law before too long. Here is how the Alliance for Natural Health, which has been valiantly fighting the Codex Alimentarius, sums up the new proposals:

The EU framework starts to really bite between 2010 and 2011 when - unless pro-natural health interests like us can continue to positively influence the process - we could see:

i) Massive restrictions on allowed ingredients, including vitamin and mineral forms, as well as botanicals
ii) Massive restrictions on maximum permitted doses of vitamins and minerals
iii) Massive restrictions on what can be said about any product with beneficial properties
iv) Imposition of pharmaceutical-type standards, making it difficult for many truly natural products to comply [4]

What this means is that if the current Codex/EU proposals are implemented, the quantity of vitamins and supplements that can legally be bought and consumed will be hugely reduced, to the point where taking the permissible amounts will be almost pointless. Full implementation is expected by 2013. The advertising of any genuine benefits to these items will also become illegal unless proven by clinical trials (bringing us back to the problem of sceptical experimenters), while even innocuous herbal remedies (such as garlic and mint) could be classified as drugs if promoted as being for health purposes. The reason for these restrictions? - to 'protect' (as ever) the public from the potential harm of natural products, the benefits of which have not, in the eyes of Codex, been scientifically verified. The fact that many of these products and substances have been used harmlessly for generations and that they involve far fewer chemical and toxic elements than most conventional pharmaceuticals (which, statistically, are far more provably harmful) seems not to count. Quite astonishing figures show that each year in the USA alone around *180,000* people die due to unexpected effects of normal medication, over-prescription or incorrect diagnosis by doctors, making these the main annual causes of death in the US - yet no outcry demands the kind of draconian measures being proposed for natural medicine, which can barely be shown to have killed anyone in its long history.[5]

There are double standards being employed here. While taking away the easy accessibility of natural health products, Codex is at the same time also weakening the rules on organic food (making it permissible to have certain amounts of non-organic ingredients included in products labelled as organic), relaxing restrictions on genetically modified constituents (which will no longer have to be indicated when included in ingredient lists), permitting higher pesticide residues in vegetable produce, and encouraging irradiation for preservative purposes. How can an authoritative body, which claims to have our health interests at heart, support such policies when so many people have expressed serious concerns over the areas in question? When aspartame is accepted as a foodstuff, but garlic is restricted as a drug, we will truly enter twisted realms.

Other inconsistent health policies affect our lives in ways that many believe are directly sinister. For instance, growing global imposition of the highly debatable fluoridation of drinking water - the very stuff of life - presupposes dental benefits that have been challenged even by some mainstream science studies (which have suggested *detrimental* effects in some experiments), but still it continues. Some believe this is yet another attempt to poison and suppress our natural immune systems, with fluoride being entirely alien to the human constitution.[6] Yet natural products, which have a long history of positive influence and very few downsides, are being withdrawn. Once again the power of choice and our right to take even small risks is being taken away by faceless quangos, which have decided on our behalf what is good for us and what is not. This is not to say that *no* protective measures should be taken to ensure our food and supplements are safe and sensibly regulated, but the current measures go much too far into draconian - and entirely contradictory - realms. Campaigners like Scott Tips, Ian R Crane, Robert Verkerk and Philip Day are doing sterling work in trying to raise public awareness and to prevent the Codex-driven agenda from being embedded into US, EU and national law (and people are encouraged to support them - see *Appendix 2*), but time is running short.

The irony is that the mainstream scientists branding natural health products and alternative medicine as potentially dangerous are often the same ones who dismiss both as meaningless nonsense. Some object on the grounds that alternative health care might prevent patients from seeking the 'proper' (i.e. pharmaceutical) attention that they may also need, but others contend merely on the basis that fringe methods, in their eyes, simply don't work, mortally offended at what they see as bad science. Yet the attempt to protect us from their possible harm (high-dose vitamins have been especially lambasted in these areas) is surely a tacit acknowledgement that these practices might have a real effect of some kind after all - or why try to stop them?

What this is truly all about, as far as many observers are concerned, is protecting the interests of the huge pharmaceutical and food industries, which do not benefit from us being healthy. Those who feel this view is too cynical might like to consider that official Codex Alimentarius publicity openly acknowledges that all its meetings (often large conferences) are attended by representatives with 'transnational corporation interests'. Conspiracy die-hards contend that neither does it suit the wider powers to have a healthy and energetic population, and that the erosion of our personal health choices is yet another part of the programme to weaken humanity into submission.

DIPHTHERIA
is deadly-

IMMUNISATION
is the
safeguard

ASK AT YOUR
LOCAL COUNCIL
OFFICES
OR
WELFARE CENTRE

Issued by the Ministry of Health
and the
Central Council for Health Education

US post-war poster promoting the happy benefits of vaccination. Yet if the practice is as safe and effective as advertised, why after all this time are so many people still concerned about possible side effects? Some even question the entire science behind immunisation. Why are these arguments not yet settled?

Immunisation Choices

With what we put into our mouths being regulated by strong-arm tactics, what we put into our bloodstream is increasingly dictated in the same way. The choice as to whether to vaccinate or not is rapidly being eroded, with countries like Australia and some states of the USA already having made it effectively compulsory for most groups. Now the UK is heading towards a mandatory MMR programme.[7] Yet this is occurring despite many concerns over the reliability of the very science of immunisation, and the serious side-effects which have been alleged to occur. It is certainly a fact that nearly all diseases supposedly eradicated by vaccination can be shown to have already been on a steep decline before its introduction, and in some cases diseases have *risen* afterwards. There also seems to be no great statistical increase of disease in unvaccinated children, despite much pharmaceutical propaganda (unsurprising, with huge profits at stake).[8]

This is a controversial area, and a very emotive one, but given the still unsettled debates around the issue, the global rush towards compulsory injections of toxic compounds (which include poisonous mercury) straight into the deepest part of a child's immune system is highly questionable. Again, the *manner* in which we are cajoled into accepting vaccination - nearly always through fear or emotional plays around the issue of 'responsibility' to our children, together with constant scare stories of epidemics that rarely arrive - takes away the concept of personal choice and suggests that any opinions outside those of government scientists are automatically wrong. With the new EU Codex proposals, even alternative methods of staying healthy and naturally boosting our immune systems are under attack, making us more vulnerable to control and prone to dependency on a state that seems to prefer chemical-based solutions. Unsurprisingly, then, many suspect that the push to vaccinate (with new vaccines being introduced and promoted with the fear-factor every year, to deal with everything now, from cervical cancer to flu) is as much about protecting the pharmaceutical industries, with all their powerful lobbyists and political influence, than protecting the individual.

Given some of the other detrimental effects of modern living, from growing electromagnetic and microwave pollution (which some believe is also contributing to the very serious disappearance of bees and other important wildlife) to the belief of some that our very planetary atmosphere is being tampered with through the 'chemtrails' phenomenon [page 68], it is not so difficult to see why some people have become convinced there is an ongoing and deliberate assault on our physical and mental well-being. But if so, there also seems to be an attack on our spiritual and social well-being. With no frontier seemingly sacred, the 'thought police' of Orwell's nightmare parable may have finally arrived.

Policing Personal Beliefs

The current tendency of governments to think they know better than the individual what is good for them has recently extended beyond health and into the realm of the spiritual. The acceptance of the esoteric within long-established religions - and elite infrastructures - is fine, it seems, but anything outside of those traditional parameters is noticeably becoming a target of persecution.

In May 2008, a new EU law entitled the 'Unfair Commercial Practices Directive' was introduced across Europe. Ostensibly in place to protect consumers from fraudulent traders, it worries those with mystical leanings for it also carries an underlying implication that - if the directive is followed to the letter - all practitioners of psychically-based religions such as Spiritualism, all forms of mediumship and mystery arts such as astrology, tarot and divination, must provide empirical proof of their effectiveness. If not, by implication these services must be classified only as 'entertainment' - or not advertised at all.[9] Sensible precautions on one level perhaps, but such blanket discrimination will always disadvantage methods that are impossible to prove in anything that might equate to clinical trials because they lie beyond standard scientific paradigms - paradigms set by minds closed to fringe thinking from the start.

Although some of the initial responses to the new law were too reactionary, the fact remains that, as with alternative health product proposals, advertisements claiming any genuine benefits to mystical services are now technically in breach of the law. If the anti-alternative lobby that seems to be growing in influence were to take a greater hold over things (especially given the traditional evangelical opposition to the mystery arts), it could use powers now firmly in place (albeit hidden in the small print) to see such activities greatly curtailed, without the need for any new public offensive. Despite a little tabloid coverage, this potentially dangerous piece of legislation was allowed to slip through Parliament without resistance, yet it amounted to an attack on the very fundamental freedom of the individual - the freedom to live a personal spiritual conviction.

Religious persecution of one kind or another has plagued history, but the introduction of Parliamentary Acts of Tolerance and the creation of the multi-faith society most of the West

Spiritualist ladies in 1906. Back then it was thought that mediumship and communication with the dead would become accepted as a mainstream religion, but a continued bias against alternative faiths has resulted in increased marginalisation, now even manifesting in legislation.

comprises today was a step towards some kind of enlightenment. However, fear of a new dark age of 'occultism', much of it promoted either by the fundamentalist Christianity that would appear to lurk behind certain policies [Chapter IV] or, conversely, by rampant scientism and debunking bodies such as the Inquisition-like CSI (Committee for Skeptical Enquiry), are seeing a new intolerance being inflicted on our society. Major religions can freely shout about their effectiveness through posters and propaganda - yet the New Age beliefs or alternative practices, with no less evidence for their provenance, are being singled out as unworthy of the same respect. Already routinely lambasted by the media, now they are under potential attack from the law.

What authority on Earth is omniscient enough to be able to pontificate as to which faith and/or spiritual practice is acceptable for promotion and which is not? Why, for example, should forces quite happy to accept the belief that wafers and wine can turn into the body and blood of Jesus Christ not also accept the (statistically supported) belief that the motions of the planets can influence moods and psychological profiles? How can a system that accepts the belief that spiritual inspiration can come from heavenly realms not also accept the belief in the presence of disembodied entities that apparently speak through mediums? Why should a culture that increasingly speaks of an 'entangled' quantum universe [Chapter XIV] that seems to defy our previous understanding of time and space close its doors to the belief that such entanglement might enable divinatory processes to work through the principle of the 'holographic universe'?

In short, what possible right can anyone have to compel another to describe their cherished convictions as being simply 'entertainment' or something similarly derisive? Regardless of the alternative world's veracity or otherwise, the growing mainstream resistance to it amounts to a new religious intolerance. It is a policing of the human spirit at its deepest level, and marks the revival of a worrying policy that tyrants and oppressors have used since time immemorial when they have felt threatened by the power of individuality and any who might step outside of the pre-approved authoritarian religions. The Soviet Union and China heavily suppressed the freedom of faith. Now the West, with its strange paradoxical mix of underlying religious fundamentalism and hard scientism (note the huge publicity given to Richard Dawkins and the promotion of aetheism in recent years - is this some kind of bizarre double-bluff at work?), is beginning to do the same to those who would choose their own inner path.

If spiritual beliefs were to become policed in the way some fear, it is one clear area that would demand some form of mass civil-disobedience. Martyrs once stood against the crushing of their personal convictions at the cost of their lives. Hopefully such a high price should not need to be paid again in these supposedly more civilised times (any legally-required disclaimers could simply be made in a tangibly sarcastic context, for instance). But who knows where a new witch-hunting mentality could lead? We must be on our guard. Acquiescing without resistance to rules that humble and humiliate personal beliefs could lead to a dangerous path.

Political Correctness

The right to choose our beliefs is closely related to the right to hold an opinion, yet this is another area of our lives that is being encroached upon as part of what some believe is an ongoing attack on our ability to function as fully-rounded human beings. The scourge of 'political correctness' has been a prime suppresser of the freedom to express our inner feelings, and for the last two decades it has notably curtailed the collective's ability to speak its mind, forcing us into a kind of false interaction with others that disables debate and blocks progress in working through social issues.

Racism and the intimidation or humiliation of any minority group, from the gay community to the disabled is plainly - to all but right-wing fanatics and advocates of eugenics - entirely unacceptable. All such ignorant prejudices should be given the contempt they deserve. But when the misplaced accusation of such intimidation is used to stifle entirely normal expressions, words or terminology that are clearly well-meant or logical ('blackboard' is no longer an acceptable terms in schools, for instance, even in ones that still have them), or to quash necessary concerns and important discussions (the issue of immigration, for instance), common sense is replaced by a field of distortion that serves no-one.

The terror of being falsely accused of political *in*correctness, with the accompanying threat of becoming a social pariah, has given birth to a climate where people are afraid to speak what is in their hearts over some issues, not helped by burgeoning 'hate crime' laws welling up across the world, which are ambiguous enough to potentially restrict legitimate questioning on many things, including 9/11. The lightest criticism of extremist Zionism is already enough to have someone marked down by the Anti-Defamation League (the understandably defensive but sometimes over-zealous Jewish rights organisation). Consequently, valid concerns and feelings can be pushed into the shadows and fester, where they are sometimes reborn in yet more extremism, albeit of a different kind (almost certainly a factor in the recent worrying rise of the far-right British National Party into mainstream channels). Other people simply sink into disillusion, where the enthusiasm to fight injustice becomes seriously sapped.

The beauty, art and wisdom of the Muslim world is all too often overshadowed in the media by an over-focus on fundamentalism and horror stories of 'political correctness gone mad', in which Christmas trees are banned to avoid offending Islam, etc. Whilst occasionally true, it is often those trying to be politically correct, rather than the minorities they are claiming to protect, that are the cause of the problems - thus spreading division. Is this a deliberate ploy?

What all this breeds, more than anything else, is resentment - resentment of the very kind of minorities political correctness is supposed to protect. Fear of other cultures, other religions, of other ways of being, are all fostered by this approach, almost as if it is *meant* to, creating more division and disunity amongst communities - and, especially in the case of criticism of Islam, helping to bolster support for the West's questionable Middle Eastern wars. Muslim fundamentalism is a problem that needs dealing with, as all fundamentalism does, but the false notion that Muslim = fundamentalist = terrorist (not helped by the media) has been allowed to grow in part by the block that political correctness has put on serious discussion of the real issues. Did political correctness thus arise through natural filters of society, or was it subtly introduced as part of a deliberate Divide and Rule policy..?

The Fracturing of Community and Families

Part Four of this book provides some fairly obvious, yet easily missed solutions to many of the issues raised throughout these pages. At the risk of holding that optimism back a little longer, some of the other ways in which society has allowed itself to be corralled into a divided and distracted state of being need a brief mention here.

   Given the devastating lengths to which the ruling elite will seemingly go when it needs to, as discussed in earlier chapters, it is not beyond the realms of possibility that a Divide and Rule strategy is being implemented, under a veneer of appearing to nurture the opposite, as seen with the political correctness issue. It is certainly hard to make sense of some of the more peculiar legislation and encouraged social trends that seem to split communities, not unite them. Brian Gerrish, a retired UK Naval officer who began to fight what seemed like simple bureaucracy in his home town of Plymouth, only to uncover a demonstrable layer of infiltration in local government from the dubious federalist-EU organisation Common Purpose, believes that concerted efforts are also being made to split families and dilute community spirit through unnecessary social services interventions and authoritative interference.[10]   Gerrish's view even extends to believing that some of the appalling civic art that has been foisted on the public in parks, road roundabouts and retail arcades in recent times is designed to lower our spirits, not raise them. If this seems to take concerns a little too far, it is hard to deny that modern culture, for all its multiple communication facilities, does often seem to encourage alienation rather than cohesiveness.

   The arrival of television (and to a degree its progeny, the Internet) has been a key factor in this process. On one level it has created a kind of community of its own, but at the same time it has taken people away from each other, holding us in cushioned, enclosed environments, voiding the social interaction previous generations once took for granted. It has also divided families, with a majority of children in the UK now said to eat dinners on laps in front of televisions without their parents, who eat elsewhere. Family meals occur only on very special occasions, creating schisms and non-communication where once there was social glue.

   The fracturing of families has inevitably been a big part of the social experiment that seems to be ongoing in the UK in particular. Divorce, split and single-parent families may have become unavoidable in the psychological climate of our times, but all the studies show that overall the end product gives us young people far more prone to problems with loneliness, rage, alchohol, drugs and teenage pregnancy. The lack of family role models (especially male ones) is seen as a major problem by some analysts, but the lack of *any* role models is another. With Christianity having lost its hold on England especially - good or bad, depending on your viewpoint, but still a social shock to the system - and with a Parliament full of particularly uninspiring personalities (now seen as generically corrupt since the expenses outrage of 2009), who should people look up to? Who is setting the standards? The 'celebrities' we so often elevate to high status are hardly beacons of virtue. [See Chapter XV for some possible remedies.]

A nation of the dispossessed may seem like something a ruling class would wish to avoid, but the counter-argument is that people entangled in their own social problems are far less likely to cause trouble in areas further afield, leaving our hidden overlords free to plan a world that doesn't ultimately include the likes of us anyway.

Media Influence and Propaganda

Although sometimes a pleasant diversion (perhaps literally), television has been one of the primary tools of our social undoing. For the first time in human history a device has been created that can focus many minds on the same thing at the same time - both a blessing and a curse. This medium could serve humanity well if put to good use, and there is nothing wrong with a little entertainment for entertainment's sake. Yet even the most perfunctory sift through the channels on any given evening will reveal the menu of violence, negativity and depression we flood the collective consciousness with every day [page 293] - something that surely cannot be good for the spirit or social stability in the long-term. The contention that television (and cinema) acts as a necessary catharsis and an outlet for our repressed aggressive tendencies can only be stretched so far. The advent of computer games, in which the player becomes the actual perpetrator of violence, now played by millions of people (especially children) around the world, *has* to raise even more serious questions - but they are for a forum beyond this book. Few would really disagree that it all makes for a more fractured society, if only through the increased physical isolation of those more used to electronic networking than direct human interaction. The question here is whether all of this is a vagary of cultural evolution or a deliberate ploy of social engineering from a ruling class adopting a bread-and-circuses policy. There are some, of course, who believe television is a direct mind-control/surveillance system and won't have one in their home at all.

Television is certainly a very persuasive medium. The power of imagery and suggestion is particularly hypnotic (obviously more so than radio, although that outlet is not guiltless) and allows a very selective version of consensus reality to be easily fed to the masses. Like the press, at its core most mainstream broadcasting endorses the official line on almost everything, with only a very few tiny cable or satellite channels daring to challenge this state of affairs (see page 354 for one example). We may say we are not influenced by what we watch, and programme makers will deny that anything they transmit really affects people, but if either of these assertions were true then billions would not be spent on the advertising commercials that part us with hard-earned money.

As a propaganda tool, the 'idiot's lantern', as television was once known, is certainly the primary frontline. Programmes that pretend to question the status quo (i.e. past 'investigative' takes on 9/11 or the Moon landings, etc.) nearly always end up avoiding the real issues and instead simply validate the standard position, usually with the obligatory sneer. Likewise, for all the Jeremy Paxmans behind the news desks, there is now a scarcity of real political incisiveness (in the UK, at least) beyond shallow critiques of individuals, especially after the BBC's neutering in the wake of the David Kelly affair [page 135]. Even during the MP expenses scandal, there was little questioning of the underlying key issues. With the consensus view continually pumped from our screens and thrown into print day after day, it is hard not to be drawn in by it on some level. It *is* eventually possible to watch or read the news with discernment and not be taken in by every underlying agenda being slid into our living rooms, but it takes practice and diligence that not everyone finds easy to maintain.

Fast food and television... Fine in moderation, but our unhealthy fascination for trivia and comfort has been a recipe for a distracted and compliant society, easy to control.

'Dumbing Down'

It is difficult to deny that the phenomenon of 'dumbing-down' has also infected the media of late. Those who believe that television can be a useful educational tool increasingly despair at the watered-down psuedo-'documentaries' that have now taken the place of once-great series. With the occasional notable exception, on the whole crashing music, thin treatments, inane animations and glamorous presenters (with unnecessarily lingering camera shots) seem to have replaced passion and informative content. Even late-night news programmes would sometimes seem more at home in the childrens' slot. Well-spoken presenters are increasingly replaced by all-purpose 'estuary' accents using very limited vocabulary to accomodate the less sophisticated among us - which on one level seems kind, but also encourages the dangerous trend of pandering to the lowest levels of culture, instead of trying to offer something potentially better. This questionable approach takes the evolution of consciousness backwards for everyone. But once again, is it evolution - or social engineering? Many suspect the latter.

Encouraging hidden talents in those with less fortunate educations doesn't have to be patronising. Treating people as idiots and bringing everything down to the level of phone-texting language certainly is. The decline of the written and spoken word is already considered to have detrimentally affected the development of speech in young people, a development already hindered by too much television in the early years, according to studies. We are at risk of entering the world of *Nineteen Eighty-Four*'s 'Newspeak', in which subversiveness is stamped out by the deliberate deterioration of English into a kind of baby-talk that makes it *impossible* to express any kind of complex idea that might challenge convention or authority. Meanwhile, attention spans have been greatly reduced to match, by the ever-faster editing of modern media techniques and flickering images which, after prolonged exposure, leave people unable to concentrate on anything for long anyway - hence, in part (on top of the chemical effect from food additives, known to produce hyper-activity), the low boredom threshold of the generations raised on frantic games and quick-fire cuts.

When young people show signs of reacting to all this over-stimulation with 'difficult' behaviour or the tellingly-named Attention Deficit Hyperactivity Disorder (ADHD), the state reaches for pharmaceutical solutions, with an astounding one in ten children in the USA now dosed up with the highly-questionable and potentially dangerous drug Ritalin to keep them docile.[11]

Instead of rousing people to aspiration and helping them to become more than they are, we are currently keeping people in stasis or, worse, reducing the population to an infantile and numbed condition that then demands the presence of a nanny state to look after it - which the authorities duly provide.

In this way we allow our senses to be quashed and our attention to be diverted from things that could really matter by media outlets that tantalise with the promise of instant riches from TV quiz shows and national lotteries ('a tax on the poor'), or eat our time and attention with essentially meaningless football scandals, celebrity gossip and cheap titillation. All the time we are mesmerised by these things, like a magician's trick we are not seeing the sleights of hand and agendas that are really shaping our world.

Physical Barriers

One of the serious issues conjured by a media obsessed with titillation is a general debasement of sex and natural human affection, created by negative associations with, or false impressions of, sexuality. These diminish its more empowering and enlightening qualities (indeed, sex was once thought in some mystic circles to connect us to higher spiritual powers). The dark shadow of AIDS first turned something wonderful into something dangerous and frightening, and now ubiquitous public information advertisements about all the other apparently rife sexual diseases seem to be doom-laden beyond the call of duty.

The reporting of sexuality in negative contexts has produced a continual run of scare stories over the rapists and paedophiles that apparently stalk every street, leading to a culture where teachers and carers can no longer make physical gestures of the most innocuous kind (permission has to be sought just to offer first-aid in some schools) and taking photographs of class plays or sports activities now invites frowns or demands from parents or staff to stop. [As it happens, few laws actually prevent normal photographs of children in most public places, but the general hysteria around paedophilia has created the *assumption* that there are such laws.] And so, yet more distance is forced between people and we find ourselves policing each other without even the need for edicts from above - a key feature of the world that has been created around us. When parents increasingly dare not take snaps of their own children on a beach for fear of being prosecuted under child pornography laws, we know we are in a society that is being led in a very unhealthy direction.

A general respect for the personal boundaries of those around us, together with wise and balanced sexual behaviour, is something sensible; an irrational fear-bound society that sees a human gift as inherently threatening, while continually obsessing over it, is inviting psychosis.

The Caged Society - Evolution or Contrivance?

In all these ways, truthseekers believe we have been tricked. Thus hypnotised, diverted by trivia, controlled by fear, anaesthetised by additives and pharmaceuticals and kept in the dark from what is really going on in the world around us, only one more ingredient is needed for the conjurer's final distraction - something provided easily in the shape of rampant materialism. This was accelerated massively in the every-man-for-himself boom years of the 1980s and has never left us since. Even in these times of deep global recession, retail therapy is one of the most popular pastimes. With spiritual matters firmly placed on the backburner in the modern Anglo-Saxon world, or warped by evangelical fundamentalism of all kinds (another kind of bondage in the opinion of many), the strings are firmly attached for our role as puppets, as we look for instant, if unenduring fixes in the only cathedrals still packed with people - the shopping malls.

What, then, will we do if a seeming economic recovery based on the voracious government borrowing that is currently propping things up in many countries turns out to be a false bubble that bursts, bringing everything down with it, as some believe is the plan [page 74]? Like birds unable to fly out when the door is finally opened, if materialism is our cage, then we will look to the same masters to make a new protective prison for us and to bring back the old comfortable fixes. And our masters will surely deliver - albeit with a world finally tailored to their exact needs.

On such fears, the conspiracy world is based. Could all this be just the chance of evolution's trial and error, then, or is the view that it is being deliberately manipulated through social engineering a realistic possibility? The truth, as ever, may lie somewhere between the extremes. Nonetheless, an uncohesive and disempowered population is clearly easier to control. But what would all this

Shopping malls, our new cathedrals. With the world in economic peril, we still distract ourselves with material comforts.

control really be needed for? Is it just about power for power's sake or is there another, more pressing, reason? We shall explore a strong possibility soon.

However, there is one more widely-promoted tool of control that is currently having the effect of creating division and alienation that we need to look at first, one flying closely under the radar as something of apparently unimpeachable good intent - that of our collective desire to save the planet from impending climate disaster.

THE TRUTH AGENDA: *The diminishment of self-responsibility and choice, even in matters of health, means that we are left at the mercy of those who seem to prefer us hooked on chemical-based symptom suppressers and dubious additives in our food and water, rather than allow us to protect our well-being by natural or common sense methods. The employment of psychological warfare also seems apparent in societal trends, with people reduced to statistics while health and safety, political correctness, family breakdown and the distractions of the media and materialism alienate people from each other and from their own sense of self-empowerment. Many believe this is a deliberate policy of Divide and Rule, creating a weaker - and therefore more malleable - society.*

Power station cooling towers loom over trees. Balancing our energy needs with concerns over the environment and climate change is one of the big discussions of the age - but have we really understood climate change, and is the global warming scenario the correct one? Many think not, but they are not being given a proper voice in the mainstream.

XI   THE GREEN DILEMMA

The widely-promoted fear of a major catastrophe due to climate change is increasingly creating a judgmental society of finger-pointing and mistrust. With man-made global warming having been decided on as the primary mechanism of our forthcoming undoing, it might be thought that all the arguments were settled. But are they? Many think not. Sensible protection of our planet and its eco-systems is a must, but climate change and green issues appear to have been hijacked for use as more tools of control through which the hands of freedom are being tied.

Policing Each Other Through Green Concerns

In the darker days of the Soviet Union and its communist associates, one successful method by which behaviour was controlled was to sow seeds of doubt and suspicion amongst the general populace by hiring urban spies and encouraging exposure of anyone showing signs of disloyalty to the state. Avoiding the need for expensive monitoring, the people simply policed each other and fear kept dissent down.

This self-policing technique is now creeping into Western society through the unexpected channel of 'green' concerns. Already we have recycling officers sifting through bins in some areas of the UK and USA, fining unfortunates who may have inadvertently thrown away inappropriate items - despite the recent weakening of the recycled materials market, which has seen much of the collected waste end up in landfill anyhow. Some councils in Britain have started placing cameras and other detectors in recycling containers, truly bringing the surveillance state to our doors - via our bins. However, due to genuine and well-intentioned concerns about the perilous state of the planet's ecology, a significant number of people seem to believe such measures are a *good thing*.

The much-encouraged hysterical response to the claimed threat of global warming (see below) and climate change in general has enabled the creation of a culture in which it is becoming perfectly legitimate to criticise and monitor other people's behaviour in the name of saving the planet. Because the aspiration seems like a reasonable one, many go along with this rise of the new green fascism, not because they feel comfortable with it, but through political correctness or fear of ostracism. People don't like to be seen raising objections against an apparently virtuous cause.

Consequently, with all the fears around greenhouse gases contributing to global warming, and the screams that 'peak oil' has been reached and that we are about to run out of the black gold that has fired our modern world, it is seemingly becoming more acceptable to be criticised for taking a holiday by aeroplane, or for buying a bigger car (or whatever) - or for not recycling properly. One is now more likely to come across a street protest against 4x4 vehicles than one about something arguably more crucial like, say, the truth about 9/11 or the growth of surveillance and the loss of freedom. In a very clever way, people have been turned inwards on each other, controlling *themselves* by policing each other's lifestyles in the name of the environment.

Recycling and sensible environmental measures are a good thing - intimidation, surveillance and social mistrust are not.

Pollution is a problem that needs tackling - but much of the responsibility for doing so seems to have fallen on the everyday person instead of the huge industries that generate much of it, thus neatly deflecting the burden of guilt and creating more mandates for control of the population.

The Guilt of Climate Change

What all this self-inflicted finger-pointing achieves for our governments is to place the guilt for environmental destruction and climate change on the small people - us. For all the climate treaties and uneasy (and possibly unattainable, especially in the current disastrous global recession) carbon reduction targets fanfared by leaders keen to be seen to be doing something, the fact is that the real polluters, the industrial giants, chemical plants and power stations, continue belching out emissions into the atmosphere and poisoning the waters while authorities turn blind eyes and society continues to function on the benefits of their doing so. Conversely, as all this carries on, as perhaps it must for a while, the feeling of personal guilt concerning our own tiny carbon contributions grows ever-more suffocating. This transference of guilt is tacitly supported by governments and regimes around the world, unsure how to balance the needs of a perilous economy and the planet.

All the time this collective guilt broods, the *appearance* that something is being done is partly maintained by the public energy expended over the issue, even though the underlying problems continue and a long-term answer remains elusive. So the common people are carrying the lion's share of responsibility instead of those entrusted with finding the solutions, who happily pass the burden back. We too often fail to notice this inequality of responsibility, because we are all too busy believing that dismantling the Aga or persuading our neighbours not to fly to Benidorm next week will make a major contribution to preventing climate change.

This distractive guilt isn't necessarily placed on us from on high. Those individuals deeply touched by the apparent plight of the Earth can be relied on to ensure local communities are kept on their environmental toes by the creation of activist groups (like the Transition Town initiative), set up in recent years to encourage communities to become greener and more self-sufficient, less reliant on oil and other resources that may become scarce.[1] In theory, the aims of such groups are entirely sensible, but in practice some campaigners' fervent tones, using aggressive words like 'unleashing' to launch environmental initiatives can risk intimidating those who feel less sure of their ultimate aims. Some green publicity statements give the strong impression that there are those who actually *want* a social apocalypse and a return to a medieval lifestyle, in a kind of non-religious echo of the end-timer philosophy explored in Chapter IV.

Resistance to open debate over issues taken for granted by the likes of Transition Towns, such as the man-made causes of climate change or the certainty that oil is about to run out (challenged by some leading truth campaigners such as Ian R Crane, who worked in the oil industry for much of his life), has generated a number of heated conflicts on Internet forums and at public gatherings. It has also bred resentment amongst those feeling bullied by new (and often young) boil-in-the-bag enviro-activists, who seem to think nothing of disrupting airports and public spaces while accosting unwitting bystanders with often third-hand platitudes they barely understand themselves but have been trained to parrot. Such public intimidation may win frightened lip-service for a while, but not genuine support. This, surely, is not the way to save the planet. Many green thinkers seem resistant to considering conspiracy theories, without seeing that they themselves may be some of the very people being manipulated to discourage free-thinking individualism.

The Global Warming Conundrum

The rise of the new green dogma has been fuelled by a huge wave of propaganda concerning man-made global warming. Climate change would seem to be a fact by simple observation, but the loose way the terms 'climate change' and 'global warming' are so often interchanged to mean the same thing is questionable, because many people believe that global warming - despite the impression continually given in the media - remains a hypothesis, and is not a proven certainty. Even when taken as a certainty, the causes of that warming are a debate in themselves.

By accident or design, it has been of great political convenience to finger man-made greenhouse gases as the primary cause of the global warming we are all being encouraged to fight, with all the requisite carbon taxes and added social controls that come with it. It also massively benefits the quietly powerful nuclear industry, which is promoted by some (even by previously green thinkers such as James Lovelock) as the only practical non-carbon answer to slowing the onset of impending global catastrophe. [Note the recent negative publicity given to alternatives such as wind farms, and consider which lobby might benefit most from this, whatever the discussions over the landscape impact of wind turbines. A nuclear waste accident might, in the long-run, have a far greater impact.] As fear of greenhouse gas doom rises - and it is plainly stirred as a fright-based mass-hysteria - we find ourselves giving in to draconian measures and granting assent to very tough carbon targets, which threaten jobs and make life generally harder. All necessary sacrifices, we are told, for the future of the planet. Yet the world is being turned upside down for something which remains unproven, and an increasing number of people are now beginning to question global warming. In 2008, a UK poll showed that nearly 60% of the population still remained doubtful about global warming or its causes, a figure condescendingly leapt on by government scientists as merely evidence of public ignorance - not of their own inability to produce firm and convincing evidence.[2]

It may be the case that man-made global warming is a reality. But the purpose of this book is to make sense of why so many people doubt the veracity of much of what they are told to believe nowadays. The fact is that applying the Truth Agenda to global warming once again gives valid grounds for questioning and reveals deep areas of confusion that are not being properly acknowledged. It is little surprise that the public remains unsure, when there seems to be such a concerted effort to keep a lid on what is, in truth, a tumultuously boiling debate.

We are repeatedly told that nearly all respectable scientists now support the idea of man-made global warming, based on firm evidence. But the truth is that there are many equally respectable scientists who have raised concerns about that evidence and the conclusions drawn. When big names come forward to voice those concerns, however, they suddenly find themselves redefined as 'mavericks' or 'fringe' - or accused of secretly working for oil companies or polluting industries, as ex-cabinet minister Nigel Lawson and TV naturalist David Bellamy, both of whom have widely questioned global warming, have found to their cost. Peter Taylor, once an environmental adviser to both the UN and the EU on climate change, as a less famous but equally notable example, eventually resigned when he realised that any statistical results they produced that didn't support the idea of global warming were being ignored, or dismissed as 'instrument error'.[3] Other government-funded climatologists have reported similar stories. Lawrence Solomon's book *The Deniers* [see *Appendix 2*] lists and interviews around twenty fully-qualfied climatologists and scientists who challenge the global warming model. Yet with nearly all official climate research now being funnelled into the concept of man-made global warming, it has become impossible to study much else with financial support - thus skewing both the figures and the weight of mainstream opinion towards one view. It has also opened the world to the disastrously misconceived policy of growing of crops for biofuels, which is destroying forests and communities as surely as global warming would.

The disproportionate and huge siphoning of funds into global warming has also allowed studies into areas of equivalent importance to be neglected. Research into the potentially devastating disappearance of bees, for example (which - once again - would harm the ecosystem as surely as global warming would), have until recently only been granted ridiculously small budgets, and even now the recently increased funding is only a desultory amount in comparison.

When the previously-eminent ex-editor of *New Scientist*, Nigel Calder, co-authored with Henrik Svensmark the 2007 book *The Chilling Stars*[4], proposing that cosmic rays and solar cycles could equally explain climate change and pointing out that past rises in ancient carbon cycles did not directly correlate with changes of global temperatures (there is generally an 800-year or more delay between the two), Calder's pedigree was

Peter Taylor, former environmental advisor to the EU and UN, is one of many qualified climatologists who challenges global warming theory and claims that data which supports an alternative scenario is being systematically ignored.

suddenly forgotten and he found himself ostracised from the science community. A UK Channel Four documentary the same year, *The Great Global Warming Swindle*, based partly on Calder and Svensmark's theories, was equally slammed as entirely worthless because of a number of errors, and claims that some of the scientists interviewed on the programme were quoted out of context.[5] However, following up the complaints, the British broadcasting regulator watchdog Ofcom ruled that the programme 'did not materially mislead the audience so as to cause harm or offence,' and accepted Channel Four's claim that 'none of the inaccuracies materially affected the argument of the film in any way'.[6]

Despite the official finding in favour of *The Great Global Warming Swindle*, it was nonetheless entirely dismissed by green pundits and quickly buried under the ongoing deluge of global warming propaganda. Yet when one Stewart Dimmock went to the British High Court to challenge the dubious use of Al Gore's hugely influential 2006 global warming-promoting film *An Inconvenient Truth* as an educational video in UK schools, and the film was indeed found to be inaccurate on nine major points (see below), this didn't prevent it continuing to be shown to children as a factual documentary. Nor did it slow its seemingly unstoppable cinematic tour of multiplexes, village halls, churches and environmental groups.

An Inconvenient Ruling

The ruling against the Al Gore movie is worth quoting in full here, because it sums up the types of misrepresentation concerning the global warming hypothesis that are all too rife. The website *www.newparty.co.uk*, key in bringing the case to court, reports the ruling thus:

The decision by the government to distribute Al Gore's film An Inconvenient Truth has been the subject of a legal action by New Party member Stewart Dimmock. The Court found that the film was misleading in nine respects and that the Guidance Notes drafted by the Education Secretary's advisors served only to exacerbate the political propaganda in the film.

In order for the film to be shown, the Government must first amend their Guidance Notes to Teachers to make clear that 1) The Film is a political work and promotes only one side of the argument. 2) If teachers present the Film without making this plain they may be in breach of section 406 of the Education Act 1996 and guilty of political indoctrination. 3) Nine inaccuracies have to be specifically drawn to the attention of school children. The inaccuracies are:

1) The film claims that melting snows on Mount Kilimanjaro [is] evidence [of] global warming. The Government's expert was forced to concede that this is not correct.

2) The film suggests that evidence from ice cores proves that rising CO_2 causes temperature increases over 650,000 years. The Court found that the film was misleading: over that period the rises in CO_2 lagged behind the temperature rises by 800-2000 years.

3) The film uses emotive images of Hurricane Katrina and suggests that this has been caused by global warming. The Government's expert had to accept that it was "not possible" to attribute one-off events to global warming.

4) The film shows the drying up of Lake Chad and claims that this was caused by global warming. The Government's expert had to accept that this was not the case.

5) The film claims that a study showed that polar bears had drowned due to disappearing arctic ice. It turned out that Mr Gore had misread the study: in fact four polar bears drowned and this was because of a particularly violent storm.

6) The film threatens that global warming could stop the Gulf Stream, throwing Europe into an ice age: the Claimant's evidence was that this was a scientific impossibility.

7) The film blames global warming for species losses including coral reef bleaching. The Government could not find any evidence to support this claim.

8) The film suggests that sea levels could rise by 7m causing the displacement of millions of people. In fact the evidence is that sea levels are expected to rise by about 40cm over the next hundred years and that there is no such threat of massive migration.

9) The film claims that rising sea levels has caused the evacuation of certain Pacific islands to New Zealand. The Government are unable to substantiate this and the Court observed that this appears to be a false claim.

Not all of the inaccuracies in the film were fully considered by the court as the judge requested a sample on which to consider the case. Professor Carter's witness statement lists 20 inaccuracies in the film.[7]

Meanwhile, in the US, John Coleman, the founder of the hugely influential Weather Channel, but also a very vocal global warming sceptic, is himself considering suing Gore and other proponents of the unproven hypothesis.[8] Coleman is especially critical of the 'carbon credits' system, a suspect corporate wheeze in which companies are allowed to continue to pollute if they simultaneously invest in environmental projects abroad. Investigation has revealed misrepresentation and outright fraud concerning the true nature and value of these supposedly balancing projects, suggesting that the carbon credits scheme is yet another distraction to deceive the unassuming, guilt-ridden public.[9]

It is worth noting here that despite the UK High Court ruling and John Coleman's threats of action in the US, that *An Inconvenient Truth* continues to be shown in UK schools (and public venues) without any of the conditions stipulated above being met. Thus, our children are provably being educated with propaganda as regards global warming (and who knows what else), not factual material.

The Confusing Data of Climate Change

What jars with those unsure as to what to believe as regards climate change is that at the time of writing, average global temperatures have actually been on a *decline* since 1998, with a notable increase in the fall in the last few years.[10] This is claimed as nothing more than a statistical blip, a cycle within a cycle in an otherwise rising trend, which may yet turn out to be the case - but it can be relied upon that if the temperature had risen in that time instead, such a statistic would now be loudly trumpeted as the final proof of global warming. Some commentators, like Peter Taylor, and Australian geophysicist and astronaut Phil Chapman, actually believe we may be entering a period of global *cooling*, which could create a new Ice Age, albeit a modest one [see also Chapter XII].[11] If so, the massive reductions of carbon being proposed could have entirely the wrong result, helping to hold back (if very minorly, on the grand scale) a mechanism for keeping the temperatures up, and contributing instead to a potentially disastrous opposite effect to global warming.

For all the hysteria over carbon pollution contributing to global warming, it can be clearly demonstrated by analysis of ice core samples and other methods that historical carbon variations in the atmosphere have very limited correlation to climate or temperature changes.

Some believe this was the idea all along. There is evidence to suggest that the global warming hysteria as we know it today had some of its seeds in a conference held in North Carolina in 1975, The Atmosphere: Endangered and Endangering, an event that hosted Malthusian-style speakers advocating the need for world depopulation [page 68] - another possible motive for creating a climate scare. An article by Marjorie Mazel Hecht on the website for *21st Century Science & Technology* magazine observes the following:

'[The conference was] *organised by the influential anthropologist Margaret Mead, president of the American Association for the Advancement of Science (AAAS), in 1974. Mead - whose 1928 book on the sex life of South Pacific Islanders was later found to be a fraud - recruited like-minded anti-population hoaxsters to the cause; sow enough fear of man-caused climate change to force global cutbacks in industrial activity and halt Third World development... ...Guided by luminaries like these, conference discussion focussed on the absurd choice of either feeding people or "saving the environment".*

...The North Carolina conference, which took place Oct. 26-29, 1975, was co-sponsored by two agencies of the US National Institutes of Health: the John E. Fogarty International Center for Advanced Study in the Health Sciences and the National Institute of Environmental Health Sciences... ...It was at this government-sponsored conference... ...that virtually every scare scenario in today's climate hoax took root.

Scientists were charged with coming up with the "science" to back up the scares, so that definitive action could be taken by policy-makers.

Global cooling - the coming of an ice age - had been in the headlines in the 1970s, but it could not easily be used to sell genocide by getting the citizens of industrial nations to cut back on consumption. Something more drastic and personal was needed.' [12]

Likewise, it is now widely believed that the once-popular 'hole in the ozone layer' public frenzy was at best a genuine misunderstanding of a natural process with little to do with man-made pollution (the hole periodically opens and closes by itself), and at worse was used as a deliberate deception to further not only the above agenda, but also to benefit industries that made billions from the introduction of CFC-free replacement technology. [13] If the report on the 1975 conference is accurate, it would explain much of the trajectory of climate propaganda we have seen since. It is interesting to note that just two years later the ITV faux-documentary *Alternative 3* posited the notion that government scientists were secretly planning to decamp to Mars and the Moon to escape devastating climate change caused by pollution. [14] Although quickly revealed as a spoof, many felt that the programme masked a genuine agenda, and if nothing else it unquestionably helped to seed fear of climate change in the public consciousness.

As for global cooling, as Mazel Hecht's conference report points out, it is true that just a few decades ago it was the environmental cooling model the public was being informed of. Yet many still adhere to that former model, if for different scientific reasons. R Timothy Patterson, professor of geology and director of the Ottawa-Carleton Geoscience Center of Canada's Carleton University is another proponent of global cooling, stating:

'CO_2 variations show little correlation with our planet's climate on long, medium and even short time scales... ... I and the first-class scientists I work with are consistently finding excellent correlations between the regular fluctuations of the Sun and Earthly climate. This is not surprising. The Sun and the stars are the ultimate source of energy on this planet... ... Solar scientists predict that, by 2020, the Sun will be starting into its weakest Schwabe cycle of the past two centuries, likely leading to unusually cool conditions on Earth... ...Solar activity has overpowered any effect that CO2 has had before, and it most likely will again... ... If we were to have even a medium-sized solar minimum, we could be looking at a lot more bad effects than 'global warming' would have had.' [15]

Recent NASA data on the very quiet sunspot activity of the current cycle and the notable reduction of solar irradiance and radio emissions [page 250] certainly points more towards a cooling process, rather than the opposite. Solar cycles are discussed more in the next chapter. Seemingly every year now, NASA releases new data that suggests the Sun, its sunspot cycles and fluctuating magnetic fields, which are in the greatest state of unpredictability ever recorded, have a far more profound effect on Earth and its climate than anyone previously thought.

At this point in the debate the traditional evidence of melting ice caps and retreating glaciers, together with the requisite tales of drowning polar bears and suchlike

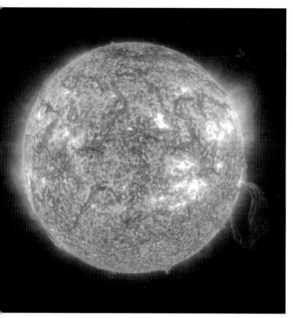

The biggest contributor to climate change..? An increasing number of scientists believe that unless we take solar cycles into the equation, we are not going to truly understand what is happening to our planet. The Sun may influence far more than is being admitted to by mainstream sources.

(see the Gore ruling on page 228) are always held up as the final proof of man-made global warming. Ice melt does appear to be rapidly occurring in the north at least, although contrary, if controversial, reports of new ice sheets *forming* elsewhere don't receive the same level of media discussion. Doubters point to increased cloud cover and changing ocean currents stimulated by factors outside of our atmosphere (as proposed by the likes of Calder and Svensmark) as being equally likely to be responsible for the dwindling northern ice, rather than a general warming process.

Even government scientists accept that the melting of the Arctic cap (largely just floating pack ice) would not directly or significantly contribute to rising sea levels. The thawing of areas like the Greenland or Antarctic ice sheets would affect the seas more seriously, but the melt rate in these places is far less than at the North Pole and it could take millennia to generate the kind of major water rises often implied.[16] The media, ever simplistic for the sake of a screaming headline, would appear to have us believe otherwise, but exciting and apparently apocalyptic footage of collapsing ice is often attributable to nothing more than standard seasonal thaw.

Despite the mounting evidence for solar influences cooling Earth, a 2006 study in the peer-review journal *Nature* (sometimes accused of being the mouthpiece for official scientific propaganda and a shop window for global warming proponents) concluded that solar changes were 'unlikely' to have much effect on our climate.

However, even that piece cautioned the following:

'Apart from solar brightness, more subtle influences on climate from cosmic rays or the Sun's ultraviolet radiation cannot be excluded, say the authors. They also add that these influences cannot be confirmed because physical models for such effects are still too poorly developed.' [17]

In other words, the climate change debate is far from being closed, yet the panic button has already been hit in favour of one theory.

  Some say we cannot afford to wait to find out for sure what will happen to the climate, and that we must take a chance and act now to save the world from catastrophe - but this is all part of the huge fear and transference of guilt that has been placed upon us, to join all the other spirit-crushing pressures previously discussed. Shouldn't all sides of the debate at least be heard properly before drastic measures are introduced that could have even worse long-term detrimental effects if the mainstream has it wrong? Public doubt concerning the science of climate change should be taken more seriously than it is. People are not as stupid as some would have us believe, and tend to know when something isn't quite right. The polls suggest that the collective psyche (more tangible than is given credit for - Chapter XIV) is touching on an meaningful unease that needs addressing, not dismissing.

The Energy Crisis
A few more successive years of falling temperatures would make it far harder to keep the global warming bubble alive and it will be interesting to see just how much longer the official position can stay skewed towards one polarity if temperatures don't begin a substantial rise soon. The UK in particular is also facing a potential energy crisis within a decade, as carbon-producing power stations are phased out to meet the new greenhouse gas targets. Experts are predicting that replacement technology (mostly nuclear) is unlikely to be ready in time to meet the 'energy gap'. How tolerant those gathered around candles in cold rooms will remain towards all the highbrow talk of saving the planet for future generations may therefore be in question in any case and eventually render all the carbon debates redundant. Many will reach for all the old dirty energies again rather than freeze. Likewise, the developing world, now leaping ahead with new technological industries, appears reluctant to put long term global environmental prospects ahead of the quality of life *now*.

  Human beings are not used to thinking long-term, and, perhaps unfortunately, there seems little prospect of this changing any time soon. No amount of bleeding-heart Western green thinking and the wish for a return to a world of

THE TRUTH AGENDA

'clip-clopping horses' (as one green pundit eulogised on BBC radio recently) is going to change the thinking of upcoming civilisations headed in the opposite direction. With only very limited climate protection being predicted to result from even the most drastic carbon emission cuts, other solutions beyond enforced energy fasting and abstinence are therefore going to have to be found to turn things around. Proponents of 'free-energy' and cleaner technologies, promised by some to be just around the corner but reputedly held back by governments and oil companies (trying to squeeze the last drops of economical control from the formerly dominant mineral slime) claim that such solutions will indeed be forthcoming. Some have even suggested the entire global warming scare has been deliberately created to lay a path for these technologies, but in a way that ensures the industrial-military complexes retain the sole right to develop them.

The Common Sense of Preservation

In debating and challenging some of the confusing data on climate change, this is *not* to say that we shouldn't be making every effort to protect the planet from pollution and environmental destruction, regardless of where climate curves do or don't take us. Respecting Mother Nature, preserving the rain forests and cleaning up the air, land and seas with wisdom and a sensible balance of priorities is plainly necessary - and sheer common sense. However, the understandable urgency some feel in wanting to avoid dangerous climate swings has led to an unfortunate situation where people are becoming divided into unhealthy factions and, without question, yet more fear is being used to force change instead of encouraging positive forward-thinking.

Nobody sane questions that the environment and its resources (especially water) must be protected. However, all the while man-made global warming is held up by governments and the mainstream as the sole primary issue of our times (besides terrorism) without convincing proof, it remains that people's genuine care for the planet is being abused to justify all manner of heavy taxes, reduced circumstances and restrictive legislation that could turn out to be unnecessary. Unless a new clean technology *is* unexpectedly revealed and sanctioned, it is not too difficult to imagine these restrictions eventually manifesting as a general constraint on global movement, as air and possibly even road travel becomes prohibitively expensive (and morally frowned upon) to all but the elite few. Note the number of rock stars who flew vast entourages around the world at great expense and with vast carbon outputs to tick us all off about global warming at the *Live Earth* concerts of 2007. Al Gore's 'carbon footprint' is also rumoured to be one of the largest amongst touring celebrities. Yet everyday folk are being discouraged from free movement.

In 2009, Lord Turner, Chairman of the Committee on Climate Change, openly called for personal flights to be rationed, prompting even Norman Baker MP, a keen climate campaigner, to caution 'there is an absolute need to recognise the serious climate change implications of aviation, but Forties-style rationing is not the way forward.'[18] Even if global warming is eventually proven and lifestyle restrictions can be shown to be an absolute requirement, the ugly and authoritarian manner by which these changes are currently being forced on us feels wrong, and a much lighter approach is needed.

What, though, of the growing number of independent scientists and researchers who see natural causes such as solar cycles and cosmic rays (not to mention huge carbon emissions from volcanoes) as being the prime drivers of *climate change*, be it global warming or cooling? Why are they not listened to more? Tellingly, the natural cause lobby - and this may be key to the current imbalance in the debate - do not offer the political benefits of the man-made greenhouse gas camp; for if in truth we are at the mercy

Questioning global warming does not equate to questioning the need to preserve places like the rain forests, nor does it mean that the doubters have no concerns over pollution, as is sometimes falsely put about by those who condemn so-called 'climate change deniers'. In fact, very few people deny climate change - it is mostly the man-made global warming model that is challenged.

of celestial cycles outside of our immediate control, then no action on Earth will make much difference to whatever is going to happen. Financial incentives and social controls would be lost if this were ever admitted - and the risk of panic and despair setting in amongst the populace would become very real. Which is perhaps why so few want to discuss the alternative view on climate change.

The Control Agenda Unfolds

Here, perhaps, is where we begin to see the control agenda unfolding into something concrete. As already touched on, and as the next chapter explores in more detail, what if the true overseers behind the scenes are aware of some impending and enormous shift, of which climate change, whatever its real cause, may be a simple precursor? If they even suspect that something might be about to occur which could upset the old order and risk unseating their long-entrenched positions of authority, they would presumably want to insure against this happening. Perhaps this explains what the control agenda is all about. We have explored in the earlier chapters all the many prophecies and predictions for these times, which have come through from many sources, psychic, celestial and religious, and are subscribed to by many influential political and spiritual leaders. These people will not take any chances on losing their hold on us.

A happy, go-ahead, independent society is much harder to keep under one umbrella of containment, and far harder to manipulate. The conspiracy view holds that to maintain the necessary control, every effort must be made to keep us distracted, docile and down, even if that means implementing draconian measures of control and surveillance and binding us in a state of fear (the actual title of a 2004 Michael Crichton novel, which heavily questions global warming and posits that the concept was created purely as a social crowbar).[19] For many years, fear of nuclear war, legitimate or not,[20] was plainly used as a political tool, and it appeared to suit authorities for entire generations to grow up in deep terror of imminent incineration. But with atomic apocalypse no longer seen as such a huge threat (although the souped-up campaigns against the nuclear programmes of Iran and North Korea taps into this nostalgia), and terrorism not quite enough in itself, the warping of climate concerns and the growing unease over the current global economic crisis may be designed to exacerbate a new all-encompassing fear as a further justification of social restrictions to keep us in our place. Rationing both travel and the availability of unlimited energy (in the name of saving the planet) would help with this. Meanwhile, restraining access to better health and reducing natural immunity while force-feeding us on junk food, junk TV and dubious chemicals, dulls the senses and takes away our spark, leaving a malleable and defenceless population.

Our beautiful Earth - a place worth looking after, because there's nowhere else to go. But our desire to save it shouldn't be used to override common sense or justify dubious restrictions in the name of very uncertain evidence and often hysterical reasoning.

Again, it must be asked - could things really be this bad? Let's hope not. But if there is the slightest danger of such an outcome developing, even on a small scale, then it would be wise to look seriously at the possibility and make efforts to prevent such a nightmare from becoming a reality. If, as the name of one truthseeking website has it, we are indeed in danger of becoming a 'prison planet', then it is time to stand up for freedom. The last part of this book explores the optimistic view that we can, and will.

Why, however, do things seem to be coming to a head now, of all times? It is necessary at this point, then, to explore more fully the 2012 prophecies.

THE TRUTH AGENDA: *Legitimate environmental concerns are being abused to create another layer of fear and restriction, which sets people against each other and undermines a cohesive societal spirit, despite the attempts to build 'green' communities. We must clearly preserve our environment with enlightened policies, but the carbon pollution propaganda threatens to restrict both freedom of spirit and freedom of movement, while the panic that is closing down our energy infrastructure too soon could plunge us into literal darkness. Man-made global warming has been presented to us as an unarguable absolute, when in truth there is a very important debate to be had in the light of much contradictory evidence. Other factors outside of our atmosphere seem to play a part in the climate changes we are seeing, suggesting some kind of impending cosmic influence beyond our control - which may explain why a ruling elite might want to ensure it retains its grip on us while it can.*

Sunrise from the air, beautiful to see. Yet the Sun could be one of the very factors that could dramatically alter life on Earth, and some think its current erratic behaviour might be part of the changes alluded to in the ancient prophecies for the year 2012.

XII 2012

Across the world, a number of ancient cultures have calendrical systems, prophecies or traditions that point very clearly to 21st December 2012 as being a hugely significant date around which some kind of global transition or shift of consciousness will occur. What exactly are the predictions and how might they come about? Regardless of what does or doesn't happen in 2012, the reality is that the anticipation surrounding it is already stimulating a new awakening process in many people. With wildly varying speculation as to what will unfold, and the date fast approaching, are those in power aware of the potential for an upsetting of the old order, and thus trying to create a world that cannot fall from their grasp?

Millennial Transference

In the decade running-up to the Millennium, with all the requisite religious fervour and anticipation of the long-awaited Day of Judgement, esoteric seekers began to look for tangible evidence that might give genuine meaning to all the prophecies and predictions. Curiously, two convincing possibilities duly presented themselves, although the second would take a little longer to percolate.

Most prominently, a sloppy formatting limitation in computer programmes raised wide fears of a technological apocalypse, rather than a religious one, in the form of the so-called 'Millennium Bug'. Developed without foresight of commercial computing's rapid proliferation, the standard electronic brain's inability to recognise a new century raised the widely-feared spectre that the first tick into the year 2000 might bring a mass-shutdown of an entire civilisation, with computers crashing in turn across the time-zones. Although the real Millennium actually occurred in 2001 (2000 technically being the last year of the previous one), it was 2000 that mattered as far as the computers were concerned, as years were generally denoted with just two digits in their core programming. What if they thought '00' meant 1900? What would occur? Doomy predictions of power-grid meltdowns and frozen databases paralysing the infrastructure of society were all lugubriously speculated on, sometimes gleefully by the end-timers or extremist green campaigners seeking their return to a romantic feudalism. Planes might plummet from the skies and food distribution could grind to a halt. Many larders and cellars were well-stocked by that New Year's Eve, with a wide expectation of the end of life as we knew it.

When the crisis failed to materialise - or enough work was done by panicked programmers to avert disaster - a strange kind of restlessness set in amongst those alternately relieved or disappointed. Was that it? No global catastrophe nor heavenly trumpets. While some speculated that the whole panic had been a massive scam to promote the sales of new 'Bug-free' hardware, others turned their attention to trying to work out what it was deep down in the collective that still seemed unresolved. A nagging sense of an impending *something* still remained. Had it all just been wild paranoia, or had the echo of another imminent but later event simply been brought forward to the Millennium by our cultural fascination with significant numbers?

At this point, interest began to gather around the second most tangible possibility that might explain all this intuitive anticipation - the 2012 prophecies. Increasingly discussed as the 1990s progressed, their potential significance had been somewhat eclipsed by the millennial angst. With the year 2000 safely cleared, perhaps a greater clarity could now be reached on possible events twelve years later. Thus began the rise in awareness, first amongst the usual demographic of mysteries enthusiasts and truthseekers, then slowly but surely amongst a more general populace, of the 2012 phenomenon, which now occupies many people's thoughts today. This interest will only increase as the year approaches

As the Millennium celebrations exploded across the time zones, many breathed sighs of relief - or disappointment - as the much-vaunted computer 'Millennium Bug' failed to bring civilisation to its knees. But a sense of expectation still seemed to remain.

and popular culture latches on, as evidenced by documentaries and disaster movies such as *2012* (from the makers of alien-invasion spectacular *Independence Day*), which may hamper or enhance comprehension of something that might have genuine meaning in the real world.

2012 - The Key Elements

The essential component of the 2012 speculation runs thus: a number of ancient cultures, most prominently the Maya (see below), developed complex calendrical systems, which appear to have been based on an observational cycle of some recurring phenomenon, probably astronomical in origin. Although there are some disputes as to the exact date, most reliable 2012 researchers (fully taking into account historical alterations to calendars and remembering to include the year zero) agree that this cycle comes to a close, and begins again, on the winter solstice of 21st December 2012, which occurs (fascinatingly, given the mystical significance which some attach to these numbers) at 11.11 UT precisely.[1]

This time cycle is recorded by a number of independent cultures around the world, in calendars, folklore and tradition. On the other side of the world from the Maya, for instance, important elements of the same cycle can be found as a prominent part of the King Wen sequence in the *I Ching*, or 'Book of Changes', the Chinese divinatory oracle.

Some of these cultures attach prophecies to this cyclical time-period, which speak of significant changes that occur to the planet and its peoples around the time of each calendrical transition. More contemporary sources, divined through spiritual, psychic or other means [Chapter IV] have added their own weight of speculation as to how these changes might manifest. Although no agreement can be reached on exactly what will transpire, it is hard to dismiss the essential fact that there is an unusual amount of cross-referencing as regards 2012, which sets the phenomenon apart from the routine cult or evangelical predictions that so often come and go without solid grounds or fulfilment.

The Maya Countdown

The most substantial and oft-referenced 2012 source derives from the wisdom of the Maya people, who were most diligent in recording the time cycle. In the last decade there has been a massive growth of interest, particularly amongst New Agers, in the culture that flourished in what is now essentially Mexico and Central America ('Mesoamerica') between 250 and 900 AD. Despite recent cultural attempts (not least in Mel Gibson's film *Apocalypto*) to characterise the Maya as a savage, degenerate race, they were in truth remarkably sophisticated in many ways, and developed highly accurate calendrical systems, apparently based on observations of the sky.

Those who wish to understand the highly complex workings of the Maya calendar must investigate elsewhere, and are referred to the indispensable work of Geoff Stray (to which this chapter is much indebted) and John Major Jenkins - see Appendix. However, in essence, the Maya counts comprise a series of three intersecting systems, the Haab (a 365-day calendar), the Tzolkin (a 260-day calendar) and, most crucially, the Long Count (a more convoluted calendar of cycles within cycles, most prominently comprising thirteen 'baktuns', or one 'Sun'). The counts originated from the earlier Olmec civilisation and were developed as the centuries went by. What matters here is that the start date of the all-important Long Count, or 13-baktun Sun cycle, equating to 5125 of our Gregorian years, has now been accurately calculated based on the workings of all three systems - giving us a precise end point. As Geoff Stray explains:

'It is now clear, after almost a century of disagreement among Maya specialists, that the Creation of the current Sun - the start-point of the 13-baktun cycle - equates to 11th August 3114 BC, and will be replaced by the next Creation on 21st December 2012.' [2]

All of which means that we are about to enter the next Sun. In itself, this should give no more cause for alarm than opening a calendar for a new year would. However, the excitement comes with the many predictions, ancient and modern, associated with this process, leading to much speculation as to what it was about the cycle (beyond its astronomy) that was thought important enough to record with such accuracy.

One thing, as first discovered and outlined by John Major Jenkins in his book *Maya Cosmogenesis 2012*, does seem very clear. Because of a periodic wobble in the Earth's tilt (which produces the cycle, known as 'precession'), every 25,625 years the winter solstice Sun, as seen from our planet, significantly aligns itself over the exact centre of the galactic equator - the 'dark rift' of our Milky Way. This is an area where fewer stars are visible due to interstellar dust, but equates to being our viewpoint of the central 'nuclear bulge' of our own galaxy. The Long Count of the Maya is a fifth of this period - 5125 years - and appears to have recorded this process of 'galactic alignment' (as Jenkins calls it). The Sun entered the alignment zone once again in 1980. Because it takes 36 years to precess through this part of the sky, it effectively stood at the precise centre of the rift in 1998 - but 21st December 2012 was the year specifically defined by the Maya calendar as the special moment for reasons not yet understood.

Was it just the Sun's movement into a notable position that was recorded in the Maya calendrical systems, with merely astrological and esoteric implications, or was it somehow known that when this point in the galactic alignment process was reached that something more tangible also occurred? On page 254 we explore some possibilities as to why the Maya may have thought it mattered. But firstly, what are the much spoken-of Maya predictions themselves?

The Maya Prophecies

Despite all the fuss now being made about the 'Maya prophecies', there is actually remarkably little information to be gleaned from true Maya sources about what exactly to expect in 2012. The clues that do exist, although much held back from circulation by mainstream archaeologists, keen to avoid any eschatological taint from mystical New Agers, nonetheless seem to indicate a clear Maya belief that something of great significance would occur. Carvings on 'Monument 6' at Tortuguero in Mexico are the only contemporary references (i.e. made while the Maya were at their height) discovered so far to record what was anticipated to occur at the end of the current 'Creation' - on what we today call 21st December 2012 - and refer to the apparently momentous descent of the 'Nine Support Gods'. Exasperatingly, damage to the carved glyphs denies us a full explanation of what the nine gods would do once here.

The more apocalyptic of the Maya prophecies can be found in much later records, largely in the writings of the *Chilam Balam*, or 'Jaguar Priests', shaman-seers from Yucatan. Although not written down until the late 1500s, they record (in Maya language, but using European script) the traditional beliefs of the Maya and include the following in the book of *Tizimin*:

'... in the final days of misfortune, in the final days of tying up the bundle of the thirteen katuns [baktuns] on 4 Ahau, then the end of the world shall come and the katun of our fathers will ascend on high... ... These valleys of the Earth shall come to an end. For those katuns there shall be no priests, and no one who believes in his government without having doubts... I recount to you the words of the true gods, when they shall come.'

Maya temple at Chichen Itza, Mexico. Although there are not as many prophecies as people think, the Maya beliefs are still the most publicised in connection to 2012, and the accompanying calendars remain the most complex and best-kept of any ancient system in the world.

There follows a colourful description of wars waged, destruction, a ravaging of the land and wild weather, during which the nine gods will 'arise in sorrow'. Put together with the above references to a loss of faith in governments and priests, and all the not dissimilar themes in St John's Revelation and other religious texts, it's clear to see why some believe this may indeed be the stage we are seeing in the world today.

Why, though, should we give credence to the Maya prophecies above other obscure oracles? The meticulous precision with which the time cycle was recorded initially sets it apart from more woolly soothsaying, but it is in the remarkable amount of secondary support sources that the 2012 prophecies become unusually grounded.

Other Historical 2012 Predictions

The Aztecs - often mixed up with the Maya but actually a later Mesoamerican civilisation that flourished from the 12th century before being destroyed by the

244

Spanish in the 1500s - derived their calendrical systems from the earlier Maya system, but added their own nuances and prophecies, and awaited the return of their god Quetzalcoatl (or Kukulcan), the feathered serpent. The famous carved wheel, the Aztec Sunstone or Calendar Stone, for example, represents the five ages of the world, the Aztecs' own take on the Suns of the Maya. Rectangular panels display the four previous Suns, while at the centre is shown the fifth and current era - believed by the Aztecs to be the very final Sun. [Geoff Stray has claimed that the Sunstone may have been based on the design of an original version with moving parts, and a remarkable animation he has prepared, available on his website *www.diagnosis2012.co.uk*, as good as proves this.]

The Aztecs recorded that each of the previous four Suns ended in some kind of epic disaster - flood; an eclipse accompanied by the descent of flesh-eating demons; volcanoes; and wind. Unfortunately, the demons, or *tzitzimime*, are expected to return again to mark the end of the fifth and last Sun - on 21st December 2012.

Other cultures, often, though not exclusively, from North and South America, held similar views. The Peruvian Incas predicted that the *pachakuti* or 'turning over' of the world and time would occur in 2012, while the Hopi Native Americans of Arizona have been awaiting the arrival of the 'Blue Star Kachina' before 'Emergence' in 2012, heralded by a time of the 'great purification'. Many believe that the blue-tinged Comet Holmes, which spectacularly entered our solar system in 2007 (its coma gases expanding to a diameter bigger than the Sun), fulfilled the prophecy of the blue star, and the purification process is believed by some tribal elders to be occurring now. Other North American and Mexican tribes have very similar traditions.

The blue-tinged Comet Holmes in 2007. At its peak, its coma was bigger than the diameter of the Sun. The Hopi tribe believe that the arrival of a blue star will herald great change - but was this the very 'star'?

If all the prophecies heralded from the Americas, they could, perhaps, simply be written off as word-of-mouth repetition from one original source. Yet, as we have already seen, the ancient Chinese recorded the same precession time cycle in the *I Ching*, and even as far away as New Zealand the Maoris believe that the Earth and Sky, broken apart during

THE TRUTH AGENDA

the Creation, will come back together again - in 2012. This moment will mark the time when '*Ka hinga te arai*' - 'the curtain will fall', or, as a recent rediscovery of the original translation has it, 'the veil will dissolve'. On yet another continent, some African Zulu shamans are expecting the appearance of 'Mu-sho-sho-no-no', a star with a long tail that in previous ages turned the world upside down and caused a deluge (ancient flood stories are rife in almost every civilisation's legends). This star is expected to return in the year of the red bull - 2012.

This is just a very small selection of all the many connected prophecies from all manner of tribes and cultures, which, when calculated into our Gregorian calendar (again, fully allowing for historical adjustments), all seem to culminate in 2012 or thereabouts. Many religions, including virtually all the Abrahamic faiths, as well as the Hindus and Buddhists, have produced their own correlations to 2012 through various means. Although there is no accordance as to exactly how it will all transpire, it seems that the multiple foretellings represent an important sense of expectation embedded deep in our collective mind - and there have also been some very direct and more contemporary visions, which may shed light on the 2012 phenomenon.

Modern 2012 Insights

In addition to the historical predictions, there have been all manner of revelations in recent years that point to some kind of significance for 2012, many of which have been reached without foreknowledge of the prophecies and have only come to larger awareness within the last decade.

A number of people have become cognisant of the approaching period's significance through 'altered state' experiences, either through imbibing hallucinogenic substances or via unplanned shifts of consciousness during out-of-body experiences on operating tables or after head injuries or lightning strikes. From these have come several vivid visions that something huge might be about to occur around 2012.

Shamanic experiences have also revealed valuable insights. It was while imbibing the South American hallucinogenic brew Ayahuasca [page 255] in the early 1970s, for instance, that the brothers Terence and Dennis McKenna gained a realisation that the *I Ching* represents a fractal 'timewave' of important historical moments (or 'an unfolding pattern of every event that ever happens', as Geoff Stray puts it) - reaching its key infinity point in 2012. The graph created by mapping the mathematical content of the *I Ching* has peaks of 'novelty' and troughs of 'habit', resembling a fractal mountain range that, from the late 1960s, curiously starts to descend towards a point of maximum novelty where it hits the baseline - with the projected end-point of the cycle falling on 17th November 2012. This is close enough to the Maya

Tools of Control

Creation date to be eerily uncanny - yet at the time of formulating their theory, the McKennas had no knowledge of the ancient prophecies.

We have already seen how a great number of psychics and mediums have been receiving information about the importance of these times. Several entirely unexplained crop formations have also made direct references to the 2012 time cycle,[3] and some claimed UFO abductees such as Jon King [page 46] have been given insights that the years around 2012 will be crucial ones for humanity (although one school of thought has it that these revelations are veiled hints at a full-scale alien invasion due for that year). Those who practice 'remote viewing', in which information on places or people can be gained through clairvoyant techniques (much explored in military experiments), also try to divine insights into the past and future. However, it is claimed that attempts to see past 2012 very often fail, as if some kind of psychic barrier is in place there.

The final sequence of the McKenna 'timewave' - the peaks and troughs mark times of historical significance ('novelty') or mundanity ('habit'). Repeating fractal patterns seem to arise from this process - but mysteriously the projected future wave seems to collapse completely as it approaches 2012 [magnified].

It is not the place of this book to be a comprehensive compendium of 2012 theories - the curious should read Geoff Stray's seminal *Beyond 2012: Catastrophe or Ecstasy* for that. But the impression should be clearly conveyed by these brief examples alone that there does seem to be something oddly compelling about all the intersecting threads that weave this strange tapestry of expectation.

What, then, is the 2012 phenomenon really all about? Will anything happen, and if so will it be a positive or negative experience? Could it all be just so much hysteria, a phantom somehow born through a deeply buried collective awareness of obscure ancient traditions, but with no real substance? Or is a verifiable phenomenon about to make a significant manifestation, knowledge of which has been bubbling up through myth, symbolism and archetype for aeons?

Cosmic Waves

There have been many possibilities put forward to account for what was being recorded by the ancients in the 2012-terminating time cycle. Most agree that some kind of astronomical factor seems likely, especially given the galactic alignment correlation. Some are betting on esoteric elements coming into play, such as the legendary return of the planet Nibiru [page 86], but although unsubstantiated sightings have been claimed, there don't appear to be any unusually large celestial bodies currently approaching (which surely would have been shouted by amateur astronomers by now, even if authorities kept quiet). Approaching comets and asteroids on huge elliptical orbits, causing gravitational or climate effects, have been cited as more likely agents of change, whilst hyperactive solar cycles and periodic shifts in the Earth's tilt have been equally discussed. However, reasoned explanations as to why the Sun or Earth should by themselves suddenly behave out of character have been lacking. At least until recently.

Of all the theories under discussion, one does appear to keep raising its head, an all-encompassing concept that could explain recent observable changes in our celestial neighbourhood. This concerns the idea that our entire solar system, forever in motion with the rest of the Milky Way (and synchronous with the galactic alignment cycle), is moving into an energetically charged region of space.

The convincing qualities of this hypothesis do not necessarily mean that it is the correct one. However, it would explain many current developments in our region of space and is worth discussion here. The Sun, especially, has been more active in the last decade than it has been since records of its activity began - more so, even, than for thousands of years - although it has suddenly hit an uncannily quiet period in recent times, as we shall see. Together with other persuasive evidence, cosmic dust levels recorded in ice-core samples taken from deep beneath Greenland and Antarctica,[4] and analysed by Dr Paul LaViolette and other researchers, suggest that we periodically experience the passing of galactic or cosmic 'waves', pulsing out from the centre of our galaxy as a result of 'galactic core explosions'. As they transit through space, it is postulated that these vast shockwaves energetically excite stars, causing an increase in the frequency and intensity of solar flares and giving rise to disrupted sunspot cycles - phenomena which our Sun has been experiencing in recent times.

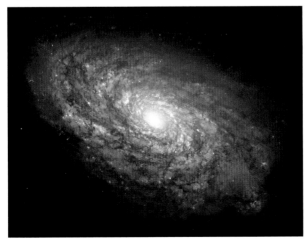

Galaxy NGC 4414, not unlike our own Milky Way. Dr Paul LaViolette believes that energetic pulses periodically emanate from the centres of galaxies, sending out shockwaves that change the behaviour of stars as they pass through. We may now be entering such a cosmic wave.

Tools of Control

The wave pattern identified by LaViolette operates on a 26,000-year and/or halfway 13,000-year schedule, and may account for the varying wobble of the Earth's tilt, which creates the cycle of 'precession' and gives us the aforementioned galactic alignment cycle, as well as playing a possible role in a number of mass-extinction events in our prehistory. Calculating on this basis means, happily, that we are not currently due for a major event ('superwave') at this time, but less severe galactic core explosions do seem to occur at more frequent intervals, which are still being studied - a pattern which may be embedded into the ancient calendars. It may be that we are now experiencing the beginning of a transit through one of these lesser - but still significant - waves. (Cosmic wave theory may also account for the supposed coming of the otherwise rather unscientific and misnamed 'photon belt' spoken of in some classic channelled information).

Given that *all* the planets in our solar system have recently been undergoing significant changes (rising temperatures, fluctuating brightness, changes in atmospheric densities and magnetic fields, new thin atmospheres developing around both Mercury and the Moon, and Mars undergoing ice cap melt are just a few of the effects), the behaviour of our Sun is a strong candidate as being the common factor here. Scientists who deny that solar cycles can significantly affect the Earth's climate might like to investigate further. But the Sun itself is probably at the mercy of a wider influence, and cosmic waves seem like a good explanation.

The most complex solar mass coronal ejection (CME) yet recorded, 4th January 2002 (seen here in a NASA composite image). The Sun has broken records for activity in recent years, although the current cycle has gone unexpectedly quiet.

Solar Activity

Sunspots (areas of intense magnetic activity, which appear relatively darker than the rest of the Sun's surface) run in eleven-year cycles (a period sometimes known as the Schwabe Cycle), peaking in number (solar maximum) at each end of the cycle, and falling back to none or very few (solar minimum) in the middle, as the Sun's natural rotation and other factors give rise to a regular pattern of convection anomalies.[5] Sunspots are associated with the manifestation of huge flares and 'coronal mass ejections'

(CMEs), which throw out voluminous amounts of solar particles and radiation into space, enveloping our entire solar system in a large protective bubble known as the heliosphere. Solar activity can have profound effects on our planet. Particularly strong ejections can cause communications problems on Earth and disrupt electrical power grids. They also generate the *aurora borealis*, or northern/southern lights, at the poles, as charged particles collide in the ionosphere.

Even if the cosmic wave theory is set aside, it remains that the Sun has until very recently displayed a sharp rise in activity. Occurrences of sunspots have been on a notable rise since they were first properly observed in the 1600s, with the requisite increase in CMEs and other coronal effects. Although there has been a slight fall in solar activity since the 1960s (in line with the general trend of a rising and falling wider cycle), the overall trajectory is an upwards one. According to David Hathaway of the Marshall Space Flight Center, 'four of the five biggest cycles on record have come in the past fifty years', and on 4th November 2003 the largest flare ever recorded (an unheard of 'X-45' in a scale that was never expected to exceed X-20 when it was developed) broke all records and expectations by being more than twice the size of anything

A heavily filtered view of the most powerful solar flare ever seen, 4th November 2003 - an 'X-45' on a scale that only previously went up to X-20. If one of these were to occur while aimed at Earth, our entire power infrastructure could be knocked out.

previously recorded. Given this kind of behaviour, could the tribal prophecies of the arrival of stars with long 'tails' and the suchlike be referring not to the coming of a new body into our solar system, but to a changed appearance of our own star?

In 2006, NASA was predicting, from computer modelling and statistical analysis of the last few solar cycles, that the peak of the current eleven-year sequence, which began a year later than expected after a strange lull between cycles - and thus appeared to fall in 2012 - would be one of the most active sunspot periods seen in modern times. Recently, however, the very slow start of 'Cycle 24' has seen a revision of this prediction to suggest that we might have the opposite effect - a very quiet solar maximum. In 2008, no sunspots were seen on 266 of its days, the least since 1913, and the early months of 2009 saw no reversal of this decline. This led NASA and the National Oceanic and Atmospheric Administration (NOAA), in May 2009, to move the expected peak of the cycle to 2013 and to forecast a 'below-average' number of sunspots, with the caveat that 'even a below-average cycle is capable of producing severe space weather'.[6]

Interestingly, periods of quiet sunspot activity have been associated with very cold periods for Earth's climate (the 'Maunder Minimum' of the 17th century, in which sunspot counts fell to very few for a long period, seemed to begin a period known as the 'Little Ice Age', a time of bitterly cold winters between 1650-1850, the source of all the Christmas card paintings showing skaters on the Thames). Given this, perhaps those scientists predicting global cooling rather than global warming [previous chapter] may yet be proved right. In 2009, NASA also released figures that showed a drop in solar irradiance - a 0.02% reduction at visible wavelengths, but a substantial 6% fall in the ultraviolet spectrum - reducing in turn the heating of the Earth's upper atmosphere. Radio emissions from the Sun also fell to their lowest level since 1955.[7] Is this an ongoing trend into another Maunder Minimum-type period - or the calm before a storm, as some scientists think? In 2009, alerted to the solar anomalies (if at opposite ends of the intellectual spectrum), both *New Scientist* and the *Daily Mail* were predicting the imminent possibility of a huge solar event that could take human society back to a new dark age by knocking out our technological infrastructure.[8]

But whether it is a period of hugely increased solar activity, or a notable quietening, the likelihood is that we are entering a cyclical anomaly, which is indicative of a noteworthy change in our local celestial backyard - one that may affect life on Earth. If we are indeed passing through the energetic shock-wave of a galactic core explosion, this theory offers one possibility as to why this change may be so marked, beyond the usual solar cycles. The same process may well be affecting not only us, but our entire heliosphere.

Fluctuations in the Heliosphere

With material from the Sun being ejected to the furthest reaches of the solar system, the protective shell it creates acts as a shield against some of the more unwelcome cosmic rays and radiation pouring out into space from other stars and active celestial bodies. Yet the heliosphere is itself behaving rather oddly at the moment, again reflecting apparent changes in our Sun.

The heliosphere pushes against the interstellar wind like a ship ploughing through the sea. Its passage through space even leaves an energetic bow-wave, with its edge known as the 'heliopause' [see diagram]. Yet Russian studies have shown that the boundary of the heliosphere, the 'termination shock', has increased in thickness by around an astonishing 1000% since the 1960s, suggesting a development of great significance. The Siberian geologist Dr Alexey Dmitriev believes the solar system is currently moving through a 'magnetized cloud of plasma' (presumably part of the cosmic wave), which is adhering to its edge to create the thickening. Dmitriev holds that this plasma (a partially ionised gas with a proportion of free electrons, known as an important 'state of matter') is the cause of so many of the changes we are seeing. He points to a notable increase of plasma in the Earth's ionosphere (the highest layer of our atmosphere), which may be affecting our weather and contributing to the current process of 'geomagnetic reversal' [see below].

Conversely, recent NASA studies have reported that, despite the apparent thickening of the termination shock, the heliosphere itself is weakening at a dramatic rate - and thus beginning to shrink in diameter. In 2008, data from the Ulysses spacecraft, which orbits the poles of the Sun, confirmed that the solar wind had decreased in general magnetic pressure by 20% since the previous solar cycle (and by an astonishing 36% in the immediate vicinity of the craft itself), making it the lowest reading since records began fifty years ago.[9] As a result of this retraction, the *Pioneer* and *Voyager* craft, sent out in the 1970s, are expected to exit the heliosphere far earlier than expected. Even usually cautious NASA scientists have expressed concern that

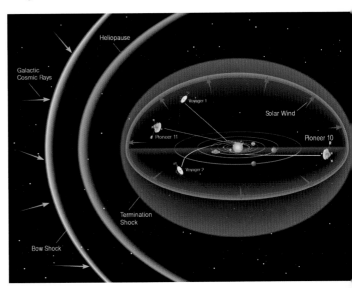

NASA diagram of the heliosphere, the protective bubble around our solar system exuded by the Sun, which ploughs through space like a ship in water, even creating a kind of bow wave ('bow shock'). In recent years the heliosphere has been notably shrinking, suggesting that we our passing through something which is affecting it - possibly a cosmic wave.

this reduced cosmic protection could make us far more vulnerable to high-energy interstellar influence, and others have speculated that this might be a factor affecting our climate (the latter point played down by official sources, as ever).

Our own local protective fields are not even as secure as was previously believed. Also in 2008, the THEMIS (Time History of Events and Macroscale Interactions during Substorms) NASA fleet of five spacecraft detected a tendency of the Earth's magnetic field to admit solar particles at completely unexpected times - therefore allowing far more in than had been previously calculated. The official NASA website describes the findings thus:

'... Our magnetic field is a leaky shield and the number of particles breaching this shield depends on the orientation of the Sun's magnetic field. It had been thought that

when the Sun's magnetic field is aligned with that of the Earth, the door is shut and that few if any solar particles enter Earth's magnetic shield. The door was thought to open up when the solar magnetic field direction points opposite to Earth's field, leading to more solar particles inside the shield. Surprisingly, recent observations by the THEMIS spacecraft fleet demonstrate that the opposite is true. "Twenty times more solar particles cross the Earth's leaky magnetic shield when the Sun's magnetic field is aligned with that of the Earth compared to when the two magnetic fields are oppositely directed," said Marit Oieroset of the University of California, Berkeley, lead author of one of two papers on this research, published May 2008 in Geophysical Research Letters. Researchers have long suspected that this "closed door" entry mechanism might exist, but didn't know how important it was. "It's as if people knew there was a crack in a levy, but they did not know how much flooding it caused," said Oieroset.' [10]

All of which seems to add to the view that not only is our local space environment now in a state of great flux, but the limitations of our understanding of it are also being revealed. This leaves the door open to the possibility that so-called 'fringe science', such as cosmic wave theory, may deserve far more serious consideration if we are to understand both what we may be about to go through and what the ancients were perhaps recording.

Geomagnetic Reversal

Another potentially massive planetary effect, almost certainly related to the phenomena being discussed here (and, again, little reported on in the mainstream), is the fact that the Earth would appear to be in the early stages of what is known as a 'geomagnetic reversal'. This is where the magnetic polarities of the planet make an abrupt switch, reversing their positions. Geological evidence reveals that it has occurred before, apparently on a major cycle of around 250,000 years, with other possible ones occurring at shorter intervals (some believe there was one 13,000 years ago, concurrent with the period the Atlantis legends may originate from, and also - as with the superwave cycle - embodying half a precession cycle). Calculations reveal that another reversal should therefore be expected any time soon, and the signs are that it has already begun.

The north magnetic pole first began to shift its location in 1904, as noted by Canadian scientists from the Geolab group, but since 1974 it has been wandering four times faster, by several hundred kilometres. Geologist Gregg Braden has stated that Earth's magnetic field has dropped 38% in the last 2000 years and that this rate of decline has risen to an average of 6% per year over the last century. This strongly suggests that 'the magnetic field is dropping at an accelerating rate towards a 'zero point' at which the polarity of the Earth will reverse', according to

Geoff Stray's report. He adds:

'French geologists have found 'a "large area of reversed magnetic flux" in the ocean off South Africa, which matches computer simulations of imminent reversal. They say that "the magnetic field seems to be disappearing most alarmingly near the poles", and there are "huge whorls" of molten iron beneath the poles that are rotating in a reverse direction, further weakening the field and accelerating the process.'

Meanwhile, in 2008, the Russian news agency *Pravda* revealed that scientists had identified more evidence of pole movement in such a fashion that it could contribute to an actual axis shift of the planet (something long channelled through by psychics and mediums, and also suggested by other researchers), giving rise to enormous climate changes and earthquake activity:

'Alexander Fefelov, a senior spokesman for the Russian Academy of Natural Sciences, said that planet Earth would have its magnetic and geographic poles relocated during the upcoming years. "Planet Earth on the orbit is a round object in weightlessness. The planet may suddenly change its axial inclination from time to time. It happens once in 23,000 years. The pole displacement angle may reach 30 degrees. The South Pole used to be located in the area of Easter Island before the latest displacement, whereas the North Pole was located in the Himalayas. That is why mammoths, rhinoceroses and sabre-toothed tigers used to inhabit Arctic latitudes. It was a very sudden displacement of poles. Archaeologists still uncover animals with undigested herbal food in their stomachs, which means that the animals died as a result of fast freezing, so to speak," the scientist said.' [11]

Although many analysts of geomagnetic reversal do *not* believe that a magnetic polarity switch will physically alter the tilt or rotation of the planet, it is clear that huge effects could be expected from such an action. The temporary collapse of the Earth's protective magnetic fields that would accompany the final stage of a polarity flip (which some believe could occur very quickly - possibly within days or even hours - after a slow build-up), could also expose us, however briefly, to a surplus of cosmic rays, with unknown results. In the worst case scenario, any huge electromagnetic pulse wave (EMP) that might emanate from the Sun during this period (*always* a major risk in any case) could also result in an entire neutralising of all electrical equipment on Earth and a wiping of databases, plunging society back into the medieval lifestyle seemingly desired by some.

All very apocalyptic, then, as the prophecies seem to suggest. Or is it? For some believe it may be these very kinds of unexplored energetic effects that might have a profound - and not necessarily negative - effect on humanity.

Galactic Alignment and Ascension

John Major Jenkins' observation that the Maya were recording the cycle of galactic alignment, in which the Sun, from the perspective of Earth, appears to stand over a particular part of the centre of the dark rift of our Milky Way every 5125 years [page 242], may offer more than just a visual nicety. According to Jenkins, the alignment may also result in an energetic resonance and a reversal of our *personal* polarity fields as well as our planet's geomagnetic ones, as its magnetic field aligns itself with the Sun. Geoff Stray explains:

'As the alignment occurs, the Solstice Meridian will align with the plane of the galaxy, or Galactic Equator, and pass onto the other side, which Jenkins says will signal a "field-effect energy reversal", allowing us to resonate with the source of the field. The source of the "energy" field (which includes the electromagnetic spectrum and beyond) is the Galactic Centre, and just as water spirals down a plughole in opposing directions in each of Earth's hemispheres, which are divided by the Earth's equator, so our changing orientation to the Galactic Equator will affect us in a similar way. This will be the completion of the "human spiritual embryogenesis" that is measured by the Maya Long Count calendar, culminating in a "pole shift in our collective psyche" and the birth of our Higher Selves.' [12]

Some have misunderstood this to mean that our entire solar system is crossing over the galactic plane, like a frisbee going up and down, but this is incorrect - the alignment in question results purely from the tilt of Earth in relation to the Sun. This, however, is not insignificant, as Jenkins insinuates. In a personal communication to this author, Geoff Stray elaborates:

'During the galactic alignment process, the Earth's axis is pointing in the direction of the Sun, and behind the Sun, to the visual centre of the galaxy (not astronomical galactic centre - the Sun will be in closest conjunction to that in another 200 years from now). The Earth's magnetic field will thus be aligned towards the Sun. It has just been discovered that there is a huge hole in Earth's magnetosphere... ...I personally think galactic alignment is just a cosmic clock that points to a time-window in which something will happen... ...Of course, this could combine with a huge influx of plasma, as in Alexey Dmitriev's scenario [page 250] - perhaps a huge flare will breach the heliosphere and let in all that interstellar plasma, which will come straight in the hole in the magnetosphere.'

It would seem likely that there is a link between the original cosmological event that started the Earth's wobble, our magnetic field's consequent periodic alignment with the Sun, geomagnetic reversal and the cosmic wave theory. It seems too much of a coincidence that these might all be falling together by chance. All the discussed phenomena ultimately speak of a cyclical reaction to a changed environment in space. But whichever consequence takes precedence, it seems reasonable to anticipate something within ourselves being affected, and this may have unexpected results.

Exposure to increased or altered electromagnetic fields can have a number of striking effects on human states of mind, creating mood swings between elation and depression, and even stimulating epilepsy or hallucinations, depending on the dosage. Some researchers believe this to be a result of the brain's pineal gland producing natural amounts of dimethyltryptamine, or DMT, as it responds to energetic changes. DMT is found in plants such as Virola, Psychotria and Acacia, and, depending on the area of the Amazon concerned, whichever DMT plant is locally available is added to the Ayahuasca brew, known for its extreme and sometimes expansive effects on the human mind (as the McKenna brothers explored). The taking of Ayahuasca is now a fashionable venture, with visitors from overseas seeking shamanic experiences.

The Ayahuasca brew being prepared in the Peruvian jungle. Ceremony and ritual is an important part of the preparation, and the drinking of it is not undertaken lightly. Ayahuasca contains DMT, which appears to expand consciousness (or distort it, depending on the viewpoint). But the brain also produces natural quantities of DMT, and some believe that an electromagnetic pulse from a cosmological event could trigger a mass hallucinogenic experience.

Dr Rick Strassman, a US professor of psychiatry, has discovered that DMT (or the 'Spirit Molecule') is also produced by the pineal gland during times of extreme physical or psychological trauma or at significant moments such as birth and death, and that it can result in people having mystical episodes or out-of-body experiences [page 34], where consciousness appears to detach from physicality. This may explain the 'unreal' feeling which can set in whilst experiencing accidents or stressful circumstances, which may be a natural protective mechanism. Debates continue as to whether DMT helps release what some would call the soul from its attachment to matter, or whether it merely produces the hallucinogenic *illusion* of such an experience - but its effect on our consciousness is claimed to be profound.

Strassman and other speculators believe that a huge rush of DMT production in our pineal glands could be stimulated across the entire global population in response to a cosmological energy spike, solar EMP or geomagnetic polarity shift, perhaps resulting in a mass out-of-body experience that affects the entire population of Earth. Given that a change in the geomagnetic field of just twenty 'nanoTeslas' (nT) is enough to trigger epileptic seizures, a major leap caused by unusual solar flares, which can already raise the field by 500 nT, could clearly result in a very dramatic effect on civilisation. Perhaps, with the rise of unexplained phenomena and psi effects we seem to have experienced in recent history [Chapter XIV], we are already seeing the beginning of such effects, as our solar system approaches the crucial moment.

Work by neuroscientist Dr Michael Persinger demonstrates that ghost and poltergeist activity notably increases at times of raised geomagnetic activity, either because more appear or because we become more attuned to them. Thus, the literal spectre is raised of a world going into mental and physical freefall around 2012 as the planet physically reacts to the final stages of the energy shift with quakes and tsunamis, atmospheric auroras shimmer overhead, our pineal glands go into overdrive and we find ourselves unable to discern between the already unusual external reality and the eccentric hallucinogenic visions that may suddenly fill our consciousness. All this would bring the world to its knees as surely as any Millennium Bug.

But will we be brought to our knees - or raised to a higher state of being? A recurring optimistic feature of New Age prognosis and psychically channelled messages has been that the 2012 changes will bring with them a 'raising of consciousness' into a 'new dimension'. Many refer to this process as 'Ascension' (although that term can have more specific connotations - see page 307). Some predictions are more specific than others, and they are hard to reconcile with each other in any fine detail, but the general thread is of a movement towards something more advanced than our current psychological and physiological state.

Some sources directly assert that, at the peak of the Earth changes, those evolved souls of a 'higher' nature will suddenly advance to the 'Fifth Dimension', to enjoy a new life on a less physical and far purer plain of existence (what happens to the rest of us is unclear), while other versions suggest that 2012 will bring a gentler transition as Gaia evolves, with normal life continuing but on an 'improved-frequency' Earth. Detail on how any of these scenarios are supposed to actually occur is usually absent, but, as with the very similar Abrahamic or evangelical aspirations to a 'New Jerusalem' after a period of tribulation (some versions of Ascension seem to be The Rapture without the religious trimmings), they universally seem to offer hope of better things for the faithful. All, at the least, reflect a feeling that nothing will be quite the same afterwards.

With all the more (relatively) science-based speculations being considered here, perhaps it is not so outlandish to imagine that passing through a cosmic wave and/

or undergoing a changed magnetic alignment with the Sun might result in some lasting effect, which leaves us in a new evolutionary state. If all the DMT-inspired pineal fireworks do result in pushing our brains to new extremes of experience, it is interesting to note that Dr Persinger also observes that during *quiet* times of electromagnetic activity incidences of telepathy and ESP phenomena seem to rise substantially. In the descent from the peak of the 2012 time cycle, as whatever disruption we might experience recedes and some kind of normality sets in until the next cosmological bump, perhaps our species might find itself with enhanced transcendental faculties that remain active, the wilder visions settling down into a new sense of telepathic intuition and communalism. Perhaps, in such a world, those of the old control agendas may suddenly find themselves marginalised and left behind by a civilisation liberated from shackles that no longer work in an altered context - which may be their greatest fear. A whole new level of evolutionary adventure may then present itself, rather as Kubrick's *2001: A Space Odyssey* muses. Indeed, the first steps towards understanding the true power of our metaphysical natures may already be taking place, as Chapter XIV outlines.

2012 - the Year of... Nothing?

All this is as maybe - and is, of course, wildly speculative, as 2012 discussion tends inevitably to be. The sifting of all these options should not be taken as any kind of endorsement of their veracity. The Truth Agenda can only be applied partially when faced with something almost entirely nebulous. The cross-referencing calendrical cycles across the globe, together with the coincidences of modern discoveries (such as the Timewave theory), definitely suggest a more substantial basis than is usual in the pantheon of prophecy, and as such are significant, but the little we have to go on reveals nothing of any solidity.

Amongst all the excited speculation, we must also, therefore, be prepared to face the mundane possibility that in the post-2012 years we might be looking back at a rather disappointing (if comforting) lack of dramatic occurrences, with all the 2012-related books stacked in the bin, this one probably included. Perhaps there will have been a few tangible effects, but only very subtle ones. What then? But that debate is for the future.

What, however, of the other day-to-day realities that awareness of the 2012 phenomenon might bring as it approaches? For, as stated before, what is more important to the hypothesis being discussed in this book is not whether any of the visions, prophecies and predictions for these times actually come true, but that the *belief that they might* may well be helping to shape the massive control agenda that seems to be so insidious - and very real.

Tying the Threads Together

It can be taken as a given that if those on high (the Illuminati, lizards, global elite or whoever may be pulling the strings of global control according to the conspiracy theorists) really are motivated by ancient beliefs and occult practices, as the Bohemian Grove rituals and other supporting evidence outlined in this book strongly suggests, then they will be very aware of the 2012 predictions. Anticipating the upheavals that could result from a fulfilment of the prophecies, potentially overturning the established order of their machinations and tipping long-term agendas into chaos, it can also be taken as a given that they would do everything in their power to ensure they remain on top. If so, this would seem to make sense of the global control scenario on a number of levels.

Notwithstanding the lure of power for power's sake, which almost certainly plays at least some part in the motivation of the controllers, there does seem to be an urgency to the placing of the chess-pieces that are forming the patterns of today's politics. Tracing the likely paths do make the notion of a one-world government a feasible ambition. And yet diversity has always been held up as a strength in the past - so why change that now? Could it be that the threat of a global catastrophe, making a mockery of borders, has shaped the new agenda?

Readiness for Civil Unrest?

Amongst all the predictive speculation, there have also been extraordinary claims that a number of countries are expecting civil disturbances on a massive scale. Some truthseekers believe that the Rex 84 (Readiness Exercise 1984) programme in the US, for instance, run in the Reagan years to test civil unrest contingency plans, led to the building of around 600 FEMA (Federal Emergency Management Agency) prison complexes, each one designed to hold thousands of inmates. It is claimed they lie empty, waiting... for what? Mainstream pundits have attacked the myths that have built up around the 'concentration camp' assertions, some alleged locations for which, when investigated, have turned out to be nothing more than water-treatment plants or dilapidated World War II internment camps. Yet the belief in these camps persists, and there does seem to be a grain of truth that the US has some worryingly draconian policies in waiting, beyond those already discussed. In a piece otherwise critical of the conspiracy theories, *PublicEye.org*, the 'Website of Political Research Associates', does concede the following:

The Spotlight... *carried the first exclusive story on "Rex 84" by writer James Harrer. "Rex 84" was one of a long series of readiness exercises for government military, security and police forces. "Rex 84" - Readiness Exercise, 1984 - was a drill which postulated a scenario of massive civil unrest and the need to round up and detain large numbers of demonstrators and dissidents. While creating scenarios and carrying out mock exercises is common, the potential for Constitutional abuses under the contingency plans drawn up for "Rex 84" was, and is, very real. The legislative authorisation and Executive agency capacity for such a round-up of dissidents remains operational.*

The April 23, 1984 Spotlight *article ran with a banner headline "Reagan Orders Concentration Camps." The article, true to form, took a problematic swipe at the Anti-Defamation League of B'nai B'rith along with reporting the facts of the story. The Harrer article was based primarily on two unnamed government sources, and follow-up confirmations. Mainstream reporters pursued the allegations through interviews and Freedom of Information Act requests, and ultimately the Harrer* Spotlight *article proved to be a substantially accurate account of the readiness exercise, although* Spotlight *did underplay the fact that this was a scenario and drill, not an actual order to round up dissidents.'* [13]

This suggests that whilst some of the conspiracy hysteria may be unfounded, contingency plans to combat 'massive civil unrest' do exist - as surely they must. Official explanations for the unoccupied camps that *have* been acknowledged in the US imply that they are mere contingencies for any unexpected surge of illegal immigrants over the US-Mexican border. But why should such an influx occur and what event might precipitate the movements of such high numbers of people? Is it merely the (possibly misplaced) worry that global warming and rising sea-levels might displace populations, which could turn up on US borders seeking refuge, or could there be a bigger disaster anticipated, in tune with all the 2012 speculation?

With so many US citizens having easy access to guns and other weaponry, and already strong units of local militias and defended communities established around the States, any destabilising event on that continent could easily see a plunge back into a feudal 'wild West' situation. It has long been predicted that a new American civil war could erupt in difficult

US Navy air crewmen survey the devastation caused by Hurricane Katrina in 2005. The anarchy that broke out in some parts of New Orleans during the disaster was an example of how quickly society can become unstable when the natural order is disrupted. Are the authorities going to be better prepared in the event of a 2012 disaster - and is their 'solution' internment camps?

times, and, for all the heroism and good community relations that surely were forged during it, the Hurricane Katrina disaster that hit New Orleans in 2005 exposed the perilous fragility of law and order when governments hesitate. With the US in its worst recession since the Depression of the 1930s, any extra 2012-related ingredients entering the powder-keg might require authorities (in their eyes) to incarcerate - or 'protect' - large numbers of its population.

It is likely that most countries will have similar contingency plans (there are also claims of empty British prison camps), and the control agenda that appears to be gripping most Western societies may have at least some of its roots in the fear that the world is about to - metaphorically or literally - turn upside down.

The Astrology of 2012

Interestingly, even without the prophecies, the astrological component of the next few years would appear to promise trouble and strife by itself, with civil unrest clearly on the cards. Statistically, astrological cycles *do* appear to have tangible influence on the collective psychological states that generate events on Earth, as the 2006 book *Cosmos and Psyche* by Richard Tarnas (previously seen as a hard-line academic and now predictably marginalised by his alleged peers), makes very clear - and 2012 would appear to be a notable period in this regard, according to other astrologers.[14]

An important 'square' aspect (a 90 degree angle) between Pluto (control, power, death) and Uranus (maverick, libertarian, unpredictable), which will be in place by 2012, put together with the zodiacal placing of both planets, is almost guaranteed, in the astrological view, to bring about an overt social struggle between these polarities, continuing the Pluto/Uranus cycle that began in the mid-1960s - a major time of revolution and unrest. All this is likely to impact the UK especially, a country which will, of course, be hosting the Olympic Games in 2012, thus focusing the eyes of the entire world on this little island [page 304]. Whatever issues are coming to a head here will be brought under the global microscope that summer and opened to the world for debate, as China found with its own Olympics in 2008. Britain could suddenly become a major flashpoint if the liberty versus control battle reaches some kind of climax, either philosophically or on the streets. In the closing chapter we shall explore further the UK's potential role in any 2012 drama.

Helen Sewell, a psychological astrologer who has made an extensive study of the 2012 aspects, elaborates on the effects of the Pluto and Uranus positions in her influential article *The Astrology of 2012*:

'If we look back in history at the Uranus/Pluto cycle, this particular one started with a conjunction of the two in Virgo in the mid 1960s. The conjunction of two planets is

An astrological 'bi-wheel', showing the chart for London on 21st December 2012 (11:11 am) on the main outer ring, and the chart of England on the inner ring, enabling comparisons and interpretations to be made [see quote]. England's 'birth date' is set for 25th December 1066 (12.00 pm) - the crowning of William the Conqueror, which changed the country forever and is thus considered to be a key start point for things as we know them today (some use the Unification chart of 1801, which, by coincidence, is strikingly similar in many respects - either way, England is a Capricorn country). See Helen Sewell's full article for the details.

like seed-planting time, when their conglomerate energies collide like nuclear fusion and new things are born. Looking at what was going on at this time gives us clues as to the potential of these seeds for both good and ill as the cycle matures. In the mid 1960s there was huge rebellion against the establishment, seen in such examples as the American student riots against the Vietnam war, and the Cultural Revolution in China. It was a time of experimentation with psychedelic drugs, the 'sexual revolution' (Pluto ruling sex and Uranus ruling revolution), and various rebellions against the social norms of the time as an attempt to 'break out' of restricting, outmoded ways of being.

In 2012, Uranus and Pluto are going to come into their first really challenging aspect to each other since the 1960s and this will create a build up of an incredible pressure - of volcanic proportions. The tension between the two forces could detonate revolution and rebellion (even Earthquakes, on a physical level), and could bring crashing down what we thought were established political structures. This will be especially so, because Uranus will be in the war-like sign of Aries, and Pluto will be in Capricorn, which represents authority, the establishment, political structures and governments.

My vision of one of the possible outcomes of the 'clash of the Titans' is this: Our freedoms are gradually and perniciously being eroded away at the moment and, with

Pluto having just moved into Capricorn in January 2008, governmental control may well become more extreme. Uranus, particularly when it moves into Aries in 2010, will no longer be able to tolerate its freedoms being curtailed and will revolt in a possibly very sudden and violent way.' [15]

So, in addition to the social unrest, these same aspects could also help trigger physical repercussions to the planet, perhaps fulfilling the predictions of Earth changes inherent in so much of the 2012 soothsaying. Given the obvious grounding in metaphysics and the occult shared by those who may be covertly pulling the global strings it is almost inconceivable that they would not also be aware of the zodiacal implications of the near future. Even in the more public face of power, Cherie Blair, for instance - and thus, by default, Tony - is known to have consulted astrologers, and Ronald Reagan allegedly built his entire schedule around astrological advice. [16] Once again (for any doubters of mysticism reading this), what is important here is powerful people's *belief* in such things, regardless of the truth. Sensing any kind of upheaval that might unseat their influence, it stands to reason that the world's secret rulers would want to cling to power at all costs and put into place every kind of control that would help achieve this.

The better news, for those open to the astrological view, is that the roles of Neptune and Jupiter in 2012 could provide the spiritual balance to all this, Neptune in particular helping with an expansion of consciousness and the 'Ascension' qualities discussed earlier. [Readers should investigate Helen Sewell's article in full to get the bigger picture.] The general thrust is clear, however - 2012, by astrology alone, would seem to be a time when the old order of things could be upset beyond recognition, bringing great difficulty but, through it, great transformation.

The Control Agenda Explained?

To summarise... A fear in high places, based on long-studied prophecies and modern predictions, that everything we have known in our recent history may be about to implode, would seem to be a plausible motivation behind the climate of control that has been cranked up so vastly in the last decade. If the agenda is not just about power in its own right, but masks instead an underlying mystic/occult conviction, passed down through endless generations, of a right-to-rule amongst an elite class (or even *believed* to have been passed down), perhaps some sense can be made of the world we live in. History records that when power is so desired, or thought to be an inherent dynastic right, no method of implementation, however deceitful or callous it may seem to the masses, is considered off-limits. If the swarming populations are seen as little more than cattle in the eyes of a pious elite (as emotionally removed as the Nazis were to the Jews), why would we be treated as anything but livestock; animals merely to be herded or slaughtered as necessary? Certainly, any possibility of individuals suddenly evolving on a spiritual level and stepping up to their own full potential would be something to be vigorously resisted at all costs, and dissuaded by whatever suppressants necessary, be they social, political or chemical.

This, at least, is the conspiracy view, the take on life this book has chosen to explore, offered for consideration, not as an absolute.

Yet if all this turns out to be the dark fantasy of our inner collective fears and we live not at the mercy of some deeply-preserved occult elite worried about mystic predictions, but merely a group of selfish manipulators milking an economic system they have learnt to play well, is the outcome likely to be very different? Sensing even the vaguest possibility of a forthcoming global shift - even if they genuinely believe that global warming alone might be the disruptor - would they not wish to ensure their influence remains strong? The Truth Agenda, whichever way it is applied, would seem to reveal unarguable control games, and in the last part of this book we will see how they can be diluted and side-stepped to create a world that benefits the many and not just the few.

2012 Squared

What of the 2012 phenomenon itself? This chapter has examined some of the more credible possibilities to account for it, but there are many other ideas to be explored elsewhere. Are we dealing with a large planetary shift, or something more introspective; an apocalypse of the heart, rather than the world? Will we be looking at social upheaval, spiritual upheaval, or both? Are we dealing with a planetary evolution, at the whim of cycles in the heavens, and if so, can we ride with it as it goes?

Some have scoffed at the New Age pretensions so often associated with the speculation regarding 2012, with all its talk of transformation and 'raising of consciousness'. After all, will people be feeling quite so elated in the midst of electromagnetic pulse waves, atmospheric upheaval and earthquakes, whilst simultaneously undergoing a traumatising hallucinogenic experience? And what does any of this mean to the oblivious millions of the 'developing world', simply trying to survive another day rather than being concerned with the raising of consciousness? The truth is that no-one knows what will happen, nor whether this chapter (or indeed the entire book, along with several other tomes) will be seen as an embarrassing footnote of fringe paranoia within just a few years. Yet the gift of it all has been that the very act of *considering* the possibility of fundamental developments to both humanity and the planet, and waking to the idea that someone might want to hold back our full potential as living beings, is in itself creating a self-fulfilling prophecy of positive change.

Through mere consideration of the concept of a great shift, many are finding their lives transformed and enhanced in ways they had never before thought possible, and these people are tipping metaphorical lines of dominoes that are having a genuine and uplifting effect on the world. The awakening process initiated by the 2012 speculation is in itself a force to be reckoned with. The realisation that truths, both political and metaphysical, have been kept from us and that we may be able to transcend the restrictive view of ourselves that has been so widely fostered, can only be the path to something better, if delusion can be forestalled and everything kept in perspective. Discernment and perspective are the biggest challenges that these times we find ourselves in bring - and there will be casualties along the way amongst those who cannot find a balance. But if enough seekers can keep themselves in a sensible questioning state, achieving a genuinely new level of consciousness and stepping up to a fresh social and planetary responsibility in a mode of true self-awareness, then the entire 2012 phenomenon will have been worthwhile, even if the key period comes and goes without great drama.

What, though, if the window that begins on (or centres around) 21st December 2012 does bring great upheaval? If so, the doom-mongers who put much weight on the more devastating predictions would do well to remember the name given to the turning of the great calendrical system by the Maya, whose beliefs above all seem to have captured the popular imagination - they called the time 'Creation Day'. So 2012, whichever way things transpire, is not about endings, but beginnings.

We need to look, then, at ways in which to ensure that something new and good can begin with these times. The recognition of our inherent power, so often trodden down or distracted from by the system we have become locked into, could balance and neutralise the agendas of those who seem to prefer us weak, and instead offer opportunities to create a new culture of hope and vibrancy.

THE TRUTH AGENDA: *The 2012 prophecies are unusually cross-referenced by many sources, ancient and modern, and seem to represent an important upwelling from the collective psyche, stimulating an awareness of imminent change. Cosmic forces and alignments may be the bringers of that change but, whether metaphor or reality, the simple self-reflection that knowledge of the prophecies is inspiring may in itself contribute to an important developmental stage for humanity. Any road to higher consciousness may be something to be fought in the eyes of a ruling elite. Its fear of losing the control and privileges maintained for so long might well be the driving force behind the erosion of liberty and programme of suppression that many believe is in place. If 2012 does bring huge events, conscious knowledge in the run-up will surely help us; if it ultimately disappoints, the speculation will still have woken many up to wanting to improve their world.*

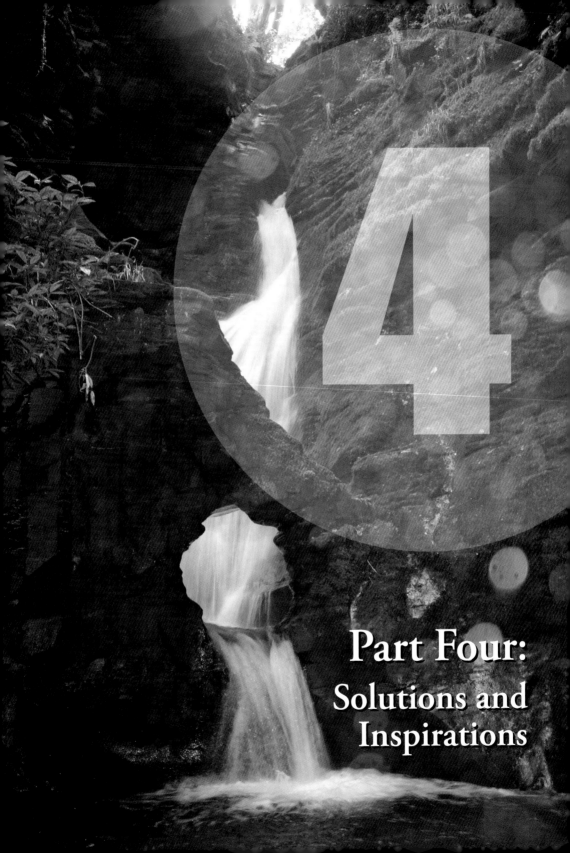

4

Part Four:
Solutions and Inspirations

To some truthseekers, overt occult symbolism such as the glass pyramid at the Louvre, Paris, suggests a boastful arrogance in the elite's attitude. But what kinds of minds would plan such things, and are they really as infallible and all-knowing as some would have us believe?

XIII   WHO ARE WE DEALING WITH?

Uncertain speculation on the ruling elite many believe is running the world can lead to the presumption that it is all-powerful and infallible. But is it? And do we really understand its motivation? Identifying the human foibles and underlying desires of those who may be planning centralised domination could lead to a greater chance to offset their agendas - if people can break the chains of apathy and step up to the task.

Lifting the Blindfold

So far in this book we have been exploring a hypothesis; what if the world *is* being controlled by a ruling elite putting its own narrow interests and convictions above ours? And what if we are about to undergo a huge change, social, spiritual or cosmological? The exploration of these ideas has thrown up disturbing possibilities and more pieces of evidence to support them than is entirely comfortable. For all this, however, it is still a hypothesis until proven beyond doubt, and the fervent who believe passionately in every aspect of conspiracy theory's most extreme frontiers would do well to remember this when trying to drive their beliefs home to doubting listeners - a balanced and sensible approach will be needed to attain credibility.

However, as has been expressed in earlier pages, if all that this troubled speculation achieves is to help prevent such a grim picture from coming true, or at least reaching full fruition, then it will have served a useful purpose. It is also crucial that a note of optimism is struck as we reach our conclusion. A common and often valid criticism of truthseekers is that their fevered investigations into humankind's worst nightmares can leave some listeners feeling *more* fearful, and risks driving them into a state of disempowered paralysis, putting up the shutters when what is needed is engagement. Yet the unavoidable truth is that looking a potentially tough situation in the eye does mean facing up to disturbing realities that may have been swept under the carpet, for they may require urgent action. Lifting the blindfold means that we might not run into the approaching wall at such a great velocity. If these pages have left some feeling shocked and reeling, the act of simply contemplating such issues may in itself spark a new awakening, whether all the ideas are agreed with or not. Looking twice at the world around us is a very good habit to cultivate. If the reader has come this far, it is likely that at least some of it has hit home.

With that established, this last part of this book steps back from detailed dissection of the symptoms to get a sense of perspective on the overall shape of the central hypothesis. In so doing, some potential solutions and strategies for dealing with it become clearer, as encouraging processes that could help us are identified and examples of past actions that have changed the world for the better emerge as the kind of transformational developments that can occur when enough people stand up to initiate them.

The Elite and its Motivations

Something too often missed in all the conspiracy speculation is the realisation that if we are being governed by a secret and powerful elite trying to twist the world to its own ends, then we are still essentially dealing with fellow human beings (putting the ET/reptilian element aside for a moment). Like every other person on the planet, they must have physical, social and emotional needs, even if the latter faculty may be too easily set aside in the kind of mind that would plan 9/11-type scenarios. The personalities involved must have loved ones of their own, and experience thoughts, feelings and cares in at least some directions - and they eat, procreate and go to the lavatory like everyone else. They also, like most of us in our lives, probably think they are doing the right thing, however much we may see their schemes as misguided.

This is an important point. We all have reasons for doing what we do, and can often justify our actions to ourselves in the face of serious challenges from the outside. Hard though it may be to comprehend the motivation of those who might think that wiping out a fair percentage of the population would be a positive move, or who believe that planning wars and economic breakdowns to effect the creation of a unifying world government is an acceptable strategy, the fact is that many seemingly well-intentioned visionaries and academics throughout history have voiced the need for such approaches. This does not make them right, of course, but there is plainly a significant, if small, stratum of humanity that believes a bigger picture should be put before the needs of the masses. Those who have expressed support for eugenics and depopulation programmes, for instance, often have deep-seated environmental concerns or feel strongly that we have lost our balance with nature and must put the planet's future ahead of the requirements of the common people (as with the attenders of the 1975 conference that seems to have been at least the partial root of the global warming scare - page 230).

One of the most prominent promoters of the term 'new world order' was the famous and much revered writer H G Wells, who believed fervently that the only answer to global strife would be the creation of the eponymous hierarchy, though he saw it as a long and nebulous process. Writing in his 1940 book *The New World Order*, Wells states:

'There will be no day of days then when a new world order comes into being. Step by step and here and there it will arrive, and even as it comes into being it will develop

fresh perspectives, discover unsuspected problems and go on to new adventures. No man, no group of men, will ever be singled out as its father or founder. For its maker will be not this man nor that man nor any man but Man, that being who is in some measure in every one of us.' [1]

The New World Order is clearly not a modern concept, and has roots going back even further than this idealistic vision of it.[2] Some believe both World Wars were deliberately coordinated, or at least used, to help bring about a mandate for world government. As early as 1913, writing in his book *The New Freedom*, President Woodrow Wilson made clear that some formidable force already underpinned the commercial, and probably political, infrastructure of the USA:

Herbert George Wells in 1943. Rightly famous for novels like The Time Machine *and* War of the Worlds, *Wells also held radical political views and believed that only a 'New World Order' and a programme of eugenics could stop the world from falling into anarchy. It is easy to condemn these attitudes, but those who hold them may see themselves as saviours.*

'Since I entered politics, I have chiefly had men's views confided to me privately. Some of the biggest men in the US, in the field of commerce and manufacturing, are afraid of somebody, are afraid of something. They know that there is a power somewhere so organized, so subtle, so watchful, so interlocked, so complete, so pervasive, that they had better not speak above their breath when they speak in condemnation of it.' [3]

What is striking in H G Wells' writings, however, is his sense of excitement and enthusiasm for the idea of a dominating collective that would put all to rights and avert 'the disastrous extinction of Mankind'. There is no sense of negative intention nor a Malthusian dislike for humanity. Yet at the same time Wells was an advocate of eugenics, writing:

'It is in the sterilisation of failure, and not in the selection of successes for breeding, that the possibility of an improvement of the human stock lies.'

Many find this view entirely repugnant, but here is the paradox - the very kinds of people truthseekers tend to single out as the enemies of humanity clearly see themselves as its saviours. It is all a matter of perspective and of where one chooses to draw the moral line.

The philosopher Bertrand Russell openly accepted the inevitability of a one world government, based on a world of hard scientific values, and was disturbingly frank about the society that would result, writing in his 1931 book *The Scientific Outlook*:

Bertrand Russell, philosopher and Nobel laureate, in 1950. Russell's views on how the future of humankind would evolve into a rigidly-managed hierarchy of 'rulers' and 'plebs' were either shockingly prescient, or are being used today as a working blueprint.

'In like manner, the scientific rulers will provide one kind of education for ordinary men and women, and another for those who are to become holders of scientific power. Ordinary men and women will be expected to be docile, industrious, punctual, thoughtless, and contented. Of these qualities, probably contentment will be considered the most important. In order to produce it, all the researches of psycho-analysis, behaviourism, and biochemistry will be brought into play... ...All the boys and girls will learn from an early age to be what is called 'co-operative,' i.e., to do exactly what everybody is doing. Initiative will be discouraged in these children, and insubordination, without being punished, will be scientifically trained out of them.'

Many feel that this exactly what is going on today. By 1953, Russell was even more direct. Writing in his book *The Impact of Science on Society*, he states:

'Diet, injections, and injunctions will combine, from a very early age, to produce the sort of character and the sort of beliefs that the authorities consider desirable, and any serious criticism of the powers that be will become psychologically impossible... ...Gradually, by selective breeding, the congenital differences between rulers and ruled will increase until they become almost different species. A revolt of the plebs would become as unthinkable as an organized insurrection of sheep against the practice of eating mutton.' [4]

On the surface, this appears to support such a world, rather than condemn it, and such thinking seems outrageous and unacceptable, even if it does come close to identifying the very philosophy that may now be actively shaping our world. However, although it seems difficult, almost distasteful, for some to contemplate, a thought to be considered here is this - what if such thinking were definitively shown to be right? What if humankind's very survival did rest on the notion of more control, not less? What if the choice were demonstrated to be between total destruction through over-population, pollution and over-stretched resources, or a selectively-bred, closely-monitored world that regulated itself and continued? What if an anarchy-ridden post-2012 apocalypse society were to stand no real chance of survival, but a tightly-controlled disciplinarian civilisation would? Uncomfortably, in the light of the world's current issues, it can be seen, at least to a small extent, how arguments could be made in these directions when looked at from a certain viewpoint. The problem comes, as ever, with the massive issue of who gets to decide. Those in comfortable circumstances looking down from on high must inevitably see things rather differently to those scraping an existence lower down the rungs, at their mercy.

We already hold the power of genetic manipulation in our hands, and it will not be too long before required characteristics of children will be able to be routinely selected and engineered. Also, with life-spans ever-increasing, and our understanding of tissue and brain cell regeneration growing by the year, how long will it be before life can be sustained indefinitely? When that occurs, the population problem will clearly explode if unlimited access to such power is allowed (that is, if the majority of the population is permitted to survive in the first place). A world of immortals would risk stagnation, but also domination from those who attained the status of immortality first. They would effectively decide who would be offered the gift from thereon. In the end, the gene pool would almost certainly be controlled by such authorities, the new eugenics having arrived through the back door. These issues are already reality, not dystopian fiction. The power of genetic engineering, which is currently changing our food, both animal and vegetable - and thus our entire eco-system, as spliced and altered genes make their way into nature through pollination and cross-breeding - means that humankind has already taken the entire planet's evolutionary destiny into its own hands, and there is no going back. Do those calling the shots have the moral compass to carry such a huge responsibility? Can they serve as the gods they are setting themselves up to be?

In a society of angels, perhaps a charter of rigid regulation, surveillance and genetic population control could be applied with compassion and the wide agreement of a common consensus - but we are nowhere near such a state of being. With the motivation of those governing our world today clearly in question, it seems impossible that the kinds of agendas many feel the ruling elite is implementing could work in any way other than being a simple attack on the larger percentage of humankind. Without common consensus, whatever the supposedly good intentions some may feel they have behind their plans, any attempt to regulate the

THE TRUTH AGENDA

world by coercion and draconian measures remains an immoral one. There may be other solutions the elite has not considered in its hermetically-sealed world of privilege and protection, ones that might be able to be constructively and routinely discussed if the agenda were thrown open to exposure and public debate.

Openness as Mitigation?

It is an irony that if the powers that be were to be entirely honest about their actions, they might find many people backing them in some areas. The public, concerned about energy, might support a long game to foment the creation of Western oil pipelines across the Middle East, for instance, if it was openly declared and decently negotiated, instead of being manipulated into being by suspect wars with false-flag origins. Similarly, an admission that 9/11 was aided by a cabal inside America might shake Western culture for a while, and risk some repercussions, but eventually things would settle into a respect for the new spirit of honesty. The bizarre Bohemian Grove ritual [page 92] might be tolerated as a harmless pageant if it were fully admitted to and discussed, instead of being oddly hidden and skirted around. Even the perfect portraits of people standing on the Moon might be a little more acceptable as acknowledged fakes if a vulnerability were admitted and it was explained why representative shots had to be reproduced to show what we *should* have seen.

Wall Street, New York. The recent banking crisis, which resulted in huge losses and unemployment across the world, revealed deep seams of dishonesty that appear to have become acceptable standard practice.

The problems with global cover-ups is that they arrive and build up - as they so often do for all of us - through a lack of honesty largely sparked by the fear of what people might think or do if they were to perceive the true vulnerability within. The elite appears to fear us and our reactions as much as we may fear them [page 317]. Many disingenuous actions are borne of inner psychosis; a lack of trust that other people will understand. Our leaders appear to have got so used to lying and playing deceptive games that they cannot now operate any other strategy. Everything from the banking system to Parliamentary expenses appears to be based on subterfuge. Right now we are clearly not trusted by those affecting our lives so strongly and as a result we do not trust them. Yet sometimes a declaration of honesty creates unexpected results.

Not that some of the elite would care a jot for our trust, nor be remotely bothered about what any of us thinks of their actions. For those who may feel that caveats to explain their motivation is too generous to those who maim, kill and deceive to get their way, for whatever reason, it should be noted that there do also appear to be those pulling the strings who seek power for power's sake. The lessons of history tell us that selfishness, greed and excited bloodlust cannot be ruled out as prime movers in some cases, at least. And, to acknowledge the not-insubstantial belief in the reptilian agenda, if it were to turn out that this highly exclusive club was indeed the result of a dominating extra-terrestrial gene seeded long ago and being exploited and/or activated by celestial visitors today, then it might explain why concern for the needs of humanity would be as low down the list of its priorities as general concern is for the welfare of livestock today.

As for what kind of people may comprise the global elite, the well-intentioned and the not-so well-intentioned, most likely we are largely dealing with high-ranking politicians, academics, intellectuals (as with Wells and Russell), monarchies - and very rich families. In other words, all the obvious candidates. Other books go into the detail, so there is little need to explore it here. Most cite the key players as being the likes of Henry Kissinger, Zbigniew Brzezinski [page 23], Dick Cheney and assorted US neo-conservatives, figures such as Tony Blair and selected world leaders, most US presidents and their hidden sponsors, magnates and corporate leaders, and other moneyed and influential business dynasties like the Rothschilds and the Rockefellers. Thinking along these lines soon enables one to speculate freely on the kinds of characters we are probably dealing with. How much of the grand plan all of them know, however, and whether there are pyramids-within-pyramids amongst even the power structures near the top, is another matter.

Factions Within Factions

The presumption is often made that the very existence of a ruling elite means that those involved must be all-powerful and of one mind, accurately manipulating domino events that hit the required spot every time, all to a predetermined agenda. But this may apportion them an unwarranted infallibility.

There is evidence to show that there are factions and disputes within the echelons of those with great influence over our lives. After all, the world is a big and complex place. Even with a general agreement on how it should move forward, the pressures of regional needs and personal biases are almost certain to blur the clarity of purpose from time to time. From the word that does sneak out of Bilderberg meetings and the suchlike, it sounds as if as many disagreements, compromises and negotiations arise there as within any supposedly democratic Parliament. If this weren't the case, the meetings would not presumably need to take place, so set would the scheming be.

As with Masonic and other secret society structures, there is also a pecking order to consider. It is doubtful that all those 'in' on a global conspiracy seeking centralised control would be party to every machination, and certain players may themselves be manipulated from within without realising it. From the outside, for example, it appears that Gordon Brown, for all his many references to creating a 'New World Order', does not have the solid support from above that protected 'Teflon' Tony Blair in his years of power. Brown seemed destined to be a fall-guy from the start, set up to come to power just as the world economy took a tumble (although he himself had clearly played a part in that - page 72). The question is, does Brown know the full plan? Is he someone faithfully playing a game with a known outcome of outward failure, while secretly ensuring that the fairly clear agenda of weakening the UK to guarantee full entry into a federal EU succeeds, or is he still clinging on in the genuine belief that all will come right and that he will one day be hailed (however unlikely) as a political hero? (The Freudian-slip Brown made in Parliament that the Labour Party had 'saved the world', in the wake of the economic crash, does suggest he has a high opinion of his own role, even if few of his elite colleagues share it.)[5]

Likewise, when Bill Clinton found himself under threat of impeachment following the Monica Lewinsky sex scandal, was this all part of a contrived drama, or a sign of factions within factions very genuinely trying to remove him after an unintentional gaffe? And did Richard Nixon go rogue or was he just playing a pre-auditioned role? On a smaller level, when a man in the crowd died after being pushed to the ground by a policeman during the 2009 G20 protests in London,[6] it took all the seemingly contrived focus away from images

Police 'kettling' (forcibly enclaving) protestors at the London G20 protests in May 2009. When a protestor died shortly after being pushed to the ground by a policeman, the media suddenly turned on the authorities. Is this evidence of a totally coordinated elite strategy to enrage the population further or, as many believe, an unexpected error? How organised can a ruling elite really be?

of a few people smashing a bank window and suddenly all the headlines became howls about police brutality. Was this an ongoing twist to stir further civil unrest [page 303] or was it (as many suspect) something going unexpectedly wrong and changing the script? Does every war and false-flag terror attack really go to plan, or is there as much cock-up involved as conspiracy?

How organised, then, is this global elite, and is it really as united as some truthseekers give credit for? The evidence suggests there are chinks in the armour and disagreements within, and weaknesses and unpredictable elements always arise in any grand plan. This offers hope. The foibles of human nature and the sheer universality of chaos theory may ensure that unexpected events and peculiar sidetracks undermine the apparent solidity of the control agenda just when they are least expected. We could therefore be dealing with something far less coordinated than feared - indeed, the wide truthseeker presumption of the elite's potency may make it seem more of a problem than it really is. But can we take the chance of becoming complacent?

We have clearly seen through the application of the Truth Agenda that certain events and trends do seem to be part of an unfolding pattern that suggests an attempt to engineer a mandate for centralised power. We must not become petrified into inaction by this. Nor, however, should we take the risk of assuming there is no real threat, if the conspirators are found to be less competent than some believe. Either way, it is important at the very least to call attention to the appalling deeds committed by those at least *trying* to be an all-powerful force.

Consent by Apathy

If plans for world domination are being laid on any level, a simple fact needs to be recognised - that it only goes on because we collectively allow it. Even with obvious governmental deceptions such as the weapons of mass-destruction debacle, such things only continue to occur as widely as they do because not enough people stand up against them or call their leaders properly to account. Through all the methods discussed in Part Three, we have allowed apathy and the distractions of (apparent) comfort, trivia and entertainment to hold us in our armchairs in the hope that anything dark 'out there' will sort itself out in time. Voter turnouts for British elections have become ever lower, meanwhile, meaning that most recent governments have come to power with the direct consent of only a tiny minority of the population - with fewer votes than those regularly cast for TV talent shows. This lack of political interest is understandable on one level, but it also sends out the message that we don't really care how we are ruled, and quietly gives permission to those who think they *do* know to do with us what they wish. After all, if we show so little regard for the democratic process, however flawed it may be, perhaps we won't mind not having one at all.

By having become so disconnected with what goes on around us in our names, we have not stood up in our collective power - and are therefore as responsible as any global elite for having created the world we live in today. With the consent granted by our passivity, we have watched obvious lies and manipulations take away our strength, resolve and liberty, and have done little or nothing about it. As such, we have given away our personal responsibility. The energy spent complaining loudly but emptily in the pub or bus queue about the shortcomings of today's society, if applied in more proactive and positive directions, could be used to offset the very things being complained about. The problem is that we have been trained to think that we cannot make a difference - when we can. The next chapter will explore an unseen mechanism that may offer some hope in this direction, while the final one provides some practical examples of people power, which could lead to solutions.

The truth is that until now, conspiracy or no conspiracy, we have collectively permitted a relatively small group of flawed individuals to foster questionable agendas that affect many lives. That this was able to happen at all is astonishing in itself, but a long game is being played and there is still time to wake up before the final pieces are put into position.

Maintaining the Flame of Optimism

Much of the awakening process that HAS been started has come from the kind of people drawn to be part of the truthseeking community, and there are many players who should be applauded for their selfless efforts to raise awareness. Instead, those often unseen efforts are generally rewarded by undeserved ridicule and sidelining by a culture that has shut its eyes and ears to anything but the skewed vision it is fed by those who prefer to keep us dumb. People who question the status quo are easily neutered in the mainstream by being inanely lumped in with those (i.e. almost nobody) who supposedly believe Elvis is alive and working in a local chip shop - false stereotypes created by a media that is all too often either controlled, fearful or just lazily stupid. Truthseeker enthusiasm has allowed itself to spill over into fanaticism and lack of discernment sometimes, no doubt, and this must be guarded against, but the fact is that there are absolutely vital questions and observations being raised by other very reasonable, very *normal* people, which could make a real and positive difference to people's lives - if ever given a chance. To get that chance, though, however small, these questions will have to be framed in the right way and targeted in the right direction.

We have already seen in Chapter I how accusations of verbal evasion had Barack Obama repeating his inaugural oath the day after taking office to avoid 'conspiracy

THE TRUTH AGENDA

theories'. This was a remarkable acknowledgment of the growing influence of conspiracy thinking. The concerns over the old-guard powers most likely behind Obama's ascension certainly demand attention. At the same time, this should not be allowed to eclipse the very real hope for something new that shone in the eyes of those who voted for change. If that positive energy is not leached away by the usual distractions, there is genuine cause for optimism because of it. The revitalised

US election enthusiasm made it feel like people were beginning to care again, people who thought that their opinion might count for something this time. The economic crisis caused by questionable banking and complacent (or complicit) politicians has woken people up in a big way to the possibility that they may not be as looked after as well as they believed before. Any tangible disappointment in the new US administration will alert them even further to the reality that the world is not being run for our

Thousands upon thousands line the Washington DC National Mall to witness the inauguration of Barack Obama. Hopes are high for something new from a very new kind of president - but if disappointment should follow, people may become more alert to seeking less conventional views on the way their lives are governed.

collective benefit. If Obama, with the wide-eyed hopes of so many people heaped on his shoulders, fails his nation, or is seen to obfuscate his people in any way, there may be a wider sea-change in how people perceive the way we are all governed.

It doesn't take long for the average person to see through manipulation once obvious anomalies are pointed out. Assuming the masses will always be dumb may be an arrogant and huge mistake on the part of our masters (as Tony Blair discovered when he attempted to feed patronising spin to the annual conference of the Women's Institute in 2000, receiving a much-deserved slow-handclap of objection in response).[7] When discussed in an accessible and objective way, the concept of a ruling global elite, which believes that some kind of catastrophic change may be imminent and has thus been implementing a regime of draconian restrictions by nefarious means to ensure it retains control, is nowhere near as far-fetched as it may at first seem to those new to the idea. It is also plain that 'fringe' areas such as UFOs, paranormal phenomena, religious apparitions, visions of the

Solutions and Inspirations

future and ancient prophecies are taken far more seriously by authorities than has ever been admitted. The connection of all these areas, as discussed in previous chapters, can be made to sound credible when expressed in balanced tones.

Tones are important. The introduction to this book has already pointed out that extreme conspiracy dogma, passionately but indiscriminately shouted, can repel potential support and plays into the hands of the mainstream's characterisation of all alternative thinkers as uneducated tinfoil-hat fanatics. Those with the power of insight who can rise above this have a responsibility to convey a user-friendly overview of the control agenda - and check their facts, or be prepared to be corrected with good grace if proven to be wrong. Bellowing loudly or preaching only to the converted won't be enough if real change is to be created and critical mass achieved. Successful outreach requires initial moderation - and compassion. Newcomers can be confused by all the many complex sources of information out there, and may shrink from the at-first shocking alternative

Confrontational protest banners at a London peace rally. Striking the right balance between making a robust point and avoiding putting people off through over-zealous in-your-face campaigning is not always easy. Understanding what diverse groups of people will respond to and having empathy for their individual sensitivities can make a big difference in making listeners more open to hearing alternative truths.

viewpoints if not properly acclimatised. Truthseekers themselves need to take this into account, find a sense of balance and exercise real discernment. The habit of questioning absolutely everything can lead to a hubristic assumption that we are *never* told the truth of anything by anyone - but this is to fall too deeply into cynicism and risks pathology. Hearts and minds must be kept open and optimism maintained if true change is to come about, whilst at the same time retaining sensible vigilance.

The uncertain era we live in now provides a unique opportunity for those with the insights to offer another view - while they can. The ongoing withdrawal of liberty and freedom of speech in Western society needs serious addressing and only greater awareness will enable the collective will to create its own catharsis, but for that to happen those with eyes to see need to take true responsibility.

The good news is that the weight of numbers believing in something, or changing a viewpoint, may have a more far-reaching effect than anyone suspects, as we shall now explore.

THE TRUTH AGENDA: *There may be more than one reason why a world of centralised control would be desired by a ruling elite, and we cannot fully presume to understand from the outside. But no strategy that imposes an undeclared agenda without transparency or choice can be right, and any regime of underhand manipulation must be resisted. To resist successfully, however, those with awareness must hold on to optimism and strike an appropriate tone if they are to be listened to and people awakened so that a minority's vision for the world is not allowed to ride roughshod over the needs of everyday people. The elite is not infallible, and this offers hope.*

We all like to think of ourselves as individuals - and we are - yet recent scientific discoveries are making it clear that our minds, when working together, have a genuine collective effect on the world, one that could be very powerful if tapped.

XIV   THE POWER OF COLLECTIVE THOUGHT

The belief that minds working together can affect the material world may be more than just New Age rhetoric. Scientific experiments with the power of thought are revealing an all-encompassing mechanism of collective consciousness, the understanding of which may be the key to forging a new world of positive change. Can we step up to the responsibility that proactive use of this process could bring?

What Are We Fighting For?

In Chapter XII we explored the hopes and fears for the year 2012. Beyond the obvious astronomical observations, we cannot yet know for sure what kind of recurring event the ancients were indicating in their calendrical systems, but it seems that a significant shift may be imminent, even if it occurs through the simple self-fulfilment of people's own expectations. A spiritual renaissance is in order either way, one that could be forged by growing social upheaval and polarisation (as the astrology alone suggests).

Yet it cannot be denied that, on past archaeological evidence, perceptible cosmological events on a scale beyond our control would seem inevitable; if not soon then at some point in the future. This leads the pessimistic to dark musings. Given that our planet has endured catastrophes, climate changes and mass-extinctions several times before, then where, in truth, is our civilisation going? Has the emergence of humankind, seemingly the most advanced intelligence Earth has yet produced, been a statistical quirk born in a time of geological and celestial stability but doomed to falter in the way most other dominant species have before it? If so, what is the point of trying to better ourselves? Why fight to build a more enlightened civilisation, free from fascistic control and complex conspiracies, only to see it knocked down again by cycles outside of our influence?

There are some who feel helpless in the dual face of cold agendas from powerful elites and pending doom from natural threats, and shrink at the seemingly insurmountable tasks our world must confront if it is to gather itself into something sane and resilient. This fearful stance is all-too-often used to justify a dangerous path of inaction and apathy. The notion that nothing we do or think can make a real difference may also be deeply misconceived.

The Evolution of Consciousness

On a practical level, all we really have in life are the basics - ourselves, our loved ones and the immediate environment around us. For some, this is all that is needed. The pragmatic approach of accepting that reality and making the very best of it to live in the now and enjoy the pleasures and little moments for what they are brings all the meaning they require. It is remarkable how even those who find themselves in situations or environments beyond their making, far from perfection, can often cultivate a sense of well-being within, their spirits kept high. For others, however, a more profound centre is needed - a sense that what they do, what they think and how they live affects a larger canvas outside of themselves. The continuing magnetic pull to religion, however misused it may have become, is evidence of how strong this human instinct is. The belief in the collective power of prayer has motivated the lives of millions (to scoffing from the likes of Richard Dawkins), yet only recently has evidence begun to emerge that there may indeed be a scientifically detectable force behind it.

A Hindu woman at prayer. Scientific experiments with the mind are proving that both individual and collective thoughts can and do alter the environment around us, and that mind-to-mind 'transmission' is a reality, thus entirely supporting the genuine power of prayer.

If it does turn out that our every thought and action is directly affecting the world around us on an energetic level, as the experiments described below suggest, then it also follows that over long aeons the human race has been evolving its consciousness to the point where the collective mind may have become a powerful 'entity' in its own right. Perhaps every strife, every debate and painful learning experience, all the pushes and pulls between right and wrong, 'good' and 'evil', have been for a higher purpose after all, as equations resolve (however agonisingly slowly) and the entity (or 'Noosphere', as Pierre Teilhard-de Chardin called it) matures into adulthood.[1] Removed from the long-held and narrow view that we live our lives merely to be judged or played with by lofty deities, be they Olympian, Norse, Hindu or Abrahamic (and all points in-between - which is not necessarily to say they don't exist on some level), we may face instead the reality that a web of consciousness itself is the ultimate force of life, binding us and propelling the universe forward, God by any other name. From this perspective, it may be the experiences and thoughts that somehow imprint themselves into the permanent fabric of the universal mind that are important, rather than the material gains or losses fought for day by day. Edgar Cayce [page 50] would have called the resulting memory-field the 'Akashic Record', a kind of eternal databank through which the universe evolves. All of this means that what occurs here and now does matter, because it will count in the future, very much so, regardless of what calamities may appear to befall. How we handle events and what we learn and radiate into the collective consciousness may be the most crucial thing of all.

Arthur C Clarke's 1954 book *Childhood's End* posits the notion that humankind may eventually evolve into something far beyond flesh and blood (as does his and Kubrick's *2001: A Space Odyssey*).[2] The story concludes with humanity's psychic progeny dissolving the Earth as they move onwards out into the universe, the cradle discarded. We appear to be nowhere near such a stage yet - although some ascensionists may disagree - and keeping the planet strong and healthy is our current responsibility (once we agree, based on correctly-assessed evidence, which way that will best be achieved - Chapter XI), but Clarke's parable illustrates that our attachments to the things we think matter most may need some reappraisal. It is our handling of what we have before us now that may determine greatly how quickly we step up the ladder of consciousness.

What, then, is the evidence that we have a tangible psychic evolution before us?

The Power of the Mind

In Dean Radin's 2006 book *Entangled Minds*, he assesses the oft-dismissed yet astonishingly substantial evidence that the human mind not only communicates with other minds on a recordable minute-by-minute basis, but that all minds working together generate a collective 'field' (for want of a better term) that can affect material reality.[3] The power of the mind has been tested and speculated on for centuries, yet mainstream science has managed to sideline and dismiss the multiple studies that have been mounted to show that consciousness can and does extend beyond the body and outwards across perhaps unlimited distances. This dismissal is unforgivable in light of the fact that many of these studies have been conducted under rigorous scientific conditions, the methodology painstakingly developed, dutifully tidying up all loopholes or any potential for inaccuracy or vagueness. Indeed, because of the need for scrupulous integrity in the face of mainstream cynicism, many of the experiments have been carried out under strictures more rigidly scientific than most peer review science. Yet still academics refuse to acknowledge the findings, or afford them only the faintest of interest, which soon sees the implications forgotten.

Conducting what is known as meta-analysis - compiling statistical studies of the studies - and factoring in even the widest possible margins of error, Radin demonstrates categorically that science *has* proved that the mind is capable of telepathy (or 'psi' phenomena) and other 'non-local' effects, as the odds against the positive results occurring by chance are simply too huge. Most strikingly, the quantum quality of 'entanglement', in which particles once joined and then separated remain in mysterious and instantaneous communication with each other, can be shown to work at a macro level too. In other words, we are all 'entangled' with each other and the world around us in a way that means we are inseparable from our fellow beings and our environment - and the universe is inseparable from us. The implications of this work are truly colossal, and many students of the 'new physics' are, however reluctantly, coming to the same conclusions.

It is worth a brief resume here of the kinds of effects that have been discovered from the numerous investigations of many different researchers into psi phenomena, fully confirmed by meta-analysis:

* Basic telepathy ('transmission' of images, feelings, etc.) can provably occur between certain individuals, and the effect is much stronger when the test participants are known to each other and therefore entangled (i.e. if they are life partners - which says much about the importance of relationships).

* Physical distance between participants can make a difference to psi effects (the further the separation, sometimes the weaker the results), but not always, and 'transmissions' are instantaneous, no matter what distance is involved.

* The instantaneous qualities of psi effects have been confirmed by wiring people up to machines that register brainwaves, skin-resistance or nervous system reactions. Incredibly, the machines record that separated participants can share identical matching reactions even when only *one* of them is being stimulated (with images or sounds, etc.) and the other is entirely unaware of what is happening to their counterpart. This is clear evidence of quantum entanglement and also suggests that 'gut reaction' is far more than an empty term.

* Results for psychokinesis (or telekinesis - the ability to influence the movement or behaviour of objects) have been less solid, but still show a success rate far beyond statistical chance. Experiments with dice, for instance, have shown that it is possible to influence the general outcome of a series of throws.

These extraordinary findings demonstrate that we live in a world where the pattern of events, relationships and emotional states must be influenced on a continuous basis by these processes, even if they are merely operating at a background level. Perhaps it is not just by mathematical coincidence that we so often know who is at the other end of the line before we pick up the telephone. Perhaps we should

THE TRUTH AGENDA

trust our initial instinctive feelings about people and places more than we do. Perhaps a run of good fortune when we are in a positive mood is more than just the perception a happy-go-lucky mindset. And when the car or lawnmower next breaks down when we are in a bad state of mind, we should perhaps consider the very real influence we may be having on the objects and environment around us.

But if all of this is indeed occurring continuously, what wider effects might it be having beyond our individual lives? The 'collective unconscious', alluded to by the likes of Carl Jung in more esoteric and psychological terms, may be more of an everyday reality than anyone has previously suspected - offering a tool that could help the current plight of civilisation.

The Global Consciousness Project

Realising that there must be a larger implication to the web of psi effects, a number of researchers have looked for ways in which such an influence can be tracked and monitored. Here is not the place for a complex study of the workings of consciousness science, and *Appendix 2* gives some necessary pointers for further research. However, open-minded physicists like Dean Radin and Robert Jahn, working at the Princeton Engineering Anomalies Research Laboratory (PEAR) in the USA, have been instrumental in developing fail-safe mechanisms of testing the powers of psi - thus also creating ones for recording collective patterns.

The standard method of reading cards with symbols and pictures and 'transmitting' the images to another person in a different room had been shown to produce positive results above statistical chance, but was not considered scientific enough to constitute absolute recordable proof. Tests on the likes of brainwaves and skin responses took things to a higher level, but more was needed. Hence the idea was developed of using computers to produce random binary sequences - entirely meaningless streams of digital ones and zeroes pouring out in an endless torrent. It was established that if a person or persons could, without any physical interaction with the computer, influence the streams into more ordered sequences, this would be a) a fairly infallible test of psi, and b) would be scientifically recordable to the finest degree. Subsequently, the 'Random Number Generator' (RNG) tests have produced the most convincing evidence yet that the mind operates on levels outside of any of the usual restrictive parameters conventional science has superimposed onto it.

It was soon realised that certain individuals could nudge the otherwise chaotic RNG data into desired sequences. Radin writes:

'In the PEAR Lab tests, participants tried to intentionally influence the RNG outputs to drift above *the chance-expected average (they called this the high aim condition,*

Solutions and Inspirations

like aiming for heads instead of tails), then below *chance (the low aim condition, like aiming for tails), and then to withdraw their mental intention entirely to allow the RNGs to behave normally as the baseline or* control *condition.*

From their experiments, Jahn's team reached several conclusions. They found that in all of their experiments using truly random sources, like those based on quantum events, the random outputs tended to match the directions that the participants intended. When wishing for high scores the RNG outputs drifted up, and when wishing for low scores the RNG outputs drifted down. By comparison, no positive results were observed when simulated random numbers were used, like those generated by software algorithms. They estimated that the magnitude of the PK [psychokinesis] effect was approximately equal to 1 bit out of 10,000 being shifted away from chance expectation. While this may seem like a tiny effect, over the entire database this resulted in odds against chance of 35 trillion to 1.' [4]

Further experiments showed that groups of people working with the RNGs had even more chance of pushing the sequences into non-random patterns. It was discovered, therefore, that the human mind appeared to have the astonishing capability of creating order from chaos, generating 'coherence', and that an increase of focused minds could affect the outcome. With this remarkable insight, the researchers began to consider whether this might be something that was occurring on a daily underlying level, as a natural output of the ever-evolving consciousness of humanity. This genius stroke of enquiry led to the creation of the now ongoing Global Consciousness Project. [5]

Four events that had the most dramatic effects on the Random Number Generators (clockwise from top left) - 9/11; the 2004 Boxing Day tsunami; The O J Simpson murder trial verdict; Princess Diana's funeral. What these seemingly unrelated occurrences have in common is that they all focused many minds on the same thing simultaneously and sent out psychic ripples across the world.

As the years have gone by an increasing number of RNGs, or 'eggs' as the global models are known, have been placed at several participating locations around the world, streaming out their meaningless sequences for the Global Consciousness Project. Each has its own power source, with no direct connection to the outside world. The latest results are collected from each individual machine at intervals and then compiled. Those results have been profound. It was quickly observed that certain collective events - i.e. when many minds were focused on the same thing at the same time - were producing notable divergences from randomness in the RNG data. The most significant areas of global focus, such as the death of Princess Diana, the Boxing Day tsunami of 2004 and, perhaps inevitably, 9/11, seemed to create the biggest ripples of all. Even bizarre events like the unexpected 'not guilty' verdict in the original murder trial of actor O J Simpson (transmitted live around the world) generated powerful spikes of coherence in the RNG output.

What this reveals is that the act of strong collective focus seems to throw something out into the wider environment that affects the workings of material components, such as computers. The generation of data coherence would seem to assert that when we think together, a more ordered universe appears to result - an encouraging thought. Although a very subtle effect in the labs, and the mechanism behind it remains unknown, it has nonetheless become clear that some process is at work, quantum, energetic or esoteric, that is at its most powerful when we are *united*. Exactly how this process can be practically tapped and manipulated is not something promoted by the Global Consciousness Project researchers, who remain cautiously laid back in their observations, but others outside the strictures of (perhaps understandably in this case) having to maintain scientific credibility have been able to speculate more freely.

Taking Back Collective Power

Many believe the RNG and other psi experiments have revealed a world in which we are incontrovertibly entangled with each other, bound together by more than just societal trends. If the Big Bang theory or all its multiple variations is correct, it must be the case that every piece of matter in the universe was once bound together in a 'singularity' - before being burst apart in a massive expansion. As particle physics has shown, once something is entangled, it is always entangled, no matter what distance is introduced. Should we really be surprised, therefore, at the discovery that we are in a constant state of instantaneous and non-local interaction with each other? This at once vindicates the beliefs of mystics throughout the ages, and supports the reality of the power of prayer. Experiments with prayer using groups and target recipients (chosen groups of hospital patients, for instance) have shown positive results of faster recovery above statistical chance, regardless of which faith or denomination might be doing the praying. [Such studies are debunked by Dawkins, but the examples he gives in his 2006 bestseller *The God Delusion* are highly selective.][6] The RNG experiments suggest a clue as to how it is that prayer can be successful. Maybe it is we ourselves - if also

Solutions and Inspirations

interacting with a larger universal collective consciousness that we could recognise as God - who are doing much of the work, rather than the outcome solely relying on the intercession of a higher power.

The realisation that working and thinking together has more than just a metaphorical consequence potentially grants us much power - but it also gives us great responsibility. If we could learn fully how the process of collective consciousness works, it could be used to great effect - perhaps even to create the Utopia that humanity has aspired to for centuries. However, it also reveals to us how easily such a mechanism could be manipulated for negative purposes. Maybe it has been deployed against us all this time. We have seen how those in powerful places seem instinctively to be drawn to occult wisdom and the metaphysical realms. Adolf Hitler famously gathered such knowledge and created massive collective ripples to a terrible effect. With a new and wider awareness of the power of united thinking, could there be a chance to take back a mechanism that was always rightfully ours? In this way we could start to forge a world we actually want, rather than settling for the prepackaged and compromised one we are being handed.

Of course, the implications of a global consciousness field have mixed consequences, for it means that however much we may try to live apart from the big wide world 'out there', we can never truly escape it. The interactive process ensures that we are always being affected, whether we are aware of civilisation's worst excesses or not. Becoming a hermit may not be the panacea of isolation it appears. If the collective is being polluted by what certain elements of humankind put into it, then we are all sullied on some level. However, the equal and happier observation is that when we project positivity and live in ways that offset darkness, the mechanism must be such that it cannot do anything but channel that back into the collective - an effect that must also reach the very people trying to enforce their agendas over the common good.

'Critical mass' is often spoken about in New Age circles - the belief that if enough people take on an attribute then that attribute is passed on to the entire human race when a certain key percentage of the population is affected. People will often (sometimes glibly) speak of the 'hundredth monkey' syndrome as an example, supposedly based on experiments with apes on South Pacific islands.[7] It can sound all too loose and easy - yet experiments by dedicated researchers like Dr Rupert Sheldrake, observing the mysterious transmission of behavioural traits amongst animal species (which he calls 'morphic resonance'), do indeed support the view that all life is surrounded by some kind of ether or field. The feeding habits of certain bird species, for instance, have been shown to have very quickly changed across the world at rates beyond that dictated by simple behavioural mimicking. Sheldrake believes the methods and information are being passed on through what amounts to being, in the populist view, a collective telepathic field. Perhaps the all-encompassing 'Force' in the *Star Wars* movies is not so far from the reality of what we are dealing with.

This all seems to suggest that the spreading of collective information and abilities is dictated by the weight of numbers alone - but in the human mechanism at least, the focus of intention seems to have equal status when strategically applied.

The Importance of Intention

Despite the apparent evidence that it is the proportion of a population focusing on something that produces the largest energetic output into the collective, it is also clear from the effectiveness of propaganda, sparked from on high and spread by the media, that the collective can be easily led, like starlings in a flock. This unfortunate effect has been responsible for much of the state of affairs we have discussed throughout these pages, and we can now see that there is far more to the process than simple word-of-mouth influence. When a certain percentage of the human race is persuaded to believe something, that belief would appear to be transmitted across the entire species through a more esoteric medium than previously suspected. It takes a strong will and keen level of awareness to break free of the tendrils being bound around each one of us, regardless of our own individual experience.

Adolf Hitler, 1932, during his ascent to power. Highly focused intention can easily lead the will of the collective, as Hitler clearly demonstrated - or override weak opposition, for all the importance of the weight of numbers in the RNG experiments.

But there is evidence to show that concentrated personal intention can override the critical-mass mechanism. Free-thinkers have fought themselves clear of the popular consensus since time began - otherwise we might still believe the Sun revolved around the Earth today - but it takes dedication and the courage to face risk. Hitler was a negative example of how one man's will was able to lead the collective, made especially susceptible given the dire circumstances in Germany at the time of his rise. Some dictators achieve their position by force alone, but charisma and the power of personal faith seems to produce the most lasting effect. This is something that plainly demands vigilance. Some seem to have the power to shape the collective to their own will, setting up lines of dominoes and tipping them to their own patterns and design, while others (like Tony Blair) have the ability to mollify the masses in the face of great opposition and obvious deception [Chapter VII]. How can this happen given that the more people who think something, the greater effect it produces on the RNGs? Why is it that some individuals are able to push past this process to impose manifestos of their own onto a majority opposition?

It is an established statistic that sportsmen or teams tend to win home games more often than when playing away. Although much of this can be put down to a familiarity of environment and a generally more relaxed attitude, the clear presence of support from a larger number of fans makes a huge difference. The players are inevitably more puffed up with pride and propelled by expectation. But it has never been entirely understood why the success rate is influenced so greatly. Perhaps the new discoveries regarding collective consciousness provide an answer. But how, then are certain individuals seemingly able to buck this trend?

Tim Henman was one of Britain's finest professional tennis players for many years, and achieved good results in tournaments around the world. Yet whenever confronted with the Wimbledon championships, on his own turf so to speak, although he did better there than anywhere else full success always eluded him. Why should this have been, with an entire stadium and a country full of eager supporters tuning in to will him to the top? Surely, according to the implications of the collective process, Henman should have won Wimbledon at least once?

Famously, in 2001, it was Croatian player Goran Ivanisevic who raised the winning cup at Wimbledon, to everyone's surprise. When Ivanisevic arrived for the start of the tournament, he was considered a rank outsider after a particularly poor season in the run-up, and had only been entered into the competition as a 'wildcard'. So how was he able to make such a comeback, defeating Henman in the semi-finals along the way? Interestingly, from the moment Ivanisevic was first interviewed for the games, he claimed that he felt confident because God 'wanted' him to win [echoes of George W Bush - page 59]. This extraordinary claim was repeated as he made his victory speech. For all the millions willing Henman to beat him, their wishes appeared to have been entirely nullified by one man's faith that God was on his side. History records many other examples of unlikely victories where the power of something greater was invoked. But did God really fix Ivanisevic's matches, or was it the personal conviction that saw the player through? Most likely the latter, but it makes a point - the numbers game, as far as the collective mind goes, is not a fail-safe mechanism for success. Something more is needed, and that something appears to be the power of *intention*. Other psi experiments support this view.[8] Projects which have tried to influence the creation of specific crop formation designs using psychic abilities also appear to demonstrate the same principle, with a number of successful outcomes.[9] Masuru Emoto, a doctor of Alternative Medicine, has even claimed that the formation of water crystals can be manipulated by telepathic intention. (Emoto's views have been influential in the New Age, although his methods have been the subject of some controversy.)[10]

Of course, it could be that *lack* of faith might also have played a part in Tim Henman's repeated inability to win Wimbledon. Subconscious thoughts are often more powerful than our conscious minds. Perhaps the innate British fear that he might *not* win, for all the bravado on the surface, coupled with an insecurity around the same thing within the player, also helped to prevent his ultimate triumph.

The quality of intention is very important here, and may explain how a global elite has managed to turn the world to its own advantage. Those fomenting the New World Order and all its grand plans must be highly dedicated if they want their schemes to work. It seems that no stone is left unturned along the way, and the cold propensity towards ruthlessness in the name of a glorious cause, sacrificing perhaps millions of lives in the process, risks them becoming invincible. It can't be denied that the adherence to moral scruples, although the higher path and the one that must be taken, can compromise the chances of instant success (although instant success is not the same as lasting success). Apathy, however, has been the biggest neutraliser of our own potency. The icy focus of highly coordinated intent gives the elite the upper hand over a collective mind that has been weakened by distraction and deception, diverted socially and chemically, and compromised by the insidious encouragement of the 'whatever' attitude - the killer of all effective societies. Our own collective power of intent has been eroded away into almost nothingness in a culture that seems no longer to know what it wants, nor is able to agree on what it thinks matters. The intent from the opposition, meanwhile, has grown ever sharper. No wonder things are they way they are.

It is time to wake up and learn how to use both the weight of numbers *and* the application of intention to change this unacceptable situation. We must become as attentive and focused as those who are shaping the world for us to our detriment - and put to positive use a mechanism that could have the potential to, literally, move mountains.

The Proactive Use of the Collective

Is it too far beyond the realm of imagination to contemplate that the practical application of the collective process could, with much greater development and understanding, be used to do more than offset the schemes of a ruling elite? With the risk of cosmological catastrophe hanging over us, an apparatus for dealing with it could be helpful right now.

In the run-up to the Millennium, one rather promising idea was pitched by the popular psychic Uri Geller. With his claims that broken watches can be fixed by collective focus and that cutlery can be physically bent by the power of the mind (both demonstrated on numerous television programmes over the years, to savage attacks from sceptics), Geller reasoned that a wider application of these abilities could make a huge difference to the world. His vision was of stadiums and living rooms full of people on the first day of the new century, focusing their minds on... attempting to defuse the world's nuclear arsenals. What better way to start a new Millennium than by cleansing the planet of one threat, at least? Sadly, the idea never came to fruition, but in the pitching of the idea, Geller had hit on an a constructive way of new thinking that could be used in a number of directions.

Given that dice rolls can be influenced by the thoughts of individuals, and that objects can be telekinetically manipulated, albeit on rare occasions, it might be worth considering the idea that this gift could be amplified massively by the focused intent of millions of minds, and used to hold back all manner of looming dangers. If dice can be influenced, why not, say, a killer asteroid or comet heading our way? Were we to be faced with such an imminent disaster (and were

Could the newly discovered effects of mass-consciousness and promising telekinesis experiments offer a way out of some of the many apocalyptic scenarios that keep some people awake at night? Could killer asteroids or comets actually be repelled by thought?

we ever to be told of it in advance), would there be any sense in *not* trying it? Could the Sun's erratic behaviour be calmed by the influence of the collective? Or the Earth's seismic movements contained?

Experiments with spiritual healing, monitored by RNGs, also show clear signs of successful influence, again backing up the reality of the power of prayer. Dean Radin describes a study conducted by Ryan Taft in which even brain cell growth in flasks was plainly stimulated by focused healing meditations.[11] This remarkable result suggests that the key to universally good health may be something else in our own hands, if we but knew it. Mental well-being has long been associated with physiological resilience. When humanity stops pumping itself full of the drugs and suppressants sold to it by the pharmaceutical giants as the sole solutions, it may find that all along it never needed them. In time, even superhero-type regenerative powers might be possible - all without genetic engineering.

These ideas may sound like insane idealism, and perhaps today they are, but the discovery that our minds do appear to influence the environment around us provides a tiny glimpse into a future that could be very different if such techniques were to be investigated and progressed. Perhaps the next revolution will not be technological, but consciousness-based - and if the hopes some have that the human race may find itself with higher psychic faculties after 2012 are realised, this revolution could come faster than we think.

Taking Responsibility

If it does become an irrefutable fact that the power of the collective mind is an integral part of shaping the world we live in, this will place a great responsibility on every person's shoulders. If what we think, what we say, what we watch and how we act is being fed into an all-encompassing matrix, then it joyfully transmits or gloomily infects every other being on the planet, on however small a scale. No-one can sidestep it. As it is likely that the resulting domino effect of this system has been misused against the populace many times, it is clear that we have played a part in allowing this to happen in an even more substantial way than supposed in the previous chapter. Therefore, we truly need to look at how we live our individual lives and identify what we are feeding into the collective - because it makes a difference to everyone around us. It is time to take greater responsibility for managing the tools that are used to focus the collective attention, and wrestle back control for a more enlightened purpose. A journey through a usual night's television viewing reveals an appalling diet of death, mutilation and misery, all being fed into the ether and dulling down the collective energy. A study in 1992 revealed that the average child of the day had witnessed around 40,000 onscreen murders by the age of 18.[12] It has probably gone up since. This is not a sensible way to live. We have been fooled into thinking that no other entertainment is as exciting as violent conflict, but we had best be sure of how we entertain ourselves in future, as it becomes ever clearer that the evolution of consciousness is at stake here in a very direct way.

The minutiae of many things we currently take for granted may have to change if the collective is to be used to its purest potential. For example, even the way we conduct our Parliaments may require a major reassessment, particularly in Britain. Most Western countries have at least deduced that the best chambers to operate in are ones set in a semi-circular layout - unlike the Westminster Parliaments, which still follow the traditional pattern of opposing benches. This creates an environment that can only encourage head-to-head conflict, instead of inspiring cooperation. By this, we have ignored the lessons of myth; even King Arthur spotted that what was needed for positive government was a round table. The distance between the front benches

THE TRUTH AGENDA

in the Lords and Commons was actually set out with the expectation of conflict, being precisely two sword-lengths *and a bit* to prevent fights breaking out in the days when weapons were as likely to be brandished as words. From these chambers decisions are made which ripple out and affect peoples' lives, yet the edicts and rulings cannot help but be shaped by their environment. More thought may need to go into what lies at the heart of the smallest domino points. As for Westminster, perhaps it is time to move out of the old buildings and into fresh premises for the new times before us (although not, preferably, to Strasbourg or Brussels - page 76). It

is often said that ghosts have a tendency to linger where the circumstances of their deaths were traumatic, as if the sudden energetic output of the events somehow imprinted themselves into the fabric of the walls and ceilings. Given this, the endless years of corruption, conflict and obfuscation in the old Parliament chambers must have an effect on those working within them today, and influence their thought patterns and moods accordingly. It is time for something different.

The Houses of Parliament and some of the people governed by its inhabitants. Both the antiquainted layout and traditions of this admittedly iconic complex are beginning to look somewhat anachronistic in these times of change - and the psychic imprint of everything that has happened there must affect the decisions made within its walls.

Echoes From the Future

Another aspect of psi phenomena that has recently come to light is the quality of 'presentiment'. This is an astonishing discovery resulting from the numerous noted experiments, including the RNG readings. It became clear, from analysing the data on brainwaves, skin responses and nervous system responses that an unexpected phenomenon was occurring - both participants in any test were registering the recorded changes in response to stimuli a few seconds (sometimes several seconds) *before* the stimulation. Initially considered an error or statistical quirk, it soon became clear this effect was repeatedly evident in many tests. Presentiment has since been identified in data even from mainstream medical response test results - previously unnoticed purely because no-one thought to analyse those parts of the data that preceded the stimulant.[13]

THE TRUTH AGENDA

The staggering conclusion that can be drawn from this observation is that, on some level, every one of us knows what is about to happen *a short while in advance.* How this works is an unknown - but it does. Does the mind exist slightly out of time? Does time not work in the way we imagined, as quantum physics is beginning to suggest? Either way, the psi tests have stumbled upon an incredible ability we never knew we had - the faculty of responding to future events.

Realising that this must also be occurring on a much greater scale, researchers applied the observation of presentiment to the global RNG data and discovered - breathtakingly - that certain large-scale events were indeed being anticipated by a large section of humanity. The highly significant RNG responses to 9/11 show that the curve into output coherence began a clear two hours before the first of the attacks. That is two hours in which, on some subconscious level, humanity already knew it was in for one of the most momentous days of modern history. The thoughts of those relative few involved in planning the attacks (whoever they were) would be unlikely to have generated such a notable pattern of non-randomness by themselves, unless the power of intention played a part. Most likely, it seems that we collectively felt the echo of a ripple coming backwards in time towards us. Indeed, there are many records of relevant dreams, visions and predictions that occurred across the world in the days and hours before the events of 9/11, which were perhaps very literal receptions of this spontaneous broadcast from the future. Similarly, the 2004 tsunami, which wiped out the coastlines of many countries on the Indian Ocean, also produced a presentiment curve of coherence in the hours before the quake took place, again with preceding dreams and intimations. Animals seemed to pick up on the future echo even more strongly, with many reports of strange behaviour and of creatures clearing away from the coasts long before the event.[14] Some believe they were simply sensing tremors beyond our senses, but others believe they may be more finely tuned into the presentiment system than we are, as Sheldrake's work might suggest. If the tsunami was a

The aftermath of the Boxing Day tsunami of 2004 in Sumatra, Indonesia. The devastation caused by the wave was apalling, but the event also created another kind of wave, a psychic one rippling backwards in time to be picked up by humankind in the hours running up to the quake, as revealed by the RNG data.

Solutions and Inspirations

truly natural event (some have claimed the quake was triggered by nuclear tests), no intention component could possibly have come into the equation that time.

Time is perhaps one of the least understood qualities of nature, and the New Physics is rapidly discovering that many of our previous presumptions about it have been wrong. High energy accelerators have produced particles that seem to travel backwards in time, and the laws of physics do not entirely rule out the possibility of negative flow. We appear on the surface to live our lives in an arrow of time that moves forward, but maybe not everything obeys those rules. If time is a river, flowing generally in one direction, perhaps a pebble thrown into that river, just as in water, momentarily produces ripples that flow in both directions, before all of them are quickly swept forwards again. It may be that this is what we are picking up on with huge events like 9/11. Some moments may be so big, so devastating to the consciousness of humanity, that they punch bigger holes in the river than others. Perhaps, if we could learn to fine-tune the reading of the data, we could even learn how to read the echoes from the future - or possible futures - and try to change the events if necessary, or avoid the worst consequences.

Stepping Up to the Task

Alternative physics, then, brings us back to one of the central themes of this hypothesis. Prophecies and predictions about these times are so strong, so ubiquitous, that it is not unreasonable to suppose that what we are tuning into is a particularly large ripple from an occurrence just around the corner, making itself known in the manner described. Only this time the ripple may be so big that we have been picking up on it for years - centuries, even. Certain sections of human society may have known this all along and kept it hidden, but maybe now the secret is leaking out. The exact nature of the change everyone seems to feel in their bones still remains elusive, but they sense it nonetheless. Can we alter it or anticipate its worst excesses (if the event turns out to have negative connotations), or can we only confront it as it arrives?

The evolution of consciousness may have been the very thing which has gifted us the ability to see further than we have before, and curves of learning and the development of technology are now enabling us to detect the presence of energetic waves, whilst revealing telling transgressions of the barriers of time. Whatever happens to us, that evolution of the collective mind has been precious, and we must not let it go to waste by giving up hope of improving ourselves. Instead, we could use a new wider awareness of the power of consciousness to help create hitherto unimaginable solutions to break the ancient cycle of mass extinctions and cosmological threats. With that awareness we could have an extra faculty that might help us enormously once its potential is fully realised. It is time for all of us to step up to the task of forging the world anew - not a New World Order, but just a new world. History alone records that when people stand up to be counted, positive change always comes - and showing up for duty is the first step.

THE TRUTH AGENDA: *Astonishing discoveries are being made in the realm of consciousness research, revealing that psychic abilities are not rare gifts, but widely-distributed effects that bind us together on a day to day basis. The realisation that collective thought is not an abstract concept but, courtesy of the Random Number Generator experiments, a recordable reality, grants us an insight into hitherto unsuspected powers we may all have to forge a better world using both the telepathic weight of numbers and the power of intention. With that realisation, however, comes a greater awareness of the huge responsibility we have to our fellow beings. What we think and do affects everyone else and what we pour into the collective helps shape it negatively or positively, as we decide.*

The US Live Aid concert, 1985, one in a network of simultaneous global events that raised millions for famine relief and set an example of what can be achieved when people stand up for a cause and work together positively.

XV   THE POWER OF POSITIVE ACTION

How can we put into practice the lessons of everything learned from the speculation over the control agenda, and live a new truth to create a better world, whilst maintaining personal integrity? What does history show us about the possibility of turning around even the most seemingly insurmountable situations through concerted collective effort? Taking the initiative and keeping the flame of optimism alive must now be our primary duty.

Personal Responsibility

A growing theme as these pages have unfolded has been that of taking collective responsibility. Whatever global cover-ups and deceptions may be occurring only do so because we allow them to occur. But, as the process of collective mind reveals, *personal* responsibility is equally as important. What manifests in the collective is a product of what we do individually. Although it is easy to point the finger at governments and ruling elites for their many misdemeanours, if we are truly honest with ourselves it is likely that we all embody many of the same issues in our own personal lives. Lies and deception occur through fear and the dominance of the ego. Can many of us say we have never once been dishonest in our lives? When we do fall from integrity, we create caveats for ourselves to justify our actions, and the caveats may sometimes even have validity. Those who rule our lives are simply projections of our own inner conflicts and issues. It is often said that we get the leaders we deserve, and there is a truth to this. They represent *us* in more ways than one. We put them there and allow them to stay in positions of influence even after the likes of the weapons of mass destruction debacle. Those we don't vote for, the mysterious elite, Illuminati, ruling class, whatever we choose to call them, still could not function in the way they do without society's tacit consent through apathy. We very often turn blind eyes to the things we fear are occurring, because engaging any more closely invites the possibility of having to do something about it ourselves - and this is where many people's resolve falters. This is a great shame, because the will to change things is there - but the fear and distractions placed on us tend to dissolve the confidence necessary to stand up and put thoughts into action.

This author had a conversation with a party guest not long back. The visitor was bemoaning the surveillance state, speed cameras, ID cards and the rise of ridiculous rules regarding the photographing of school football matches. Venturing the suggestion that perhaps he should join the growing movement trying to alert people to such concerns, offering mention of a few websites and publications that might help, I was met with an immediate and dramatic withdrawal of interest.

Suddenly, there was a backtracking and the guest's entire demeanour changed. He went as far as to say that actually he wasn't really bothered by any of the things he had just been loudly lamenting and that he didn't think things were really too bad. It would all be alright in the end. Excuses were made and he shuffled away, eyes to the ground.

This cautionary tale encapsulates the problems faced in trying to create change - many people want it, but are either too scared or too habitually passive to stand up and be counted. Once again, our collective cultural intent is so much weaker than the highly focused intent of those making the rules for us, that the imbalance of power becomes inevitable. This has to change if the worst excesses of the control agenda are to be avoided.

Facing the Fear of Ridicule

Many people will not voice their concerns for the world they live in because they fear ridicule from a society that has been trained not to question, brainwashed by a media that pours scorn on anything remotely 'alternative'. Yet the curious fact is that when a risk is taken and personal feelings about potential 'other' reasons for the state of things are voiced, it is remarkable how many people will agree with the viewpoints expressed. It doesn't take too long to find someone at work, on the bus or in the family who will agree with what may at first seem like an extreme view, though it can take time for the barrier to be broken. At first, there may be a reluctance to engage with the issue, if the results of doing so are initially uncertain. Given the confidence, however, that by openly assenting to a supposedly heretical view they will not be met with mocking humiliation, supportive personal views and anecdotes are often forthcoming, even in unexpected places. As a prolific lecturer on unexplained mysteries and cover-ups, the author has witnessed this phenomenon many times - faced with someone risking more ridicule than they are, audience members will often share a view or an experience (often to do with ghosts or UFO

Speakers forum at the first Alternative View conference [page 354] in 2008. Faced with people publicly willing to speak their minds at events such as this, listeners will often be encouraged to share thoughts or anecdotes previously kept private, revealing quite a different take to official 'consensus reality'.

sightings) they may never have spoken of before. It is quickly revealed by this kind of admission, or by venturing into unusual personal conversations with friends and colleagues, that society's self-image of 'consenus reality' is entirely false. We live in a world underpinned by mysteries and deceptions, as this book has revealed, but a facade is presented to give the opposite impression, and most of us quietly agree not to rock the boat.

To shatter this fraudulent artifice, then, we need to be willing to take risks. We have to step into our real power and learn to face opposition with confidence and courage. So what, if someone doesn't agree with your view on, say, 9/11 or the Moon landings? So what, if you challenge the official version of a major news story and are taken to task on it? A little resilience and obstinacy is called for. The odds are that any returning verbal attack will be based on loosely-held perceptions of the issues rather than any firm knowledge, so why not take a small chance and guess that you will be in possession of more facts than your critics? If you are *not* familiar with those facts, of course, then you are on shaky ground. All truthseekers owe it to themselves to be properly informed on the subject of their passion. Views ranted without foundation are soon rounded on for demolition, and rightly so. But when there is a firm basis for an argument, when one has gathered more information (or at least serious points to raise) than most, authority is often quietly conceded to those whose power of intent, combined with informed arguments, radiates clearly. *Un*informed challengers will often back down in the face of supreme confidence, and a strong personal conviction can be admired even if the viewpoint isn't agreed with. In a society where most opinions are based on third-hand tabloid sources, ones that the majority of the public know in their hearts aren't really reliable, someone who knows their subject is in good stead.

This is not to say that voicing unusual views in the pub or in the office, in an attempt to air important issues, isn't sometimes going to be an uncomfortable experience. Some will take up the gauntlet and attempt to demolish you with equal conviction, in the same way that this book will doubtless be torn apart by those who have firmly placed themselves into the camp of the mainstream 'consensus' view. But so be it. Questioning convention isn't for the faint-hearted. However, adopting the right tones and being as non-confrontational as possible can make a huge difference. Offer a truth, never attempt to sell it. But if this doesn't work, comfort yourself with the thought that if Tony Blair could get over a slow hand-clap by the Women's Institute and still be voted back in, anyone can handle a little humiliation here and there.

If readers of this book have concluded that a ruling elite is indeed trying to warp the world's needs to its own deceptive manifestos, then our very civilisation, our very planet, our very lives, may all be at stake. What price a little philosophical confrontation here and there? For those with eyes to see, it is time to step up to the full responsibility demanded by the simple awareness that a serious debate needs to take place. We have already established that the collective effect of doing this could be massive - but the fight to apply the Truth Agenda to many levels of life now needs to begin in earnest.

Personal Integrity

Personal integrity is vital in all of this. Trying to make the world a better place whilst living a life full of the same mistakes one is hoping to correct in others can only take one so far. None of us is perfect, but we owe it to ourselves to take a good long look in the mirror before setting out to right the wrongs of others. It is not an easy process, nor one that will ever be fully won - we are only human after all. But a habit of occasionally checking for false projections, correcting even the smallest step into the kind of behaviour we may abhor on the outside, is a healthy one worth cultivating.

If we are all contributing to a growing entity of shared mind that imprints itself on the universe, it is also our collective responsibility to create a world that operates from a positive centre - and this can only be done by operating from the correct place in our own personal centre. If some of the more dire predictions about 2012 were to be realised, we might find ourselves in a society that rapidly developed into a dog-eat-dog situation (it is often said we are only two meals away from revolution). The question we must ask ourselves is, do we want to be one of the dogs? Cultivating a compassionate demeanour, if resolute and resilient, whilst helping to set up a cooperative network of like-minded people unwilling to fall into anarchy and chaos, could make a huge difference in the event of a global crisis.

The maintenance of personal integrity also extends to living out our ideals, not just preaching them. So if the crumbling of communities and families is a personal concern, then making active efforts to create strong communities and families should become a priority. If the denigration of speech and the dumbing down of society worries us, then we need to make the effort to use a wider vocabulary and keep ourselves educated and sharp. If global deception creates a pain in our hearts, then we need to live as honestly in our own lives as we can. And so on. Put more simply, universally applying the adage 'be the change you want to see' to all areas of life will stand more chance of manifesting an improved world than not doing so.

Guarding Against Mob Rule

Given the propensity for civil unrest in hard times, the rise of the mob-rule mentality should be actively guarded against. We have seen that it is very likely that a social upheaval of some kind may erupt before too long, as economic conditions and concern for control agendas exacerbate the problem. There will always be those who will use these situations to indulge delightedly in violence and anarchy. There may also be *agent provocateurs* stirred into the mix by governments which could, by 2012, be looking for any excuse to install even more draconian restrictions on their citizens. It is interesting to note how often in recent times the concept of potential rioting has been planted into the public mind by politicians and the media, under the guise of not wanting it.

The wide coverage of the G20 London summit seemed to beg for trouble, resulting only in the smashing of a bank window in the end - but the feeling was that far more was hoped for. When stones were thrown through the window of a prominent executive in the wake of the banking crisis, the television coverage as good as announced the address of the house, seeming to encourage more of the same. The media thrives on conflict, while the ruling forces want more control, which makes for a powerful mix we should be very suspicious of. In June 2009, even Conservative leader David Cameron (very likely to be the next Prime Minister) voiced an expectation of street riots.[1] What is going on? Is this some kind of mind-control technique designed to create that very outcome?

Riot police at the G20 protests, 2009. The concept of British rioting seems to have been increasingly placed in the public mind since the economic recession began. Such events would enable the justification of more extreme draconian laws, and we must guard against a fomented mob mentality.

The problem is that there may well be very good reason to take to the streets - with peaceful protest - if restricted liberty, injustice and financial imbalance in society remain unaddressed. And the new resistance, in Britain at least, is as likely to come from 'Middle England' as from extremist groups - there is a growing unrest (especially amongst the elderly, who have seen hard-earned pensions crumble) in a previously quiet demographic that might not have been taken into account by the powers that be. But armed revolution and mob rule will not solve anything - instead it would simply play into the hands of those waiting to use all the many civil unrest measures gathered in the wings since the War on Terror began. Perhaps the claimed secret internment camps [page 258] may yet find some occupants. We must not make it so easy for any such plans. What is needed now is a rebellion of the heart, not one of hate and anger. Non-violent action has nearly always shown itself to have the longest-lasting effect in fomenting global change, as we shall shortly see. We must stand in the light and look to the highest aspirations if we want to make a better civilisation.

Come the summer of 2012, southern England in particular is going to be gripped with anti-terror clampdowns, as the Olympics take place. The games will almost certainly be used to cement many new restrictions into place. It is considered by some conspiracy theorists that Britain is being used as a guinea pig, the focus of a huge social experiment in control techniques. We certainly have more surveillance cameras than anywhere else in the world, and sweeping anti-terror laws that have raised eyebrows even in the US. The climate of restriction and suppression has seemed especially strong here. Why might this be?

The British Factor

There are some who feel it was no accident that Britain won the bid for the 2012 Olympics. It wasn't expected to - France was the front-runner, and there were allegations of vote-rigging amongst the Olympic panels. It seems to have been important to someone that the eyes of the world should be on the UK in 2012, and the UK wasn't complaining. The jubilation in the country was short lived, though - just one day after the announcement in July 2005, the 7/7 bombings took place, instantly neutering any pride or joy. Some believe this was a message in itself, a foreshadowing of what may come with the games themselves - celebration tempered with a grim recognition of the hard realities of life. A morbid coincidence was noted by many when the mock double-decker, carrying London Mayor Boris Johnson and guitarist Jimmy Page (amongst others) into the Beijing Olympic stadium in its 2008 closing ceremony, mechanically opened up at the top to resemble, rather disturbingly, the exploded bus in Tavistock Square. Was this making a point?

Many fear that the 2012 Olympics, in that year of such expectation and the focus of so much prophecy (even though Creation Day doesn't fall until 21st December), will be used to send out a message to the world. If British social unrest is in full swing by then, especially if the dispossessed become outraged by the cost and security measures of the games, the temptation for a ruling elite to make a show of strength could be high. Some fear a British false-flag terrorist attack taking place to crank the security even higher, perhaps in a fulfillment of the Nostradamus quatrain that refers to 'games of slaughter, not far from the age of the great millennium'.[2] (Astrologically, the Full Moon of 4th June is seen as a potential flash-point, although the Olympics take place in July-August.)

Others even think the possible faked alien invasion [page 40] will be launched during the Olympics, and it is interesting to note that the promotional videos for the London Olympic bid featured flying saucers hovering over the city. However

THE TRUTH AGENDA

things pan out, the expectation for a misuse of power in the summer of 2012 is strong. So are these just paranoid fears, or could there be something to it?

What constellates in the UK in 2012 will, just as during the Beijing Olympics in 2008, be disseminated across the world for analysis and debate. It is almost inconceivable that the powers that be will not have considered this. But why select Britain to be the focus of the world's attention in 2012? Why was the Olympic favourite Paris not chosen, say, with all its overt occult architecture and secret society connections, if a full message of elite dominance needs to be delivered?

Misplaced patriotism aside, there has always been something specific about the UK that has made it a world leader in so many areas. Somehow, this little country even managed to create an Empire that spanned the globe. Unfortunately, that empire was founded on slavery and oppression, but the fact that it was created at all was still remarkable. Perhaps it is something in the British psyche

The Olympic stadium under construction for the 2012 London games. The eyes of the world will be on London in 2012, and what is happening here will be widely discussed around the world. The security clampdown that will accompany the games and the fears of a false-flag terror stunt during them or in the weeks before lead some truthseekers to be concerned.

- we always look outwards and retain a keen awareness of the wider world. We are not insular, but always seek outreach, whether it be through trade, colonisation or the spread of pioneering culture (modern music especially). The British don't keep things to themselves. We may be protective of our borders (hence the EU's exasperation at our reluctance to give away sovereignty, and the apparent programme to erode it from the inside), but we always want to talk to the world on the other side of them. We stand between the Americas and Europe and have often provided a bridge between the two, politically and philosophically. We also display a healthy balance of cynicism and open-mindedness. Despite the impression given by our media, most British citizens *will* listen to unusual viewpoints if backed up by evidence and reasoned debate.

The fact that Britain is seen by some in the New Age movement as the 'heart chakra' of the world is interesting. Certainly, it is curious that this country attracts (or generates depending on one's viewpoint) more crop circles than any other - and this is just one example of some peculiarly British (although often English)

Solutions and Inspirations

mysteries on the boundaries of the inexplicable that have ignited many discussions about the entire nature of reality. For all the inevitable scepticism, the enduring fascination with the crop formations (even by non-believers) is a fine example of national bloody-mindedness in the face of opposition. The presence of a network of stone circles and 'earth energy' sites has also attracted many alternative thinkers to the country, and the continuing flirtation with Arthurian myths, stories of Jesus visiting Glastonbury, and belief in fairies and a whole undercurrent of mystical beings that supposedly inhabit these isles, seems to add to the feeling of something special residing here. Britain has survived threatened invasion in several wars, most

notably the Second World War, and many feel there must be some underlying esoteric reason for its having been so protected in recent centuries. And now, with all the vast speculation, both social and metaphysical, about the possible turning-points of 2012, it seems that the UK is about to play a major role in the focus of attention in that potentially pivotal year.

Gazing out from the top of Glastonbury Tor, considered by some to be the Isle of Avalon, King Arthur's final resting place. This 'green and pleasant land' is rich with myths, legends and contemporary mysteries such as the crop circles, and many feel that Britain is a special place, which will play a major role in 2012, not least because the Olympics will focus attention here.

Yet at the same time (lest the reader fear jingoism creeping in), could it be that the control experiment is being specifically concentrated here because the British are particularly susceptible, rather than enlightened? It does seem to have been recognised by at least one of the great visionaries that there is more to the role of the British than meets the eye. Speaking in Switzerland in 1917, while addressing the issue of secret societies, the Austrian philosopher and mystic Rudolf Steiner described the British as being the 'bearer of the consciousness soul', but he also identified the vulnerability of some British 'elements' to manipulation:

'What is the aim of these secret brotherhoods? They do not work out of any particular British patriotism but out of the desire to bring the whole world under the yoke of pure materialism. And because... ...certain elements of the British people as the bearer of the

consciousness soul are most suitable for this, the brotherhoods want, by means of grey magic, to use these elements as promoters of this materialism. This is the important point. Those who know what impulses are at work in world events can also steer them. No other national element, no other people, has ever before been so usable as material for transforming the whole world into a materialistic realm.

Therefore, those who know want to set their foot on the neck of this national element and strip it of all spiritual endeavour - which of course lives equally in all human beings. Just because karma has ordained that the consciousness soul should work here [in Britain] particularly strongly, the secret brotherhoods have sought out elements in the British national character. Their aim is to send a wave of materialism over the Earth and make the physical plane the only valid one. A spiritual world is to be recognised only in terms of what the physical plane has to offer.' ³

This uncannily accurate foresight would appear to be borne out by today's programme of control and the distraction of materialism, which seems so powerful in the UK. It may also explain why 2012 could be used to make a demonstration of quelling the human spirit here - we may have the 'consciousness soul', but we are also easy to manipulate in certain ways.

It must be stressed that placing this emphasis on the British does not mean that other countries have nothing to offer these times - far from it. Each nation has its strengths and weaknesses and doubtless its own important part to play. But it does seem as if something important is destined to be constellated in Great Britain in or around 2012, and its inhabitants should be ready to step up to whatever task is appointed them.

The Waiting Game

As we appear to approach the times alluded to for so long in prophecies and visions, however they may manifest themselves, a sense of anticipation needs to be matched with a schedule of proactive action to lay the ground positively. Yet some in the spiritual community seem determined to wait for everything to be done for them. This problem has been endemic amongst certain Christian elements awaiting an imminent Second Coming, and it also compromises some in the New Age community.

As far back as the early 1990s, channellings were being widely received from an apparently space-borne spiritual collective known as the Ascended Masters. Led by Sananda, a incarnation of the Christ, and accompanied by the commander Ashtar, Saint Germaine and an assortment of holy avatars, the messages generated a popular belief that spaceships were orbiting the planet, waiting to rescue the chosen ones before the predicted Earth changes began in earnest. Vivid predictions

Solutions and Inspirations

of the San Andreas fault demolishing California and of a chain of subsequent earthquakes, volcanoes and hurricanes led many to believe the end was nigh. All would be well for the more spiritually-advanced, however, who would be beamed up onto the ships at the crucial time. Except that the time never came - or if it did, no-one noticed. Some devotees had sold their belongings, left partners and quit jobs, and gone into holy exile to wait for their 'ascension'. Presumably they still wait today. Perhaps it was 2012 the channellings were referring to, but it seemed clear at the time that the changes were expected within the 1990s.

Unfulfilled prophecies have been letting down the devout for generations, and the same potential disappointment could be relevant to the 2012 schedule [page 257]. However, the personal purification process the Ascension followers went through might still have counted for something for those who put them into practice there and then. Some, sensibly, used the learning gleaned from *considering* the possibility of huge change as a self-fulfilling programme of personal development, similar to that discussed at the end of Chapter XII, and as such they didn't waste their time. Others, however, waited, putting entire lives on hold, abdicating responsibility to improve the world they lived in - the Ascended Masters would put all to rights when they arrived, and who were they to interfere with their plans? Better to sit quietly and wait. And wait.

When it was pointed out that perhaps Ascension wasn't coming after all, new channellings started to come through, which intimated that the rescue programme *had* indeed occurred. No-one had noticed though, because the memory of ascended friends and family had been 'erased' from our minds. On one level, this ludicrously unlikely let-out devastated those aghast at having been left behind, but on another it effectively ended the Ascension movement as was, as most woke up to the possibility that they might just have been had by some trickster thought-form. Belief in Ascension continues today, and has strong resonance with the evangelical Rapture movement, but for many it seems to have become something more sensibly nebulous and rather less dogmatic.

This phenomenon of being on eternal hold, doing nothing but waiting, is something that occurs in a number of new spiritual movements, and it feels fundamentally wrong. Surely, any higher being would demand some active participation from us to make a better world, rather than just offer salvation on a plate? And for those awaiting the Second Coming, is it unreasonable to consider that Jesus himself might also want some positive change instigated in the run-up to his arrival? Waiting for beings from above to come down and put everything straight, be they Jesus, Maitreya, Ashtar or all manner of anticipated extra-terrestrial landings, risks becoming yet another excuse not to do anything ourselves to sort things out.

Making a Stand

It is time to make a stand. Regardless of what other powers may be out there watching over us, we cannot take the chance that they really exist or that they will be there for us when it counts. WE have to create change, and it has to happen now. Any ruling elite (sometimes blamed for encouraging belief in celestial rescuers) will not be waiting for something else to do its work for it. There are identifiable problems that could be tackled here and now with enough people willing to play their part and make it happen. We must also set our own standards. The supposed testimony of gods and prophets have made it pretty clear over the centuries what is required of us for better lives, and we ourselves are canny enough to be able now to make the choice between right and wrong. The cradle has fallen and we have to stand on our own feet.

Taking personal responsibility can be the moment of epiphany. In his 1983 book *People of the Lie*,[4] psychiatrist Dr M Scott Peck cites a lack of anyone taking responsibility as one of the reasons for the appalling 1968 My Lai massacre, in which US soldiers rampaged through a Vietnamese village, indiscriminately raping and killing hundreds of civilians, mostly women and children. Each participant simply deferred responsibility to another in the chain of command, who then did the same, *ad infinitum*. Few wanted to risk being seen as objectors. Meanwhile, bloodlust reigned and men found themselves doing the unthinkable. In the end, only one military commander was ever prosecuted for the atrocity, and even then Richard Nixon stepped in to reduce his sentence.[5]

This far-from-isolated example says much about the reason why we all too often live under the strictures of evil, or even incompetence - because not enough are willing to put their heads above the parapet, to stand up for what is so clearly right. Yet when they do, and the collective takes hold, the successful results can be striking. Perhaps the oft-stated, and yet underestimated, adage (generally attributed to the 18th century political philosopher Edmund Burke) says it best: 'All that is necessary for the triumph of evil is that good men do nothing.'

When people do decide to take a role in shaping their community and environments, it makes a huge difference. Being proactive in voicing views on both the small and the large things in life, and creatively campaigning for necessary changes, generates a web of focused intent that binds people together more positively and breaks the stagnation of laziness and apathy. Everyone feels better in an active state, and energy expended positively is never wasted - it seems to be a universal law that it comes back a thousandfold in the end, refreshing those who give it; and the Random Number Generators have now shown that such focused activity reshapes the world on measurable levels. Far more energy is expended in a much less healthy way enduring yet another heavy night of television in the armchair.

Doing something, anything, even just once a week, could make a substantial contribution to the world. For the truly enthusiastic, US film-maker Michael Moore recommends that all people with strong views on the incapability of authorities should stand for election themselves, even on small local councils - lest those on power trips are always the ones left in charge. Otherwise, writing letters to MPs, newspapers, councillors or web forums could nudge the odd domino here and there. Taking part in peaceful protests and spreading leaflets for campaigns is another outlet - they may not get instant results but do transmit the fact that someone cares about the decisions that are made. Joining collectives and organisations of like-minded people can be more influential than working alone, and getting involved with positive local projects, social or environmental, can produce unexpected results (the planned erection of many local microwave masts have been successfully fought this way, for instance). If even that seems too much, just willfully introducing a 'difficult' subject into the bar room or across the dinner table might transform at least one person's life. And if there is no possibility of social interaction, then the simple act of changing one's own attitude on a daily basis might feed something good back into the collective. However much or little we choose to do, let us not go passively into our cages.

For the bolder participants, Moore's idea of putting oneself up for even minor elections may have identified something important. All the while those who want power are allowed to dominate the electoral system, the big egos and the dangerous climbers most likely to be recruited by the elite will continue to rise to the top, and we will suffer accordingly. Installing a system that compels a certain number of people who do not have political ambitions to be part of any vote might at least prevent some of the more dubious manipulated decisions that have coloured our view of authorities throughout history. Perhaps one day (with our full idealist glasses on) the technology that already allows a large proportion of the population to vote for their favourite singers or entertainers, might be broadened to allow us all more of an everyday say in governmental matters. If electronic voting is seen as safe enough to be used for general elections, why should many big decisions not be influenced by Internet-referenda, with everyone voting from home on the issues of the day? If that is not practical, laws could be passed to ensure that at least a portion of every Parliamentary vote has to be cast by members of the public, perhaps being called into the Houses on a jury-service basis. This would at least ensure far fewer partisan decisions. To put things right we may have to take part ourselves in the systems we feel threatened by.

The Positive Lessons of Recent History

Throughout these pages we have explored the connection between unexplained mysteries, conspiracy theories and future prophecies, trying to see where the truth of it all lies. One thing, it would seem, has become clear; that whatever the underlying reality there does appear to be a concerted effort to control humankind through subterfuge and oppression. For a long time this scheme has been flying 'under the radar', but now it appears to be emerging unapologetically into full vision - a worrying sign that its sponsors are becoming confident of a successful outcome. But this arrogance may have revealed their hand too soon. They may have underestimated the strength of feeling that could be galvanised with enough public consciousness. There is still time to awaken the world to what is going on.

History records many instances when seemingly hopeless cases have been quickly turned around by the sudden rising of awareness and mass action, and it is helpful here to remind ourselves of a few of them:

* In 1989, within weeks, political shift within the Eastern Bloc saw the opening of the border between East and West Germany and the fall of the Berlin Wall. Thousands took to the previously impregnable barrier and stood defiantly on top of it, unable to believe that such an enduring symbol of division and oppression had been rendered impotent overnight. It is true that by this point it was politically and economically convenient for the wall to be removed, but the flood of hope and transformation that ran through the population of the alienated German sides was very real and enabled the change to take place more swiftly and painlessly than ever might have been imagined; in the end, seeing growing bureaucratic delays and painfully slow political manoeuvring, citizens took things into their own hands and the armies stood back. No-one could have foreseen such a development even a year or so before.

Suffragette Emmeline Pankhurst is arrested in London, 1914. The struggle to attain votes for women was hard won - but successful. The suffragette movement is one of the best examples of great change achieved through dedication and tenacity, and its motto is timely today: 'deeds, not words.'

* The suffragette movement in the late 19th and early 20th century saw a huge step forward for the rights of women in the West. Arrests, abuse and intimidation failed to douse the spirit of the suffragettes, one of who (Emily Davison) threw herself

under the King's race horse to make her point, losing her life in the process. Change did not come easily for the women's movement, but it did come. After slow and reluctant legislative amendments, in the end equal voting rights were won. Finding a candidate one *wants* to vote for is more of the problem today, but it shouldn't be forgotten how hard-won the universal ability to do so was. It took the rise of a large and concerted movement to achieve the end, and the journey wasn't comfortable - but it worked.

* Nelson Mandela was incarcerated for 27 years and it seemed for a long while that he would die in captivity. Although some to this day still believe that his original tactics with the armed wing of the African National Congress did amount to terrorism, perception had changed by the 1980s and Mandela had become a symbol of freedom for the disempowered black majority. Dedicated and relentless campaigning, aided by international awareness, helped push South Africa into unexpected social shift. An upsurge of support humbled and undermined the white minority government and Mandela was released in 1990. Within four years he had become President of South Africa. Few would have predicted such an astonishing development in such a short time.

* Oppressed Poland saw the unexpected rise in the early 1980s of the dockyard union Solidarity. Breaking all the rules of the then Communist regime, and led by the tenacious figure of Lech Wałęsa, Solidarity inspired a huge national freedom movement in the face of violent threat and harsh penalties. Although the union suffered severe repression, the flame didn't go out, and the dissolution of the Soviet Union (helped in part by the example set by Polish workers) saw the incredible development of a Solidarity-led coalition effectively forming the first post-oppression government, with Wałęsa as its president. Poland had many social problems still, but it was free at last to work out its issues on its own democratic terms - largely because enough people had risked all to make it happen.

* It is easy to be cynical about the now ubiquitous charity bonanzas of today, but the Live Aid concerts of 1985 were a remarkable example of mass consciousness in action. Realising that the governments of the world were not doing enough to prevent an appalling humanitarian crisis due to famine and conflict in Ethiopia, a conglomerate of rock stars led by Bob Geldof and Midge Ure (whose role is often understated) mounted first an all-star charity Christmas record in 1984 (*Band Aid*), and then the massive network of live concerts around the world on 13 July 1985, led by the London concert in Wembley Arena and linked by global satellite transmissions. Huge amounts of money were raised to help directly alleviate some

of the suffering, while governments dithered and made excuses (although Geldof has since been accused of becoming a NWO puppet). Some believe that the coming together of so much goodwill made a lasting impression on the collective field. The Global Consciousness Project [page 285] wasn't running at that point, but the Random Number Generators would surely have been producing significant results if it had been. Other examples of collective focus, such as the

'Harmonic Convergence' of 1987, which was one of the first global-meditation projects, have been rightly cited as important moments in mass consciousness, but it could be argued that the many millions more involved in Live Aid created the largest wave of compassion and joy to flow through the collective, the first to be stimulated on such a scale by the medium of modern communications - an example of their best use.

Crowds gather for the 'Orange Revolution' in Ukraine, 2004. Weeks of determined and non-violent protest in harsh weather conditions saw the overturning of a highly questionable election result and the ultimate victory of the challenging movement - another encouraging example.

* The 2004 'Orange Revolution' in Ukraine (reflecting the political colour of the democratic movement) saw thousands take to the streets in protest at what was clearly a rigged election by the incumbent regime. Led by opposition leader Viktor Yushchenko, a man facially disfigured by a recent claimed attempt to poison him (presumably by government spies), the crowds remained laudably non-violent at his behest. The authorities surrounded the protestors in Kiev's aptly-named Independence Square, but (with echoes of the scenes in Russia as the Soviet Union fell) faltered in their response, perhaps seeing the conviction in the eyes of the demonstrators. After nearly a month of sometimes continuous protest, in which astonishingly dedicated people stood in freezing conditions with few facilities, the government blinked first and backed down. The election was re-held and Yushchenko became president. Problems continued in Ukraine, but it had been made clear than peaceful demonstration could make its point as strongly as any armed struggle. Things don't always work out so well, of course, with the tragic Tiananmen Square events of 1989 being a bad example, but even in China change is coming. Softly and slowly, dedication and the willingness to take risks eventually undermines even the most rigid edifices of power.

* The Northern Ireland peace process has been a long and very difficult path, and still provokes strong emotions. Yet it is clear that something had to give. After so many deaths, injuries and bereavements on all sides of the divides, the efforts of those who believed a unity of vision could still be forged have paid off. Who would ever have envisioned, even just a few years before the 1998 signing of the Good Friday Agreement, that hardline unionist Ian Paisley and Sinn Fein leader Gerry Adams would finally be able to sit at a table together, smiling for cameras? Or that Paisley would actually become friends with once arch-enemy and IRA member Martin McGuinness? It wasn't easy, and much pride and anger has had to be swallowed, but if this situation is not a sign that great change *can* come even in the most dire of circumstances - when enough people put their minds to creating it - then what is? Yesterday's men still keep some of the old emnities going, but they have been reduced to the status of small criminal organisations, with little support from the wider community, and it is unlikely that the 'troubles' of old will return at the same level.

Naturally, some will interpret a number of the above situations as being conspiracy manipulations in themselves, and there is certainly far more complexity to the events than discussed here. But there does comes a point during seismic social shifts where it becomes clear that people are taking matters into their own hands and generating change that seems beyond engineering. These few examples show how quickly and how massively the world can (and does) alter for the better with the application of proactive dedication, passion, compassion - and highly focused intent. Facing seemingly insurmountable odds, the steely facade of oppression or authoritative stagnation CAN be taken down when these qualities are stirred.

There are many more examples of successful and dramatic changes that could be mentioned here; the spread of genetically modified food has been massively held back in the UK by a basic consumer resistance which has said 'no' to overt tinkering with our food, for instance. Sadly, it is coming in through the back door courtesy of the best efforts of the likes of the Codex Alimentarius 'food safety' body [page 209], but large companies like Monsanto have struggled to get this far. On a smaller scale, but thematically related, groups like the British Campaign for Real Ale have helped save a number of independent breweries from bankruptcy by mounting boycotts of pubs that refuse to install local brews at the pumps, along with other actions.[6] Economic pressure alone often sees the will of the people triumph. On the larger scale, peace protests may have made a huge difference to the world, when seen with the long view. The CND marches from the mid-20th century onwards may not have seen off nuclear weapons, but the fact that so many people made their feelings known may have prevented an even worse proliferation. Likewise, the huge show of feeling around the 2003 invasion of Iraq [Chapter VII] may not have dissuaded the decision-makers to call off the war, but it certainly made it harder for them to achieve their aims without conscience or cause - hence, perhaps, the need to generate the weapons of mass destruction lie. Had those millions around the world not made it clear that the war in Iraq was being perpetrated against their wills, perhaps Western bombs would have started falling on Iran several years ago. All the time that the elite and their elected puppets see that people care, though they may ignore their ultimate wishes, it must, however irritatingly for them, hold back the plans they might otherwise implement to even more devastating effect. The spread of the surveillance state and the ID culture, although insidiously creeping onward, has also been held back more than it might have been if no-one had ever objected, with some of the more extreme proposals having to be at least temporarily rescinded for vote-winning reasons alone.

An Interlude

As the author composes this closing chapter, the sun is shining outside, the birds are singing and life appears to be going on as normal. It all seems so serene and secure. Things appear easy enough, beyond the usual stresses and strains of modern life and the complexities of human relationships. Some readers may be having a similarly nonchalant experience as they read this. So what's the problem? Why worry about any of this control agenda stuff?

It is clear that life in some parts of the West, if nowhere else (paradise compared to many places on Earth, it must be admitted) is not yet *overtly* compromised by the issues examined under the Truth Agenda. The question is, will this last? The very veneer of normality and the relative comfort of Western society can keep us distracted from seeing below the surface to the very concerning issues bubbling away underneath, not yet on the boil, but not far off. Even when the news is full of fear and disaster, we still have a general propensity to switch it off and go back into our little worlds of comfort. But with some kind of shift, cosmological or social, possibly imminent, and with signs and wonders in the skies and fields, underlying religious and occult agendas influencing the corridors of power, and the now apparent engineering of an Orwellian society, how long can this deceptively appealing normality be maintained?

An alarm clock is ticking, getting nearer to ringing. Many of us are already awake, though, one eye opened, dazedly watching the clock from under the duvet. Do we wait for the inevitable heart-thumping shock of the bell - or do we get up early while we still can and switch the alarm off, making for a more gentle awakening? It is, after all, the early bird that catches the worm.

Prometheus Unbound

What is the very worst that can happen if we make a stand against any rise, any hint, of a global fascist state? A few unpleasant scenarios come to mind. But perhaps the question that should be asked is - what is the worst that can happen if we do not make a stand? That option paints a picture too bleak to contemplate further, as previous chapters have examined. Which means that there are limited choices in the matter. If we collectively do nothing, we risk losing the freedom we have left and put ourselves at the mercy of forces that may wish to remove us entirely from their world. It may be that the worst fears of the conspiracy theorists are never realised and that they have fallen too far into paranoia. But what if even a few of those fears are founded in a level of reality? Wouldn't it be better to head them off before such plans come to maturity?

We need to put our fears aside and deal with the things we can see in front of us now. If there is something to be done, we must do it, and rise above the threatening darkness - and not expect any thanks. In Greek myth, Prometheus' reward for stealing fire from the gods to enlighten humankind was to be chained up on a rock whereby an eagle pecked out his ever-regenerating liver each day. Hopefully we will not meet quite such a gruesome fate, but the task of trying to enlighten humankind does always seem to have been a somewhat thankless one. Do we want friends in the short term, or an enduring world of freedom? Sacrifices may have to be made - but as many of those involved in the positive history-making events listed above discovered, the resulting dividends can be huge. If time and energy is given in a spirit of service, with no expectation of personal gratification, the rewards deliver themselves in due course. And Prometheus was released from his rock in the end.

Confidence and High Spirits

A commonly-heard lament amongst those with awareness of the issues discussed throughout these pages is whether we should really be bringing children into the world right now, with all its present and coming traumas. But this is a narrow view. From many people's spiritual perspective, souls which incarnate here choose to do so, and in that view who would we be to halt their journey? Indeed, children of those awake to the issues may be needed more than ever as the grand equation works itself out.

Fear must be replaced with confidence - the confidence that we are astonishing beings with often untapped qualities and the ability to cope with whatever is thrown at us. The irony is that the ruling elite, whatever and whoever it may comprise, clearly recognises this, when many of us don't. It is plain that those who distract us from our true selves and crush the human spirit with social controls and chemical suppression must do so because they *know how powerful we really are*. Otherwise, why bother? Those in the elite would appear to fear us as much as we may fear them - and there are far more of us.

Some who study the legends of extra-terrestrials visiting Earth in ancient times, with all the tales of the Annunaki, the Nephilim and beyond, believe that humankind was genetically accelerated from ape-like beings (again, shades of *2001*) to be a slave race for the 'gods'. To achieve this, however, through gene control and breeding, they had to cut us off from our innate connection to the higher spiritual forces, to keep us energetically mute, and thus malleable. Many believe that we are now regaining those lost faculties through an imminent evolutionary leap and that the battle for the soul of humankind is still being fought. Even if the myths are just myths, the metaphor is clear and the lesson the same - we are more than we think we are. Hence the fight-back from those who fear us. The gods have lost control and we now have our own power to turn the world from darkness to light, if the will can be galvanised and focused.

There are good grounds for optimism and high spirits are recommended. We must always hold up a light in the shadows. Perhaps Mahatma Gandhi said it best when he wrote:

'When I despair, I remember that all through history the ways of truth and love have always won. There have been tyrants, and murderers, and for a time they can seem invincible, but in the end they always fall. Think of it - always.'

If, then, we ever find ourselves asking 'who are we to stand up to all this?', perhaps we should rephrase the question and ask - who are we *not* to?

THE TRUTH AGENDA: *Collective positive action works. It may take time and dedication, but the rewards are worth it - and what will be the price of not challenging tyranny and subterfuge? The ultimate reality of the conspiracy scenario probably lies between two points of extreme, but valid questions have been asked and it is time to step out of fear and stand up for liberty and truth. Take the best from the journey ahead, wherever it may take us.*

Light at the end of the tunnel...

APPENDIX 1 - Notes

A Note on the Notes

Reading sparse reference-only notes, which require constant flicking between the middle and the back of the book to glue together what is referring to what, can be frustrating, so these notes are written in a prose style and are as self-contained as possible. They also contain some relevant snippets that almost made it into the main chapters.

As for the references cited, we currently live in an age where the Internet has taken over from libraries, so although books still feature both here and in the *Further Information* section that follows, those without computers must forgive the electronic bias. Unfortunately, some links do vanish after a while (although if this happens, try searching for them at: *www.archive.org*), but all of the ones listed here were live at the time of publication. Today, of course, search engines give access to a huge vat of information on most topics, and many news websites, especially, cover the same events. Discerning the best sources to reference is a time-consuming business of observing the detail and diligence of any report, and involves a degree of gut instinct. So the references here are merely the ones I found helpful - it goes without saying that searches can be run and numerous alternatives will keep readers busy.

Throughout the book, I have tried to access the most mainstream channels where possible, rather than relying on conspiracy databanks, which can be prone to recycling of unreferenced material or over-reactionary filtering. Given the book's repeated theme that information in the mainstream is highly biased and often manipulative, some readers may be puzzled by this. The advantage of such an approach is that if even the official media is tuning into something, however lightly or unwittingly, it serves as an indication that the matter in question must truly warrant investigation and is therefore more likely to alert the attention of those just setting out on the path of questioning consensus reality. This is not to say that truthseeker channels are always inherently unreliable, and they are also included here for some areas, but I denote the type of source used where it is not obvious.

Readers will also note that I liberally use *Wikipedia* - the online encyclopedia that anyone can edit - as a reference tool. *Wikipedia's* notorious inclination to mainstream bias and editing by dubious hands (especially over things like 9/11 or paranormal phenomena) may at first make this seem a strange choice, but the point above stands here too; when even *Wikipedia* hints at doubts in an official version of events, then something interesting is definitely going on (see note 2, Chapter IX, on Waco, for instance). In any case, because of the 'peer-review' editing system, its reporting of 'normal' subjects, at least, is generally balanced and fair, and even with its sceptical takes on more interesting matters it is sometimes good to see what the everyday view on something is before exploring the more conspiratorial channels. *Wikipedia* pages are also very good as a first-stop for useful links that may lead to deeper areas with a bit of web-surfing. Ditto the BBC News website; many truthseekers are now critical of the BBC, but if one takes some of the reporting with a pinch of salt it still acts as one of the main windows into what the average household is being fed as reality, and the links are useful.

As for the books mentioned here and in the *Further Information* section, publication details are generally for first print-runs unless otherwise noted. Sometimes it can be hard to define whether these are UK or US editions, but where this is known I state it, and Internet retailers like Amazon make all but the most obscure books pretty easy to find.

It should also be mentioned that the references given for documentaries are usually their home websites, but most of them can also be found on *You Tube* and *Google Video*, although these are not always strictly legal. Supporting the original filmmakers (some of whose creations are still free on their websites, but they get advertising revenue from those hitting their sites) obviously helps them to fund further useful works.

I MAKING SENSE OF OUR WORLD

1) David Aaronovitch's *Voodoo Histories*: Aaronovitch's conspiracy-debunking book (Jonathan Cape, 2009), subtitled *The Role of the Conspiracy Theory in Shaping Modern History*, is best summed up by Ian Kershaw's endorsement of it on the back cover as '[a] witty demolition of numerous conspiracy theories and an analysis of why otherwise intelligent people are so ready to believe in them'. Unfortunately, this claimed analysis seems to plump for the usual lazy view of many conspiracy theorists as being inherently anti-Zionist (or worse, anti-Semitic) fanatics, and, in the case of 9/11, evades a discussion of the actual evidence with limp arguments that could be easily knocked down if the detail of that evidence were actually addressed. The book's hardback jacket promises 'to provide ammunition for those who have found themselves at the wrong end of a conversation about moon landings' - on this alone readers should ask for their money back, as Aaronovitch's discussion of this subject amounts to nothing more than a few short general paragraphs that address not one jot of evidence.

2) Polly Toynbee on conspiracies: Polly Toynbee is quoted from her article in *The Guardian*, *A growing state of mind that needs a firm rebuttal - conspiracy theories provide easy answers, but rarely much insight*, 31 August 2005. The full article and a good critical dissection of this piece can be found at: *http://www.julyseventh. co.uk/july-7-conspiracy-theorists.html*.

3) Obama's inaugural speech: Barack Obama's oath-taking fluff is discussed in Ewen MacAskill's article *Obama retakes oath to quell conspiracy theories*, 23 January 2009, which can be read at: *http://www. guardian.co.uk/world/2009/jan/23/obama-presidential-oath*. In essence, when Obama repeated back the all-important words, as recited by the chief justice John Roberts, Roberts accidentally (or not, according to the conspiracy version) said 'I do solemnly swear that I will execute the office of president of the United States *faithfully*' [my italics], words which Obama dutifully, if falteringly, repeated. However, what should have been said by both was 'I do solemnly swear that I will *faithfully* execute the office of president of the United States'. A simple misplacement of a single word can mean a lot at such a crucial moment in history - see also comments on page 125 about Neil Armstrong's iconic words, spoken as he supposedly first set foot on the Moon.

3) Robert M Gates retained as US Defense Secretary: Obama's unexpected and much questioned retention of the Republican Robert M Gates as US Defense Secretary is analysed by Peter Baker and Thom Shanker in the article *Obama Plans to Retain Gates at Defense Department*, 25th November 2008, which can be found at: *http://www.nytimes.com/2008/11/26/us/politics/26gates.html?hp*.

4) Conspiracy doubts over Obama: In 2009, Alex Jones put out an Internet documentary entitled *The Obama Deception*, which squarely points the finger at Barack Obama's administration as being a full continuation of the New World Order agenda, with no allowances whatsoever made to those who believe Obama himself may want to create positive change from the inside. Download the film from Jones' website *www.prisonplanet.com*.

II MYSTERIES ANCIENT AND MODERN

1) Were internal ramps used to build the pyramids?: In 2007, Jean-Pierre Houdin, a French architect, proposed an interesting theory, supported by many verifiable observations, that the Great Pyramid (and by implication the others) may have been built using an ingenious system of *internal* ramps and counterweights to hoist the huge blocks into place. This certainly makes more sense than the external ramps theory, for which there is no clear evidence, and if proven to be correct would force an uncomfortable revision of much Egyptological dogma. The initial theory is reported in the piece *Mystery of Great Pyramid 'Solved'*, 31 March 2007, at: *http://news.bbc.co.uk/1/hi/world/middle_east/6514155.stm*. In the piece, even Egyptologist Bob Brier, tellingly, states:

'This goes against both main existing theories... ...I've been teaching them myself for 20 years, but deep down I know they're wrong.'

A supportive article by Brier explains the internal ramps theory further at: *http://www.archaeology.org/0705/ etc/pyramid.html*. In 2009, BBC 2's *Timewatch* series featured the theory in the programme *Pyramid: The Last Secret*, information on which is available at: *http://www.bbc.co.uk/timewatch/pyramid.shtml*.

2) *Giza: The Truth*: Ian Lawton and Chris Ogilvie Herald's book *Giza: The Truth - The Politics, People and History Behind the World's Most Famous Archaeological Site* (Virgin Books, 1999) attempts to objectively assess all the alternative theories of Hancock, Bauval, Gilbert, etc. (see next note and the *Ancient Mysteries* section in *Further Information*), but ends up as a suspiciously partisan advert for orthodox Egyptology, with the one caveat that the possibility of levitation as a building technique is considered. It is worth a read for a round-up of conventional archaeology's views on unconventional theories, but caution is advised for those seeking an unbiased assessment. More information can be found on Ian Lawton's website at: *http://www. ianlawton.com/gttindex.htm.*

3) The Giza-Orion correlation: The theory that the Giza pyramids were laid out to represent the belt of the constellation Orion received its first full airing in Robert Bauval and Adrian Gilbert's book *The Orion Mystery* (Mandarin Books, 1994). Many have since criticised the detail (especially Lawton and Ogilvie-Herald - see previous note), but the general idea of an astronomical correlation at Giza remains popular.

4) Alternative views on the pyramids: Some interesting facts and figures that serve as a concise compendium of some of the less conventional views on the Giza pyramids can be found at: *http://www.welcomethelight. com/2009/03/amazing-pyramids-of-modern-times*, from where this quote is taken.

5) Heretical archaeological theories: Some believe that humankind originated millions of years earlier than we are usually told, and claim that important archaeological discoveries proving this have been deliberately kept from us. Those wishing to explore the idea further should explore *Forbidden Archaeology: The Hidden History of the Human Race*, by Michael A Cremo and Richard L Thompson (BBT Science, 1996). At 952 pages, it isn't a light read by any means, but does include some tantalising evidence to suggest that archaeological cover-ups of 'inconvenient' findings (such as clearly-tooled objects found in supposedly pre-human strata) *do* occur. Michael Cremo's website offers other related titles and information at: *http://www. mcremo.com/fa.htm.*

6) Crop circle disinformation: George Wingfield's investigation into the non-existence of the press agency that issued the Doug and Dave debunking story led him to believe there might be an MI5 plot in operation, as outlined in his article *The Doug 'N' Dave Scam*, published in *The Cerealogist*, issue 5 (Winter 1991-92), pages 3-6.

7) Ministry of Agriculture crop circle investigation: Interestingly, the department of ADAS (Agricultural Development and Advisory Service) that discovered soil anomalies beneath crop circles was shut down in mysterious circumstances soon after announcing its results, as recounted in my book *Swirled Harvest: Views from the Crop Circle Frontline* (Vital Signs Publishing/S B Publications, 2003), Chapter 6, *End Game*, pages 43-46.

8) Astronomical crop formations and the Sun: An analysis of the possible connection between astronomical crop formations and Sun cycles can, again, be found in my book *Swirled Harvest: Views from the Crop Circle Frontline*, Chapter 15, *Galaxy Legacy*, pages 123-129.

III UFOS

1) UFOs and nuclear bases: Robert Salas was a military officer present at the US Malmstrom Air Force Base in 1967 when an unidentified aerial object temporarily rendered the nuclear missiles there inoperable. Since going public about it, Salas has become a regular on the UFO conference circuit, and several ex-officers have backed up his story. Similar occurrences have also been reported at other military bases, and the implications of an outside force that can neutralise nuclear weapons are clearly huge. The details of the Malmstrom event are told in Salas' book *Faded Giant* (BookSurge Publishing, 2005), while a potted version of the account can be read at: *http://www.cufon.org/cufon/malmstrom/malm1.htm.* The claimed presence of nuclear missiles at the UK Rendlesham base at the time of its own UFO sighting has never been officially acknowledged, but privately confirmed by insiders.

2) The Gary McKinnon extradition case: A straightforward record of UFO enthusiast Gary McKinnon's battle against extradition, which is attempting to send him to the US to stand trial for hacking military computers in search of information on ETs, can be found at *http://en.wikipedia.org/wiki/Gary_McKinnon.*

3] The Disclosure Project: Full details of Steven Greer's Disclosure Project, which aims to stimulate UFO-related testimony from military and civil aviation personnel, are available on its official website at: *http://www.disclosureproject.org*.

4] UFOs and animal mutilations: The laser-precision animal mutilations are a disturbing and largely unexplained mystery. Despite many attempts to dismiss the missing organs and/or flesh as the results of natural causes (such as infestations from blow-fly maggots), it is very hard to explain all of the effects in this way, and the many related sightings of strange aerial phenomena take things into different territory. Although many believe that extra-terrestrials are responsible, others believe the UFO connection is a mask for secret military experiments.

The first serious study of the phenomenon was made by Linda Moulton Howe in her book *Alien Harvest* (Littleton/Co., 1989). A concise round-up of the traditional paranormalist view on the animal mutilations can be found at *http://www.crystalinks.com/animal_mutilation.html*, while a more mainstream but perhaps rather too sceptical view is available at: *http://en.wikipedia.org/wiki/Cattle_mutilation*.

5] Billy Meier's ET-inspired prophecies: Claimed UFO contactee Billy Meier's future predictions are rounded up by Michael Horn in *The Henoch Prophecies from the Billy Meier Contacts* at: *http://www.galactic-server.com/rune/meierpredict.html*. This in itself appears to have been extracted from *Nexus Magazine*, Volume 11, Number 5.

6] Jon King's 'Earthshift' schedule: A good summing up of claimed ET contactee Jon King's 'Earthshift' schedule can be found in Geoff Stray's *Beyond 2012: Catastrophe or Ecstasy* (Vital Signs Publishing, 2005), Chapter 15, *UFOs and ETs*, pages 167-169. King's own book, *Cosmic Top Secret: The Unseen Agenda* (New English Library, 1999), fills in his own general views on extra-terrestrial activities.

IV MIRACLES AND PROPHECIES

1] Nostradamus and Mother Shipton's predictions: Geoff Stray gives a good resume of the Nostradamus and Mother Shipton prophecies in *Beyond 2012: Catastrophe or Ecstasy*, Chapter 18, *Nostradamus*, pages-186-193. The basics on Nostradamus can be found at: *http://en.wikipedia.org/wiki/Nostradamus*.

2] Edgar Cayce's predictions: More details on the Cayce prophecies can be found at the website for the Edgar Cayce Association for Research and Enlightenment: *http://www.edgarcayce.org*. A more mainstream (and less partisan) view on Cayce can be found at: *http://en.wikipedia.org/wiki/Edgar_Cayce*.

3] Bar Codes do NOT represent 666: The urban myth that bar codes embody the biblically significant number 666 is, disappointingly for some, convincingly exploded at *Bar Code 1: A Web Of Information About Bar Code* at: *http://www.adams1.com/pub/russadam/new.html*. Asked 'Is there a hidden 666 in bar code?', the website robustly responds with the following:

*'NO! I get this question asked at least once a week. What people really mean is "does UPC found on grocery products have a hidden 666 (mentioned in Revelation 13:16 in the New Testament)?" People have thought that the three guard bars used to specify the start, middle and end of a UPC bar code looked like the bar code sequence for a "6" found in the UPC symbol table... ...These guard bars are not "6" and carry no information. Even if you don't believe that guard bars carry no information and insist on applying the code table, you have to determine whether the digit is on the left side or the right side of the symbol. That's because the sequence of bars and spaces are different depending on whether the digit is on the left of the symbol or the right of the symbol. The LEFT guard bar would have to be **smallest space, smallest bar, smallest space, WIDEST BAR** in order to be a "6". The guard bar on the left is actually **space of undetermined wide (left side digit must always start with a space element), smallest bar, smallest space, smallest bar**. That sequence of bars and spaces is undefined and is not a "6" even using the table. The middle guard bar is not on the left or the right ('cause it is used to divide the symbol), so it is undefined by the table.'*

4] The Bible Code: Michael Drosnin's somewhat doom-laden but influential book *The Bible Code* (Simon & Schuster, 1997), which purports to have found a code of apocalyptic prophecies scattered throughout the Bible, has frightened many readers, but has been savagely attacked by sceptics. An anonymous Amazon review by 'A Customer', which can be read at *http://www.amazon.com/Bible-Code-Michael-Drosnin/ dp/0684849739*, sums up the main case against it:

'Researchers Dror Bar-Natan, Maya Bar-Hillel, Gil Kalai and Brendan McKay published an article in the journal Statistical Science, *edited by the Institute of Mathematical Statistics, in which they proved the Bible Code to be non-existent. There is no single, agreed-upon original Bible. Even the oldest versions of the Bible vary from one another. Therefore, any attempt to pick out, for example, every fifth word, would be different for each Bible. Besides, even these versions of the Bible are not the original texts, but highly edited versions of more ancient works. The procedures followed by the Bible Code team were not in compliance with scientific standards because they were repeatedly changed with the goal of finding a code. Such statistical tuning can eventually find a few apparently meaningful codes in any long book, but for every such coherent fragment there is a huge amount of gibberish. The focus on the tiny bit of apparent coherence to the detriment of the huge amount of nonsense is a biased attempt to interpret white noise into a supposedly divine message.'*

Despite this, and despite the slightly self-deflating claim from Drosnin that the predicted events may be avoidable, the book, and its sequel, *The Bible Code II: The Countdown* (Penguin, 2002), have been huge hits with Christian end-timers in particular.

5] The Virgin Mary and earth energies: Interesting links between Marian apparitions and earth mysteries are made by Richard Leviton in his book *Signs On The Earth: Deciphering The Message of Virgin Mary Apparitions, UFO Encounters, and Crop Circles* (Hampton Roads, 2005). Leviton concludes that natural earth energy 'hot spots' help stimulate connections with other levels of consciousness.

6] The Fatima apparitions of 1917: There are, of course, myriad Internet references to the 1917 Fatima events, many of them inevitably somewhat religiously biased, but I found these ones particularly useful:
http://members.aol.com/bjw1106/marian6.htm
http://www.theotokos.org.uk/pages/approved/appariti/fatima.html
http://en.wikipedia.org/wiki/Our_Lady_of_Fatima

7] George W Bush says 'God' told him to invade Iraq: Ewen MacAskill recounts Palestinian Foreign Minister Nabil Shaath's testimony that George W Bush claimed divine inspiration concerning the invasion of Iraq in the article *George Bush: 'God told me to end the tyranny in Iraq' - President told Palestinians God also talked to him about Middle East peace*, 7 October 2005, which can be read at: *http://www.guardian.co.uk/ world/2005/oct/07/iraq.usa*.
   Shaath and Abu Mazen, Palestinian Prime Minister, give on-camera descriptions of their meeting with President Bush in the BBC series *Elusive Peace: Israel and the Arabs*, broadcast on BBC 2 in October 2005. Details can be found at: *http://news.bbc.co.uk/1/hi/programmes/elusive_peace/4268184.stm*.

8] More on Bush and God: Bush also told author Bob Woodward, author of the book *Plan of Attack* (Simon & Schuster, 2004 - an account of the administration's invasion of Iraq), that, after giving the order to invade, he went into the White House garden and prayed 'that our troops be safe, be protected by the Almighty', adding 'I was praying for strength to do the Lord's will.'

9] The Astrology of George W Bush: The astonishing identical placement of George W Bush's astrological Sun to America's Sun is discussed further in Helen Sewell's article *The Astrology of 2012*, originally published at: *www.diagnosis2012.co.uk/astro.html* and updated slightly at: *http://goldenagetoday.com/departments/ golden-age-articles/36-article-page/376-the-astrology-of-2012*. See also Note 16 of Chapter XII for general information on astrology.

10] Evangelist Ted Haggard: More background on the controversial evangelical preacher Ted Haggard can be found at *http://en.wikipedia.org/wiki/Ted_Haggard*.

11] Jeff Sharlet on Ted Haggard: Haggard and the creeping influence of fundamentalist Christianity in US politics is examined in Jeff Sharlet's book *The Family: The Secret Fundamentalism at the Heart of American Power* (Harper, 2008), from which this quote is taken.

THE TRUTH AGENDA

12) Hillary Clinton and 'The Family': Jeff Sharlet's book (above note) also claims that Hillary Clinton is a member of one of the 'cell churches' that make up the slightly sinister evangelical 'Family' referred to in the title, which acts as a kind of pyramid-scheme for religious 'dominionists' trying to infiltrate all levels of US society. Further thoughts on this can be found in the article *Hillary Clinton member of "cell church" run by "The Family"*, 4 April 2008, at: ***http://www.dailykos.com/story/2008/4/4/133640/8678/994/490211***.

13) Did Tony Blair and George W Bush 'pray together'?: In a famous BBC TV *Newsnight* interview (screened on 6 February 2003) with then Prime Minister Tony Blair in the run-up to the Iraq invasion, the following curious exchange took place between Blair and television nemesis of UK politicians Jeremy Paxman:

PAXMAN: I want to explore a little further about your personal feelings about this war. Does the fact that George Bush and you are both Christians make it easier for you to view these conflicts in terms of good and evil?
BLAIR: I don't think so, no. I think that whether you're a Christian or you're not a Christian you can try to perceive what is good and what is evil.
PAXMAN: You don't pray together for example?
BLAIR: [awkwardly, with a sheepish grin] No, we don't pray together Jeremy, no.
PAXMAN: Why do you smile?
BLAIR: Because - why do you ask me the question?
PAXMAN: Because I'm trying to find out how you feel about it.
BLAIR: [strangely] Possibly.

The full transcript of this interview (and a link to the broadcast), which in any case makes for fascinating reading in the light of the disaster in Iraq that followed and all the later revelations about the deceptions behind it, can be read at: ***http://news.bbc.co.uk/1/hi/programmes/newsnight/2732979.stm***.

V GRAND CONSPIRACIES

1) Concerns over vaccinations: Many qualified medical experts have questioned the safety and science of the vaccination program - and have been unfairly debunked and accused of quackery as a result. Internet searches will reveal a lot of important information that should be read before parents decide (while they still have the power of decision) to allow the immunisation of their children.

One of the most thorough questioners has been Trevor Gunn, author of the influential booklet *Mass Immunisation - A Point in Question*, first published by Cutting Edge Publications in 1992 and reproduced many times since. Gunn (corresponding on behalf of *The Informed Parent* magazine) contributes an important dialogue with Dr C J Clements EPI of the Global Programme for Vaccines and Immunisation, identifying some serious issues with immunisation propaganda, in a piece entitled *Response to WHO Evidence for Vaccine Safety and Effectiveness*, which can be found at: ***http://www.whale.to/m/gunn.html***.

A comprehensive presentation by Trevor Gunn can be audio downloaded at: ***http://www.changingtimes.org.uk/Lectures/TrevorGunn/TrevorGunn.htm***. Some other sources on vaccination concerns can be found in Appendix 2, in the *Health* section.

A concerted effort to debunk MMR questioners has centered around the work of Dr Andrew Wakefield, who produced a 1998 paper in the medical journal *The Lancet* asserting links between the MMR jabs and cases of autism. Subsequent allegations of professional misconduct in his research methods have resulted in Wakefield being vilfied in the media (the same media that made screaming headlines of his original findings), but many parents who believe their childrens' autism is directly attributable to MMR continue to support him and Wakefield is currently fighting to clear his name. *Wikipedia*'s cautious view on Wakefield can be found at ***http://en.wikipedia.org/wiki/Andrew_Wakefield***, while Wakefield himself mounts a robust defence of his views (defending himself against his arch-nemesis, journalist Brian Deer) in the article *Autism, bowel disease and MMR vaccination: In his desperation, Deer gets it wrong once again*, 9th February 2009, at: ***http://www.rescuepost.com/files/deer-response.pdf***.

2) AIDS conspiracy theories: There are too many alternative theories on the possible origins and 'purpose' of AIDS to go into here, but a handy (if largely sceptical) round-up of some of them is available in Juliet Lapidos' report *The AIDS Conspiracy Handbook*, 19 March 2008, at: ***http://www.slate.com/id/2186860/***, while a good example of the total conspiracy view can be found at the website *The AIDS Conspiracy*, at: ***http://sonic.net/~doretk/ArchiveARCHIVE/Aids/Aids.html***.

3) The overpopulation controversy: The threat of planetary overpopulation is seen by some (including TV naturalist David Attenborough) as one of the major issues of our times, or at least is being promoted as such, raising truthseeker fears that drastic action might be taken by a ruling elite to 'solve' the problem. Typical of such reports was an interview with Professor John Beddington on BBC Radio 4's *Today* programme, 19 March 2009, which can be heard at: *http://news.bbc.co.uk/today/hi/today/newsid_7952000/7952148.stm*. Promotion for the interview reads as follows:

'The government's chief scientific officer has warned that a "perfect storm" will occur in the year 2030, with simultaneous shortages of energy, food and fresh water devastating an over-populated planet. Professor John Beddington explains how he reached this conclusion and puts forward his solutions.'

On the other hand, some conspiracy theorists believe the over-population scare is another engineered myth spread to further the control agenda, and there have been claims that the world is nowhere near reaching resources capacity, despite trouble in more densely-populated areas. Some of these views may, of course, be pushed by religious hardliners with an anti-contraception stance, but the arguments are worth a listen. An interesting article on this can be found at: *http://www.lifeissues.net/writers/kas/kas_01overpopulation.html*.

4) Dr Eric Pianka denies advocating mass-extermination: The controversy over Dr Eric Pianka's 2006 lecture to St Edwards University, which some took as a recommendation that a human extermination programme should be instigated, is discussed at: *http://en.wikipedia.org/wiki/Mims-Pianka_controversy*. Denying this interpretation, and in an effort to clear his name, Pianka issued a statement on the University of Texas website, which included the following paragraph:

'I have two grandchildren and I want them to inherit a stable Earth. But I fear for them. Humans have overpopulated the Earth and in the process have created an ideal nutritional substrate on which bacteria and viruses (microbes) will grow and prosper. We are behaving like bacteria growing on an agar plate, flourishing until natural limits are reached or until another microbe colonizes and takes over, using them as their resource. In addition to our extremely high population density, we are social and mobile, exactly the conditions that favor growth and spread of pathogenic (disease-causing) microbes. I believe it is only a matter of time until microbes once again assert control over our population, since we are unwilling to control it ourselves. This idea has been espoused by ecologists for at least four decades and is nothing new. People just don't want to hear it... I do not bear any ill will toward humanity. However, I am convinced that the world WOULD clearly be much better off without so many of us... We need to make a transition to a sustainable world. If we don't, nature is going to do it for us in ways of her own choosing. By definition, these ways will not be ours and they won't be much fun. Think about that.'

5) Dr Leonard Horowitz on flu anti-virals: Horowitz's view that it is the anti-virals that are as much the problem as swine flu itself was expressed in a presentation given at The Alternative View conference at Heathrow, UK in May 2009. Horowitz's book, *Emerging Viruses: AIDS and Ebola - Nature, Accident or Intentional?* (Healthy World Distributing, 1996), explores the idea that the viruses in question were 'by-products of a genetic engineering program'. His personal website can be found at: *http://www.drlenhorowitz.com*.

6) Side-effects of Tamiflu: The worrying and numerous neuropsychiatric effects reported in people taking Tamiflu, especially children and young adults, which have resulted in suicides and self-harming, appear to be accepted in the mainstream, as discussed in detail in *Wikipedia*'s current entry on oseltamivir (Tamiflu) at: *http://en.wikipedia.org/wiki/Oseltamivir*. So why isn't there more of a debate about it in the media? Public fear, as ever, has overridden common sense.

7) UK government stockpiles Tamiflu / Extended Tamiflu lifespan: The news that the UK government spent £100 million on buying up to 50 million doses of Tamiflu at the height of the first swine flu scare can be read in David Rose's article *Tamiflu might not work against swine flu, Government's own scientists warn*, 23 May 2009, at: *http://www.dailymail.co.uk/news/article-1186913/Tamiflu-work-swine-flu-Governments-scientists-warn.html*.
The very unusual announcement, also in May 2009, that Tamiflu was going to have its shelf-life extended by two years is seen by many as a diversion from the fact that the swine flu scare did begin just as the current stocks needed to be used. Did the panic not use up as much as was anticipated? Andrew Jack's short report *Tamiflu can be used past 'sell by'*, 9 May 2009, at *http://www.ft.com/cms/s/0/e96d7460-3c30-11de-acbc-*

00144feabdc0.html, states the following:

'The European Medicines Agency said for the first time ever that a medicine could remain safe to use for seven years, in response to concerns of a global shortage of a drug [Tamiflu] that could help prevent and treat a pandemic flu virus. "The recommendation is don't throw it away," a spokeswoman said.
The move may reduce short-term pressure for additional stockpile orders by governments from Roche of Switzerland, which produces the drug.'

8) Donald Rumsfeld and Tamiflu: The claimed flu antidote Tamiflu was developed by Roche Laboratories, and former US Secretary of Defense Donald Rumsfeld (seen by many as a main NWO operative, and a key architect of the George W Bush Iraq and Afghanistan campaigns) was indeed chairman of Gilead Sciences Inc. when his company bought the patent for Tamiflu in 1996. This has obviously raised suspicions in a number of directions, and Rumsfeld's involvement in the production of the dubious sweetener Aspartame (see Note 3 of Chapter X) has added to the speculation. A discussion on the truths and myths of the details can be read on the page *The Tamiflu/Rumsfeld Connection*, April 2006, at: *http://urbanlegends.about. com/library/bl_bird_flu.htm*, while another revealing piece on Rumsfeld's profiteering from Tamiflu can be found in Geoffrey Lean and Jonathan Owen's article *Donald Rumsfeld makes $5m killing on bird flu drug*, 12 March 2006, at: *http://www.independent.co.uk/news/world/americas/donald-rumsfeld-makes-5m-killing-on-bird-flu-drug-469599.html*.

9) The Georgia Guidestones: This US stone monument with inscriptions that appear to recommend a massive reduction of the global population, along with other apparent New World Order platitudes, is discussed basically at: *http://en.wikipedia.org/wiki/Georgia_Guidestones*. For a fuller conspiracy view on the stones, have a look at: *http://www.theforbiddenknowledge.com/hardtruth/thegeorgiaguidestones.htm*.

10) The 'Amero' currency: Information on the 'Amero', the claimed single currency that will supposedly one day encompass the USA, Mexico and Canada, can be found at: *http://en.wikipedia.org/wiki/North_American_currency_union*.

11) Doubts over the Federal Reserve: Many conspiracy websites inevitably have something to say about the astonishing illegality of the US Federal Reserve, but for a non-conspiratorial critical take on it, go to: *http://www.abolishthefederalreserve.com*.
  Another intelligent and critical piece on President Obama's decision to give yet more control to the Federal Reserve can be read in John Nichol's article *Don't Cede More Economic Authority to Unaccountable Fed*, 18 June 2009, which can be read at: *http://www.thenation.com/blogs/thebeat/444471/don_t_cede_more_economic_authority_to_unaccountable_fed*.

12) *The Money Masters* documentary: Information on the film *The Money Masters*, which takes a highly critical and illuminating look at the history of banking, can be found at its official website: *http://www.themoneymasters.com/synopsis.htm*.

13) House of Lords bribes scandal: The failure of the House of Lords to properly punish two of its members, exposed by undercover journalists from the *Sunday Times* for the verbal admission that they would accept bribes to influence legislation, was at least partially corrected in May 2009 when Lord Truscott and Lord Taylor of Blackburn were temporarily suspended from the House. Many others think they should have been permanently ejected, but in the mess of the MPs' expenses scandal no-one was going to throw stones in their own glasshouse. These two made the mistake of getting caught - how many other Lords are equally corrupt, however? A good resume of the bribes scandal can be read in the article *Britain's House of Lords suspends members in "bribe" probe*, 20 May 2009, at: *http://www.monstersandcritics.com/news/uk/news/article_1478521.php*.

14) 'Common Purpose': Although supposedly a harmless 'educational charity' that promotes 'leadership and networking development training', many believe the organisation Common Purpose masks an attempt to subvert democracy and introduce federalist-EU policies and other murky agendas through a back door. Several websites are now dedicated to exposing it, including the *Stop Common Purpose* website at: *http://www.stopcp.com*. A more concise article calling attention to problems with CP can be found at *http://*

www.tpuc.org/node/107, and a full presentation by CP's most public nemesis, Brian Gerrish, can be audio downloaded at: *http://www.changingtimes.org.uk/Lectures/BrianGerrish/BrianGerrish.htm*.

15) ID Cards: The basics on the issues surrounding the forthcoming UK ID-card scheme can be found at: *http://en.wikipedia.org/wiki/British_national_identity_card*.

16) More on ID Cards: An excellent fictional account of what could happen in a society entirely based around ID cards and surveillance was featured in a now-rare flash of BBC risk-taking with the series *The Last Enemy*, broadcast on BBC 1 in February-March 2008. The effect of the lead character being deliberately deleted from the ID database, reducing him to the status of a street tramp, gives a chilling demonstration of what could happen to anyone considered 'problematic' by any future fascist state. Details of the series can be found at: *http://www.bbc.co.uk/drama/lastenemy/welcome.shtml*.

In the non-fictional world, human rights campaigner Peter Tatchell gives an excellent presentation on the perils of the ID system and its potential abuses in a video that can be downloaded at: *http://www. changingtimes.org.uk/Lectures/PeterTatchell/PeterTatchell.htm*.

17) Bloodlines of presidents and monarchs: A good compact guide revealing the complex but fascinating genealogical connections between various presidents, politicians and monarchs, with many links and references, can be found at: *http://groups.google.com/group/total_truth_sciences/browse_thread/thread/ f3c944726cb1f283*. Amongst the more worrying news from this is that Barack Obama is claimed to be related to Dick Cheney (believed by many to be one of the key architects of 9/11 - see Chapter VIII), and that the British Royal Family are descendants of Vlad the Impaler, the cruel 15th century Transylvanian/ Romanian tyrant on which Bram Stoker based the character of Dracula!

18) '6000 people run the world': The mainstream exposure that just 6000 people essentially run the world was first revealed in David Rothkopf's book *Superclass: The Global Power Elite and the World They Are Making* (Farrar, Straus and Giroux, 2008). Although largely non-conspiratorial in tone, it manages to identify many of the same people truthseekers point to as being key elements in the One World Government agenda, adding a few celebrities like *U2*'s Bono into the mix as well as identifying other names one might expect, such as Rupert Murdoch and Bill Gates. Interestingly, the book received a fair bit of media coverage from some of the same journalists who usually scoff at conspiracy theories, showing that revelations of what amounts to partisan manipulation can be reportable - but only if couched in certain terms and put through the right intellectual filters. An informative review of Rothkopf's book, by Laura Miller, can be read at: *http://www.salon.com/books/review/2008/03/14/superclass/*. Miller comments:

'Rothkopf announces that he and his researchers have identified "just over 6,000" people who match his definition of the superclass - that is, who have met complicated (and vaguely explained) metrics designed to determine "the ability to regularly influence the lives of millions of people in multiple countries worldwide." These include heads of state and religious and military leaders... ...but the core membership is businessmen: hedge fund managers, technology entrepreneurs and private equity investors.'

19) The US military damage ancient Babylon: News that the US military willfully camped on the ancient site of Babylon, creating untold harm to an important archaeological site, did actually go mainstream. The BBC's coverage of it, *Army base 'has damaged Babylon'*, 15 January 2005, can be found at: *http://news.bbc. co.uk/1/hi/world/middle_east/4177577.stm*.

20) The Tower of Babel: The story of the Tower of Babel is taken from *The Bible - Revised Standard Version* (quoted from the 1952 edition).

21) Freemasonry: The Internet is crammed full of conspiracy takes on Freemasonry, naturally, but for a straightforward and fair assessment (which includes critical observations), *Wikipedia* is probably the best starting point for an all-round history: *http://en.wikipedia.org/wiki/Freemasonry*.

22) The mystical layout of famous cities: Greater awareness of occult symbolism being encoded into architecture and city planning was aroused by the publication of Graham Hancock and Robert Bauval's book *Talisman: Sacred Cities, Secret Faith*, Element Books (US), Michael Joseph (UK), 2004.

An informative conversation with Robert Bauval, which makes for a concise insight into the subject, can be read in the article *Robert Bauval: A Man For All Seasons - Conversation with Robert Bauval on the Subject of Egyptian and Masonic Symbolism as Incorporated into the Master Plan of the District of Columbia*, at: **http://www.opencheops.org/page18.htm.**

23) Princess Diana conspiracy theories: There appear to have been people queuing up to assassinate Princess Diana, if the many, many conspiracy theories doing the rounds are to be believed, and amongst which Mohammed Al Fayed's Prince Philip allegations seem tame in comparison. Although claims that Diana's lineage from the Stuart dynasty was not acceptable to hardline elements from the House of Windsor may not be entirely without foundation, alternative versions involve the belief that Diana's growing involvement in anti-landmine campaigns was an important element (Dodi Al Fayed's mother was the upper class Saudi Samira Khashoggi, sister of major armaments dealer Adnan Khashoggi - perhaps someone in the family didn't want a peacenik at their table), or comprise confused tangles concerning the preservation of specific extra-terrestrial bloodlines.

Seeing the entire assassination set-up as a kind of modern ritual sacrifice, with heavy secret society overtones, others have speculated on everything from Diana's supposed genealogical connections to Mary Magdalene and the Merovingian dynasty, to extraordinary (if darkly entertaining) claims that she was murdered on the orders of Hillary Clinton to prevent Diana being forcibly married in an occult ceremony to then President Bill (!). The problem is that so much has now been stirred into the pot of mythology and partial-truths that Diana's admittedly suspicious death will probably now never be solved, as with the JFK shooting.

Of all the Diana conspiracy books available, the most grounded and convincing is Jon King and John Beveridge's *Princess Diana: The Hidden Evidence* (SPI Books, 2001), which makes clear, if nothing else, that staged car-crashes are indeed a tried-and-tested method of assassination in the intelligence world.

24) Modern pyramids: Pyramid building now seems to be all the rage again, for good or ill. A good collection of photos showing recently constructed pyramids from around the world can be found at: **http://www.welcomethelight.com/2009/03/amazing-pyramids-of-modern-times/.**

25) The 'Cremation of Care' ceremony at Bohemian Grove: A mainstream view of The Bohemian Club and the Cremation of Care ceremony can be found at: **http://en.wikipedia.org/wiki/Bohemian_Grove#cite_note-21.** This article notes that in response to a heckler who raised the subject of Bohemian Grove at one of his public appearances in 2007, Bill Clinton (laughing) said:

'The Bohemian club! Did you say Bohemian club? That's where all those rich Republicans go up and stand naked against redwood trees right? I've never been to the Bohemian club, but you oughta go. It'd be good for you. You'd get some fresh air.'

26) Mysterious deaths and the Clintons: It is easy to joke about the Clintons, but a glance at the list of their ex-associates and colleagues who have met untimely ends in unusual or unexplained circumstances is a sobering experience. The morbidly curious should look at *The Progressive Review's Arkansas Sudden Death Syndrome*, which lists over 50 people who have fallen into this unfortunate category: **http://www.freerepublic.com/focus/f-news/1142670/posts.**

27) Jon Ronson and Bohemian Grove: Journalist Jon Ronson remains non-committal about the significance of what he witnessed at Bohemian Grove, but he was impressed enough to base an entire chapter of his bestselling book *Them: Adventures With Extremists* (Simon & Schuster, 2002) on his experience of sneaking into the Cremation of Care ceremony with Alex Jones, as well as showing the footage on the noted Channel 4 documentary.

VI ONE GIANT LEAP..?

1) JFK's intention to land astronauts on the Moon: President John F Kennedy announced his aims to send men to the Moon by the end of the 1960s in a speech known as the *Special Message to the Congress on Urgent National Needs*, 25 May 1961. The entire text of this very influential speech can be read and heard at: **http://www.jfklibrary.org/Historical+Resources/Archives/Reference+Desk/Speeches/JFK/003POF03NationalNeeds05251961.htm.**

2) Inconsistencies in the claimed visibility of stars: In his book *NASA Mooned America!* (self-published, 1992), Chapter 5, *Star Light - Star Bright*, pages 29-36, Ralph René draws a series of curious comparisons highlighting astronauts' often contradictory statements about either the brightness or dimness of stars as seen from space, and struggles to reach a definitive conclusion on the ultimate truth of the matter. For instance, he quotes Harry Hurt III's book *For All Mankind* (Atlantic Monthly Press, 1988), in which Hurt writes of the Apollo 14 mission:

'The astronauts had a hard time seeing the stars even with the help of a special "monocular" (half a binocular) used to supplement the scanning telescope and the sextant. Due to the absence of an atmosphere to refract and filter light, the stars do not twinkle in cislunar space. Rather, as Stu Roosa puts it, "The stars look like little points of light or fuzzy little dots".'

On the other hand, these kinds of statements need to be contrasted with comments such as this from Apollo 11 astronaut Michael Collins, who writes (describing his thoughts at the time of being in space):

'My God, the stars are everywhere, even below me. They are somewhat brighter than on Earth.'

There are numerous examples, equally at odds with each other, leading many to question the testimony of the astronauts.

3) Gus Grissom: Astronaut Virgil 'Gus' Grissom's running critique of the Moon programme, his subsequent untimely demise in the Apollo 1 fire and his son Scott Grissom's attempts to piece together what happened is discussed at length in Gerhard Wisnewski's worryingly credible book *One Small Step? - The Great Moon Hoax and the Race to Dominate Earth from Space*, Clairview Books, 2007.
   Scott Grissom's public breaking of the news that he believed his father was murdered first appeared in Steve Herz's article *Apollo Astronaut was Murdered, Son Charges* in the US magazine *Star*, issue dated 16 February 1999, and is summed up in a similarly-titled piece by Christopher Ruddy at: ***http://www.theforbiddenknowledge.com/hardtruth/astronaut_murdered.htm***.

4) Thomas Ronald Baron's damning report on Apollo safety: Although Baron's final 500-page report on poor safety at North American Aviation (NAA) has never been seen since he and his entire family were killed in a suspicious car crash, his preliminary paper is available to read. This alone makes it clear that the Apollo missions were hardly being planned with the kind of efficacy and diligence surely required to safely get men to the Moon and back. Notes on the Baron affair and the paper itself can be found in Steve Garber's article *Baron Report (1965-1966)*, 3 February 2003, at: ***http://history.nasa.gov/Apollo204/barron.html***.

5) James Irwin: The claims that astronaut James Irwin was about to make a public statement exposing the Moon missions as a fraud, but died suddenly before he could do so, were made by one Lee Gelvani (apparently a friend of moon-hoax theorist Bill Kaysing - see ***http://billkaysing.com***), who claimed to have been in direct contact with Irwin. However, 'Lee Gelvani' appears to be a pseudonym and no direct proof of his allegations exist.

6) Earthly contamination in 'Moon' material: Astrobiologist Andrew Steele's discovery that the lunar sample he was sent for analysis contained obvious earthly particles is reported in Gerhard Wisnewski's *One Small Step?*, Part Two: *The USA*, pages 207-208.

7) Laser reflectors on the Moon: Gerhard Wisnewski's revelation that scientists cannot pinpoint the exact location of the laser-reflectors supposedly left on the lunar surface by the astronauts is again discussed in *One Small Step?*, Part Two: *The USA*, pages 209-218.

8) Incorrect horizon line behind Aldrin: The impossibility that an aesthetically perfect horizon line could run through Aldrin's visor reflection to match the real horizon behind him, if taken with a camera at chest height, is incontrovertibly demonstrated in Mary Bennett and David Percy's dense and detailed book *Dark Moon: Apollo and the Whistleblowers* (Aulis Publishers, 1999), Chapter 1, *Photo Call*, pages 40-41.

9) Original Moon videos lost: The astonishing news that NASA had lost the original videotapes of the Moon missions (before suspiciously finding them again in time for the 40th anniversary) was originally published in the Australian newspaper *The Sydney Morning Herald* in the report *One giant blunder for mankind - how NASA lost moon pictures*, 5 August 2006. *Wikipedia's* take on it can be found at: ***http://en.wikipedia.org/wiki/Apollo_program_missing_tapes.***

10) Fake space walk photo: The provably-doctored photo of astronaut Michael Collins, taken on a terrestrial training flight but altered to represent a Gemini space walk, features prominently in Collins' 1974 autobiographical book *Carrying the Fire: An Astronaut's Journeys* (republished 2001 by Cooper Square Press). Curiously, the same shot is cut out *again* and superimposed over 1970s spacey artwork on the original cover.

11) Fake Moon golf photo: The obviously montaged shot of Alan Shepard and companion supposedly playing golf on the Moon is analyed and taken apart (literally) bit by bit by Mary Bennett and David Percy at: ***http://www.aulis.com/nasa12.htm.*** The book in which the photo features is *Moon Shot: The Inside Story of America's Race to the Moon*, by Al Shepard and Deke Slayton (Turner Publishing Inc., 1994).

12) Ed Mitchell's ET claims: The first interview in which astronaut Edgar Mitchell claimed that NASA and the US authorities had covered-up evidence of ET activity was made on *Kerrang Radio*, 23 July 2008, and can be heard at: ***http://www.youtube.com/watch?v=RhNdxdveK7c.***

The *Daily Mail's* take on the story, *Apollo 14 astronaut claims aliens HAVE made contact - but it has been covered up for 60 years*, can be read at: ***http://www.dailymail.co.uk/sciencetech/article-1037471/Apollo-14-astronaut-claims-aliens-HAVE-contact--covered-60-years.html.***

Mitchell has gone on to be very vocal on this issue, leading some to acclaim him as the whistleblower everyone has been waiting for, while others are suspicious, fearing that his claims may in themselves be a set-up of some kind.

13) Radiation hazards in space: Radiation is the 'show stopper' in the manned exploration of space, according to Mary Bennett and David Percy, who use it as one of the key arguments against the official story of the lunar missions in *Dark Moon*. Chapter 3, *Radiant Daze*, pages 77- 114, sifts many of the issues. Ralph René also discusses the problem at length in *NASA Mooned America!,* Chapter 15, *Sunstroke*, pages 125-136.

14) Were the space suits radiation-proof?: Given the high doses of radiation in space and on the lunar surface, one might reasonably expect that the astronauts' space suits were radiation-proof. Yet no fully-protective suit has yet been devised that can handle prolonged exposure in a terrestrial radiation zone (i.e. in a Chernobyl-type disaster), let alone a space-bound one - raising further questions about how the astronauts survived on the Moon.

15) Marcus Allen: The UK's most high-profile challenger of NASA, and UK publisher of *Nexus Magazine*, Marcus Allen has appeared widely on television and radio, managing to disarm even TV Rottweiler Jeremy Clarkson. A full video presentation by Allen can be downloaded at: ***http://www.changingtimes.org.uk/Lectures/moonlandings/moonlandings.htm.***

16) Jack White's Moon photo analysis: Jack White's exhaustive and very convincing deconstruction of the NASA lunar image bank can be sifted through at ***http://aulis.com/jackstudies_index1.html***, and is almost impossible to peruse without feeling at least slightly shaken after. Amongst more obvious anomalies, White also identifies peculiarities such as photographic prints of the Apollo 11 mission seen lying on the foot of the Apollo 15 lander (a horizontally-flipped version of NASA photo reference AS11-40-5948) - something never explained, and items that presumably wouldn't be able to survive the harsh lunar environment of high-temperature sunlight in a vacuum without some serious curling if nothing else. Gerhard Wisnewski demonstrates the same problem in *One Small Step?*, Part Two: *The USA*, pages 158-159, in which a print photograph showing the family of Apollo 16 astronaut Charles Duke can be seen lying on the lunar surface, apparently unaffected in any way. Leaving an unframed print photograph in even terrestrial sunlight for a short time will soon affect it, so how did those on the Moon stay so pristine?

17) Pete Conrad's 'spotlight' comments: Pete Conrad's curious commentary on the Sun resembling a 'super-bright spotlight' is quoted from Mary Bennett and David Percy's *Dark Moon*, Chapter 1, *Photo Call*, page 27.

18) Did Yuri Gagarin really go into space?: There is evidence to suggest that a number of manned space flights were secretly attempted by the Russians before the famed Gagarin mission, but that the cosmonauts involved were either killed or injured. Some believe that in wanting to claim a first and realising that the US might officially achieve the feat of manned spaceflight before them, the Soviet authorities used air officer Gagarin as a publicity front until real cosmonauts could eventually make it into space. Not as unlikely as it sounds, Gagarin only had a few flying hours' experience when he was chosen, his observations about the historic flight were notably inconsistent with the official claims, photos of him allegedly sitting in the capsule appear to have been doctored, and it seems slightly odd that no camera was used to look outwards into space during the flight itself to record such an incredibly important moment. Gagarin himself was said to have been injured in a fall from a balcony just six months after his supposed feat and suffered behavioural problems thereafter. He reportedly died in a mysterious military plane crash in 1968. No plane wreckage was ever photographed or publicly exhibited, and hardly anything of Gagarin's body was left - yet the flight suit that identified him was supposedly discovered in treetops nearby.

Gerhard Wisnewski writes at length about the Gagarin anomalies and other Soviet cover-ups in *One Small Step?*, Part One: *The Soviet Union*, but a brief resume (from a somewhat evangelical source) can be found at *http://www.biblebelievers.org.au/gagarin.htm*, and reports the following:

'*On 12 April 2001, the Russian senior engineer Mikhail Rudenko, at the Experimental Design Office 456, in Khimki in the Moscow region, admitted in* Pravda *that three cosmonauts had died in space before Gagarin was sent up, namely Alexei Ledovskikh (1957), Serenti Zhaborin (February 1958), and Andrei Mitkov (flight attempt January 1959).*'

On top of this astonishing announcement, it is rumoured that an additional seven cosmonauts were lost in pre-'Gagarin' flights, with Italian radio hams claiming to have picked up plaintive SOS messages from Russian personnel that could only have come from space.

19) John F Kennedy instructs NASA to cooperate with the Soviets: The remarkable memorandums in which President Kennedy orders NASA to set up joint missions with the Soviet Union, releasing the CIA's UFO files into the bargain, are discussed by Michael Salla PhD in the article *Kennedy linked US-USSR space missions with classified UFO files*, 27 May 2009, at: *http://www.examiner.com/x-2383-Honolulu-Exopolitics-Examiner%7Ey2009m5d27-President-Kennedy-linked-joint-lunar-missions-with-classified-UFO-filed*.

VII WEAPONS OF MASS DECEPTION

1) The Suez crisis: A good timeline of the 1956 Suez crisis, which reveals many of its more dubious aspects, is available at: *http://www.bodley.ox.ac.uk/dept/scwmss/projects/suez/suez.html*.

2) The 'fake bin Laden' video: The Osama bin Laden seen in the alleged '9/11 confession' video is almost certainly not the real man and the footage is convincingly debunked at many websites, including *http://www.welfarestate.com/binladen/surprise/* and *http://www.911lies.org/fake_bin_laden.html* (this also covers the interesting fact that to this day bin Laden is not on the FBI's 'wanted' list for perpetrating 9/11).

3) Turkmenistan-Afghanistan-Baluchistan oil pipeline?: A good forum discussion, putting forward the pros and cons of the theory that the US wants a major oil pipeline running through these regions, hence some of its recent military strategies, can be found in the thread *Free Baluchistan*, started 6 April 2005, at: *http://www.moonofalabama.org/2005/04/free_baluchista.html*. Another piece, which gives some clarity on the matter, Alex Bigham's *Why Baluchistan Matters*, 4 July 2006, can be found at: *http://www.guardian.co.uk/commentisfree/2006/jul/04/whybaluchistanmatters*.

4) Increased opium production in Afghanistan: The huge rise in opium production in Afghanistan since Western troops arrived has been widely-acknowledged in the media, if sheepishly ignored by politicians, leading many to wonder what the motive is in having allowed this to occur. Two good mainstream sources on this can be read at: *http://news.bbc.co.uk/1/hi/world/south_asia/6239734.stm* and *http://www.independent.co.uk/news/world/asia/the-big-question-why-is-opium-production-rising-in-afghanistan-and-can-it-be-stopped-960276.html*.

5) Ron Suskind's revelations on the Iraq war: Ron Suskind has been an important mainstream challenger of the official record of the events leading up to the 2003 invasion of Iraq, and his revelations that WMDs were already known not to exist there deserve more attention. Information on Suskind is available at: *http://en.wikipedia.org/wiki/Ron_Suskind.*

More recent leaks firmly back-up Suskind's discoveries, with the 2009 exposure of certain Whitehall e-mails making clear that both politicians and bureaucrats knew full well that the all-important 'dossier' was being (at the very least) over-enhanced to prop up an otherwise shaky case for war. Nigel Morris writes candidly on the deception in his article *Secret emails show Iraq dossier* was *'sexed up' - Intelligence chiefs criticised 'iffy drafting' of key document*, 13 March 2009, at: *http://www.independent.co.uk/news/uk/politics/secret-emails-show-iraq-dossier-uwasu-sexed-up-1643960.html.*

6) Norman Baker MP on David Kelly: Norman Baker's investigation into the shameful David Kelly affair and the weapons inspector's very dubious death is one of the very rare conspiracy theories to go mainstream without blanket ridicule, largely because of Baker's high-profile as a Parliamentary reformer and an outspoken (for an MP) liberty campaigner. Some see his conclusion that Iraqi dissidents alone killed Kelly as a polite evasion of possible deeper truths, but going public with such views was still a brave move for a man in his position. Partly as a result of Baker's revelations, it is now hard to find too many people willing to believe the official 'suicide' verdict on Kelly's demise.

Baker's bestselling book *The Strange Death of David Kelly* (Methuen Publishing, 2007) is the main source to go to, but for a concise version of his findings, the article *Why I know weapons expert Dr David Kelly was murdered, by the MP who spent a year investigating his death*, 20 October 2007, is a good round-up and can be read at: *http://www.dailymail.co.uk/news/article-488667/Why-I-know-weapons-expert-Dr-David-Kelly-murdered-MP-spent-year-investigating-death.html.*

An audio download of Norman Baker presenting his findings in a lecture can be heard at: *http://www.changingtimes.org.uk/Lectures/NormanBaker/NormanBaker.htm.*

7) Brian Haw's eight-year Parliament protest: In what must be one of the longest-running unbroken anti-war protests in history, peace campaigner Brian Haw has managed to keep his impassioned, if unsubtle, information stalls on the Iraq war and other recent Western military ventures standing at the edge of Parliament Square (opposite the Houses of Parliament) since July 2001. In raising awareness of sanctions and bombings on Iraq even before the WMDs were used to justify a full war two years later, Haw met a continual onslaught of police intimidation and attempted legislation to move him, but public support, court cases and legal loopholes have enabled him to stay and the battle still goes on. Find out more about his impressive tenacity at: *http://www.parliament-square.org.uk*. The right to protest in Westminster has been massively curtailed in recent years, so Haw's success in staying there is particularly satisfying, while poignant.

VIII 9/11

1) Did the FBI aid the 1993 WTC bombing?: The chilling testimony of agent Emad Salem that the FBI deliberately supplied live explosives to the perpetrators of the 1993 WTC bombing has not received the coverage it demands, not even amongst 9/11 truth campaigners. Information on Salem is available at: *http://en.wikipedia.org/wiki/Emad_Salem.*

2) Lack of aeroplane debris at the Pentagon: The strange absence of obvious plane wreckage inside or outside of the Pentagon was noted by several reporters and eye-witnesses at the time. Quotes such as 'there's no evidence of a plane having crashed anywhere near the Pentagon' (James McIntyre, CNN News), 'I don't recall at any time seeing any plane debris' (April Gallop, Pentagon staff survivor), 'There weren't seats or luggage or things you find in a plane' (Judy Rothschadl, documentary maker) and 'I got in very close, got a look early on at the bad stuff. I could not, however, see any plane wreckage' (John McWethy, ABC News) are typical statements. McWethy was one of the first to coin the phrase that the plane had 'basically, vaporised', a view entirely encouraged by official sources since - and something quite impossible in the circumstances. The debris that has been identified from photos seems not to be from a Boeing 757 [page 149]. Quotes extracted from David Ray Griffin's *Debunking 911 Debunking* (Olive Branch Press, 2007), Chapter Four, *Debunking 9/11 Myths*, pages 269-270.

3) NIST's shotgun tests: The bizarre revelation that NIST (National Institute of Standards and Technology) conducted its supposedly 'scientific' analysis of how fireproofing might have been removed from steel supports at the WTC by firing shotgun rounds at metal plates in plywood boxes is reported in David Ray Griffin's *Debunking 911 Debunking*, Chapter Four, *Debunking 9/11 Myths*, page 251.

4) Fire temperatures should not have weakened steel supports: The quoted statistics on the temparatures needed to weaken steel, as set against the probable maximum temperatures of the fires in the twin towers, are based on data produced by the 9/11 Commission's own Thomas Eagar, professor of Materials Engineering and Engineering Systems at MIT, as quoted in the article by R Herbst BAAE, ME, *Mysteries of the Twin Towers: A Survey of Available Evidence on the Collapse of the World Trade Center Towers*, 12 February 2009, point 5.2.3, *Refutation of Early Fire and Heat Theories*, which can be found at: *http://www.seattle911visibilityproject.org/rwtcpdf.pdf*.

5) Steven E Jones & Richard Gage: The calibre and qualifications of those questioning the physics of 9/11 is now very high, and the work of Dr Steven Jones and Richard Gage has been important in alerting the upper echelons of physicists and architects (respectively) to the unignorable anomalies in the observable processes of the WTC's destruction. Yet there have been attempts to denigrate the reputations of Jones and Gage as a result of their high-profile work for the 9/11 truth movement, with Jones being suspended from his teacher's position at Brigham Young University as a result, before taking early retirement. To dispel any doubt about their credentials, here are their official biographies:

STEVEN E JONES: Jones earned his bachelor's degree in physics, magna cum laude, from Brigham Young University in 1973, and his Ph.D. in physics from Vanderbilt University in 1978. Jones conducted his Ph.D. research at the Stanford Linear Accelerator Center (from 1974 to 1977), and post-doctoral research at Cornell University and the Los Alamos Meson Physics Facility. [*http://en.wikipedia.org/wiki/Steven_E._Jones* - see also *http://911scholars.org*]

RICHARD GAGE: Richard Gage, AIA is the founding member of ae911Truth.org [Architects and Engineers for 9/11 Truth]. *He has been a practicing architect for 20 years and has worked on most types of building construction including numerous fire-proofed steel-framed buildings. He is employed with a San Francisco Bay Area architecture firm and has most recently performed Construction Administration services for a new $120M High School campus including a $10M steel-framed Gymnasium. Most recently he worked on the Design Development for a very large mixed use urban project with 1.2M sq.ft. of retail and 320K sq.ft. of mid-rise office space — altogether about 1,200 tons of steel framing.* [*http://www.ae911truth.org*]

6) Delayed release of the WTC blueprints: The blueprints for the WTC were mysteriously held back from circulation until 27 March 2007, when they were finally, and revealingly, released, as discussed at: *http://stj911.org/press_releases/blueprints.html*.

7) Thomas Eagar on support columns: MIT professor Thomas Eagar's view that the remaining support columns at the WTC should have been enough to hold the towers up is, interestingly, quoted from *Without Precedent: The Inside Story of the 9/11 Commission*, by Thomas Kean and Lee H Hamilton, with Benjamin Rhodes (New York, Alfred A Knopf, 2006) - a book written by the main authors of the official 9/11 Commission report!

8) Richard Gage demonstrates flawed physics in the official 9/11 story: A video presentation by architect Richard Gage, *9/11: Blueprint for Truth*, which by itself nails the case that the WTC could not possibly have fallen due to natural collapse, can be downloaded at: *http://www.ae911truth.org*.

9) Human remains found several blocks from the WTC: The discovery of new body parts on a New York skyscraper rooftop as long after 9/11 as 2006 (demonstrating to doubters the sheer propulsive force exuded in the destruction of the towers, far more than a simple collapse could generate), is reported in Amy Westfeldt's article *9/11 human remains found on skyscraper rooftop*, 6 April 2006, at: *http://www.mg.co.za/article/2006-04-06-911-human-remains-found-on-skyscraper-rooftop*.

10) More evidence of propulsive forces at the WTC: Rick Siegel's documentary *911 Eyewitness*, based on his own amateur footage of the WTC collapses taken from across the Hudson at Hoboken, spends some time analysing the physics of the extraordinary force apparently employed. Some truth campaigners have criticised the film's scientific reliability and take issue with Siegel's belief that helicopters seen hovering near the towers are in some way responsible for their falls. Nonetheless, there are some interesting observations here, including seismic readings on rumbles and deep booms heard on his soundtrack shortly before the towers fall (suggesting large explosions taking out the infrastructure), although these remain as yet unverified by cross-referencing with other footage. Information on the film can be found at: *http:// www.911eyewitness.com.*

11) Pulverisation of all objects in the WTC debris: The testimony of Robert (Bobby) Gray, crane operator in the clear-up operation at the WTC, that even filing cabinets and other office equipment didn't appear to survive the tower collapses, is quoted from his co-authored book (with Glenn Stout, Charles Vitchers and Joel Meyerowitz) *Nine Months at Ground Zero: The Story of the Brotherhood of Workers Who Took on a Job Like No Other* (Scribner, 2006).

12) Thermite found in 9/11 dust: A good resume of the discovery of thermitic particles in the dust near Ground Zero - effectively proving the presence of explosives at the WTC on 9/11 - can be read in Gregg Robert's article *Scientists Find Unignited Explosive Residues in WTC Dust: Red/Gray Chips Match Advanced Thermitic Materials Developed in US Government Labs*, 22 April 2009, at: *http://www.ae911truth.org/info/57.*

13) Toxic dust deaths from 9/11: The scandal that rescue workers and the public were admitted back into the WTC disaster area long before it was safe to breathe the contaminated air has been widely attacked in the US. It seems the authorities were keen to get nearby Wall Street back up and running again so that the economy wasn't held back, but people have died for it. One of many articles decrying the situation, Paul Krugman's *Dust and Deception*, 26 August 2003, can be read at: *http://healthandenergy.com/dangerous_ 9_11_dust.htm*, while Penny Little's film on the issue, *911: Dust and Deceit*, can be downloaded at: *http:// www.911dust.org/.*

14) Fire Captain witnesses explosions: Fire Captain Karin Deshore's testimony of 'popping' explosions at the WTC is quoted from David Ray Griffin's *Debunking 911 Debunking*, Chapter Three, *The Disintegration of the World Trade Center*, page 177.

15) Firemen silenced about 9/11: Paul Isaac's depressing claim that NYC firemen have been forbidden by fire authorities from discussing their witnessing of explosions at the WTC is reported in an article by Randy Lavello, *Bombs in the Building*, at: *www.prisonplanet.com/analysis_lavello_050503_bombs.html.* Encouragingly, the recent creation of Firefighters for 9/11 Truth seems at last to be taking a stand against this situation - see *http://firefightersfor911truth.org.*

16) More on the 1993 WTC bomb: The (official) story of the 1993 bomb that attempted to bring down the WTC can be read at: *http://en.wikipedia.org/wiki/World_Trade_Center_bombing.*

17) More on Rick Seigel: See Note 10 above.

18) WTC Janitor's testimony: Janitor William Rodriguez's reporting of the bomb blast in the basement just before the first plane hit the WTC is quoted from Greg Szymanski's article *WTC Basement Blast and Injured Burn Victim Blows 'Official 9/11 Story' Sky High*, 24 June 2005, at: *www.arcticbeacon.com/24-Jun-2005. html.* Rodriguez, now a major campaigner for 9/11 truth, has his own website at: *http://www.william911. com*, where details of his DVD *What Really Happened on 9/11?* can be found.

19) Light aircraft hits NYC tower block: A report on the plane that hit a New York apartment block on 12th October 2006, entirely failing to raise fears that the building might collapse due to the subsequent fires, can be read in Ed Pilkington and Andrew Clark's report *Manhattan plane crash reawakens spectre of 9/11 - Baseball star's aircraft flies into apartment block/Fighter jets scrambled as smoke pall hangs over city*, at: *http:// www.guardian.co.uk/world/2006/oct/12/usa.edpilkington.*

20) Demolition experts' WTC 7 observations: Demolition experts' remarks that the video of the fall of

WTC 7 (played to them without foreknowledge of where the footage was taken) must have been showing controlled demolition at work are recounted in David Ray Griffin's *Debunking 9/11 Debunking*, Chapter 3, *The Disintegration of the World Trade Center*, pages 200-201.

21) Fire Captain reports warning of WTC 7's demise: Fire Captain Michael Currid's report that he had been warned by Mayor Giuliani's Office of Emergency Management that WTC 7 was 'a lost cause' and ordered to evacuate is quoted in Dean E Murphy's *September 11: An Oral History* (Gale Group, 2003), pages 175-176.

22) Barry Jennings reports early evacuation and explosions in WTC 7: City Housing Authority worker Jennings' claim that he and colleague Michael Hess entered the emergency command centre in WTC 7 only to find it already evacuated by 9.03am, together with their subsequent experiencing of explosions inside the building, are described by Jennings himself in an interview with Dylan Avery, which can be seen at: *http://www.youtube.com/watch?gl=GB&v=VQY-ksiuwKU*. A timeline of Jennings' account can be read at: *http://www.historycommons.org/entity.jsp?entity=barry_jennings_1*. The BBC *Conspiracy Files* programme on WTC 7 distorted Jennings' testimony, twisting the timeline and implying that no-one else witnessed the claimed explosion.

Jennings died of unknown causes in 2008, age 53, leading to inevitable conspiracy speculation that an important eye-witness had been done away with, as discussed in Joe DeFranceschi's piece (with subsequent forum comments) *Barry Jennings, Key 9/11 Witness Dies*, 17 September 2008, at: *http://www.groundreport. com/US/Barry-Jennings-Key-9-11-Witness-Dies*.

23) Remote control used for 9/11 planes?: The notion that enforced remote control might have been used to guide the planes in on 9/11 may seem far-fetched, but today's wide usage of US military drone planes and the fact that the supposed Al Qaeda hijackers were reported by their flight schools as being such poor pilots (as with Hani Hanjour - page ??) make it something that has to be considered. Some good information links on this can be explored at: *http://911research.wtc7.net/resources/web/remote.html*.

24) 9/11 Commission director's friendship with Condoleezza Rice: Philip Zelikow's all-too-close links with then US Secretary of State Condoleezza Rice - hardly making the 9/11 Commission an 'independent' inquiry - can be explored at: *http://www.antiwar.com/sperry/index.php?articleid=2209*.

25) Editing and misrepresentation of air traffic control tapes: The inconsistencies and apparent subsequent altering of the NORAD air traffic control transcripts and recorded conversations from 9/11 constitute some of the most serious and glaring problems of the official account, but to do them any justice here would take up another quarter of the book. Instead, readers are once again directed to David Ray Griffin's essential book *Debunking 9/11 Debunking*, in which the entire first chapter, *9/11 Live or Distorted?*, is taken up with exploring the NORAD transcript issues in fine and shocking detail, between - tellingly - pages 27-94.

26) Norman Mineta's report on Dick Cheney: Norman Mineta's discarded yet crucial testimony to the 9/11 Commission regarding the very strange 'do the orders still stand?' incident with Dick Cheney, by which it seems that a plane was being deliberately allowed to approach the Pentagon, is recounted at: *http:// en.wikipedia.org/wiki/Norman_Mineta*. However, this report also mentions an entirely different - and totally contradictory - retelling of the incident later made in the *Washington Post*, 22 January 2002, in which a more heroic slant is put on the actions allegedly taken in the Presidential Emergency Operating Center, suggesting yet another rewriting of history taking place.

27) A K Dewdney's cell phone experiments: Science writer A K Dewdney's experiments with cell phones (mobiles) in aircraft, which determined that none of the alleged cell calls from Flight 93 could possibly have been made in that way, can be read in detail at: *http://physics911.net/projectachilles*. The general anomalies and all-round strangeness of the calls allegedly received by relatives of the hijacked victims is discussed in another article by Dewdney at: *http://physics911.net/cellphoneflight93*.

28) Barbara Olson's claimed calls from Flight 77: David Ray Griffin's critique of the contradictions inherent in the claims that Barbara Olson made calls to her husband Ted from Flight 77 is quoted from his article *Ted Olson's Report of Phone Calls from Barbara Olson on 9/11: Three Official Denials*, 1 April 2008 (and very much *not* an April Fool's gag), at: *http://www.globalresearch.ca/index.php?context=va&aid=8514*.

29) Rice denies warnings of planes-as-missiles: Condoleezza Rice initially denied that intelligence warnings had ever been given that planes might be used as missiles in a terrorist attack. However, when presented with evidence that such warnings were given, this was her response to the Independent National Commission on Terrorist Attacks Upon the United States on 13 May 2004:

'I think that concern about what... we might have known was provoked by some statements that I made in a press conference... ...And I said, "No one could have imagined them taking a plane, slamming it into the Pentagon" - I'm paraphrasing now - "into the World Trade Center, using planes as a missile." ...I probably should have said, "I could not have imagined," because within two days, people started to come to me and say, "Oh, but there were these reports in 1998 and 1999. The intelligence community did look at information about this." To the best of my knowledge, Mr. Chairman, this kind of analysis about the use of airplanes as weapons actually was never briefed to us.'

30) Air Force One threatened?: The story of presidential aeroplane Air Force One being threatened with destruction, initially publicised on 9/11 before being quietly withdrawn, is discussed at length in Webster Griffin Tarpley's [no relation to David Ray Griffin] book *9/11 Synthetic Terror: Made in USA* (Progressive Press, 2005), Chapter IX, *"Angel is Next" - The Invisible Government Speaks*, pages 272-310.

Tarpley believes the use of the code-word 'Angel' to describe Air Force One in the threatening message allegedly received by the White House on 9/11 is evidence that the terrorism of that day was firmly home-grown, because the likes of Al Qaeda would not have known such codes. Tarpley holds that this was the moment Bush was brought into the confidence of the neo-con plotters he claims were the architects of 9/11 (led by Dick Cheney). Tarpley's intimation is that if Bush hadn't agreed to go along with their plans, then Air Force One might not have returned from its trip that day.

31) US poll shows a majority believes 9/11 was allowed to occur: On 23 November 2007, Kevin Crowe and Guido H Stempel III of the Scripps Howard News Service website (*www.scrippsnews.com/node/28533*) reported the following result from a poll taken from 'a national survey of 811 adult residents of the United States' conducted by Scripps and Ohio University:

'Nearly two-thirds of Americans think it is possible that some federal officials had specific warnings of the Sept. 11, 2001, terrorist attacks on New York and Washington, but chose to ignore those warnings.'

32) George Monbiot on 9/11 truthers: 'Green' pundit Monbiot's borderline-offensive and clearly uninformed views on 9/11 questioners can be read in his article *9/11 fantasists pose a mortal danger to popular oppositional campaigns*, 20 February 2007, at: ***http://www.guardian.co.uk/commentisfree/2007/feb/20/comment.september11.*** As a typical media response to very valid questions about 9/11, this pitifully ignorant and dismissive piece by itself illustrates why the issue will never receive a proper airing in the mainstream media.

IX THE WAR ON LIBERTY

1) Pearl Harbor conspiracy: A good resume of Pearl Harbor conspiracy theories, *Pearl Harbor: Mother of all Conspiracies*, is available at: ***http://www.geocities.com/Pentagon/6315/pearl.html.***

2) The Waco siege: The idea that the fires at the Waco siege of 1993 were deliberately caused by FBI officers was initially dismissed as fringe paranoia. However, the release of the documentary *Waco: The Rules of Engagement* in 1997 (directed by William Gazecki) and its subsequent nomination for an Academy Award, together with the emergence of other credible sources, saw a growth of mainstream awareness that the situation may well have been contrived by the authorities, leading even *Wikipedia*'s current entry at the time of writing (***http://en.wikipedia.org/wiki/Waco_Siege#See_also***) to state the following:

'Mainstream media tended to discount the critical views presented in early documentary films, because they were seen as coming from the political fringes of the right and left. This changed in 1997, when professional film makers Dan Gifford and Amy Sommer produced their Emmy Award winning documentary, Waco: The Rules of Engagement. *This film presents a history of the Branch Davidian movement and, most importantly, a critical examination of the conduct of law enforcement, both leading up to the raid and through the aftermath of the fire. The film features footage of the Congressional hearings on Waco, and juxtaposition of official government spokespeople with footage*

and evidence often directly contradicting the government spokespeople. The documentary also shows infra-red footage demonstrating that the FBI likely used incendiary devices to start the fire which consumed the building and that the FBI did indeed fire on, and kill, Branch Davidians attempting to flee the fire.'

3) Anomalies in the Oklahoma bombing: A concise report on the evidence that other forces must also have been at work to wreak the devastation seen in the Oklahoma City bomb of 1995 can be found in the article *The Oklahoma City Bombing: Were there additional explosive charges and additional bombers?* at: ***http:// whatreallyhappened.com/RANCHO/POLITICS/OK/ok.html***.

Further evidence of anomalies in the official Oklahoma story are discussed in Ambrose Evans-Pritchard's article *Did agents bungle US terror bomb?* at: ***http://whatreallyhappened.com/RANCHO/POLITICS/OK/ok2.html***.

4) Authorities involved in Moscow apartment bombs?: Emmy-award winning journalist John Sweeney's illuminating, if disturbing, allegations that Russian authorities were involved in setting up the bombs that destroyed Moscow apartments in 1999 (supposedly planted by Chechen terrorists) can be read in his article *The Fifth Bomb: Did Putin's Secret Police Bomb Moscow in a Deadly Black Operation?* - John Sweeney on the evidence that the old KGB deliberately planted bombs in Moscow and blamed them on Chechen terrorists, 24 November 2000, at: ***http://cryptome.info/putin-bomb5.htm***.

5) The Gulf of Tonkin incident: A good account of the spurious Gulf of Tonkin incident, which helped spark the Vietnam conflict, can be found at: ***http://en.wikipedia.org/wiki/Gulf_of_Tonkin_Incident***. However, whilst it is now accepted that the events never happened as reported, an apologist culture has arisen in which the incident was misrepresented not to politically mislead anyone, but, as *Wikipedia* has it, 'to cover up honest intelligence errors'. This view was highlighted in comments by National Security Agency historian Robert J Hanyok to the *New York Times*, which can be read in Shane Scott's article *Vietnam War Intelligence 'Deliberately Skewed,' Secret Study Says*, 2 December 2005, at: ***http://www.commondreams.org/headlines05/1202-06.htm***. Needless to say, many truthseekers do not accept this tamer justification of the cover-up.

6) *The Power of Nightmares* TV series: Adam Curtis' courageous and excellent BBC 2 television series *The Power of Nightmares: The Rise of the Politics of Fear*, which exposed the fact that much of what we are told about 'Al Qaeda' is modern myth-making spread by Western sources to create disproportionate fear of Middle Eastern terrorism, was broadcast in late 2004. The series reveals the real Al Qaeda to be a mass of squabbling factions incapable of the organisation required to constitute the huge threat it has been presented as. *The Power of Nightmares* was later transmitted in various countries, but never, perhaps unsurprisingly, in the US.

Much praised at the time, and at one point re-cut for an edited cinema version (which was shown at the 2005 Cannes festival, but never distributed thereafter), it has vanished from circulation in recent years and has never been officially released on DVD, leading many to wonder why (although Curtis cites copyright clearances for the many archive clips used as being one of the problems). Unofficial DVDs and downloads have been widely distributed around truthseeker networks. Detailed information on the series is available at: ***http://en.wikipedia.org/wiki/The_Power_of_Nightmares***.

7) The US Patriot Act: A good critique and deconstruction of the draconian Patriot Act can be found in constitutional attorney John W Whitehead's article for The Rutherford Institute, *How Liberty Dies: The Patriot Reauthorization Act*, 13 June 2005 (from where the given quote comes), at: ***http://www.rutherford. org/articles_db/commentary.asp?record_id=343***.

8) Attempts to create a 42-day detention law: The House of Lords' defeat of the proposed 42-day detention period for suspected terrorists is well reported in the article *House of Lords deals fatal blow to 42-day terror detention plans*, 14 October 2008, at: ***http://www.timesonline.co.uk/tol/news/politics/article4938637.ece***.

9) *Private Eye* magazine: The semi-satirical magazine *Private Eye* has become required reading in the UK for its endless uncovering of corruption and intrigue within local and national authorities, as well as inside the media infrastructure. However, its frustrating inability to believe that the very conspiracies it revels in reporting at those levels could possibly be happening at a global scale, its constant characterisation of conspiracy theorists as moronic anoraks or, worse, far-right fanatics, and its endless crusade against alternative medicine, reveals a deep and frustrating seam of ex-Public School conservatism (small 'c') at its editorial core, which compromises its supposedly subversive credentials for many. Truthseekers reading *Private Eye* for vital information therefore suffer exasperating swings between fascination or laughter, and wanting to throw the thing out of the train window in rage. Anyone curious to share this experience can find out about the magazine at: *http://www.private-eye.co.uk*.

10) 82-year old activist forcibly removed from Labour conference: The disgraceful incident that saw veteran Labour party activist Walter Wolfgang evicted from the 2005 party conference by security heavies under a misuse of anti-terrorism laws is reported by the BBC in the article *Labour issues apology to heckler*, 28 September 2005, at: *http://news.bbc.co.uk/1/hi/uk_politics/4291388.stm* and analysed more deeply by Nick Assinder in the piece *Wolfgang highlights deeper disquiet*, 29 September 2005, at: *http://news.bbc. co.uk/1/hi/uk_politics/4293502.stm*.

The revelation that of 1,721 arrests under the Terrorism Act between 2007-2008 only 73 were for actual terror offences can be read in Robert Verkaik's article referenced in note ?? of this chapter.

11) Restrictions on photographing the police: A new law, which could be used to prevent civilians from taking photographs of the police and other enforcement personnel if held to the letter, was brought in under Section 76 of the Counter Terrorism Act in 2009. Press photographers staged a mass protest in response, as reported in Victoria Bone's article *Is it a crime to take pictures?*, 16 February 2009, at: *http:// news.bbc.co.uk/1/hi/uk/7888301.stm*. The article states:

'It [the new law] permits the arrest of anyone found "eliciting, publishing or communicating information" relating to members of the armed forces, intelligence services and police officers, which is "likely to be useful to a person committing or preparing an act of terrorism".'

The government legalese employs very vague wording that some fear could be abused to prevent legitimate filming of police misbehaviour, such as that which occurred during the G20 protests, when one Ian Tomlinson died shortly after being deliberately pushed over by an officer. The footage of this moment, together with discussion of the fallout from it, can be read in the article *Video reveals G20 police assault on man who died*, 7 April 2009, at: *http://www.guardian.co.uk/uk/2009/apr/07/video-g20-police-assault*. No prosecutions were attempted for the filming of this, but some wonder how long it will be before a test case comes to court. (Some PR tact was clearly required for the G20 incident, although another factor might be that the police didn't want to draw attention to the fact that many of the anti-riot officers were - quite illegally - not wearing identification numbers).

12) CCTV doesn't prevent crime: A useful US journalistic view on the ineffectiveness of CCTV as a crime-prevention tool in the UK can be read in Marcus Baram's article *Eye on the City: Do Cameras Reduce Crime? - NYPD Readies 3,000 Surveillance Cameras; Have They Worked in Other Cities?*, 9 July 2007, at: *http:// www.abcnews.go.com/US/Story?id=3360287&page=1*.

13) Government monitors electronic communications: The announcement that plans for a centralised government database monitoring the entire population's e-mail and Internet movements would be scrapped, in favour of asking communications firms to keep records to be made available to authorities instead, is reported in Dominic Casciani's article *Plans to monitor all internet use*, 27 April 2009, at: *http://news.bbc. co.uk/1/hi/uk_politics/8020039.stm?b*.

14) Impending regulation of the Internet: There are numerous pieces out there outlining the current threats to the continuing freedom of the Internet, but a good video summing-up of the issues, *The Death of the Internet?*, can be found at: *http://uk.youtube.com/watch?v=G5RQrxkGgCM*.

15) Troops surround Heathrow: The never-explained incident in which tanks rolled up to surround London's Heathrow airport in 2003 was reported in the moment by the BBC in the article *Heathrow threat real says Blunkett*, 14 February 2003, at: *http://news.bbc.co.uk/1/hi/uk_politics/2758753.stm*. In the continuing absence of any given reason for the sudden arrival of troops at a major UK airport, many believe this was simply an exercise in maintaining public fear in the earlier years of the War on Terror. If we were genuinely being protected from something, it seems strange for even the basic nature of the threat never to have been revealed.

16) Few convictions after terror arrests: The official figures announcing that hardly anyone arrested under British terror laws is ever convicted are reported well in Robert Verkaik's article *Just one in eight terror arrests ends with guilty verdict, admits Home Office,* 14 May 2009, which can be read at: *http://www.independent.co.uk/news/uk/home-news/just-one-in-eight-terror-arrests-ends-with-guilty-verdict-admits-home-office-1684580.html.*

17) Anomalies of the 7/7 bombings: A good resume of the key issues surrounding doubts over the official story of the London 7/7 bombings can be found at the July 7th Truth Campaign's website at: *http://www.julyseventh.co.uk/july-7-truth-campaign-flyer.html.*
An interesting 2006 documentary that outlines many of the problems with 7/7, *Mind the Gap,* can be watched at: *http://www.officialconfusion.com/77/index.html,* while another, shorter, film, *Ludicrous Diversion,* is also worth seeing at: *http://google.com/videoplay?docid=4943675105275097719.*

18) Terror exercises on 7/7: Peter Power's astonishing (and since confirmed) claims that terror exercises were taking place at the very locations of the bombs on 7/7 are dissected at: *http://www.julyseventh.co.uk/july-7-terror-rehearsal.html.*

19) The bus at Tavistock Square on 7/7: A claimed survivor of the bus bombing, Daniel Obachike, has controversially stated that two cars appeared to deliberately block the path of the bus up the Euston Road, necessitating a diversion that led to its entering Tavistock Square, where the explosion then occurred. Obachike also asserts a number of anomalies concerning the strange behaviour and injuries of certain bystanders outside the bus, and states that what appeared to him to be intelligence operatives seemed to be already present in the Square, as if expecting an event. Some have challenged the reliability of Obachike's testimony, which remains uncorroborated - however, it can be read in his book *The 4th Bomb - Inside London's Terror Storm* (Floran Publishing, 2007). A precis of the claims can be found in Steve Watson and Alex Jones' article *7/7 Bus Bomb Survivor Describes "Agents" at Scene in Immediate Aftermath,* 29 January 2007, at: *http://www.infowars.net/articles/january2007/290107Exclusive.htm.*

20) The shooting of Jean Charles De Menezes: The disheartening refusal of the Judge to allow an 'unlawful killing' verdict in the case of Jean Charles De Menezes, shot on 22nd July 2005 at point-blank range on the London Underground under (false) suspicion of being a terrorist, is reported by Helen Pidd in the article *No charges over De Menezes shooting - Police officers will not face trial over killing of Brazilian they mistook for a suicide bomber, says Crown Prosecution Service,* 13 February 2009, at: *http://www.guardian.co.uk/uk/2009/feb/13/police-no-charges-de-menezes-shooting.*

21) Taser-related deaths: The unacceptable blanket use of 'Tasers' (electronic stun guns), now all too often being used by police around the world in needless situations, has led to many deaths, where the victims' constitutions have been unable to withstand high-voltage electric shocks, often ineptly deployed. Human rights organisation Amnesty International states the following at *http://blog.amnestyusa.org/tag/taser/*:

'The controversy surrounding Tasers is well-documented. Between July 2001 and August 2008, Amnesty International studied more than 334 deaths that occurred after police-use of Tasers. So many of the deaths were needless. Police frequently used Tasers inappropriately, especially considering that in well over 90% of the cases, the person on whom the Taser was used did not even have a weapon. Medical examiners have cited Taser as a primary or contributory cause of death in at least 50 cases.'

The same article goes on to describe a new and worrying Taser 'shockwave' device that will be able to electrocute entire crowds at once. Science-fiction this isn't. More Amnesty information on Tasers, with further links, can be found at *http://www.amnestyusa.org/us-human-rights/taser-abuse/page.do?id=1021202.* See also: *http://en.wikipedia.org/wiki/Taser.*

22) Ambiguous knife crime statistics: The much-claimed increase in UK knife-crime remains unproven, despite all the media coverage, leading to confusion, but an inevitable deepening of fear in the population. It is hard to know what is really going on, and the stats don't seem reliable in either direction. Two articles are worth reading in this regard, Elizabeth Stewart's *Knife crime 'not increasing',* 13 May 2008, at *http://www.guardian.co.uk/uk/2008/may/13/ukcrime.boris,* and Knife Crime Facts UK at *http://www.insight-security.com/facts-knife-crime-stats.htm.*

X CAGING THE HUMAN SPIRIT

1) The effects of Health and Safety restrictions on children: The findings that too-rigorous risk-assessment restrictions are harming children is reported in James Slack's article *Health and safety 'extremists' damaging children's development*, 11 November 2007, at: *http://www.dailymail.co.uk/news/article-493019/Health-safety-extremists-damaging-childrens-development.html*. The piece includes this quote:

'Author Alan Pearce has also collated examples of extreme health and safety rules for his book, Playing It Safe: The Crazy World of Britain's Health and Safety Regulations. *These include swings being removed in one playground in case children were blinded by the sun, and pupils being banned from cycling to school because local roads were too narrow.'*

2) Criticisms of alternative medicine: A critique of the manipulatively selective way biologist and arch-sceptic Richard Dawkins dismisses alternative medicine trials is contained in an interview with doctor-turned-'punk-scientist' Dr Manjir Samanta-Laughton at: *http://www.i-c-m.org.uk/news/news/*. See also *http://www.punkscience.com*.

3) The claimed dangers of aspartame: The highly questionable artificial sweetener aspartame (often marketed as NutraSweet) seems to have sneaked itself into so many foodstuffs and drinks now (especially, but far from exclusively, diet drinks), that it is hard to get away from without close scrutiny of tiny-print ingredients on packaging. Authorities insist that it is safe to use, and yet there is huge evidence from studies that it has great potential dangers for human health, and some countries have attempted to ban or restrict it. Good links on the controversial issues surrounding aspartame can be found at: *http://www.dorway.com*.

One area of suspicion that leads some to question the impartiality of the decisions that led to the general acceptance of aspartame (even from bodies such as the World Health Organisation) is the fact that one-time US Secretary of Defense Donald Rumsfeld (see Note 8 of Chapter V) was chairman of G D Searle & Company when it was helping to develop aspartame, and actively pushed for its approval through his political connections. A useful quick guide to Rumsfeld's aspartame connections can be read at: *http://www.newswithviews.com/NWVexclusive/exclusive15.htm*. Rumsfeld, of course, also owns major stocks in the company that owns the patent for the controversial anti-flu 'antidote' Tamiflu [page 69].

4) Codex Alimentarius' controls on health supplements: An excellent source of detailed information and links concerning the Codex Alimentarius food safety body and its proposed controls on vitamins and health supplements can be found on the website of the Alliance for Natural Health at: *http://www.anhcampaign.org/campaigns/codex*. A precise list of the impending restrictions and how they will affect different countries is available at: *http://www.anhcampaign.org/campaigns/freedom-health-choice*.

An audio download of a comprehensive presentation on Codex Alimentarius by Robert Verkerk of the ANH can be found at: *http://www.changingtimes.org.uk/Lectures/RobertVerkerk/RobertVerkerk.htm*.

5) Conventional medicine is the main cause of death in the US: The staggering statistic (compiled by *The Journal of the American Medical Association*) that an average of 783,936 deaths occur each year due to the effects of prescribed drugs and medical misdiagnosis, along with other remarkable figures, is referenced and summed up well in Rebecca Sato's article *Is the US Fighting the Wrong War on Drugs?*, 16 January 2008, at: *http://www.dailygalaxy.com/my_weblog/2008/01/is-the-us-fight.html*.

6) The dangers of Fluoride: So many studies have cast doubt on the effectiveness or safety of fluoride that one has to question the motive of its continued introduction into global drinking water supplies. To pursue this policy without proper investigation is sinister at worst, and stupid at best. One good fluoride link is given in *Appendix 2*, but another very good resource for multiple web links on the problems with fluoride can be found at: *http://www.eves-best.com/fluoride-dangers.htm*.

7) MMR vaccine to be made compulsory in the UK?: In June 2009, Sir Sandy Macara, former chairman of the British Medical Association, called for the MMR jab to be made a necessary requirement for all children attending state schools - or they should be excluded from the system. A number of MPs backed the call and television coverage gave virtually no space to opposers. This was reported with the usual emotional blackmail and entirely unproven statements implying that recent measles outbreaks in the UK were due to the one in four children who remain unvaccinated due to parents' concerns. Graham Satchell's report on Macara's statement, *Call to Make MMR Jab Compulsory*, 2 June 2009, can be found at: ***http://news.bbc. co.uk/1/hi/health/8078500.stm***.

8) More on vaccinations: Readers are referred to note ? of Chapter V for references to vaccination issues.

9) The Unfair Commercial Practices Directive: Although many spiritualist mediums reacted with anger and dismay over the potential discrimination that could be caused by full implementation of the Unfair Commercial Practices Directive, others have taken a more moderate line on it, such as the articles *New Legislation for UK Spiritualists*, 10 March 2008, at: ***http://www.spiritualist.tv/news/mar08/new-law.html***, and *Astrology, that EU Directive and Consumer Law*, by Roy Gillett, *Transit* journal, July/August 2008, pages 16-18, which contend that only truly fraudulent or misrepresentative practitioners have anything to fear. Nonetheless, there is a worrying degree of ambiguity in the wording of the new directive that could be misused if so desired, and it reduces the status of any alternative religion or therapist to being merely that of a merchant - which might be more acceptable if all religions were treated equally, but the singling-out of certain spiritual practices is plainly discriminatory.

It has been contended that the previous Fraudulent Mediums Act of 1951 (which the 2008 directive effectively replaced) already compelled the required disclaimer 'for entertainment purposes only' in some cases. However, the Unfair Commercial Practices Directive changes the emphasis of responsibility. A posting from 'Jack of Kent' on the *Bad Psychics* forum on 21 March 2009 at ***http://moh2005.proboards.com/ index.cgi?board=conpow&action=display&thread=4739&page=5*** lays the issues out a little more clearly:

'The new regulations are in many ways an advance on the old Fraudulent Mediums Act. Under the FMA, the prosecution had to prove fraud (which is difficult to do at law, as the Serious Fraud Office often find out); and even if fraud was proved, then entertainment was a complete defence. There were few prosecutions under the FMA. Indeed, the ineffectiveness of the FMA worked to the credit of Psychics; the argument was that, as there were no prosecutions, an unprosecuted psychic was legitimate.

Under the new regulations, there is no need for the prosecution to show fraud - just that consumers could be misled regardless of the trader's intent - and entertainment is not now an automatic defence. Psychics charging for their "services" will be treated like a double-glazing salesperson. So, as long as Psychics are clear and accurate in their "commercial practices" then their exposure to legal risk is low under the new regulations.

On the other hand, exploiting people who are vulnerable (which presumably includes those who are bereaved) is an "aggressive" unfair commercial practice under the regulations. It is not yet clear whether this is being enforced against Psychics by Trading Standards. However, by shifting the focus from the intention of the (fraudulent) medium to the effects (or likely effects) on the consumer, the new regulations have taken the legal context for dealing with dodgy Psychics into an entirely new direction.

I think it is too soon to see if Trading Standards will allocate their (limited) resources to scrutiny of commercial psychics. It may well be that there is no general crack-down. But it is new and significant that they are now to be treated just as traders.'

10) Brian Gerrish on the destruction of communities: Readers are referred to note ? of Chapter V for references to Gerrish's views on the EU's Common Purpose initiative. However, he also believes, on a more extreme level, that authorities are taking children from their parents and putting into 'care' for reasons that are unclear or unnecessary (beyond obvious abuse cases), and sees this as a) a terror tactic designed to show what the state can do if anyone steps out of line, and b) as a further method of breaking up families, and thus communities, to weaken UK society's resistance to more centralised control.

11) Children on Ritalin: The shockingly high statistics of children - particularly in the USA - being put on the drug Ritalin, together with the many known detrimental side effects, are discussed in a series of informative articles at: ***http://www.ritalindeath.com***. The name of the website (run by parents who believe their son died due to administration of the drug) gives a clue to its general stance.

XI THE GREEN DILEMMA

1) The Transition Town initiative: The Transition Town movement, which encourages communities to become less dependent on transport and energy infrastructures and more focused on local initiatives, especially environmental ones, began in Totnes, Devon, and was first set up as a national UK network in 2007. Its official website is at: *http://www.transitiontowns.org*.

Transition Town, for all its obvious good intentions, has attracted critics for its rigid adherence to green dogma. An example of the conflicts that have arisen can be found in a fascinating debate, *Peak Oil: Myth or Reality?* (recorded for Glastonbury Radio) between truthseeker Ian R Crane, Transition Town founder Rob Hopkins and interviewer Ross Hemsworth on 18 March 2008. Hear it at: *http://www.revver.com/video/752266/peak-oil-myth-or-reality-recording-from-glastonbury-radio-part-one/*. This in itself was a follow-up to a live debate of the same title between Crane and Forest Row Transition Town spokesman Mike Grenville for the Changing Times organisation that took place on 4 September 2007, and this can be audio downloaded at: *http://www.changingtimes.org.uk/Lectures/IanCrane/IanCrane-PeakOil.htm*.

2) Public doubts over global warming: Despite an obvious national concern about climate change in general, opinion polls reveal that faith in man-made global warming as the cause is nowhere near as strong as the media and governments would usually have us believe, as was demonstrated in a 2008 survey reported in Juliette Jowitt's article *Poll: most Britons doubt cause of climate change*, 22 June 2008, at: *http://www.guardian.co.uk/environment/2008/jun/22/climatechange.carbonemissions*. This article reports:

'Ipsos MORI polled 1,039 adults and found that six out of 10 agreed that 'many scientific experts still question if humans are contributing to climate change', and that four out of 10 'sometimes think climate change might not be as bad as people say'. In both cases, another 20 per cent were not convinced either way. Despite this, three quarters still professed to be concerned about climate change.'

A previous survey reported by the BBC in *'Scepticism' over climate claims*, 3 July 2007, at *http://news.bbc.co.uk/1/hi/sci/tech/6263690.stm* found much the same thing:

'The Ipsos Mori poll of 2,032 adults - interviewed between 14 and 20 June - found 56% believed scientists were still questioning climate change.'

This poll prompted a typical response, quoted in the same piece:

'Royal Society vice-president Sir David Read said: "People should not be misled by those that exploit the complexity of the issue, seeking to distort the science and deny the seriousness of the potential consequences of climate change".'

In other words, to many academics the trend of continuing doubt is merely evidence of deliberate distortion and of people being 'misled' (and not caring, which is untrue) - not the fact that the evidence for man-made global warming is still unclear and confusing, even to some qualified climatologists.

3) Nigel Lawson questions global warming: Ex-cabinet minister Nigel Lawson's book *An Appeal to Reason: A Cool Look at Global Warming* (Gerald Duckworth & Co Ltd, 2008) logically questions the man-made global warming hysteria and political reactions to it, suggesting that even if global warming were eventually proved to be real, the proposed policies currently being implemented to deal with it are the wrong ones. The book has received high praise in many quarters for its well-reasoned (as the title would suggest) arguments, but Lawson has inevitably been lambasted by green campaigners and branded a heretic by those hell-bent on forcing unrealistic carbon reduction targets in the face of much evidence that other strategies would be better at tackling general climate change.

4) Peter Taylor on global cooling: Peter Taylor's book *Chill: A Reassessment of Global Warming Theory* was due for publication in summer 2009 by Clairview Books.

A full presentation by Taylor from 2008, outlining his credentials and criticisms of global warming propaganda, can be audio downloaded at: *http://www.changingtimes.org.uk/Lectures/PeterTaylor/PeterTaylor.htm*.

5) *The Chilling Stars* book: Henrik Svensmark and Nigel Calder's book *The Chilling Stars: A New Theory of Climate Change*, which challenges the man-made global warming theory, was published by Icon Books/Totem Books, 2007.

6) *The Great Global Warming Swindle* documentary: Channel Four's controversial programme *The Great*

Global Warming Swindle was first broadcast in March 2007 and stirred up huge - and mostly closed-minded - angry reaction from predictable quarters. Although the minor inaccuracies and claims of context-bending were widely used against it, these were as nothing compared to the spurious and ill-informed criticisms of the programme that did the rounds in the green community afterwards. Not that this stopped *The Great Global Warming Swindle* being nominated for the Best Documentary Award at the 2008 Broadcast Awards, and Channel Four reported that phone calls it received about the film were '6 to 1' in favour of it. Either way, the programme acts as a good round-up of some of the key issues in the debate.

Wag TV, the production company involved in the programme's making, outlines some of the prejudice they encountered even before its broadcast, with some interesting remarks, at: *http://www.greatglobalwarmingswindle.co.uk*.

An extended version of the film was planned for DVD release ('despite the strenuous efforts of those who support the theory of global warming to prevent its release', according to Wag TV) in summer 2009, but the original film can be seen at: *http://video.google.com/videoplay?docid=288952680655100870*.

7) OfCom's ruling on *The Great Global Warming Swindle*: Television regulator Ofcom's detailed official ruling on The Great Global Warming Swindle, which essentially supported the veracity of the programme, can be read at: *http://www.ofcom.org.uk/tv/obb/prog_cb/obb114/*.

8) The British High Court's ruling on *An Inconvenient Truth*: The full UK High Court ruling on the nine major inaccuracies in Al Gore's film *An Inconvenient Truth* can be read at: *http://www.newparty.co.uk/articles/inaccuracies-gore.html*, from which this adjudication is quoted.

9) Founder of the Weather Channel threatens to sue Al Gore: Weather Channel founder John Coleman's (as yet unfulfilled) assertions that Al Gore should face a US court of law for his claims on global warming gets a mainstream airing in the piece *Weather Channel Founder: Sue Al Gore for Fraud*, 14 March 2008, at: *http://www.foxnews.com/story/0,2933,337710,00.html*.

10) Doubts over 'carbon credits': The concerns over the effectiveness or honesty of the suspect 'carbon credits' scheme, designed to allow industries to pollute in exchange for supposedly instigating environmental projects, are voiced well in Nick Davies' article *Abuse and incompetence in fight against global warming - Up to 20% of carbon savings in doubt as monitoring firms criticised by UN body*, 2 June 2007, at: *http://www.guardian.co.uk/environment/2007/jun/02/energy.business*.

11) Global temperatures in decline: The decline of global temperatures in recent years is discussed by *World Climate Report* in the article *Musings on Satellite Temperatures*, 8 January 2008, at: *http://www.worldclimatereport.com/index.php/2008/01/08/musings-on-satellite-temperatures/*.

For a more conspiratorial take on matters, Paul Joseph Watson's article *No Global Warming Since 1998 as Planet Cools Off*, 4 April 2008, doesn't pull its punches, and can be read at: *http://www.prisonplanet.com/articles/april2008/040408_cools_off.htm*.

12) Australian geophysicist claims global cooling: Australian geophysicist and astronautical engineer Philip Chapman's predictions that we are entering a period of global cooling can be read in the article *Sorry to ruin the fun, but an ice age cometh*, 23 April 2008, at: *http://www.theaustralian.news.com.au/story/0,25197,23583376-7583,00.html*.

13) 1975 conference begins global warming scare?: Marjorie Mazel Hecht's account of the US government-sponsored event, The Atmosphere: Endangered and Endangering, is quoted from her article *Where the Global Warming Hoax Was Born*, and can be read in full at: *http://www.21stcenturysciencetech.com/Articles%202007/GWHoaxBorn.pdf*.

The same website hosts another scientifically credible and devastating demolition of global warming theory in an article by Zbigniew Jaworowski, a senior advisor at the Central Laboratory for Radiological Protection in Warsaw. *CO_2: The Greatest Scientific Scandal Of Our Time* can be read at: *http://www.21stcenturysciencetech.com/Articles%202007/20_1-2_CO2_Scandal.pdf*.

14) Hole in the ozone layer: The recent official silence on the once end-of-the-world scenario feared due to the hole in the ozone layer, supposedly caused by man-made CFCs (chlorofluorocarbons), used in refrigeration and propellants, speaks volumes. It is now almost certain that the hole is a natural function of the planet and that it opens and closes due to entirely normal cycles. A good summing-up of the issues involved can be found in Robert G Williscroft PhD's article *The Great Ozone-Hole Hoax* (in itself a sample chapter from his book *The Chicken Little Agenda - Debunking Experts' Lies*, Pelican Publishing, 2006), which can be found at: *http://thrawnrickle.argee.net/2006/11/08/ch-2--the-great-ozonehole-hoax-part-2-of-8.aspx.*

15) The fake documentary *Alternative 3*: Made by Anglia Television and broadcast on the British ITV network in June 1977 (and shown once since in New Zealand), *Alternative 3* made a convincing case that top scientists were secretly preparing to abandon Earth due to impending climate change. Supposedly intended to be shown as an April Fool's programme, but delayed in broadcast due to industrial action, showing it in a normal slot was bound to cause confusion. Consequently, despite the almost immediate revelation that it was a hoax, many remained convinced that the show was a double-bluff that masked a genuine plan. The first two 'alternatives' given in the programme can't help but raise eyebrows today, given the current conspiracy concerns (1 - eliminate a large proportion of the world's population. 2 - build huge underground shelters for governments to weather the changes - something numerous truthseekers believe is really happening.) The third alternative was to escape into space. The continuing speculation on the show is laughed at by many but, whatever else, it did help create a new fear of climate change that has been built on since. Information on the programme can be found at: *http://en.wikipedia.org/wiki/Alternative_3*, while a classic full-on conspiracy take on it can be explored at: *http://www.thule.org/alt3.html.*

Another supposed spoof, this time a book, *Report From Iron Mountain* (Dial Press, 1967), stirred similar controversy over its origins. Purporting to be a secret report from a government panel recommending the deliberate creation of wars and the encouragment of the fear of alien threats amongst other scares to keep society in line, it was later claimed as a hoax by author Leonard Lewin, but some believe this was a double-bluff. Information on the book can be found at: *http://en.wikipedia.org/wiki/Report_from_Iron_Mountain.*

16) Canadian geologist also claims global cooling: The opinions of professor of geology and director of the Ottawa-Carleton Geoscience Center, R Timothy Patterson, that imminent global cooling is more likely to occur than global warming due to weak Schwabe cycles in the Sun, are recorded concisely in the *Investor's Business Daily* article *The Sun Also Sets*, 7 February 2007, at: *http://ibdeditorial.com/IBDArticles.aspx?id=287279412587175*, and expressed more fully in a *National Post* article by Patterson himself, *Read the Sunspots: The mud at the bottom of B.C. fjords reveals that solar output drives climate change - and that we should prepare now for dangerous global cooling*, 20 June 2007, at: *http://www.nationalpost.com/story.html?id=597d0677-2a05-47b4-b34f-b84068db11f4&p=1.*

More information on Patterson, who has impressive credentials, can be found at: *http://en.wikipedia.org/wiki/Tim_Patterson.*

17) Sea level rise: *Wikipedia*'s current entry (summer 2009) on *Current sea level rise* is a good indicator of the contradictions inherent in the data that supposedly shows significant rises to be occurring due, in part at least, to man-made global warming. Starting with that assumption, the piece (partially to its credit, but also confusingly) then goes on to provide intriguing evidence and observations that appear not to prove the case at all. Until the pleasure beaches begin to vanish under water, and all the time Blackpool sands donkey rides continue, the British public, at least, will probably remain dubious about sea level rise. Certainly, the data is far from settled. We shall see. Find the article at: *http://en.wikipedia.org/wiki/Sea_level_rise.*

18) *Nature* says climate effects from cosmic sources cannot be excluded: *Nature*'s reluctant admission that the possibility of climate effects resulting from cosmic rays or solar ultraviolet radiation 'cannot be excluded' (despite the study appearing to state the opposite) appears in the article *Variations in solar luminosity and their effect on the Earth's climate*, by P Foukal, C Frohlich, H Spruit and TML Wigley, Nature, 14 September 2006. The findings are summed up on the UCAR (University Corporation for Atmospheric Research) website at: *http://www.ucar.edu/news/releases/2006/brightness.shtml.*

19) Lord Turner says flights should be rationed: A summary of Lord Turner's desire to see limits put on individuals' flights can be read in John Swaine's piece *Flights could be rationed, says environment tsar Lord Turner - Families could see the number of flights they can take rationed in order to cut greenhouse gas emissions, Gordon Brown's "environment tsar" has warned*, 6 February 2009, at: *http://www.telegraph.co.uk/travel/travelnews/4536352/Flights-could-be-rationed-says-environment-tsar-Lord-Turner.html.*

20) Michael Crichton's *State of Fear*: Michael Crichton's novel *State of Fear*, in which fear of global warming is used to create a global mandate of industrial and political control - precisely what many people believe is occurring today - was published by Harper Collins in 2004. Although mainly fictional, Crichton's non-fictional footnotes and appendices make very clear his doubting views on global warming, leading to the book being used as a supportive tool by other global warming sceptics. This in turn actually led to Crichton (before his death in 2008) being called before the Senate Committee on Environment and Public Works on the invitation of supporter Senator Jim Inhofe, only to find himself being lambasted by the likes of Hillary Clinton for 'muddy[ing] the issues around sound science'. More on Crichton's novel and the subsequent controversy can be read at: ***http://en.wikipedia.org/wiki/State_of_Fear***.

Jim Inhofe himself once described global warming as 'the greatest hoax ever perpetrated on the American people', and as such has not won himself many friends in the White House, although he has been one of the few voices in Congress to raise objections to its growing obsession with global warming. On the other hand, his hardline right-wing views and close ties to oil and gas industries (***http://en.wikipedia.org/wiki/Jim_Inhofe***) cloud the issue for many, providing unhelpful ammunition to greens who claim that all questioners of man-made global warming are 'working for the other side', which, in general, is patent nonsense.

21) Is a nuclear war possible?: Former New Zealand airline pilot Bruce Cathie's books *The Energy Grid - Harmonic 695: The Pulse of the Universe* [*The Investigation into the World Energy Grid*] (Adventures Unlimited Press, 1997) and *The Harmonic Conquest of Space* (Adventures Unlimited Press, 1998) put forward the intriguing idea that an all-out nuclear war is an impossibility. This hangs on Cathie's theory that the Earth is surrounded by an energetic 'harmonic grid' that requires the forces needed to create a nuclear explosion to be activated only at very specific times and places. A review of *The Energy Grid* by Kenneth James Michael Maclean at: ***http://www.amazon.com/Energy-Grid-Harmonic-Universe-Investigation/dp/0932813445/ref=pd_sim_b_1*** sums up the theory thus:

'[Cathie] *asserts the impossibility of nuclear war, because, he claims, a nuclear device, in order to detonate, must be placed not only in a precise geometric position relative to the Earth, but also to the Sun, and that the timing of the detonation is crucial. He says that all of the possible places and times for nuclear explosions have been worked out by the governments of the Earth in advance! This from a man who predicted beforehand the dates and times of the French nuclear tests at Mururoa Island in the South Pacific in 1968.*'

Cathie's extraordinary claims to have accurately predicted the times and places of many nuclear tests, if true, suggest the almost relieving idea that the whole global 'nuclear holocaust' scenario was yet another hoax used for political gain and social control, and that such a disaster could never have happened. Needless to say, Cathie's views have been attacked as extreme eccentricity, but they are worth hearing.

Bruce Cathie's official website can be found at: ***http://www.brucecathie.com***, and a video presentation, *Bruce Cathie - Calculating an Atomic Bomb Test: Bruce Cathie explains why we can't have a nuclear war*, can be downloaded at: ***http://www.livevideo.com/video/ConspiracyCentral/4985FBA692174AF2A9A3613BF66A9625/bruce-cathie-calculating-an-.aspx***.

XII 2012

1) The Maya end-point and 'adjusted' calendars: There have been many arguments that have raged through the 2012 community concerning the exact end-point of the current Mayan 'Creation', with the majority having settled on 21st December 2012. However, some argue for 23rd December 2012 and others even dispute the *year* and support other surrounding dates. Part of the problem comes with those who have adapted the Maya calendar to create their own idealised versions of it, causing much confusion. One such version is the 'Dreamspell' calendar and was developed by prominent 2012 researcher Jose Arguelles to work with his own theories on the Maya prophecies; another has been recalculated by Carl Calleman, who believes 28th October 2011 to be the end point. These edited versions may or may not have merit, but cannot be said to be the true 'Maya Calendar', as they are all-too often referred to.

Geoff Stray's *Beyond 2012: Catastrophe or Ecstasy*, (Vital Signs Publishing, 2005) pretty much nails these arguments once and for all (see especially Chapter 19, *The New Age*, pages 203-207, together with numerous other clarifications throughout Stray's book). Despite the continuing ubiquity of 'adjusted' calendars that still do the rounds, most have concluded that 21st December 2012 is the most definitively accurate of all the calculated end-points. See also the many debates on Stray's website at: ***http://www.diagnosis2012.co.uk***.

The exact time of the 2012 Winter Solstice, meanwhile - 11.11 am precisely - is the source of endless fascinated speculation, with many ascribing universal significance to the appearance of these numbers throughout life, especially the influential US mystic Solara, whose website can be found at: ***http://www. nvisible.com***. The strange 'coincidence' that the Maya end-point falls with these digits at the centre of it all is yet one more intrigue of the 2012 phenomenon.

2) Geoff Stray on the Maya end-point: Geoff Stray's quote about the now (almost) agreed end point of the Maya calendar comes from his book *2012 in Your Pocket* (Straydog Books, 2008 [UK], 4th Dimension Press, 2009 [USA]), a handy notebook derivation of *Beyond 2012*. Another of Stray's books, which is useful in understanding the Maya calculations, is *The Mayan and Other Ancient Calendars* (Wooden Books/ Walker & Company, 2007).

3) Crop circles with 2012 connotations: Formations with connections to 2012 are fully explored in *Beyond 2012*, Chapter 16, *Crop Circles*, pages 172-182. See also my book *Vital Signs: A Complete Guide to the Crop Circle Mystery* (SB Publications, 1998/2002 [UK], Frog Ltd, 2002 [US]).

4) Ice core samples suggest 'galactic superwaves': The work of Dr Paul LaViolette in identifying cosmic dust from ice core samples, which he uses to support the galactic superwave theory, is explained in his book *Earth Under Fire* (Starlane Publications, 1997). It is also summed up (as ever) throughout Geoff Stray's *Beyond 2012*, especially Chapter 7, *Astronomical Claims*, pages 89-92.

5) Sunspots: A good basic explanation of how sunspots are formed is available at: ***http://en.wikipedia. org/wiki/Sunspot***.

6) NASA predictions of solar activity for 2012-2013: In 2006, NASA was predicting big things for the Sun in the run-up to 2012, as outlined in the article *Scientists Predict Big Solar Cycle,* 21 December 2006, at: ***http://science.nasa.gov/headlines/y2006/21dec_cycle24.htm***. The article states:

'Solar cycle 24, due to peak in 2010 or 2011, "looks like its going to be one of the most intense cycles since record-keeping began almost 400 years ago," says solar physicist David Hathaway of the Marshall Space Flight Center. He and colleague Robert Wilson presented this conclusion last week at the American Geophysical Union meeting in San Francisco.'

However, by 2009, due to the very late and quiet start of cycle 24, NASA and the National Oceanic and Atmospheric Administration (NOAA) had revised this prediction, forecasting the peak to occur in 2013 and with an expectation of very few sunspots, as explained in the article *New Solar Cycle Prediction*, 29 May 2009, at: ***http://science.nasa.gov/headlines/y2009/29may_noaaprediction.htm***.

7) Sharp fall in solar output: The slightly perturbing 2009 finding that solar irradiance, ultraviolet and radio emissions were falling at an unusually fast rate were announced by NASA in the article *Deep Solar Minimum*, 1 April 2009, at: ***http://science.nasa.gov/headlines/y2009/01apr_deepsolarminimum.htm?list1123206***.

8) Media predicts 'solar superstorm': In 2009, the possibility of a huge solar flare destroying the infrastructure of civilisation, if simply through the effect on power grids, went mainstream. *New Scientist* magazine began the trend in issue 2700, 21 March 2009, with Michael Brooks' article *Gone in 90 Seconds*, and this was followed by Michael Hanlon's rather less subtle *Daily Mail* article - making a 2012 connection clearer - *Meltdown! A solar superstorm could send us back into the dark ages - and one is due in just THREE years*, 19 April 2009, at: ***http://www.dailymail.co.uk/sciencetech/article-1171951/Meltdown-A-solar-superstorm-send-dark-ages--just-THREE-years.html***.

Around the same time, Alex Proyas' film *Knowing* (starring Nicolas Cage), despite lukewarm reviews, did well at the box office in the US and the UK, and posits the notion of a massive solar flare extinguishing life on Earth. In fact, the film, often genuinely shocking in places and seemingly playing on evangelical end-times themes, captures well the apocalyptic zeitgeist of the age, and its success says something about the contemporary mood welling up in the collective.

9) Decrease in the solar wind: The recent and striking decrease in the solar wind is reported in the article

Ulysses Reveals Global Solar Wind Plasma Output at 50-Year Low, 23 September 2008, at: *http://www.jpl. nasa.gov/news/news.cfm?release=2008-178*.

10) Earth open to more solar particles than previously thought: The news that the THEMIS spacecraft had detected an unsuspected propensity for the Earth's magnetic fields to let in solar particles at completely unexpected times was first reported in the piece *Sun Often "Tears Out A Wall" In Earth's Solar Storm Shield*, 16 December 2008, at: *http://www.nasa.gov/mission_pages/themis/news/themis_leaky_shield.html*.

11) Russians say actual pole shift could occur: The Russian Academy of Natural Science's somewhat apocalyptic view that a geomagnetic reversal could physically change the tilt of the Earth's axis is reported in *Pravda*'s happily-titled article *Displacement of Earth's magnetic poles may turn planet into giant Hiroshima*, 23 October 2008, at: *http://english.pravda.ru/science/earth/23-10-2008/106612-magnetic_poles-0*.

12) The effects of galactic alignment: Geoff Stray's explanation of what could happen during the galactic alignment process is quoted from *Beyond 2012*, Chapter 1, *The Maya Calendars*, pages 23-24. In his book *Maya Cosmogenesis 2012* (Bear & Company, 1998), John Major Jenkins puts it thus:

'The "energy" field emanates from the Galactic Center and includes the entire electromagnetic/photon field in which our planet exists. There are dimensions of subtlety within this field - the telluric or astral realms - extending beyond the physical forces of science to include spiritual planes of being. If we imagine this field as being similar to the lines of force surrounding a magnet, we can understand that our changing orientation to this field has immediate consequences, and little to do with cause-and-effect transmission of energy between us and Galactic Center. We are instead in a relationship of resonance with our source, one that connects us deeply within to each other, and, in fact, to all other beings in this galaxy. Based upon these considerations, I would like to emphasize that the Galactic Equator - the precise edge of our spiralling galaxy - is the Zero Point location of the turnabout moment in the cycle of precession. This World Age shift occurs when the solstice Sun crosses over the Galactic Equator, and thus the galactic alignment in 2012 is about a field-effect energy reversal.'

13) Rick Strassman's DMT theories: Strassman's potentially crucial findings on the brain's natural production of dimethyltryptamine (DMT) are outlined in his book *DMT: The Spirit Molecule - A Doctor's Revolutionary Research into the Biology of Near-Death and Mystical Experiences* (Park Street Press, 2001). His personal website is: *http://www.rickstrassman.com*.

14) Dr Michael Persinger on geomagnetic activity and ghosts: Information on Persinger can be found on his webpage at: *http://oldwebsite.laurentian.ca/neurosci/_people/Persinger.htm*, while his impressive CV and a list of published books and papers can be found at: *http://oldwebsite.laurentian.ca/neurosci/_files/ MAP%20CV%202005.pdf*.

15) Secret concentration camps and civil order contingencies?: *PublicEye.org*'s analysis of the alleged secret concentration camps and the Rex 84 program is quoted from the article *The Right-Wing Roots of Sheehan's "Secret Team" Theory* at: *http://www.publiceye.org/rightwoo/rwooz9-14.html*.
  To read a total conspiracy view of the US concentration camps furore, which includes some common sense challenges in the forum that follows it to some of the more extreme claims, have a look at *US Concentration Camps - FEMA and the Rex 84 Program*, thread started 14 June 2004, at: *http://www.abovetopsecret.com/ forum/thread59023/pg1*.
  The related US civil order program 'Operation Garden Plot' is also worth perusing. A comprehensive article on this, by Frank Morales, *US Military Civil Disturbance Planning: The War at Home*, 5 August 2000, can be read at: *http://cryptome.info/0001/garden-plot.htm*.

16) Astrological cycles and evidence for astrology: In a world where astrology had not been sidelined by scoffing intellectuals who refuse to look at the compelling statistical evidence for a genuine effect of astrological influences on both psychological profiles and global events, Richard Tarnas' book *Cosmos and Psyche: Intimations of a New World View* (Barnes and Noble, 2006) would be seen as a crucial tool for understanding historical cycles and where we are headed today. As it is, the book has attracted little interest in academic circles, but has at least gained respect amongst serious students of astrology. Information on the book can be found at its official website: *http://www.cosmosandpsyche.com/index.php*.

Those curious to know what the actual evidence to support the veracity of astrology is are advised to start with John Anthony West's book *The Case for Astrology* (Viking Adult, 1991), which effortlessly demolishes most of the allegedly 'scientific' arguments against the art and provides a good round-up of important statistical studies carried out by the likes of Michel and Francoise Gauquelin. Sceptics have long attacked the Gauquelin studies as flawed, but most of these objections are based on widely-spread *myths* about the studies, rather than the facts. A good article that sets the record straight on the Gauquelin findings (which are by no means the only ones to support astrology's relevance), by Ken Irving, *Misunderstandings, Misrepresentations, Frequently Asked Questions & Frequently Voiced Objections About the Gauquelin Planetary Effects*, can be found at: *http://www.planetos.info/mmf.html*.

In the opinion of some, astrology can only fully be explained in terms of thought-forms being projected into the collective consciousness, something which the scientific work of Dean Radin and others is making more likely as a possibility [Chapter XIV]. However, those looking for a more reductionist but still semi-supportive view on astrology might like to read the books of Percy Seymour, especially *The Scientific Proof of Astrology* (Quantum/Foulsham, 2004). A respected astronomer and astrophysicist, Seymour believes that fluctuations in the Earth's magnetic field, caused by the planets moving through the solar wind, may affect brain development in the womb, thus accounting for recurring personality traits amongst people born at certain times. Seymour's theories can only go so far in accounting for all the claimed attributes of astrology, but they identify some possible real-world components to explain the cycles, which may explain why belief in astrology simply refuses to go away despite all the best efforts of naysayers like Richard Dawkins.

17) The astrology of 2012: Helen Sewell's comments on the astrological influences of 2012 are quoted from her article *The Astrology of 2012* - see Note 9 of Chapter IV.

18) World leaders use astrology: In an article on Percy Seymour (*Star Movements* Can *Influence Us: The Planets may control your future after all*, 16 May 2004, which can be read at: *http://www.astrology.co.uk/news/percy.htm*), Jonathan Leake of the *Sunday Times* points out that astrology has been used by several prominent politicians to influence decisions (we have already noted Cherie Blair's interest), stating:

'Among the powerful who have admitted consulting astrologers to make decisions are Ronald and Nancy Reagan, who allowed the astrologer Joan Quigley to dictate the presidential agenda, including the take-off times for Air Force One. Reagan's chief of staff reportedly had a colour-coded calendar around which he was expected to organise the President's schedule: green for "good" days and red for "bad". Even Margaret Thatcher once told MPs: "I was born under the sign of Libra; it follows that I am well-balanced."'

Some may argue that the very last point is not such good proof that astrology works (!), but it is clear that the subject, like so many other supposedly 'occult' practices, is taken perfectly seriously by many in high places.

XIII WHO ARE WE DEALING WITH?

1) H G Wells on the New World Order: The entire text of Wells' 1940 book *The New World Order* can be read at: *http://www.theforbiddenknowledge.com/hardtruth/new_world_order_hgwells.htm*. It is clear that Wells was an idealist, which may have clouded his morals at times, but it is also plain from this and much of his writing that he passionately cared about the future of humankind.

2) The origins of the New World Order: An excellent timeline charting the development of the NWO, D L Cuddy's *A Chronological History of the New World Order*, can be found at: *http://www.constitution.org/col/cuddy_nwo.htm*. Another good guide is available on the webpage *The New World Order (NWO)* at: *http://www.anomalies.net/object/io_1174433802417.html*.

3) Woodrow Wilson warns of a secret dominating force in the US: President Wilson's comments are from his book *The New Freedom: A Call For the Emancipation of the Generous Energies of a People*. Originally published in 1913, it can be freely downloaded in full at: *http://www.gutenberg.org/ebooks/14811*.

4) Bertrand Russell on science and world government: These and other disquieting quotes from the likes of Russell and other intellectuals advocating control by stealth, suppression and drugs for the good of humankind, can be found on the webpage *Exposing the NWO* at: ***http://www.uscrusade.com/forum/config. pl/noframes/read/1562.***

5) Gordon Brown 'saves the world': Gordon Brown's unfortunate but priceless Parliamentary gaffe in which he claimed Labour had 'saved the world' is discussed well in Martin Kettle's piece *Crash Gordon 'saves the world'*, 10 December 2008, at: ***http://www.guardian.co.uk/commentisfree/2008/dec/10/gordon-brown-save-world-pmqs.***

6) Man dies at G20 protests: See Note 11 of Chapter IX for details of this incident.

7) Blair slow-handclapped by WI: Tony Blair's excruciatingly embarrassing but fully deserved drubbing at the hands of the Women's Insitute annual conference is discussed in the article *WI gives Blair hostile reception*, 7 June 2000, at: ***http://news.bbc.co.uk/1/hi/uk_politics/780486.stm.***

XIV THE POWER OF COLLECTIVE THOUGHT

1) The Noosphere: The belief of Pierre Teilhard-de Chardin, a palaeontologist and Jesuit priest, that the mass-consciousness of humankind was evolving into a merged state of being with the planet, forming a 'layer' that he called the 'Noosphere', is outlined well in Geoff Stray's *Beyond 2012*, Chapter 12, *Fringe Science*, pages 140-141

2) *Childhood's End* by Arthur C Clarke: Clarke's seminal and very influential novel, which envisions the ultimate evolution of humankind into a race of higher (if unreachable) telepathic entities, was first published by Harcourt in 1953 and remains in print today. A summary is outlined in full at: ***http://en.wikipedia. org/wiki/Childhood's_End***. Clarke (who became increasingly attached to plots based only on hard science as the years went by, and thus grew rather less interesting) updated the book in 1990 to allow for recent scientific developments, but the essential story remains intact.

3) Dean Radin's *Entangled Minds*: This straightforwardly-written and very convincing assessment of evidence for psi phenomena (full title: *Entangled Minds: Extrasensory Experiences in a Quantum Reality*) was published by Paraview Pocket Books in 2006. This in itself picks up on themes from Radin's previous book *The Conscious Universe: The Scientific Truth of Psychic Phenomena* (HarperEdge, 1997), which won the 1997 Book Award from the Scientific and Medical Network.
  See also Radin's website at: ***www.deanradin.com***

4) Dean Radin describes the RNG experiments: Radin's description of the Random Number Generator studies is quoted from *Entangled Minds*, Chapter 9, *Mind-Matter Interaction*, page 154.

5) The Global Consciousness Project: The ongoing latest results of this extraordinarily important and ongoing study of mass consciousness can be read on its website at: ***http://noosphere.princeton.edu/***. Why isn't this kind of science also being taught in schools?

6) The power of prayer: There have been many scientific studies that have produced positive results to show that prayer can work (despite what Richard Dawkins very selectively reports in his book *The God Delusion*, Bantam, 2006). Readers are recommended to search the Internet for the evidence, but a good starting point is Debra Williams' article *Scientific Research of Prayer: Can the Power of Prayer Be Proven?*, which can be read at: ***http://www.plim.org/PrayerDeb.htm.***

7) 'Hundredth Monkey' syndrome: The 'hundredth monkey' effect is often widely quoted in New Age circles as proof of collective consciousness. The story is that colonies of apes being studied on a Japanese island in the 1950s began to wash their sweet potatoes before eating them. When a certain critical mass of monkeys was reached (one hundred being a metaphorical round-up), the same behaviour was suddenly reported amongst apes on other, entirely separate, islands, as if the new ability had been 'transmitted' somehow. However, despite the wide popularity of the concept, sceptics have rounded on the original story as being much misquoted and misunderstood, and doubt now surrounds the details. Nonetheless, later and better documented studies of collective animal behaviour by the likes of Dr Rupert Sheldrake have demonstrated that such a 'transmission' capability may well exist, so even if the hundredth monkey story itself is dismissed, it still seems to embody a general truth.

The monkey controversy is discussed at: *http://en.wikipedia.org/wiki/Hundredth-monkey_effect*.

8] The power of intention: Many experiments into the power of psychic intent have been conducted over the years, but Lynne McTaggart's *The Intention Experiment* (Harper Element, 2008) is probably a good place for a resume, together with its accompanying website *www.theintentionexperiment.com*.

9] Psychic experiments with crop circles: Attempts to influence the creation of specific crop circles with the power of the mind have thrown up some interesting results over the years, with several claims of success after meditations or visualisations carried out under controlled conditions. This author took part in such experiments in the early to mid-1990s, with intriguing results that were written up in the book *Quest For Contact: A True Story of Crop Circles, Psychics and UFOs* (Andy Thomas and Paul Bura, SB Publications, 1997). The book is long out of print, but copies turn up on *e-Bay* from time to time.

?] Masuru Emoto's water crystal experiments: The work of Emoto, in which the power of thought is claimed to influence the shape of forming ice crystals, is another much-quoted piece of 'proof' for psychic influences (largely in the New Age realms, and promoted widely in the not uninteresting 'alternative' 2004 semi-documentary *What the Bleep Do We Know?*). Sceptics have inevitably attacked the work as being seriously flawed. It can't be denied that there are many unanswered questions - no full description of the applied methodology has ever been forthcoming and, as far as anyone can tell, no-one else has managed to reproduce the exact same experiment, despite unsubstantiated claims.

Assuming that a real psychic or vibrational effect *is* occurring, big questions still arise; for instance Emoto points out that 'heavy metal' music, when played to water, produces irregular and unpleasant crystal structures, whereas classical music produces beautiful ones. However, taking the quantum observer effect into account, along with Emoto's obvious distaste for heavy metal, how can it be ensured that he is not himself psychically affecting the outcome of the experiment? This is not to dismiss all of Emoto's findings, but clearly more detailed research needs to be conducted before the water crystal method can be used as proof of anything.

Emoto's website can be accessed at: *http://www.masaru-emoto.net/english/e_ome_home.html* and his best-known book is probably *The Hidden Messages in Water* (Beyond Words Publishing, 2004).

4] Dean Radin on healing experiments: Radin's findings regarding the effect of mind on healing processes and brain cells are outlined in *Entangled Minds*, Chapter 11, *Gaia's Dreams*, pages 185-191.

5] Children exposed to TV murders: The shocking result of a 1992 survey in the *Journal of the American Medical Association*, which found that around 40,000 onscreen murders had been witnessed by the average 18-year old, is discussed in the article *Violence in the Media*, at: *http://www.enotes.com/violence-media-article*.

6] 'Presentiment' in the RNG experiments: Dean Radin reports at length the astonishing evidence that human beings can sense the future in *Entangled Minds*, Chapter 10, *Presentiment*, pages 161-180.

7] Animals sensed the 2004 tsunami: The news that animals seemed to have picked up on the imminent and devastating tsunami long before it arrived is reported in Maryann Mott's piece *Did Animals Sense Tsunami Was Coming?*, 4 January 2005, at: *http://news.nationalgeographic.com/news/2005/01/0104_050104_tsunami_animals.html*.

A rather more sceptical but still interesting take on the story can be read in Roger Highfield's article *Did They Sense the Tsunami?*, which can be read at: *http://www.telegraph.co.uk/scienceandtechnology/3337851/Did-they-sense-the-tsunami.html*.

XV THE POWER OF POSITIVE ACTION

1] David Cameron predicts street riots: Conservative leader David Cameron's 2009 warnings of civil unrest are reported in Andrew Porter and James Kirkup's article *Deceit over cuts will lead to riots', says David*

Cameron: Britain faces "riots on the streets" if Gordon Brown's "dishonesty" over public spending enables him to win the next election, 29th June 2009, at: *http://www.telegraph.co.uk/news/newstopics/politics/5690836/Deceit-over-cuts-wil-lead-to-riots-says-David-Cameron.html*.

Interestingly, a Labour minister, Hazel Blears (ironically just before being singled out for criticism during the MPs expenses row) had also warned of similar unrest a few months before, as reported in James Chapman's article *Recession could spark riots and civil disorder, minister warns*, 30th April 2009, which can be read at: *http://www.dailymail.co.uk/news/article-1174955/Recession-spark-riots-civil-disorder-minister-warns.html*.

Are these genuine fears being voiced, or is some kind of seed being planted in the public consciousness?

2) Nostradamus and the 'Games of Slaughter': Geoff Stray discusses this curious prophecy, which some think may refer to the 2012 Olympics, in *Beyond 2012*, Chapter 18, *Nostradamus*, p191, although it should be noted, of course, that two games have already passed since the referenced 'Millennium' in the quatrain.

3) Rudolf Steiner on the British: Steiner's words were spoken on 15 Jan 1917 in Dornach, Switzerland and are included in the series of lecture transcripts published as *The Karma of Untruthfulness - Secret Societies, the Media, and Preparations for the Great War Vol. 2* (Rudolf Steiner Press, 2005, p.133).

In a personal communication to this author, Steiner scholar Terry Boardman clarifies the lecture's comments on the British, making some interesting comments on the continuing influence of old bloodlines today:

'By 'grey magic', Steiner meant such things as newspapers, publishing and various forms of propaganda (including political speeches in and out of Parliament, articles, etc.) - 'the media' of that time. In my presentations [on Steiner] *I emphasise the word 'elements' to draw attention to the fact that he was NOT saying that EVERYTHING about Britain and the British was eminently suitable to promote materialism, but that there were certain elements within the British national makeup that could be used to do this.*

In the same course of lectures Steiner focuses on what happened at the time of Henry VII and Henry VIII, especially the latter, when a new, more commercially-minded aristocracy replaced much of the older aristocracy. Steiner pointed out that a number of the aristocrats who were prominent in ruling circles in Britain in his own time could trace their lineage back to Tudor times. One thinks of the Cecils, Russells, Howards, etc. In very recent times, we've seen Michael Ancram and Theresa Villiers to name but two on the Tory front bench, and the remaining hereditary Tory Lords are led by Viscount Cranbourne: the families of these three all go back to the court of James I. I think the point is that there have always been a number of families and heads of institutions that regard themselves as being responsible for the nation - as constituting the nation, in fact. The rest of us are essentially servants and foot-soldiers. This was certainly the case at the time of the Great War and may arguably still be true.'

4) Dr M Scott Peck's *People of the Lie*: *People of the Lie: The hope for healing human evil* (Century Hutchinson, 1983), Scott Peck's psychological analysis of what constitutes as evil in the modern world, is a valuable contribution to a long-running debate, although the book's announcement that the author had recently converted to Christianity didn't go down so well with some of his previous admirers, who felt it coloured his ability to retain a detached view. New admirers, however, were won.

5) The My Lai massacre: This shocking blot on US military history, which saw many innocent civilians indiscriminately raped and killed on one day during the Vietnam War is discussed well at: *http://en.wikipedia.org/wiki/My_Lai_Massacre*.

6) Pub boycotts: In my home town of Lewes, East Sussex, one of the key central pubs, under the influence of its new corporate owners, made the mistake of throwing out the beer of a famous Lewes-based brewery from the pumps. The resulting furore made any previous local protest on anything at all seem like, well... small beer. It even made national headlines (see Tim Minogue's article *Last orders*, 23rd March 2007, at: *http://www.guardian.co.uk/uk/2007/mar/23/britishidentity.travel*). A several-month boycott - complete with protesting picketers at the doors of the pub in question - decimated clientele to the point where the owners had to relent and the brew was restored. This is a fine lesson that people power *does* work. At the same time, it's disturbing that it takes the sudden absence of good alcohol to really kick people into action... If that same resolve could be universally applied to rather larger matters, we might get somewhere. Go to it.

APPENDIX 2 - Further Resources

Introduction

Appendix 1 includes most of the works referenced during research for this book, and gives clear pointers for those seeking more on the subjects covered within these pages, but a few at-a-glance sources of key information are rounded-up here for convenience. Be aware that this is just a very small selection to act as a starting point for further investigation. Readers should also note that my listing of these books, websites and documentaries is not necessarily an endorsement of their full content. Discernment, as ever, will be required.

I have emphasised the sources on 'general conspiracy' and 9/11, as the two are inextricably linked in many people's minds. With the blatant anomalies of 9/11 being seen by many as the most vulnerable and potentially exposable global manipulation in recent history, it warrants particular scrutiny.

GENERAL CONSPIRACY

Books (alphabetically by authors)

William Cooper: Sometimes known as Milton William Cooper or Bill Cooper, if you want to go back to the book that in many ways began the current trend of fascination with conspiracy theories, Cooper's book *Behold a Pale Horse* (Light Technology Publications, 1991) is pretty much it. Not an easy read by any means, and controversial for including risky discussion of the ever-incendiary and hoaxed *Protocols of the Elders of Zion* [page 82], it nonetheless started many down the line of New World Order speculation, with all the traditional elements, and therefore has become an important icon in its field. Cooper was shot dead by Arizona police in 2001 after some kind of firearms struggle (see *http://en.wikipedia.org/wiki/Milton_William_Cooper*), leading, perhaps appropriately, to his death becoming the subject of yet more conspiracy theories.

David Icke: Most of Icke's substantial works cover similar ground, but with gradual shifts of emphasis and additional material as each book goes by. Most are long and very detailed, but if you want to know the general ins and outs of who most conspiracy theorists think is responsible for what and where, his books are definitely the place to start, even if one doesn't agree with the more contentious views (reptilians, etc.). Their (non-religious) spiritual content is often under-emphasized by truthseekers, so the books are not all gloom and doom and do offer ways out of the problems. Readers are advised to begin with one of his more all-encompassing titles, *The David Icke Guide to the Global Conspiracy (And How To End It)* (Bridge of Love, 2007), and work outwards from there.

Jim Marrs: Marrs began very much down the ET investigation route, but gradually expanded into other subjects, as many mystery researchers do, becoming one of the more prominent writers on the global control agenda. His books act as a good US take on modern conspiracy thinking, and there are several titles to choose from. *Rule by Secrecy* (HarperCollins, 2002) and *The Terror Conspiracy: Deception, 9/11 and the Loss of Liberty* (Disinformation Company Ltd, 2006) probably cover the general ground best. *Alien Agenda: Investigating the Extraterrestrial Presence Among Us* (HarperTorch, 1998) pulls together the big picture on UFOs and alleged US goverment knowledge of extra-terrestrials.

Jon Ronson: Ronson is considered a non-committal lightweight in the conspiracy world (and has disappointingly dismissed 9/11 truthers), and is more interested in quirky people who believe in conspiracies than in the conspiracies themselves, but it can't be denied that his books have taken several subjects into the mainstream (such as the Bohemian Grove rituals) in a way that others have failed to achieve. They also act as a handy, if wafer-thin, glimpse into darker areas for those nervous about getting in too deep. Ronson is best known for *Them: Adventures With Extremists* (Simon & Schuster, 2002), but the follow-up, *The Men Who Stare at Goats* (Picador, 2005), is an interesting delve into the dubious world of US military experiments with psychics, remote viewing and 'unconventional' interrogation techniques.

Websites (alphabetically)

www.changingtimes.org.uk
Website of the author's own organisation, which arranges Truth events in the south east of England. A growing pantheon of very informative past presentations (audio and video) by various excellent speakers on many of the subjects covered in this book can be downloaded here.

www.davidicke.com
Icke's illuminating insights and often darkly humorous thoughts on the latest global events and the selective way they are reported are always worth reading on his news page, which can be a tonic in times of obvious social manipulation. Whatever anyone thinks of Icke and his more extreme views, a website like this needs to exist in the UK, and is excellently presented.

www.edgemediatv.com
This is the website of Sky TV's UK channel 200, Edge Media TV, which exists 'as a platform for people to share alternative views and discuss suppressed viewpoints'. For such a mainstream outlet, it has managed to buck the trend of most bland, controlled channels and features uncensored (so far) conspiracy, truth and liberty broadcasts unavailable elsewhere in the UK. Schedules can be accessed here, as well as downloads of past programmes.

www.ianrcrane.co.uk
Information on Crane's ongoing and striking live presentations dedicated to uncovering the hidden side of key current issues, with many downloads of past lectures available, is regularly posted here, together with articles, news and opinions. Crane also organises the now annual Alternative View conferences, and information on these can be found here.

www.nexusmagazine.com
The monthly publication *Nexus Magazine* has been one of the longest-running and most consistent exposers of cover-ups and alternative views on everything from conspiracies and metaphysics to health and science. Although its head office is based in Australia, the magazine is available in several international editions, and information on them all can be found at this website.

www.prisonplanet.com
www.infowars.com
The websites run by truthseeker Alex Jones, and the main US stops for the total conspiracy view on current affairs. The strident tones can be too much for newcomers, but even if readers don't go with all of it, it can't be denied that the dramatic presentation serves well the sites' laudable aim of unapologetically blasting open the control agenda for public exposure.

www.rense.com
Jeff Rense is another important player in exposing the tools of global manipulation, and the site always gives numerous links to alternative views on the important topics of the moment.

http://wearechange.org (US)
http://wearechange.org.uk (UK)
We Are Change is a global collective of (mainly youthful) truth campaigners, initially born from the 9/11 movement, who have gone on to take a stand on many questionable control agenda issues, often confronting well-known authority figures with video cameras, firing awkward questions at them and then posting the footage on their websites. The results are highly interesting, to say the least. WAC often arrange protests and public events, and networking details can be found on their many branch websites. Start with these ones and follow the links to their groups in other countries.

Documentaries

Exploring the above websites will provide links to numerous documentaries on conspiracies of all kinds, freely available on the Internet, but three stand out as good starting points. Nearly all can be seen on their home sites, but otherwise are easily found on *You Tube* or *Google Video*.

The hard-hitting *Terrorstorm: A History of Government Sponsored Terrorism*, by Alex Jones, sums up the feelings of many truthseekers about the War on Terror and its apparently contrived causes. The 2007 'final cut' version can be downloaded from Jones's website listed above.

For a good insight into how international banking is used as a key component of global control, the aforementioned *The Money Masters* is crucial viewing, and can be seen at: *http://www.themoneymasters.com/synopsis.htm*.

However, for the best all-round guide to the conspiracy view of the current state of the world, the much-praised *Zeitgeist* is a mind-blowing trip through the hidden history of control agendas and sums up the issues very well, including an excellent section on 9/11. It is long and detailed, but well worth the journey, although the religiously devout should beware, as it is highly critical of both the origins of religion and its misuse through the ages. The 'Remastered Final Edition' of *Zeitgeist* can be watched at its official website at: *http://www.zeitgeistmovie.com*.

Meanwhile, although fictional and not a documentary, most conspiracy theorists point to the 2005 movie *V for Vendetta* as being the nearest Hollywood has come to making a radical statement about the way the world may really be run. Produced and written by the brothers Laurence and Andrew Wachowski (who also created the not irrelevant *Matrix* films) and inspired by the more complex graphic novel by Alan Moore and David Lloyd (Vertigo, 1995, which in itself is a recommended read), *V for Vendetta* is set in a near-future fascist Britain and seems increasingly relevant as the years go by. The down side of it is that it appears to support terrorism (which this author most certainly does not) and it has been attacked by critics for that, but if this can be overlooked there are many salient lessons in the film. Given its strong anti-establishment tone (although anti-fascist might be a more accurate term), how the producers obtained permission to shut the roads around Whitehall and film for three nights outside the Houses of Parliament is a puzzle. The now popular wearing of stylised Guy Fawkes masks at liberty events, in honour of the central character, 'V', was directly inspired by this ultimately uplifting, if ideologically ambiguous, film, which is a must-see for anyone concerned about the current control trajectory. Good information and discussion of the film can be found at: *http://en.wikipedia.org/wiki/V_for_Vendetta_(film)*.

9/11

Books

David Ray Griffin: As a respected academic (feeling obliged by his Christian faith to turn his attention to a glaring immorality he felt he could no longer ignore), Griffin is the most important attribute that the 9/11 truth movement has, always remaining fully grounded and steadfastly adhering to the discussion of hard facts. A stickler for detail, his flawless analyses leave no stone unturned, and no discontinuity or defect of logic gets by him. If the Western cartel that appears to have operated on 9/11 isn't worried by the astonishingly convincing case against the official story that Griffin has laid out in his ever-growing series of books on the subject (six full tomes to date), it should be. Where he speculates, he does so carefully and clearly denotes this, but mostly the books stay firmly in the realm of dissecting the known. Anyone who can read Griffin's works and afterwards still believe *every* facet of what he calls 'the official conspiracy theory' (i.e. the assertion that Al Qaeda acted alone) is either in a state of extreme denial or in a coma.

Griffin's first and best-known book on *9/11, The New Pearl Harbor: Disturbing Questions about the Bush Administration and 9/11* (Interlink Books, 2004) has essentially been superseded by the semi-sequel/update *The New Pearl Harbor Revisited: 9/11, the Cover-Up and the Expose* (Olive Branch Press, 2008), which acts as Griffin's best all-round guide to the anomalies of 9/11. However, more dedicated students sometimes choose *Debunking 9/11 Debunking: An Answer to Popular Mechanics and Other Defenders of the Official Conspiracy Theory* (Olive Branch Press, 2007) as their defence tool, for its robust addressing of media and government attempts to demean and debunk questioners of the official story. Those who want to hear Griffin take apart almost line-by-line the official 9/11 inquiry should read *The 9/11 Commission Report: Omissions And Distortions* (Olive Branch Press, 2004) - the subtitle tells you all you need to know about the book's take on it. In essence, every Griffin book on 9/11 is worth reading, and completists should seek out *9/11 Contradictions: An Open Letter to Congress and the Press* (Interlink Publishing Group, 2008), *Christian Faith and the Truth Behind 9/11: A Call to Reflection and Action* (Westminster John Knox Press, 2006), and *9/11 and American Empire: Intellectuals Speak Out, Vol. 1* (Olive Branch Press 2006, with Griffin as editor).

Other authors: It is not Griffin alone who has important things to say about 9/11, and there are many books out there by various authors which make for valuable research. However, among these I would particularly cite Ian Henshall and Rowland Morgan's *9.11 Revealed: Challenging the Facts Behind the War on Terror* (Robinson Publishing, 2005), Ian Henshall's solo sequel *9.11: The New Evidence* (Robinson Publishing 2007), Webster Griffin Tarpley's *9/11 Synthetic Terror: Made in USA* (Progressive Press, 2005), and not forgetting David Icke's delightfully-named *Alice in Wonderland and the World Trade Center Disaster: Why the Official Story of 9/11 is a Monumental Lie* (Bridge of Love, 2002), which, although now inevitably slightly dated due to years of later research, was one of the first books out there challenging the official story and quickly identified the key issues. In this regard, Thierry Meyssan's *9/11: The Big Lie* (originally published in France, 2002, and first published in the US by Carnot USA Books, 2003) should also be mentioned as an important early entry into the canon. Michael Ruppert's *Crossing the Rubicon: The Decline of the American Empire at the End of the Age of Oil* (New Society Publishers, 2004) is also worth reading, although it borders more on geopolitics rather than straight 9/11 conspiracy writing.

Websites

There are now so many 9/11-questioning websites out there that it is almost impossible to keep track of them. But the ones run by academics and professionals in their field, who know about buildings, aeroplanes and fires, and the way they should behave, are probably the most important, because they carry weight beyond the usual conspiracy channels. Here is a selection of sites that will keep readers seriously in the loop of the latest 9/11 revelations, and include some very important articles, scientific studies, videos and interviews, which make up an unquestionable case that a fully independent reinvestigation is essential. Something has hit a spot in the collective, which cannot be ignored forever. Most titles in the following (alphabetical) list are self-explanatory, but clarifications are given where not:

www.911blogger.com
www.911building7.co.uk (Martin Noakes' 9/11 campaigning song)
http://911forum.org.uk
http://911research.wtc7.net
http://911scholars.org (Scholars for 9/11 Truth)
www.911truth.org
www.ae911truth.org (Architects & Engineers for 9/11 Truth)
www.CSI911.info
http://firefightersfor911truth.org
www.journalof911studies.com
http://lawyersfor911truth.blogspot.com
http://patriotsquestion911.com
www.stj911.com (Scholars for 9/11 Truth & Justice)
www.visibility911.com
www.william911.com (William Rodriguez, WTC janitor)
www.wtc7.net
www.youtube.com/watch?v=uSBYdRRuLxl (*9/11's a Lie* - satirical song by 'The Freebies')

Documentaries

Many good 9/11 documentaries are available, too many to list here, but searches through the websites will soon reveal them. However, although later findings and research have now begun to date some of the detail, many still maintain that the best starting point for newcomers is Dylan Avery's obscurely-named but hugely influential *Loose Change II*. This replaced a first version, and *Loose Change Final Cut* came along after, but the third instalment, although valuable, is essentially a different and more detailed film and takes too much knowledge for granted to really be for beginners. Go for the mark two version first. The issues are necessarily simplified to get it into an easily accessible format, and debunkers have attempted to attack it for this, but it makes all the points it needs to without at any point being disingenuous. *Loose Change II* was, after all, the documentary that really burst open the gates for the 9/11 truth movement, with its circulation via the Internet and DVD-copying networks quickly becoming massive. The official website *http://www.loosechange911.com* tends to default to the final version of the film, but the second one is easily found on *You Tube* and *Google Video*.

For the best dissection of the issues around the highly questionable collapse of the towers at the WTC, however, *911 Mysteries Part 1 - Demolitions* is excellent, calmly presenting the viewer with almost indisputable observations regarding the footage of the destruction, analysing the physics as it goes. Part 2 has yet to materialise, but this film does enough by itself. The documentary's official website is: *http://www.911weknow.com/911-mysteries-dvd.*

Less focused on the science of the events, but representing an important element of the truth campaign, the film *9/11: Press for Truth* tells the story of the 'Jersey widows', a group of partners and wives of 9/11 victims who campaigned for an official investigation into the attacks, only to see the subsequent 9/11 Commission entirely fail to answer their key questions about how the events came to pass. The official website is at: *http://www.911pressfortruth.com*.

In a not dissimilar vein, but more global in its coverage, Dean Puckett's documentary about the 9/11 truth movement, *The Elephant in the Room*, demonstrates the intense feelings and dedication of campaigners in the US and UK and is an impressive reminder that the 9/11 issue isn't going to be dropped by those concerned anytime soon. The film can be found at: *http://deaddeanfilms.com*.

OTHER GENERAL INFORMATION

A small but useful selection of books on other subjects covered in these chapters are listed here (in alphabetical order of subject), together with a tiny but helpful scattering of websites from what is obviously a huge pool - again, many further links can be followed from most of them.

ANCIENT MYSTERIES

Books:

Christopher Dunn's *The Giza Power Plant: Technologies of Ancient Egypt* (Bear & Company, 1998) is one of the best-expressed alternative theories on the title's subject, while the works of Graham Hancock are also particularly strong in reassessing mysteries such as the pyramids and other ancient artefacts, taking them out of traditional archaeology's narrow confines and speculating more freely, but in a scholarly fashion. His best-known book is probably *Fingerprints of the Gods* (originally Crown, 1996, updated by Century, 2001), but *Heaven's Mirror: Quest for the Lost Civilisation* (Michael Joseph, 1998, co-authored with Santha Faiia) and *Keeper of Genesis: A Quest for the Hidden Legacy of Mankind* (Arrow Books Ltd, 1997, co-authored with Robert Bauval), amongst other works, all provide insights into a different view of ancient history. Bauval and Adrian Gilbert's aforementioned *The Orion Mystery* (Mandarin Books, 1994), which first proposed the much-argued Giza/Orion correlation, is also worth reading, although Lynn Picknett and Clive Prince's book *The Stargate Conspiracy: The Truth about Extraterrestrial Life and the Mysteries of Ancient Egypt* (Berkley Trade, 2001) puts an interesting spin on things, claiming that the likes of Hancock, Bauval and Gilbert are fronting a secret consortium that is actively planning for the imminent return of ancient god-like beings. Meanwhile, the ever-growing 'Earth Chronicle' books of Zecharia Sitchin, beginning with *The Twelfth Planet* (originally published 1976, current edition Harper, 2007), though much criticised by sceptics, purport to tell the hidden story of humankind's history as a genetically-engineered slave race (as Sitchin interprets it), as derived from ancient Sumerian and other supportive texts. Whatever their veracity, the books have been influential and pretty much gave birth to the modern speculation on the return of the 'Annunaki' and the lost-planet 'Nibiru' [page 86].

Websites:
www.gizapower.com (Christopher Dunn)
www.grahamhancock.com
www.mcremo.com
www.robertbauval.co.uk
www.sitchin.com

CLIMATE CHANGE (ALTERNATIVE THEORIES)

Books

We have already seen that ex-chancellor Nigel Lawson's *An Appeal to Reason: A Cool Look at Global Warming* (Gerald Duckworth & Co Ltd, 2008) puts a sensibly argued and pragmatic case that the policies being pursued to deal with perceived global warming are misplaced and damaging, ecologically and economically, even if its existence were to be proven. Henrik Svensmark and Nigel Calder's book *The Chilling Stars* (Icon Books/Totem Books, 2007) actively proposes a different model of climate change based on the theory of cosmic influences causing worldwide cooling, not warming, while on a similar theme Peter Taylor's book *Chill: A Reassessment of Global Warming Theory* (Clairview Books, 2009) was imminent at the time of writing. Other sources include Mitch Battros' *Global Warming: A Convenient Disguise* (Earth Changes Media, 2007), which, together with his earlier volume *Solar Rain: The Earth Changes Have Begun* (Earth Changes Press, 2005), points to the Sun as being the major driver of climate change and other effects, not greenhouse gases. Meanwhile, Canadian environmentalist Lawrence Solomon's impressively scholarly *The Deniers: The World Renowned Scientists Who Stood Up Against Global Warming Hysteria, Political Persecution, and Fraud (*And those who are too fearful to do so)* (Richard Vigilante Books, 2008) focuses on the surprisingly long and eminent list of climatologists and scientists who challenge the global warming theory. How so many qualified people can take a stand against it and not be listened to, while the likes of Al Gore – an ex-politician, not a scientist - gets his film shown in schools, is a complete mystery. Roy Spencer's *Climate Confusion: How Global Warming Hysteria Leads to Bad Science, Pandering Politicians and Misguided Policies that Hurt the Poor* is a lighter read, but ably deconstructs the myths and indeed confusions of misplaced climate fear-mongering.

Websites

www.drroyspencer.com
www.dsri.dk/~hsv/ (Henrik Svensmark)
www.earthchangesmedia.com (Mitch Battros)
www.global-warming-and-the-climate.com
www.globalwarminghoax.com
www.urban-renaissance.org (Lawrence Solomon)

CONSCIOUSNESS/PSI STUDIES

Books

For a balanced and calmly presented assessment of the impressive evidence that human minds are inextricably linked in some kind of collective energetic process, continually communicating by instantaneous 'non-local' means and producing unexpected 'psi' phenomena, Dean Radin's *Entangled Minds: Extrasensory Experiences in a Quantum Reality* (Paraview Pocket Books, 2006) puts the firmest of cases, based on provable science, not New Age speculation. A good round-up of Radin's and many other researchers' work into collective psi effects, while speculating more openly on the implications and possibilities the recognition of a truly proactive collective consciousness could bring (based on the concept of the 'Zero Point Field'), can be found in Lynne McTaggart's *The Field: The Quest for the Secret Force of the Universe* (updated edition, Harper Paperbacks, 2008). Rupert Sheldrake is another researcher who has made important steps in bridging the divide between science and metaphysics (though he would never call it that), and his 'morphic resonance' theory to account for collective species development has been very influential. In terms of exploring consciousness and psi effects, the best starting points are probably *The Sense of Being Stared At (and other unexplained powers of the human mind)* (Crown Publishing Group, 2004), and *Seven Experiments That Could Change the World* (Inner Traditions, 2002). For the fundamentalist hard-science adherents for whom even these very grounded books push the envelope too much, Bruce Rosenblum and Fred Kuttner's *Quantum Enigma: Physics Encounters Consciousness* (Oxford University Press, 2008) should placate. An exploration of straight (if there is such a thing) quantum physics, its balanced and cautious analysis of the role consciousness appears to actively play in shaping reality still makes the point that the New Physics now needs to look outside of its old parameters to embrace a new understanding of the importance of mind. Meanwhile, those interested in the transformative effects of natural dimethyltryptamine in the brain, and what stimulates its production, are again directed to Rick Strassman's *DMT: The Spirit Molecule - A Doctor's Revolutionary Research into the Biology of Near-Death and Mystical Experiences* (Park Street Press, 2001).

Websites
www.deanradin.com
http://noosphere.princeton.edu (Global Consciousness Project)
www.livingthefield.com (Lynne McTaggart)
www.rickstrassman.com
www.sheldrake.org (Rupert Sheldrake)
www.whatthebleep.com

CROP CIRCLES

Books
The earliest books are still some of the best, with Colin Andrews and Pat Delgado's *Circular Evidence* (Bloomsbury, 1989) and the Ralph Noyes-edited *The Crop Circle Enigma* (Gateway, 1991) providing good insights into the initial development of the phenomenon. In later years, the most balanced and informative book, free of unhelpful 'croppie' generalisations, has been Eltjo Haselhoff's *The Deepening Complexity of Crop Circles: Scientific Research and Urban Legends* (Frog Ltd, 2001), which makes an excellent case for a non-human cause, using sensible empirical reasoning. Readers may also like to investigate my own *Vital Signs: A Complete Guide to the Crop Circle Mystery* (SB Publications 1998/2002 [UK], Frog Ltd, 2002 [US]), kindly described more than once as 'the definitive guide'.

Websites
www.bltresearch.com (scientific analysis)
www.cropcircleconnector.com
www.kornkreise-forschung.de (also known as *www.cropcirclescience.org*)
www.swirlednews.com (archive articles edited or written by this author)
www.ukcropcircles.co.uk
www.x-cosmos.it/cropcircles

GEOPOLITICS

Books
Generally outside the realm of conspiracy theory, but still incisively questioning of political

corruption and global intrigues, a few titles are particularly relevant. Any political non-fiction by Gore Vidal is worth reading, but two shorter books were particularly picked up on by truthseekers in the wake of 9/11 (although Gore appears to accept the official line on it), *Perpetual War for Perpetual Peace or How We Came To Be So Hated*, and *Dreaming War: Blood for Oil and the Cheney-Bush Junta* (both by Thunder's Mouth Press, 2002). Someone who did go on to question 9/11 and become very active in truth campaigning is Annie Machon, whose book *Spies, Lies and Whistleblowers: MI5, MI6 and the Shayler affair* (Book Guild Ltd, 2005) is an expose of her time as an MI5 officer, detailing a number of dubious British plots, including an attempt to hire Al Qaeda to assassinate the Libyan leader Colonel Gaddafi. (Her then partner David Shayler was sent to prison for trying to reveal what he and Machon considered to be immoral actions.) David Rothkopf's book *Superclass: The Global Power Elite and the World They Are Making* (Farrar, Straus and Giroux, 2008) has already been mentioned, as has Norman Baker's *The Strange Death of David Kelly* (Methuen Publishing, 2007 - although this could almost be in the conspiracy section), but other works of interest include Ron Suskind's *The Way of the World: A Story of Truth and Hope in an Age of Extremism* (Harper, 2008), which uncovers the corruption behind the 2003 invasion of Iraq amongst other revelations, and John Pilger's *The New Rulers of the World* (Verso, 2003) and *Freedom Next Time: Resisting the Empire* (Nation Books, 2007), which demonstrate the massive issues around loss of freedom due to globalisation and aggressive Western trade and military policies. Likewise, any work by noted academic Noam Chomsky tells much the same story; *Manufacturing Consent: The Political Economy of the Mass Media* (Pantheon, 2002) exposes the way politicians exploit a complicit media to manipulate the public, and *Failed States: The Abuse of Power and the Assault on Democracy (American Empire Project)* (Holt Paperbacks, 2007) takes apart the George W Bush administration's aggressive and oppressive policies. However, Chomsky's admittedly puzzling inability to even consider the 9/11 inside-job view has enfuriated many truthseekers, who cannot understand why such a keen critic of US government corruption refuses to investigate further, leading to accusations that he has been 'got at'. Perhaps Chomsky and people like him just can't bring themselves to face *that* depth of pessimism about their rulers. This caveat probably covers most of the authors listed in this geopolitics section, not to mention US film maker/political agitator Michael Moore, whose 2004 documentary *Fahrenheit 9/11* is very good for making things like the business connections between the Bush and bin Laden families more than clear (and in general is well worth watching), but shies away from questioning 9/11 itself. Frustrating though their reticence in some areas can be, in the end it is a matter for individuals where they want to go with their views, but at least there are people in the mainstream exposing any of the darker levels at all.

Websites
www.chomsky.info
www.johnpilger.com
www.michaelmoore.com
http://www.pitt.edu/~kloman/vidalframe.html (Gore Vidal)
http://www.ronsuskind.com/about

HEALTH

Books
The threat to the free availability of natural health products is discussed at length in Scott Tips' *Codex Alimentarius: Global Food Imperialism* (National Health Federation, 2007), a compendium of crucial articles on the impending restrictions and what can be done to combat

them. In regard to vaccinations, Trevor Gunn's *Mass Immunisation - A Point in Question* (Cutting Edge Publications, 1992) and Wendy Lydall's *Raising a Vaccine Free Child* (AuthorHouse, 2005) have already been cited as important reading, while Neil Z Miller's *Vaccines: Are They Really Safe and Effective?* (New Atlantean Press, revised edition 2008) is another vital contribution. In terms of adult health, and the questionable pharmaceutical solutions often pushed on us above other options, Lynne McTaggart's *What Doctors Don't Tell You: The Truth About The Dangers Of Modern Medicine* (Avon, 1999) is a seminal title and encompasses many of the problematic issues without blanket condemnation of conventional methods. Meanwhile, the many books of Philip Day (it's impossible to pick out one) embrace alternative methods of keeping healthy and avoiding the likes of cancer and arthritis by maintaining healthy diets and eating specific foods, and have been sworn to by many who have followed the advice – see his website below.

Websites
www.anhcampaign.org (Alliance for Natural Health)
www.credence.org (Philip Day)
www.fluoridation.com (excellent resource on fluoride issues)
www.informedparent.co.uk
www.naturalnews.com
www.thenhf.com (National Health Federation/Scott Tips)
www.wddty.com (Lynne McTaggart)

NASA CONSPIRACY

Books
We have already seen that two books are particularly prominent on this subject: Gerhard Wisnewski's *One Small Step? - The Great Moon Hoax and the Race to Dominate Earth from Space* (Clairview Books, 2007) is the most real-world case yet presented that the evidence for the lunar missions may be faked, while Mary Bennett and David Percy's *Dark Moon: Apollo and the Whistleblowers* (Aulis Publishers, 1999) is a denser, more esoteric take on it, but still makes for vital reading (see also the accompanying 2000 documentary *What Happened on the Moon?* - details can be found on their website below). Ralph René's self-published book *NASA Mooned America!* (1992) is equally uncompromising in its deconstruction of the lunar claims, and Philippe Lheureux's *Moon Landings: Did NASA Lie?* (Carnot USA Books, 2003) offers a more simplistic, but handy round-up of the main issues. Taking a rather different line, but worth a look for a balancing view, is Richard Hoagland and Mike Bara's *Dark Mission: The Secret History of NASA* (Feral House, 2007), which postulates that NASA *did* go to the Moon, but that they covered up evidence of ET structures they found there. Hoagland (formerly a NASA staff member) was one of the first promoters of the 'face on Mars' photos from the 1977 Viking mission, and still claims (despite vigorous NASA debunking based on later photos) that Mars is also covered in ancient structures we are not being told about. The authors assert (as do Bennett and Percy) that the power infrastructure of NASA is riddled with secret society and occult undercurrents.

Websites
www.aulis.com (Mary Bennett & David Percy)
http://billkaysing.com
www.enterprisemission.com (Richard Hoagland)
www.moonmovie.com

2012

Books
Geoff Stray's *Beyond 2012: Catastrophe or Ecstasy* (Vital Signs Publishing, 2005) has already been firmly indicated as a key source on 2012, so little more needs to be said on it (although beware two inferior imposter books, which have appropriated its title - make sure it's the Stray version you read), but John Major Jenkins' work *Maya Cosmogenesis 2012: The True Meaning of the Maya Calendar End-Date* (Bear & Company, 1998) is also a vital entry, and was the first serious book to alert wider attention to the beliefs of the Maya people, and defined the galactic alignment process. The current problem with 2012 books is that there are now many very poor cash-ins being produced as the year approaches, full of calendrical errors and misunderstandings about the nature of the true prophecies (even from surprisingly well-known authors). The imminent disaster movie *2012* won't help matters and discernment is definitely required in this regard. However, a book containing good overviews of 2012 from several different and respected researchers (including Stray and Jenkins) is *The Mystery of 2012: Predictions, Prophecies and Possibilities* (Sounds True Incorporated, 2009), edited by Gregg Braden. Browsing this is an ideal way to get an overall perspective on what a diverse group of people are expecting, fearing or hoping for in 2012.

Websites
www.alignment2012.com (John Major Jenkins)
www.december212012.com
www.diagnosis2012.co.uk (Geoff Stray)
www.greatdreams.com/2012.htm
http://tech.groups.yahoo.com/group/timewavezero2012/

UFOS & ETS

Books
UFOs and government cover-ups of them are well-assessed in Timothy Good's seminal works *Above Top Secret: The Worldwide UFO Cover-Up* (Sidgwick & Jackson Ltd, 1987), *Beyond Top Secret* (Pan Books, 1997), and his most recent update, *Need to Know: UFOs, the Military and Intelligence* (Pan Books, 2007). The alien abduction phenomenon is assessed very intelligently by John E Mack in *Passport to the Cosmos: Human Transformation and Alien Encounters* (Crown, 1999), while Whitley Strieber's *Communion* (Avon, 1988) and its sequels give good first-hand accounts of his claimed experiences with ETs. Stanton T Friedman and Don Berliner's *Crash at Corona: The U.S. Military Retrieval and Cover-Up of a UFO* (Marlowe & Co., 1997), meanwhile, describes itself as the 'definitive study' of the Roswell incident, and appears to be generally treated as such.

Websites
www.earthfiles.com (Linda Moulton-Howe)
www.realufos.net
www.ufocasebook.com
www.ufoevidence.org
www.ufomystic.com

PICTURE CREDITS

Image authors and/or sources as below - all other photos by Andy Thomas.

Page 7, Thomas Paine mural, Lewes, East Sussex, painted by Julian Bell (c/o Francis Kyle gallery, *www.franciskylegallery.com*).

Page 8, montage by Jason Porthouse & Andy Thomas (individual photos credited below)

Page 10, filming of *The One Show*. Photo: Helen Sewell

Page 277, Barack Obama's inaugural oath. Photo: Petty Officer 1st Class Chad J McNeeley, US Navy (*http://www.defenselink.mil/homepagephotos/homepagephotos.aspx?month=200901*). Source: Wikimedia Commons, public domain.

Page 15, Egyptian temple. Photo: Heather Thomas

Page 22, The White House, Washington DC. Photo: Tony & Ann Woodall

Page 26, Giza monuments. Photo: Daniel Mayer. Source: Wikimedia Commons, under the GNU Free Documentation License (*http://commons.wikimedia.org/wiki/Commons:GNU_Free_Documentation_License*).

Pages 28-29, Giza pyramids. Photos: Heather Thomas

Pages 30-32, aerial crop circle photos. Photos: Andreas Müller (*http://www.kornkreise-forschung.de*)

Page 34, crystal skull. Photo: Jordan Thomas

Page 36, Area 51, 1968. Photo: USGS Aerial imagery. Source: Wikimedia Commons, public domain.

Pages 38-40, Little A'le'inn, Groom Lake Road & Area 51 sign. Photos: Mike Oram

Page 42, black triangle UFO, 1990. Photo: J S Henradi (*http://www.abduct-anon.com/AUTHENTIC%20PHOTOS.htm*). Source: Wikimedia Commons, public domain.

Page 45, UFO, 1952. Photo: Central Intelligence Agency (*https://www.cia.gov/csi/studies/97unclass/p69.gif*). Source: Wikimedia Commons, public domain.

Page 48, Fatima statue. Photo: Lucas Mello Schnorr. Source: Wikimedia Commons, public domain.

Page 50, Edgard Cayce, 1910. Author unknown. Source: Wikimedia Commons, public domain.

Page 52, Revelation mural. Painting by Matthias Gerung. Source: Wikimedia Commons, public domain.

Pages 55-56, Fatima children, crowds and orb, 1917. Authors unknown. Source: Wikimedia Commons, public domain.

Page 60, Bush meets Pope John Paul II. Photo: Eric Draper, United States Federal Government. Source: Wikimedia Commons, public domain.

Page 71, George Orwell, 1933. Photo: Branch of the National Union of Journalists (c/o *http://www.netcharles.com/orwell/*). Source: Wikimedia Commons, public domain.

Page 73, Canary Wharf by night. Photo: Dave Pape. Source: Wikimedia Commons, public domain.

Page 76, Strasbourg Parliament. Photo: Cédric Puisney. Source: Wikimedia Commons, public domain.

Page 80, micro-chipped cat. Photo: Joel Mills (*http://en.wikipedia.org/wiki/User:Joelmills*). Source: Wikimedia Commons, under the GNU Free Documentation License (*http://commons.wikimedia.org/wiki/Commons:GNU_Free_Documentation_License*).

Page 86, Sumerian seal/Annunaki. Author unknown. Source: Wikimedia Commons, public domain.

Page 87, Tower of Babel. Painting by Pieter Bruegel. Source: Wikimedia Commons, public domain.

Page 88, Egyptian needle. Photo by Ronald Thomas

Page 88, The Washington Monument. Photo by Tony & Ann Woodall

Page 92, One Canada Square, Canary Wharf. Photo: Matt T (*http://commons.wikimedia.org/wiki/User: Matt.T*). Source: Wikimedia Commons.

Page 95, Operation Ivy nuclear test, 1952. Photo c/o NARA (National Archives and Records Administration). Source: Wikimedia Commons, public domain.

Page 97, World Trade Center. Photo by Tony & Ann Woodall

Pages 102-103, Apollo 1 crew and burnt capsule. Photos: NASA (National Aeronautics and Space Administration). Public domain.

Page 104, Lunar Landing Training Vehicle accident. Film image: NASA. Public domain.

Page 106, Moon rocks. Photo: NASA. Public domain.

Pages 109-112, Aldrin/Bean on the Moon. Photos: NASA. Public domain. (Contrast-enhanced edit by Andy Thomas)

Page 113, Hasselblad 500 EL camera and camera height tests. Photos: Marcus Allen

Pages 114-117, various lunar shots/space shuttle. Photos: NASA. Public domain.

Pages 119-120, Collins 'spacewalk'/Moon golf. Photos: NASA. Public domain.

Page 122, Apollo 16 lander in orbit. Photo: NASA. Public domain.

Pages 124-125, lunar buggy/Yuri Gagarin. Photos: NASA. Public domain.

Page 128, lunar lander conceptual art. Painting by NASA. Public domain.

Page 132, Armoured vehicle in Bagram, Afghanistan, 2006. Photo: Dexter D Clouden, US Army (DOD 061027-A-5420C-041). Source: Wikimedia Commons, public domain.

Page 133, bin Laden. Photo c/o FBI (Federal Bureau of Investigation). Source: Wikimedia Commons, public domain.

Page 134, Saddam Hussein, 2004. Photo: US Army (DOD 040701-O-9999X-008). Source: Wikimedia Commons, public domain.

Page 137, Marines Firing M198 Howitzer at Umm Qasr, Iraq, 2003. Photo: Matthew J Decker USMC (DOD 030324-M-9933D-002), US Army. Source: Wikimedia Commons, public domain.

Page 140, World Trade Center from the streets. Photo by Tony & Ann Woodall

Page 142, World Trade Center wide view. Photo by Tony & Ann Woodall

Pages 145-146, Pentagon after strike. Photos: Cpl Jason Ingersoll, US Army. Source: Wikimedia Commons, public domain.

Page 148, still (4 of 8) from security video purporting to show Flight 77 striking the Pentagon. Video c/o Department of Defense (*http://www.defenselink.mil/pubs/foi/index.html*). Source: Wikimedia Commons, public domain.

Page 149, exit hole in Pentagon. Photo: Jocelyn Augustino. Source: FEMA (Federal Emergency Management Agency). Public domain.

Page 150, World Trade Center burning. Author unknown. Source: Wikimedia Commons, public domain. (*http://memory.loc.gov/pnp/ppmsca/02100/02121/0012v.jpg*)

Page 152, wreckage at Ground Zero. Photo: Larry Lerner. Source: FEMA. Public domain.

Page 155, lattice remains at Ground Zero. Author unknown. Source: FEMA. Public domain.

Page 156, fireman clearing WTC dust. Photo: Andrea Booher, Source: FEMA. Public domain.

Page 160, aerial view of WTC 7 as tower collapses. Author unknown. Source: FEMA. Public domain.

Page 162, WTC 7 burns. Photo: Arquelio "Archie" Galarza (*http://www.fema.gov/pdf/library/fema403_ch5. pdf*). Source: FEMA. Public domain.

Page 164, aerial view of Ground Zero. Author unknown. Source: FEMA. Public domain.

Page 165, smoke plume as WTC 7 collapses. Author unknown. Source: Courtesy of the Prints and Photographs Division, Library of Congress (*http://hdl.loc.gov/loc.pnp/ppmsca.02121*). Public domain.

Page 166, Mohamed Atta al-Sayed. Author unknown - driver's licence photo. Source: FBI (*http://www.fbi. gov/pressrel/penttbom/aa11/11.htm*). Source: Wikimedia Commons, public domain.

Page 169, debris on roof of WTC 5. Author unknown. Source: FEMA. Public domain.

Page 172 (two images), crash site of Flight 93. Author unknown. Source: US Government. Public domain.

Page 175, more WTC wreckage. Author unknown. Source: FEMA. Public domain.

Page 180, Liberty Bell, Philadelphia. Photo: Tony & Ann Woodall

Page 182, Pearl Harbor, 1941. Photo: Lloyd C Duncan. Additional source and credit info from the National Archives, US District Court for the District of Hawaii. Source: Wikimedia Commons, public domain.

Page 184, Oklahoma bomb, 1995. Photo: Staff Sgt. Preston Chasteen, US Army (*http://www.defenselink. mil/multimedia/*). Source: Wikimedia Commons, public domain.

Page 188, Guantanamo Bay, 2002. Photo: credited to Ron Sachs/CNP/Corbis, but may be part of a sequence taken by Petty Officer 1st class Shane T McCoy, US Navy. Source: Wikimedia Commons, public domain.

Page 196, Brighton bomb, Grand Hotel, 1984. Author unknown (uploaded by 'D4444n' at *http:// en.wikipedia.org/wiki/User:D4444n*). Source: Wikimedia Commons, under the GNU Free Documentation License (*http://commons.wikimedia.org/wiki/Commons:GNU_Free_Documentation_License*).

Page 199, passengers escape smoke on 7/7. Photo: Adam Stacey (*http://moblog.co.uk/view.php?id=77571*). Source: Wikimedia Commons, under the Creative Commons Attribution 2.5 License (*http://creativecommons. org/licenses/by/2.5/*).

Page 201, advanced M26 Taser stun pistol. Photo: US Army (*http://www.pica.army.mil/PicatinnyPublic/ highlights/archive/FastTrack.asp*). Source: Wikimedia Commons, public domain.

Page 204, tablets. Photo: Sage Ross (*http://en.wikipedia.org/wiki/User:Ragesoss*). Source: Wikimedia Commons, under the GNU Free Documentation License (*http://commons.wikimedia.org/wiki/Commons: GNU_Free_Documentation_License*).

Page 211, post-WWII US poster promoting vaccination against diphtheria. Artist unknown (*http://www. nationalarchives.gov.uk/imagelibrary/medical/03.htm*). Source: Wikimedia Commons, public domain.

Page 213, Edwardian spiritualists, Chicago, Illinois, 1906. Photo: *Chicago Daily News* (DN-0003152 - *Chicago Daily News* negatives collection, Chicago Historical Society). Source: Wikimedia Commons, public domain.

Page 215, sunrise by mosque. Photo: Heather Thomas

Page 224, smoke stacks. Photo: Alfred T Palmer. Source: Wikimedia Commons, public domain.

Page 232, the Sun. Photo: NASA. Public domain.

Page 236, the Earth, photographed by the Galileo probe, 1990. Photo: NASA (*http://www-pm.larc.nasa. gov/triana/Earth.galileo.jpg*). Catalogued by Jet Propulsion Lab of the United States National Aeronautics and Space Administration (NASA) under Photo ID: PIA00728.

Page 249, fireworks over Sydney Opera House, Australia. Photo: Chris Greenberg (*http://www.whitehouse. gov/news/releases/2007/09/images/20070908-1_p090807cg-0360-515h.html*), United States Federal Government. Source: Wikimedia Commons, public domain.

Page 243, Maya temple, Chichen Itza. Photo: Lee Anderson

Page 244, Comet Holmes. Photo: Rick Jackimowicz. Source: Wikimedia Commons, public domain.

Page 246, the McKenna timewave. Diagram by Geoff Stray, from *Beyond 2012: Catastrophe or Ecstasy*, Vital Signs Publishing, 2005.

Page 247, Galaxy NGC 4414 (Hubble Image). Photo: NASA, The Hubble Heritage Team, STScI, AURA. Public domain.

Pages 248-249, solar CME/flare. Photos: NASA. Public domain.

Page 251, the heliosphere. Artist unknown. Source: NASA (*http://www.nasa.gov/centers/ames/news/releases/ 2001/01images/Pioneer10/pioneer10.htm*). Public domain.

Page 255, Ayahuasca being brewed. Photo: Debbie Marriage

Page 259, Hurricane Katrina damage, Pensacola, USA. Photo: Larry W Kachelhofer, US Navy (*http://www. navy.mil/view_single.asp?id=27629*). Source: Wikimedia Commons, public domain.

Page 261, astrological bi-wheel for 21st December 2012/UK. Chart prepared by Helen Sewell, using *Solar Fire* software.

Page 269, H G Wells, 1943. Author unknown - c/o the Youssuf Karsh collection at the Library and Archives, Canada. Source: Wikimedia Commons, public domain.

Page 270, Bertrand Russell, 1950. Photo: Nobel Foundation (*http://nobelprize.org/nobel_prizes/literature/ laureates/1950/russell-bio.html*). Source: Wikimedia Commons, public domain.

Page 274, London G20 protests, 2009. Photo: Charlotte Gilhooly. Source: Wikimedia Commons, under the Creative Commons Attribution 2.0 License (*http://creativecommons.org/licenses/by/2.0/*).

Page 277, crowds at Barack Obama's inauguration. Photo: Senior Master Sgt Thomas Meneguin, US Air

Force (*http://www.defenselink.mil/dodcmsshare/homepagephoto/2009-01/hires_090120-F-6184M-007a.jpg*). Source: Wikimedia Commons, public domain.

Page 282, Hindu woman at prayer. Photo: © Claude Renault (*http://www.flickr.com/photos/clodreno/39525690/*). Source: Wikimedia Commons, under the Creative Commons Attribution 2.0 License (*http://creativecommons.org/licenses/by/2.0/*).

Page 286, Pentagon on 9/11. Photo: Cpl Jason Ingersoll, US Army. Source: Wikimedia Commons, public domain.

Page 286, Tsunami striking Malé, the Maldives, 2004. Photo: Sofwathulla Mohamed (*http://www.darkmoon.mv/wave/*). Source: Wikimedia Commons, public domain.

Page 286, O J Simpson visiting US troops during Operation Desert Shield. Photo: Gerald Johnson (*http://www.dodmedia.osd.mil/DVIC_View/Still_Details.cfm?SDAN=DNST9103444&JPGPath=/Assets/Still/1991/Navy/DN-ST-91-03444.JPG*), US Army. Source: Wikimedia Commons, public domain.

Page 286, Princess Diana's funeral, 1997. Photo: Paddy Briggs. Source: Wikimedia Commons, public domain.

Page 289, Adolf Hitler, 1932. Author unknown (c/o/Deutsches Bundesarchiv [German Federal Archive]). Source: Wikimedia Commons, public domain.

Page 292, asteroid strike. Painting: Don Davis (*http://www.donaldedavis.com/PARTS/allyours.html*). Source: NASA. Public domain.

Page 295, aftermath of 2004 tsunami. Photo: Michael L Bak, US military (*http://www.defenseimagery.mil/imagery.html#guid=5e24f570d0bc5a851ac2182993e5d33b5f8ff005*). Source: Wikimedia Commons, public domain.

Page 298, Live Aid USA, 1985. Photo: 'Squelle'. Source: Wikimedia Commons, under the Creative Commons Attribution 3.0 License (*http://creativecommons.org/licenses/by-sa/3.0/*).

Page 300, The Alternative View conference, Totnes, UK, 2008. Photo: Helen Sewell

Page 303, riot police at G20 protests. Photo: Chris Brown. Source: Wikimedia Commons, under the Creative Commons Attribution 2.0 License (*http://creativecommons.org/licenses/by/2.0/*).

Page 305, 2012 London Olympic stadium under construction. Photo: Nigel Chadwick (c/o the Geograph Project collection, *http://www.geograph.org.uk*). Source: Wikimedia Commons, under the Creative Commons Attribution 2.0 License (*http://creativecommons.org/licenses/by/2.0/*).

Page 311, Emmiline Pankhurst arrested, 1914. Author unknown. Source: Wikimedia Commons, public domain.

Page 313, 'Orange Revolution' protests. Author unknown (*http://maidan.org.ua/news/view.php3?site=maidan&bn=maidan_foto&key=1101124510*). Source: Wikimedia Commons, under the GNU Free Documentation License (*http://commons.wikimedia.org/wiki/Commons:GNU_Free_Documentation_License*).

Page 370, Egyptian pillar. Photo: Heather Thomas

With the exception of the noted public domain or licensed images, authors retain full copyright on the featured photographs, which have been reproduced here with permission.

INDEX

Aaronovitch, David, 18, 177, 319
Adams, Gerry, 314
ADAS, 321
ADHD, 219
Afghanistan, 23, 131, pic 132, 133, 139,185, 187, 200, 331
African National Congress (ANC), 312
Agriculture, Ministry of, 32
AIDS, 68, 220, 324
Air Force One, 174, 336
Akashic Record, 283
Aldrin, Edward 'Buzz', 108, pics 109-111, 112, 114
Al Fayed, Dodi, 328
Al Fayed, Mohammed, 9, 18, 328
Allen, Marcus, 9, 108, 123, 330
Alliance for Natural Health, 209
All-Seeing-Eye, pic 89
Al Qaeda, 19, 23, 131-133, 141, 147, 150, 166, 169, 173, 185-187, 200, 335-337
Al Takriti, Tahir Jalil Habbush, 134
Alternative View Conference, pic 300
American Airlines, 173
'Amero', the, 71, 76, 326
An Inconvenient Truth, 228
Ancram, Michael, 351
Animals sensing the 2004 tsunami, 350
Annunaki, the, 86
Antarctica, 107
Anti-Defamation League, 215
Apollo 1, pics 102, 103
Apollo 11, pics 109-111, pics 114-116, 329
Apollo 12, pic 112
Apollo 14, pic 120, 329
Apollo 16, pic 117, 122
Apollo 17, pic 124
Area 51, pics 36, 38, 39, 40
Arguelles, Jose, 345
Armstrong, Neil, 99, 102, pic 104, 108, 109, 125, 320
Arthurian Myths, 306
Ascended Masters, 307, 308
Ascension, 256, 262, 308
Ashtar, 308
Aspartame, 326, 340
Astrological bi-wheel, 261
Astrology, 60, 260-262, 347, 348
Atheism, 214

A3 Sky Warrior, 149
Atlantis, 50, 88
Atta, Mohammed, pic 166
Attenborough, David, 325
Australia, 211, pic 240
Avatars, 307
Avebury, 35
Ayahuasca, 245, pic 255
Aztecs, 243, 244,

Babylon, 137, 327
Baker, Norman, pic 135, 136, 235, 332
Baker, Peter, 320
Bar Codes, 322
Baram, Marcus, 192, 338
Baron, Thomas Ronald, 103, 104, 329
Bauval, Robert, 321, 327, 328
BBC, 9, pic 10, 59, 135, 161, 162, 166, 177, 186, 198, 234, 319, 320, 335
Bean, Alan, pic 112
Beddington, Prof. John, 325
Bellamy, David, 226
Bennett, Mary, 111, 120-122, 124, 329, 330
Berlin Wall, 311
Beveridge, John, 328
Beyond 2012: Catastrophe or Ecstasy, 246, 349
Bible, The, 85, 87
Bible Code, 52, 53
Bigfoot, 34
Bigham, Alex, 331
Bilderberg Group, 66, 95, 274
Bill of Rights, 187
Bingham, Mark, 170
Bin Laden, 19, 132, pic 133, 141, 143, 175, 176, 185, 186, 331
Bird (Avian) Flu, 69
Blair, Cherie, 262
Blair, Tony, 59, 62, 81, 93, 134, 139, 262, 273, 274, 277, 289, 301, 324, 349
Blears, Hazel, 351
Blue Star Kachina, 244
Boardman, Terry, 351
Boeing 757, 144-149, 169, 332
Bohemian Club, 92, 93, 328
Bohemian Grove, 66, 94, pic 95, 134, 258, 272
Bonfire Night, pic 19

Braden, Gregg, 252
Braun, Wernher Von, 119, 126
Brier, Bob, 320
Brighton Bomb, pic 196, 197
Britain, 17, 293, 303, 304, 307
British, 306, 307
British National Party (BNP), 215
British Royal Family, 327
Brooks, Michael, 346
Broucher, David, 136
Brown, Dan, 90
Brown, Gordon, 63, 71, 72, 75, 274, 349
Brown, Willie, 173
Brzezinski, Zbigniew, 23, 273
Bura, Paul, 350
Burke, Edmund, 309
Burrell, Paul, 136
Bush, George W, 21, 59, 60, 61, 88, 89, 93, 132, 134, 139, 143, 159, 173, 174, 176, 181, 186, 323, 336
Bush, Marvin, 154

Calder, Nigel, 227, 232, 342
Calleman, Carl, 345
Cameron, David, 303, 350
Campaign for Nuclear Disarmament (CND), 314
Campaign for Real Ale, 314
Campbell, Alastair, 135
Canary Wharf, pic 73, pic 92
Cape Canaveral, 103, pic 127
Carbon Credits, 229
Carbon Pollution, pic 230
Card, Andrew, 174
Carter, Professor, 229
Casciani, Dominic, 338
Castro, Fidel, 183
Cathie, Bruce, 345
Cayce, Edgar, 49, pic 50,
CCTV, 192, pic 193, 198, 282, 322
Cenotaph Protest, pic 138
Chaffee, Roger, pic 102, 103
Changing Times Organisation, 342
Chapman, Phil, 230, 343
Chardin, Pierre Teilhard-de, 282, 349
Chechnya, 184
Childhood's End, 283, 349
China, 214, 260, 313
Chomsky, Noam, 138

Christianity, 217, 351
Chronological History of the New World Order, 348
CIA, 127, 173
Clark, Andrew, 334
Clarke, Arthur C, 283
Clements, Dr C J, 324
Climate Change, 224, 225, 235, pic 235
Clinton, Bill, 93, 274, 328
Clinton, Hilary, pic 62, 93, 324, 328, 345
Club of Rome, 66
Cockpit Voice Recorders, 168
Codex Alimentarius, 67, 68, 209-211, 314, 340
Cold War, 101, 107, 186
Coleman, John, 229, 343
Collective Unconscious, 285, 288, 290, 291
Collins, Michael, pic 119, 329, 330
Comet Holmes, pic 244
Common Purpose, 75, 326, 341
Conrad, Pete, 125, 330
Conservative Party, 303, 350, 351
Consciousness, 281, 283, 288, 290, 296
Conspiracy Hysteria, 258, 259, 278
Conspiracy Theories, 18-20, 25, 65, 66, 277, 311
Cosmic Wave Theory, 247-250, 252
CO2, 228, 231, 231
Council on Foreign Relations, 66, 95
Counter Terrorism Act 2009, 192
Counter Terrorism Bill 2008, 190
Cranbourne, Viscount, 351
Crane, Ian, 40, 210, 225, 342
Creation Day, 264, 304
Credit Crisis, 71
Cremation of Care, 93, 94, 328
Cremo, Michael A, 321
Crichton, Michael, 236, 345
Critical Mass, 288, 289
Cronkite, Walter, 94
Crop Circles, 29-33 (pics 30-33), 290, 305, 321, 346, 350
Crowe, Kevin, 336
Crystal Skull, pic 34
CSI, 213
CSICOP, 32
Cuba, 183
Currid, Michael, 164, 335
Curtis, Adam, 337

D-Notices, 32
Daily Telegraph, 74

Dark Moon, 111, 117, 121
Davies, Nick, 343
Davis, David, MP, 190
Davison, Emily, 311
Dawkins, Richard, 214, 282, 287, 340, 349
Day, Philip, 210
De Menezes, Jean Charles, 200, 201, 339
Dearlove, Richard, 134
Deer, Brian, 324
De Franceschi, Joe, 335
Deshore, Karin, 158, 334
Dewdney, A K, 169, 335
Dimmock, Stewart, 227
Disney, Walt, 119
Dmitriev, Dr Alexey, 250, 254
DMT, 255, 257
Dogon Tribe, 85
Doug & Dave, 31, 321
Drosnin, Michael, 52, 322, 323
Duke, Charles, 330
Dyke, Greg, 135

Eagar, Professor Thomas, 152, 333
Earth, pic 236, 281
Earth Changes, 50
Ebola Virus, 69
Eden, Anthony, 137
Electoral System, 310
Electromagnetic Pulse Wave (EMP), 253, 263
Elite, 262, 264, 267, 268, 271, 272, 275, 277,
281, 291, 299, 301, 309, 310, 315-317
Emoto, Masuru, 290, 350
Empire, British, 305
End Times, 58, 59, 61
Entangled Minds, 283, 349, 350
Environment, pic 222
EU Codex, 209, 212
Eugenics, 269, 271
Europe (EU), 11, 75, 139, 274
European Union, 67, 305
Extra-Terrestrials (ETs) 43-48, 50, 268, 317, 321,
322, 330

FAA, 167
FAO, 209
Fatima Children, pic 55,
Fatima Crowds, pic 56, 57, 58
Fatima, Portugal, pic 48, 53,
Fatima Prophecies/Apparitions, 54, 323

Fawkes, Guy, 9, 19
Fayed, Dodi, Al, 9
FBI, 143, 170
Federal Reserve, US, 326
Fefelov, Alexander, 253
FEMA, 258
Fifth Dimension, 256
Flight 75, 149,152
Flight 77, 166, 170, 171
Flight 93, 169-171, pic 172
Flight 175, pic 169, 171
Flight Data Recorders, 168
Fluoride, 67, 68, 210, 340
Forbes, Scott, 154
Fraudulent Mediums Act, 341
Freedom of Information Act, 43
Freemasonry, 13, 88, 89, 90, 274, 327
Friedman, Stanton T, 37, 38
Fundamentalism, 13, 216

Gagarin, Yuri, 102, pic 125, 126, 331
Gage, Richard, 151-154, 333
Gaia, 256
Galactic Alignment, 248, 254
Gallop, April, 332
Gandhi, Mahatma, 317
Garber, Steve, 329
Garrett, Joseph, 57
Gates, Bill, 327
Gates, Robert M, 23, 320
Gauquelin, Michel & Francoise, 348
Geldof, Bob, 312, 313
Geller, Uri, 291, 292
Gemini 10, pic 119
Genesis, Book of, 85, 87
Genetic Engineering, 271
Genetically Modified Food, 314
Geomagnetic Reversal, 252, 253
Georgia Guidestones, 70, 326
Germany, 126, 289, 311
Gerrish, Brian, 216, 327, 341
Gibson, Mel, 241
Gilbert, Adrian, 321
Gillet, Roy, 341
Gilligan, Andrew, 135
Giuliani, Mayor, 164, 335
Giza, pic 26, 27, 29
Global Axis Tilt, 28, 253, 347
Global Consciousness, 51, 286-288, pic 292,

THE TRUTH AGENDA

313, 349
Global Warming, 226, 227, 234, 268, 342
God, 282, 288, 290
God Delusion, The, 287, 349
Golden Age, 50,
Google, 194, 195
Gore, Al, 60, 227-229, 234, 343
Gray, Bobby, 155, 334
Great Global Warming Swindle, 227, 343
Great War, 351
Greenhouse Gases, 223, 226, 233
Greenland, 232
Greer, Dr Steven, 43, 322
Grenville, Mike, 342
Griffin, David Ray, 12, 141, 150, 166, 167, 170, pic 176, 333-335
Grissom, Betty, 103
Grissom, Scott, 103
Grissom, Virgil 'Gus', 102-104 (pic 102), 329
Ground Zero, pic 152, pic 155, pic 156, 334
G20 Summit, 23, pic 274, pic 303, 338, 349
Guantanamo Bay, 132, pic 188, 189
Gulf Stream, 229
Gulf of Tonkin, 184, 337
Gunn, Trevor, pic 67, 324
Gunpowder Plot, pic 19, 182

HAARP Project, 68
Habeas Corpus Act, 189
Haggard, Pastor Ted, 61, 62, 323
Hamilton, Lee H, 333
Hancock, Graham, 327
Hanjour, Hani, 147, 166, 335
Hanlon, Michael, 346
Harmonic Convergence, 313
Harrer, James, 258, 259
Hathaway, David, 346
Haw, Brian, 139, 332
Health and Safety, 205, 206, 207, 340
Heathrow Airport, 338
Heliosphere, 249, 250, pic 251
Hemsworth, Ross, 342
Henman, Tim, 290, 291
Henry VII, 351
Henry VIII, 351
Hertz, Steve, 329
Hess, Michael, 164, 335
Hidden Messages in Water, The, 350
Highfield, Roger, 350

Hill, Betty and Barney, 44
Hitler, Adolf, 183, 288, pic 289
Hopi Native Americans, 244
Hopkins, Rob, 342
Horn, Michael, 322
Horowitz, Dr Leonard, 69, 325
Houdin, Jean-Pierre, 320
House of Commons, 190, 294
House of Lords, 190, 294
'Hundredth Money' syndrome, 288, 349
Hurricane Katrina, 228, pic 259, 260
Hurt, Harry III, 329
Hussein, Saddam, pic 134, 137
Hutton Inquiry, 136

Ice Ages, 230, 250
I Ching, 241, 244, 245
Icke, David, 81, pic 82, pic 83, 187, pic 190
ID Cards, 78, 79, 81, 84, 191, 202, 315, 327
Illuminati, 66, 71, 77, 185, 188, 258, 299
Immunisation, 67, 68, pic 211, 212
Incas of Peru, 244
Inhofe, Senator Jim, 345
Intention, power of, 290, 291, 295, 301
Intention Experiment, The, 350
Internet, 77, 194, 195, 196
IRA campaign, 196, 197
Iran, 137, 187, 236, 315
Iraq, 86, 131,132, 134, pic 137, 138,139, 185, 200, 323, 315
Ireland, 76
Irving, Ken, 348
Irwin, James, 104, 107, 329
Isaac, Paul, 158, 334
Islamic Fundamentalism, 186
Israel, 50, 183
Ivanisevic, Goran, 290

Jack, Andrew, 325
Jacobs, David M, 44
Jahn, Robert, 285, 286
James I, 351
Japan, 181, 182, 349
Jaworowski, Zbigniew, 343
Jenkins, John Major, 242, 254
Jennings, Barry, 164, 335
Jesus, 306, 308
Johnson, Boris, 304
Jones, Alex, 94, 320, 328

Jones, Dr Steven, 151, 155, 156, 333
Journal of the American Medical Association, 350
Jowitt, Juliette, 342
Jung, Carl, 285
Jupiter, 262

The Karma of Untruthfulness, 351
Kashoggi, Adnan, 328
Kean, Thomas, 333
Kelly, David, 135, 136, 139, 332
Kelly, Ruth, 63
Kennedy, John F, 19, 91, 101, 126, 328, 331
Kennedy Space Centre, 101
Kenya, 21
Kerry, John, 84, 88
Kershaw, Ian, 319
Khalid, Sheik Mohammed, 132
King Arthur, 293, 306
King, Jon, 46, 246, 322, 328
Kirkup, James, 350
Kissinger, Henry, 93, 273
Knife Crime, 202, 339
Knights Templar, 91
Koresh, David, 184
Krugman, Paul, 334
Kubrick, Stanley, 118, 119, 257, 283

Labour Party, 274, 349, 351
Lake Chad, 228
Lapidos, Juliet, 324
Lavello, Randy, 334
LaViolette, Dr Paul, 247, 248, 346
Lawson, Nigel, 226, 342
Lawton, Ian, 27, 320, 321
Leake, Jonathan, 348
Lean, Geoffrey, 326
Leviton, Richard, 323
Lewes, 351
Lewinsky, Monica, 274
Liberty Bell, pic 180
Liberty Bell 7, 103
Little, Penny, 334
Live Aid Concerts, 312, 313
Loch Ness Monster, 34
London bombings (7/7), 198, pic 199, pic 200, 304, 339
London Heathrow Airport, 338
London 2012 Olympic logo, 82
Lovelock, James, 226

Lubbe, Marinus van der, 183
Lunar Excursion Model (LEM), 114-117, 119, 122
Lusitania, 182, 183

Macara, Sir Sandy, 340
MacAskill, Ewan, 320, 323
Mack, John E, 44
MacKenzie, Kelvin, 9
Madrid, 160, 200
Magnetic Pole, 252, 253
Maitreya, 308
Mandela, Nelson, 312
Mandelson, Peter, 75
Manhattan Project, 94
Marcel, Major Jesse, 37, 38, 102
Mary Magdalene, 328
Maunder Minimum, 250
Mazel Hecht, Marjorie, 230, 231, 343
Mazen, Abu, 323
McCann, Madeleine, 80, 202
McGuinness, Martin, 314
McIntire, James, 332
McKenna Brothers, 245, pic 246, 255
McKinnon, Gary, 41, 42, 321
McTaggart, Lynne, 350
McVeigh, Timothy, 183
McWethy, John, 332
Malmstrom Air Force Base, US, 321
Maoris of New Zealand, 244
Mars, 35, 248
Maya Calendar, 241, 242, 345
Maya Prophecies, 240-242, 254, 264
Maya Temple, pic 243
Medjugorje, 54
Meier, Billy, 46, 322
Mercury, 248
Mesoamerica, 241, 244
Meta-analysis, 283
Mexico City, 42
Middle East, 11, 272
MI5, 31
Milky Way, 242, 247, pic 247, 254
Millennium, 53, 239, pic 240, 351
Millennium Bug, 239, 256
Mineta, Norman, 168, 335
Ministry of Defence, 32, 41
Minogue, Tim, 351
Mitchell, Ed, 121, 330
MMR Programme, 211, 324

THE TRUTH AGENDA

Monbiot, George, 177, 336
Money Masters, the, 326
Monsanto, 314
Moon Landings, 20, 99, 100, 101, 104, 108, 116, 124, 128, 129, 144, 301
Moon Photos, 108-120, 122, 124, 272
Moon Rocks, 105, pic 106, 107, 208
Moon Shot, 120
Moore, Michael, 174, 310
Morales, Frank, 347
Morris, Nigel, 332
Morphic Resonance, 288
Mossad, 173
Mother Nature, 234
Mother Shipton, 49, 322
Mott, Maryann, 350
Moulton Howe, Linda, 322
MPs, British, 22, 74, 326, 351
Mumbai, 185
Murdoch, Rupert, 327
Muslim Minaret, pic 215
My Lai Massacre, 309, 351

NAA, 104, 329
NASA, 99, 100-102, 104-112, 115, 116, 118, 120-128, 175, 231, 232, 249-251, 329, 346
NASA Media Services, 111
National Identity Register (NIR), 78, 191
NATO, 187
Natural Health, 207, 209, 210
Nature Journal, 232, 344
Naudet Brothers, 158, 174
Nazi Germany, 183
Nephilim, 45, 85
Neptune, 262
New Age, 81, 203, 212, 213, 242, 256, 263, 281, 288, 291, 305, 307
New Freedom, 269, 348
New Jerusalem, 51, 61, 256
New Testament, 51
New World Order, 71, 74, 75, 82, 83, 139, 142, 181, 187, 188, 196, 268, 269, 274, 291, 296, 313, 320, 348
New World Order, 268, 348
New York, 24, 62
New Zealand, 244
newparty.co.uk, 228
Nibiru, Planet, 86, 247
Nichol, John, 326

9/11, 9, 11, 19, 79, 124, 128, 129, 131, 132, 138, 139, 141, 142, 144, 149, 150, 166, 178, 182, 183, 268, 272, 287, 296, 301, 320
9/11 Commission Report, 178
9/11 tribute film, 158
9/11 Truth Campaign, pic 177
Nine Support Gods, 243
Nineteen Eighty-Four, 77, 186, 219
NIST, 150, 151, 152, 159, 162, 333
Nixon, Richard, 93, 105, 131, 309
NOAA, 249, 346
'Noosphere', the, 282, 349
NORAD, 167, 175, 335
Northern Ireland, 314
Nostradamus, 49, 52, 304, 322, 351
NSA, 184

Obachike, Daniel, 339
Obama, Barak, 11, 21-23, 60, 62, 72, 133, 142, 143, 186, 187, 189, 276, 277, 320, 326, 327
Ofcom, 227
Ogilvie-Herald, Ian, 27, 320
Oieroset, Marit, 252
Oklahoma City, 183, pic 184, 337
Old Testament, 52
Oliver, Jamie, 209
Olson, Barbara, 170, 335
Olson, Ted, 170
Olympics, Beijing, 304, 305
Olympic Games 2012, 26, 351
Olympic Stadium, pic 305
One World Government, 71, 258, 327
Operation Northwoods, 183
Opium Trade, 133, 331
'Orange Revolution' 2004, 313, pic 313
Orion, belt of, 28
Orwell, George, pic 71, 186, 193
Orwellian Society, 315
Ossetia, 186, 187
Owen, Jonathan, 326
Ozone Layer Hole, 231

Page, Jimmy, 304
Paine, Thomas, 7, 13
Paisley, Ian, 314
Pakistan, 185, 187
Pankhurst, Emmeline, pic 311
Paris, pic 13, 18, pic 64, 91
Patriot Act, 187, 188, 189, 337

Patterson, R Timothy, 231, 344
Paxman, Jeremy, 62, 218, 324
Peak Oil, 223
PEAR, 285
Pearce, Alan, 340
Pearl Harbour, 181, pic 182, 336
Pentagon, 141, 144, pic 145, pic 146, pic 148, pic 149, 169-171, 182, 332
People of the Lie, 309, 351
People Power, 276
Percy, David, 111, 120-122, 124, 329, 330
Persinger, Dr Michael, 256, 347
Pharmaceuticals, 69, pic 204, 207, 209-211
Pianka, Dr Eric, 68, 325
Pidd, Helen, 339
Pilkington, Ed, 334
Pineal Gland, 255, 256
Place de la Concorde, pic 13, pic 64, 91
Pluto/Uranus Cycle, 260, 261
PNAC, 181
Poland, 187, 312
Political Correctness, 214, 215
Pollution, pic 224
Pont d'Alma, pic 18, 91
Pope Benedict XV, 54
Pope Benedict XVI, 58, 62
Pope John Paul II, 55
Pope, Nick, 41
Porter, Andrew, 350
Power, Peter, 198, 199, 200, 339
Pravda, 253
Prayer, pic 282, 287, 349
Presentiment, 294
Princess Diana, 9, 18, 91, 136, 287, 328
Prince Philip, 18
Private Eye Magazine, 191, 337, 338
Project Blue Book, 42
Project Mogul, 38
Prometheus, 316
Protocols of the Elders of Zion, 82
Proya, Alex, 346
Psi Phenomena, 256, 283-285, 287, 290, 294
Psychically-based Beliefs, 212
Psychokinesis, 284, 286
PublicEye.org, 258
Pubs, 314, 351
Putin, Vladimir, 186
Pyramid, Giza, pics 26, 28, 29, 92, 321
Pyramid, Louvre, Paris, pic 90, pic 266

Pyramid, The Great, 320
Pyramids, 328

Quantum Entanglement, 284
Queen, The, 84
Quest For Contact, 350
Quigley, Prof. Carroll, 72
Quigley, Joan, 348

Rabin, Yitzhak, 53
Racism, 215
Radin, Dean, 283, 285, 292, 348-350
RAF, 41
Random Number Generators (RNGs), 285-287, 292, 297, 309, 313
Random Number (RNG) Occurrences, pics 286, 290, 294
Rapture, the, 51, 61, 137, 256, 308
Ratzinger, Cardinal, 58
Read, Sir David, 342
Reagan, Ronald, 93, 262, 348
Reichstag Parliament, 183
Rendlesham Forest incident, 41, 321
Rene, Ralph, 329
Republican Party, 23
Revelation, Book of, 49, 51, pic 52, 58, 243
Rex 84, 258, 259
RFID Chips, 80
Rhodes, Benjamin, 333
Rice, Condoleeza, 166, 172, 335, 336
Riots, threat of, 303, 350, 351
Ritalin, 341
Roberts, Gregg, 156, 334
Roberts, John, 320
Roche Laboratories, 326
Rockefellers, 66, 273
Rodriguez, William, 159, 334
Ronson, Jon, 94, 328
Roosa, Stuart, pic 120
Rosicrusians, 91
Roswell, 37, 38
Rothkopf, David, 327
Rothschadl, Judy, 332
Rothschilds, 66, 273
Ruddy, Christopher, 329
Rumsfeld, Donald, 69, 70, 326, 340
Russell, Bertrand, 76, pic 270, 273, 348
Russia, 186, 187
Rutherford Institute, 188

THE TRUTH AGENDA

Salas, Robert, 321
Salem, Emad, 143, 199, 332
Salla, Michael, 331
Samanta-Laughton, Dr Manjir, 340
Satchell, Graham, 341
Sato, Rebecca, 340
Saturn V Rocket, pic 98, 101, 126, 127
Schwabe Cycle, 248
Scott Peck, Dr M, 309, 351
Scott, Shane, 337
Sea Levels, 232
Second Coming, 53, 61, 307, 308
Sewell Helen, 260, 262, 323, 348
Sexual Behaviour, 220
Seymour, Percy, 348
Shaath, Nabil, Palestinian Foreign Minister, 59, 323
Shakespeare, 20
Shanker, Thom, 320
Sharlet, Jeff, 323, 324
Sheldrake, Dr Rupert, 288, 350
Shepard, Al, 103, pic 120, 330
Shopping, pic 221
Siegel, Rick, 159, 333, 334
Silverstein, Larry, 163, 173
Simpson, OJ, 287
Sitchin, Zecharia, 86
Six-Day War, 183
Slack, James, 340
Slayton, Deke, 120, 330
Smith, Jacqui, 190, 193
Solar Activity, 231, 247, pics 248, 249, 346
Solidarity Movement, 312
Solomon, Lawrence, 226
Son of God, 81, 85
Sotham, Danny, 381
South Africa, 312
Soviet Space Programme, 107, 126
Soviet Union, 23, 214, 312, 313
Space Race, 126, 127
Spaceships, pic 86, 307
Spiritual Healing, 292
Spiritualism, 212, pic 213, 214
Stamp, Sir Josiah, 73
Star Wars, 289
Steele, Andrew, 106, 329
Steiner, Rudolf, 306, 351
Stempel, Guido H, 336
Stewart, Elizabeth, 339
Strange Death of David Kelly, 135

Strasbourg Parliament, pic 76
Strassman, Dr Rick, 255, 347
Straw, Jack, MP, 192
Stray, Geoff, 241, 244-246, 254, 322, 345-347, 349, 351
Streiber, Whitley, 46
Suez Crisis, 131, 137, 331
Suffragette Movement, 311
Sumerian Legends, 86
Sun, Cycles of, 33, pic 232, 247, pic 248
Sunrise, pic 237
Sunspots, 248-250, 346
Suskind, Ron, 134, 332
Svensmark, Henrik, 227, 232, 342
Swaine, John, 344
Sweeney, John, 184, 337
Swine Flu, 325
Switzerland, 351
Syria, 137
Szymanski, Greg, 334

Taft, Ryan, 292
Taliban, 132, 185, 187
Tamiflu, 69, 70, 325, 340
Tarnas, Richard, 347
Tarpley, Webster Griffin, 175, 336
Taser Stun Gun, pic 201, 339
Tatchell, Peter, 327
Tavistock Institute, 66
Tavistock Square, 199, 304
Taylor, Peter, 226, pic 227, 230, 342
Taylor, Lord, of Blackburn, 326
Teilhard-de-Chardin, Pierre, 282
Telepathy, 257, 283, 284
Television, effects of, 217, pic 218, 219, 293, 350
Thatcher, Margaret, 197, 348
THEMIS, 251, 252, 347
Thompson, Richard L, 321
Tiananmen Square, 313
Time, 296
Times Square, pic 24
Tipps, Scott, 210
Tomlinson, Ian, 338
Tower of Babel, pic 87, 88, 137, 327
Toynbee, Polly, 20, 21, 177, 320
Transition Towns, 225, 341
Treaty of Lisbon, 76
Trilateral Commission, 66
Truscott, Lord, 326

Truthseekers, 240, 267, 270, 276, 278, 301
Tsunami of 2004, 287, 350
Tudors, 351
Turner, Lord, 234, 344
2001: A Space Odyssey, 118, 283, 317
2012 Olympics, 304, 305
2012 Prophecies, 33, 46, 237, 238, 240, 241, 245, 246, 256-259, 263, 264, 281, 293, 302, 303, 306, 307, 345, 346

UFOs, 9, 37, 39, 40, 41, pic 42, 43, pic 45, 47, 57, 121, 277, 300, 322, 350
UFO Contactees/Abductions, 43, 44, 51, 246
UK, 11, 77, 79, 223, 260, 274, 306
UK Parliament, 75
Ulysses Spacecraft, 251
Unfair Commercial Practices Directive, 212
Ure, Midge, 312
US Federal Reserve, 72
US National Institutes for Health, 230
USA, 11, 77, 79, 223, 269
USA Military Base, Nevada, pic 36
United Airlines, 173
United States Air Force, 42

Vaccination Programme, 67, 324, 341
Van Allen Belts, 122
Vatican, 32, 55, 58
Villiers, Theresa, 351
Verkerk, Robert, 208, 210, 338, 339, 340
Veterans' Day Parade, pic 130
Vietnam War, 351
Visor Consultants, 198
Voodoo Histories, 18
V2 Missiles, 126

Waco Siege, 183, 336
Wakefield, Dr Andrew, 324
Wałęsa, Lech, 312
Wall Street, pic 272
Warminster, 41
War on Liberty, 181,185
War on Terror, 11, 77, 131, 133, 139, 141, 178, 181, 185-187, 196, 197, 203, 303
Washington DC, pic 88, pic 277
Watson, Paul Joseph, 343
Weapons of Mass Destruction (WMDs), 123, 131, 133, 134, 137-139, 275, 299, 315, 332
Weather Channel, 229

Websites, 194
Weiss, Philip, 95
Wells, H G, 76, 268, pic 269, 273, 348
West, John Anthony, 348
Westfeldt, Amy, 333
Westminster Parliament, 293, pic 294
What The Bleep Do We Know?, 350
White, Edward, pic 102, 103
White, Jack, 124, 330
Whitehead, John, 188, 337
White House pic, 22, 25, 59, 60
Wikipedia, 319
Williscroft, Robert, G, 344
Wilson, Robert, 346
Wilson, Woodrow, 269, 348
Wimbledon, 290, 291
Wingfield, George, 321
Wisnewski, Gerhard, 107, 127, 329, 330, 331
Wolfgang, Walter, 192, 338
Women's Institute, 277, 349
Woodward, Bob, 59, 323
World Economic Forum, 66
World Trade Centre, pic 140, pic 142, 149, pic 150, 154-159, 171, 174, pic 175, 199, 332-334
WTC1, 152, 153
WTC2, 152, 153
WTC 7, pic 160, 161, pic 162, 163, 164, pic 165, 334, 335
WW1, 351
WW2, 37, 50, 183, 258, 306
Wren, Sir Christopher, 92

Young, John, 116, pic 117
Yushchenko, Viktor, 313

Zelikov, Philip, 166, 335
Zionism, 82, 83, 215

Index does not cover *Appendix 2* or *Picture Credits*

THE AUTHOR

Andy Thomas is one of Britain's leading authors and lecturers on unexplained mysteries and global cover-ups.

Andy is author of seven books exploring the unexplained, including *Vital Signs: A Complete Guide to the Crop Circle Mystery* (1998, revised 2002), which has been described by many as the definitive guide to its subject and was nominated for *Kindred Spirit* magazine's 2002 Best Book award.

Andy has written articles for many publications, and regularly contributes to the journal *Nexus Magazine*. He is also author of four books about his historical home town of Lewes in East Sussex, England, once the residence of libertarian Thomas Paine and site of the world's largest annual Guy Fawkes celebrations.

Andy is the founder of Vital Signs Publishing, which in 2005 produced Geoff Stray's acclaimed and greatly influential book *Beyond 2012: Catastrophe or Ecstasy*, edited by Andy. He is also co-founder of the Changing Times organisation, which holds events to spread alternative views on important political and social issues, as well as being a gigging keyboard player with guitarist Phil Light.

A busy lecturer, Andy is renowned for his striking presentations on cover-ups and the unexplained, and speaks extensively across Britain. He has also presented in many other parts of the world, including America, Australia, Peru and various European countries, and is co-presenter of The Glastonbury Symposium, one of the UK's longest-running and largest annual alternative conferences.

Andy has made numerous radio and TV appearances, including UK television spots on *Richard and Judy*, *Esther*, *GMTV* and BBC 1's *The One Show*, and has featured in many programmes in countries around the globe.

Website: www.vitalsignspublishing.co.uk